Louise R. Atherton,
Norwich,
September 1900

GW01458866

SWEDISH DIPLOMATS AT CROMWELL'S COURT, 1655–1656

SWEDISH DIPLOMATS AT CROMWELL'S COURT, 1655–1656

the missions of Peter Julius Coyet
and
Christer Bonde

Translated and edited by

MICHAEL ROBERTS

CAMDEN FOURTH SERIES
VOLUME 36

LONDON
OFFICES OF THE ROYAL HISTORICAL SOCIETY
UNIVERSITY COLLEGE LONDON
GOWER STREET WC1E 6BT
1988

British Library Cataloguing in Publication Data

Coyet, Peter Julius
  Swedish diplomats at Cromwell's court, 1655–1656: the missions of Peter
Julius Coyet and Christopher Bonde. (Camden fourth series; v. 36).
  1. England. Political events, 1655–1656
  I. Title II. Bonde, Christer III. Roberts, Michael, *1908*– IV. Series
  942.06′4

ISBN 0–86193–117–3

Printed and bound in Great Britain by
Butler & Tanner Ltd, Frome and London

CONTENTS

ABBREVIATIONS

Abbott	W. C. Abbott, *Writings and Speeches of Oliver Cromwell* (4 vols. Cambridge, Mass. 1937–47)
BL	British Library
Brieven	*Brieven geschreven ende gewisselt tusschen de Heer Johan de Witt . . . ende de gevolmaghtigden van de Staet der Verenigde Nederlanden* (6 vols. 's Gravenhage, 1723–5)
CSP (Dom)	*Calendar of State Papers Domestic*
CSP (Ven)	*Calendar of State Papers Venetian*
EHR	*English Historical Review*
PRO, SP	Public Record Office, State Papers
Pufendorf	Samuel von Pufendorf, *Sju böcker om Konung Carl X:s bragder*, trans. Adolf Hillman (7 vols. Stockholm 1913–15)
RRP	Svenska riksrådets protokoll (Handlingar rörande Sveriges historia, 3rd series) (18 vols. Stockholm 1873–1959)
Thurloe	*A Collection of the State Papers of John Thurloe, Esq.*, ed. Thomas Birch (7 vols. 1742)
Urk. und Act.	*Urkunden und Actenstücke zur Geschichte des Kurfürsten Friedrich Wilhelm von Brandenburg*, ed. E. Erdmannsdorffer *et al.* (21 vols. Berlin 1864–1915)

The place of publication of the other works cited in the footnotes, unless otherwise indicated, is London.

INTRODUCTION

The history of the foreign policy of the protectorate in the years 1655–56 depends, to an unusual degree, upon the evidence of foreign diplomats. That this should be so arises from the relative paucity of domestic records. Among the extremely exiguous collection of documents in the Public Record Office relating to Anglo-Swedish relations in these years, the only items having any reference to Coyet's and Bonde's mission are a handful of petitions from merchants claiming reparation for damage and loss alleged to have been sustained in the course of the recent Anglo-Dutch war.[1] With one well-known exception, we have no record of the discussions in Cromwell's council of state, nor of those in the Committee of Trade and Plantations; though occasional lights as to their proceedings may be collected from the *Calendar of State Papers (Domestic)* for these years. They were years when Oliver was ruling without a parliament, so that we have neither protectoral allocutions nor parliamentary comment on foreign affairs. Until Lockhart was sent to France in May 1656, England had no permanent representative abroad, apart from Charles Longland at Leghorn and Sir Thomas Bendyshe at Constantinople, and they lay somewhat peripheral to the main centres of diplomatic activity. The *State Papers* of John Thurloe do indeed now and then afford glimpses of his attitudes—for instance, in letters to Henry Cromwell—besides convenient translations of the correspondence of foreign diplomats, furnished by Thurloe's agents; but on English foreign policy they have, surprisingly enough, very little to say.[2] Bulstrode Whitelocke's *Memorials of the English Affairs* provides a detailed account of the commercial negotiations of 1656, but it becomes fully intelligible only when read in conjunction with Bonde's despatches. And Thurloe himself, in his 'Concerning the Forraigne Affairs in the Protector's Time', and other memoranda written after the Restoration for the guidance of Hyde, provides a short-range retrospective view of some aspects of the foreign policy of the period, which however needs to be read with some caution.

Thus if a coherent record of the doubts and hesitations of protectoral policy is required, we must seek it in foreign sources: in the correspondence of Bordeaux and Mazarin, of Nieupoort and de Witt, in

---

1. PRO, SP, Foreign, Sweden, 1655–56 (SP 95/5B). The 'Proposicion for the manageing the Trade of Sweden', and the 'Propositions in Order to a Treaty with Sweden' (fos. 152–156) are both—the former probably, the latter certainly—to be dated to 1657.

2. I.e. in 1655–56: it was a different matter in 1657–8.

the reports of Schlezer to the Great Elector, and even occasionally in the flood of newsletters sent off by Venice's representatives in London. Much of this is readily available in print: in the *Lettres du Cardinal Mazarin* and the appendixes to Guizot's *History of Oliver Cromwell and the English Commonwealth*, in the three collections of de Witt's correspondence, in the *Urkunden und Actenstücke zur Geschichte des Kurfürsten Friedrich Wilhelm von Brandenburg*, and in the *Calendar of State Papers (Venetian)*. But the correspondence of Nieupoort and de Witt (for instance) is only one side of a story; and the other side is provided in the despatches of Coyet and Bonde. Apart from the extremely meagre *Christer Bondes Diarium*, most of which was printed in 1889 in the *42nd Annual Report of the Deputy Keeper of the Public Records*, Appendix II, and some despatches from Fleetwood and Friesendorff in 1657, which were printed in *Handlingar rörande Skandinaviens historia*, (40 vols. Stockholm, 1816–60), v, 205–20, little Swedish diplomatic correspondence having any relation with Bonde's mission is available in print. A few letters from Johan Ekeblad, who made one of Bonde's suite, which are printed in *Johan Ekeblads brev*, ed. N. Sjöberg (Stockholm 1911), give characteristically lively sidelights on Cromwell's England. In 1851 N. C. E. Treffenberg transcribed and published (as an Uppsala dissertation) Charles X's instructions to Coyet;[1] and in the same year appeared the brief and jejune dissertation of Pehr Kalling,[2] which printed paraphrases of or excerpts from some of Bonde's despatches, though only down to the end of 1655. The same thing was done, on a much fuller and more satisfactory scale, by J. Levin Carlbom, who in addition printed, in whole or in part, many of the orders sent by Charles X to London.[3] Much the same kind of assistance had long ago been provided in Samuel von Pufendorf's massive *De rebus a Carolo Gustavo Sveciae rege gestis commentariorum libri septem* (Stockholm 1694), since 1913 available in a full Swedish translation.[4]

There has long existed, however, a transcript of these despatches which is readily accessible: Add. MS 38100 in the British Library. It covers the following collections in Riksarkivet, Stockholm: Diplomatica, Anglica, vols. 10 (letters of Coyet to Charles X), 13–14 (letters of Bonde to Charles X: some gaps in the series being supplied by the transcriber from copies in Bonde's *Register*), and portions of vols. 17 (Barkman's letters to Charles X), and 515 (Bonnel's reports). It was made at some time during the late nineteenth century for S. R.

1. N.C.E. Treffenberg, *K. Carl X Gustafs instruction för Secreteraren Coijet under dess beskickning till England 1654*, (Uppsala 1851).
2. *Om Riks-Rådet Frih. Christer Bondes Ambassad till England 1655* (Uppsala 1851).
3. J. Levin Carlbom, *Sverige och England 1655–aug. 1656* (Göteborg 1900).
4. Samuel von Pufendorf, *Sju böcker om Konung Carl X:s bragder*, trans. Adolf Hillman, (7 vols. Stockholm 1913–15): I have used this version.

Gardiner; but otherwise the only information available about it on enquiry is that it was donated to the British Museum by Sir Charles Firth; who does not, however, seem to have used it. Gardiner on the other hand did, as appears from Chapter XLVII of his *The History of the Commonwealth and Protectorate 1649–1656* (2nd edn. 4 vols. 1903). Guernsey Jones used it also in his less than satisfactory *The Diplomatic Relations between Cromwell and Charles X* (Lincoln, Neb. 1898). Wilbur C. Abbott, in his monumental *The Writings and Speeches of Oliver Cromwell* (4 vols. Cambridge, Mass. 1937–1947) drew on it, not too profitably; for the translations he incorporated are crude, and not seldom simply wrong; his frequent paraphrases are unsatisfactory and sometimes misleading; and the essential points at issue do not emerge clearly from his pages. It therefore seemed that it might be appropriate to present a translation of these despatches in print. The translation is full, except as regards some of the despatches of Coyet, which fall into two distinct categories. Coyet wrote all the despatches dealing with his negotiation in Swedish; but those which were essentially newsletters designed to be sent to a number of recipients are in German; and since it seemed probable that most historians might be able to read these in the original (which perhaps is not the case in regard to despatches written in Swedish) it was thought sufficient to present a full summary of them, on the lines of those offered in the *Calendar of State Papers (Venetian)*. The letters of Benjamin Bonnel, who acted as commissioner during the first half of 1655, and those from Johan Barkman, who acted as secretary after Bonde's departure, are omitted: Bonnel's because they are really newsletters of small importance; Barkman's because at the time when they were written the essential object of Bonde's negotiations—an Anglo-Swedish alliance—had been temporarily abandoned, and they have therefore little interest either for Swedish or for English policy.

The treaty of Uppsala, which Whitelocke concluded on 11 April 1654, made a Swedish mission to England necessary: partly on formal and ceremonial grounds—to exchange ratifications, to give notice of Charles X's accession—but also to resolve points which in 1654 had been left unsettled, of which much the most important was the nature and terms of the alliance between the two countries which had been suggested, and agreed on in principle, during Whitelocke's sojourn in Sweden. For such negotiations it was clearly necessary that Sweden be represented in London by diplomats of higher rank, and with a greater knowledge of the aims of Swedish policy, than Commissioner Benjamin Bonnel: hence the despatch first of Coyet and then of Bonde.

Peter Julius Coyet (1618–67), who was accredited as *envoyé* pending the arrival of Christer Bonde as ambassador-extraordinary, had attended the university of Leiden, where he had been a pupil of Salmasius, and from him had acquired a command of international and civil law of which he found opportunities to avail himself on occasion during his stay in London; and when he returned to Sweden he found appropriate employment in the appellate division of the council of state. He had also, while in Holland, received a general grounding in practical politics in the chancery of Frederick Henry of Orange. He served as secretary to a Swedish embassy to Moscow in 1647; and thereafter was engaged in various minor diplomatic activities in Sweden. He was ennobled in 1649. In 1652 he was appointed assessor in the newly-established College of Commerce; and this—and perhaps the fact that he counted Erik Oxenstierna as his 'patron'— may explain his selection for the post in London, since many of the matters with which he would be called upon to deal were of a commercial nature. His position after Bonde's arrival was anomalous and embarrassing, for he had received no letters of recall (nor arrears of pay), and his relations with Bonde seem at first to have been cool, the ambassador preferring to form his judgments for himself. But Bonde soon came to appreciate Coyet's good sense and his grasp of the political situation in England: from December 1655 he admitted him to some of his audiences with the protector, and to the meetings of the commissioners. Thereafter there was an informal division of labour between them, Bonde writing the policy-despatches, Coyet managing the recruiting of mercenaries and providing surveys of the domestic situation. When at last he succeeded in his protracted attempts to get away from England, Bonde wrote warmly and generously of the assistance he had received from him. Thereafter he was prominent in Swedish diplomacy in the years 1658 and 1659, and in the negotiations with Denmark after the peace of Roskilde could be relied upon to take the hard line which Charles X himself preferred.[1] By the historian Anders Fryxell he was credited with the authorship of the propaganda piece—famous or notorious in its day, and termed by Fryxell 'a masterpiece of its kind'[2]—which attempted to justify to international opinion Charles X's second war with Denmark. He returned to England in 1666 on a fruitless mission designed to obtain an alliance on terms hardly less optimistic than those which Charles X had earlier put forward. But though he failed in this, contemporaries

---

1. Cf. Mémoires du Chevalier de Terlon pour rendre compte au Roy de ses Négociations (Paris 1681), pp. 188, 197.
2. Anders Fryxell, Berättelser ur svenska historien (new edn., 43 vols. Stockholm 1901), xi. 88–9; Georg Landberg, in Den svenska utrikespolitikens historia, I:3, 1648–1697 (5 vols. Stockholm 1956–61), p. 46. But the authorship was also claimed by Edvard Ehrensteen: [S. Loenbom], Anecdoter af Namnkunniga och Märkwärdiga Swenska Män (3 vols. Stockholm 1770–1775), I_v. 71.

thought highly of his diplomatic ability: they are even said to have called him (surely somewhat extravagantly) 'a second Salvius'. He was a cultured man and an enthusiastic bibliophile. When he left England he took with him a large library of books on law, philosophy, politics, history, geography, and English institutions; a collection of the protector's Ordinances; a copy of the writ of *habeas corpus*; the works of Grotius and Selden; and twenty-three accounts from English booksellers: one is tempted to wonder whether the financial straits of which he sometimes complained may not in part have been related to these massive purchases. At all events, it is recorded that his private library was in its time esteemed the best in Sweden.[1]

His successor, Christer Bonde (1621–59) was, as Coyet was not, a member of the high aristocracy which was to continue to dominate Swedish political life until the 1680's; and perhaps it was this difference in social standing that contributed to his initial attitude to Coyet. Hitherto his career had been wholly domestic: as assessor in the Office of Mines; as provincial governor; as assessor in the College of Commerce; as speaker of the house of nobility (*lantmarskalk*) at the diet of 1652. Since 1653 he had been a member of the council of state. When in 1655 the great question of the *reduktion* was due to be considered he had drawn up a carefully-argued memorial discussing alternative methods of repairing the crown's finances: it may possibly have provided one of the bases for Charles X's proposals, though it was considerably less rigorous than they.[2] As a member of the council of state he had naturally been made fully aware of the options available to Swedish foreign policy; and in the great council debates of December 1654 the custom of conducting discussions on crucial issues on the lines of an academic disputation had led to his being put up to argue the case for war against Denmark, rather than against Poland, though it does not follow that this was his real opinion.[3] At all events, he must have left for England fully apprised of Charles X's plans, and well primed with the appropriate arguments. As a diplomat, though not prepared to compromise on the claims of the Swedish crown to due precedence, in his private relations he refrained from insisting too rigidly on his rank: the Venetian ambassador Sagredo reported that he was 'equally distinguished for his birth, abilities and courtesy', and that he 'cared nothing for formalities, and had no scruples about visiting Paulucci [Sagredo's predecessor], although he

1. Details from Carlbom, *Sverige och England*, p. 9. *n*. 1.
2. Robert Swedlund, 'Krister Bonde och reduktionsbeslutet 1655', *Karolinska Förbundets Årsbok* (1937); Stellan Dahlgren, *Karl X Gustav och reduktionen* (Uppsala 1964), pp. 38, 55.
3. *Svenska riksrådets protokoll* (Handlingar rörande Sveriges historia, 3rd Series) (18 vols. Stockholm 1873–1959), xvi. 6–7, 15, 18.

was not a qualified Resident'.[1] Whitelocke, recording Bonde's lunch with Admiral Ayscue just before his departure, noted that he 'did according to his custom endeavour to improve his own knowledge by his discourse and questions to the company, according to their several capacities and abilities', and subjected Ayscue to close questioning on naval architecture and the most serviceable type of frigate, displaying at least some knowledge of what he was talking about.[2] One great advantage he had above all other diplomats then in England: he had the ability (and the self-confidence) to talk freely to the protector in his own language. He had learnt English in Oxford, where (as also at the university of Leiden) he had studied in 1638–9.[3] He then acquired a considerable knowledge of the country, and a great liking for it: Whitelocke, meeting him in Sweden in 1654, remarked on the pleasure he took in talking English and speaking of England.[4] Coyet, it is true, undoubtedly understood English; and there are in the Coyet Papers in Stockholm copies of letters in English to Thurloe, Leven and Cranstoun;[5] but it must be uncertain whether the originals were of his own composition, and on the only occasion on which we have information as to the language he used in public he is reported to have employed Latin. The Brandenburg envoy, Schlezer, knew English too; but he seems to have spoken to Cromwell in a Latin which (in the interests of intelligibility) was deliberately bad.[6] But neither he nor Coyet, whatever their command of the language, was able (and perhaps did not try) to use it to establish any sort of personal relationship with Cromwell. Bonde, on the other hand, from the beginning exploited the opportunity to do so. The comfort of talking English meant much to Cromwell, who, as he ingenuously confessed, had been 'so ill educated that he scarcely ventured to speak any other language than English',[7] but who was forced on all too many occasions to express himself in a Latin which (if Burnet is to be believed) was 'very vicious and scanty'. Bonde was thus in a position to provide a relatively intimate account of the protector's impulses and vacillations. They seem to have been on a footing of personal friendship: so much so, that Bonde did not hesitate to give unsolicited advice for the protector's own good, and could even on occasion say 'I told you so',

1. *Calendar of State Papers (Venetian) 1655–1656* (1930), pp. 133, 152.
2. Bulstrode Whitelocke, *Memorials of the English Affairs* (4 vols. Oxford 1853), iv. 270.
3. His name does not appear in J. Foster, ed., *Alumni Oxonienses* (2 vols. Oxford 1891–2): I am indebted to Dr G. D. Ramsay for checking this for me.
4. Bulstrode Whitelocke, *Journal of the Swedish Embassy* (2 vols. 1855), i. 296; ii. 42.
5. Riksarkivet, Stockholm, Coyetska samlingen, E. 3400, Vol. 4 (unfoliated).
6. *Urkunden und Actenstücke zur Geschichte des Kurfürsten Friedrich Wilhelm von Brandenburg*, ed. E. Erdmannsdorffer *et al.* (21 vols. Berlin 1864–1915), vii. 745.
7. *Infra*, no. IV (3 August 1655).

without disturbing for more than a moment their amicable relations. Bonde was understandably proud of the friendship; and if on occasion he demonstrably exaggerated the special courtesies and social amenities which were afforded him, that was to be attributed not only to vanity, but also to the need to demonstrate to all the world that his country was now one of the great powers, and was treated as such. If his own account is to be believed, his eloquence on a number of occasions extorted Cromwell's cordial assent to propositions which it might seem surprising that he ever seriously entertained. After returning to Sweden he played an active part in governing the country during Charles X's absence abroad, and his contributions to council debates make it clear that he was listened to as an authority on commercial matters: on the death of Erik Oxenstierna he succeeded him, in October 1656, as president of the College of Commerce. In August 1658, at Charles X's request, he drew up an exhaustive and acute survey of conditions in the provinces ceded to Sweden by the peace of Roskilde.[1] He ended his career once more in double harness with Coyet: this time in the fruitless negotiations with Philip Meadowe in the spring of 1659; and it was in the course of these negotiations that he was carried off by typhus, and died in Helsingör in May of that year.

The Anglo-Swedish negotiations of 1655–56 arose directly from the terms of the treaty of Uppsala. Whitelocke's instructions had ordered him to reach agreement on reciprocal trading-privileges, compensation for damage suffered by Swedish merchantmen at the hands of English privateers, fishing-rights off the English and Scottish coasts, and other matters of this kind, most of which had been raised in 1652–3 by successive Swedish envoys or commissioners in England. It had proved impossible, however, to obtain agreement on some of them—for instance, on the definition of contraband, and the form of sea-passes—and it was provided in the treaty that they were to be defined by further negotiation within four months of the treaty's ratification: a provision which proved unduly optimistic.

Apart from such matters as these, Whitelocke's embassy had had a more important object. It had been designed to obtain 'a more strict alliance and union than hath hitherto been' between the two countries;[2] and the aim of such an alliance was to ensure that the Sound should be opened, and should be kept open: at the close of 1653, when Whitelocke was given his instructions, the Danes still kept it shut to

1. Printed in *Handlingar rörande Skandinaviens historia* (40 vols. Stockholm 1816–1860), vi. 85–175.
2. Whitelocke, *Journal*, i. 87.

English ships. In order to effect this essential object, Whitelocke was ordered to declare that England would be ready to send 'a fleet so considerable that [it] may be able, through God's blessing, to defend itself against the contrary party';[1] and he was to enquire what assistance could be expected from the Swedes in such an event. Whitelocke's enquiry was well received by Queen Christina (in private) and by Axel Oxenstierna (more officially), and the treaty of Uppsala was in fact an alliance; but—as with other matters of less importance—the precise nature of the assistance which each ally was to render to the other was left to be settled by future negotiation.

In 1655 Sweden was diplomatically almost isolated. The alliance of 1645 with the Dutch was as good as dead; for that alliance was implicitly directed against Denmark, and Denmark had since then been bound to the United Provinces by two treaties, and had been their ally in the recent war with the commonwealth. Though Sweden had succeeded in escaping involvement in that war, her statesmen were always nervous of a Danish war of revenge aimed at the recovery of the losses sustained at the peace of Brömsebro (1645); and the 'Redemption Treaty' which the Dutch concluded with Denmark in 1649 had been in effect and in intention an anti-Swedish arrangement. In regard to Sweden's relations with Poland, the truce of Stuhmsdorf (1635) was not due to run out until 1661, and the Swedes were anxious to reach a firm settlement of outstanding differences before it did so; but there seemed little disposition for it on the Polish side: intermittent negotiations at Lübeck in 1651–3 petered out with nothing achieved. France was indeed still an ally; but Christina's flirtation with the Habsburgs had sacrificed much French good-will, while her war with Bremen had alienated protestant Germany.[2] Despite the triumphs of Westphalia—indeed, because of them—Swedish statesmen did not feel secure. There was a widely-dispersed feeling that the country needed another war: Christina herself on more than one occasion gave expression to it.[3] Certainly it was by no means peculiar to Charles X. Very soon after his accession such a war was determined on, and preparations for it begun; though the enemy to be attacked remained uncertain at least until the end of 1654.

---

1. Whitelocke, *Journal*, i. 90.

2. Gustaf Jacobson, *Sverige och Frankrike 1648–1652. Alliansens upplösning efter Westfaliska freden* (Uppsala 1911); Sven Ingemar Olofsson, *Efter Westfaliska freden. Sveriges yttre politik 1650–1654* (Kungl. Vitterhets Historie och Antikvitets Akademiens Handlingar. Historiska serien 4) (Stockholm 1957). On relations with the German protestant states the Brunswicker Schwarzkopf commented that the Swedish attack on Bremen had revealed them as '*latrones, raptores et invasores alienarum ditionum*': Birger Fahlborg, *Sveriges yttre politik 1660–1664* (Stockholm 1932), p. 91.

3. E.g. *Sveriges rikes ridderskaps och adels riksdags-protokoll* (17 vols. Stockholm 1865–1902), v. 116; *RRP.*, xiv. 307.

But for an offensive war on the other side of the Baltic Charles at the moment of his accession had neither the men nor the money. His aggressions were certainly not inspired by the need to give occupation to a burdensome armament which only a war could hope to pay for; this was a very different case from Cromwell's '160 ships swimminge', and the Western Design as the best hope of avoiding the immediate payment of their crews' wages. In 1654 the Swedish army, as provided for in the Form of Government of 1634, was in no great need of payment—or of employment either: in peacetime it mostly subsisted satisfactorily enough without being a burden to the state. Though Christina's alienations of farms which ought to have been reserved for its officers to live on had decreased its efficiency and hampered its training, for the defence of Sweden against attack it may well have been adequate. But decidedly not for the war—or wars—that Charles X had in mind. For the waging of these there must be massive recruitment of mercenaries; and from the start of the reign Charles concluded agreements with Swedish enterprisers—Königsmarck, Gustav Otto Stenbock, Robert Douglas—and sought to make similar agreements in that traditional recruiting-market, Germany.[1] Once begun, one might hope that the war would pay for itself, as it had done in the great days after Breitenfeld; though this time the French subsidies might be doubtful unless the war should be directed against the Habsburgs, and that was no longer a primary Swedish interest. The real financial problem was the large initial expenditure required to hire, arm, muster and trans-ship a strong fighting force to the other side of the Baltic. The thing could be done—must necessarily be done—on credit; but the credit of the Swedish crown at the close of Christina's disastrous reign was poor; the crown lands and revenues available for pawning had been catastrophically diminished; and hence for the successful prosecution of a policy of military adventure a drastic reform and rearrangement of domestic finances was an essential prerequisite. The business which occupied Charles's first diet of 1655, therefore, was not only foreign affairs, but the imposition, by the direct exercise of royal authority, of that partial *reduktion* which goes by the name of the 'quarter-part retribution' (*fjärdepartsräfsten*). The next prospective source of revenue was the tolls which could be levied at ports along the southern Baltic shore—either ports already in Swedish possession, or ports which it was intended to conquer in pursuance of the long-standing aim of establishing a Swedish control of all that coastline. It must have been apparent to Charles X from the beginning that such a programme was bound to involve him in a clash with the Dutch, who would be the main sufferers by it. In

1. Lars Tersmeden, in *Carl X Gustafs armé* (Carl X Gustaf-studier, 7) (Stockholm 1979), pp. 10–12, 28, 75, 119.

the period after 1627 the levying of these so-called *licenter* had been systematically developed by Gustav Adolf and Axel Oxenstierna, and had had a good share in making Swedish victories possible.[1] At that time the Dutch had loudly protested; but they were then deeply involved in their war with Spain, and they must endure what they lacked the power to amend. But now the case was altered: the war was over; with its ending Dutch trade to the Baltic was booming; and this time they would certainly not passively accept any interruption of their traffic—in particular, of their trade to Danzig; for Danzig was the main supplier of those grainstuffs which provided not only a revenue for their freighters, but the indispensable stay of their stomachs.

It was therefore important to Charles X to secure the alliance of England, in the hope that the Dutch would not risk a breach with him if he obtained it. To England—or at least to Scotland—he could look also with reasonable confidence for the raising of mercenary troops: there had been Scots in the Swedish service since the 1560s; in the Thirty Years War they had been ubiquitous; they knew the Swedes, and the Swedes knew them; and already great Scots families— Hamiltons, Douglases, Fleetwoods, Ruthvens, Ramsays, Leslies—had become domesticated in Sweden and Finland. Scottish troops, no doubt, were liable to be comparatively expensive, since they required sea-transport;[2] and the numbers that could be expected were relatively insignificant in relation to the size of Charles's demands;[3] but their established reputation—and their protestantism—offset these dis-advantages to some extent. Moreover, recruitment on the continent proceeded exasperatingly slowly: partly because German princes, anxious to give some military credibility to the federative movement, were tending to ban the levying of troops by foreign powers; partly

---

1. See the full study in Einar Wendt, *Det svenska licentväsendet i Preussen 1627–1635* (Uppsala 1933).

2. The normal monthly rate on the continent was 6–9 *rdr.* for footsoldiers, 30 *rdr.* for cavalry: *Carl X Gustafs armé*, pp. 118, 120. But for Cranstoun's levies the asking-price was eventually 12 *rdr.* for a footsoldier—twice Coyet's original estimate: *infra*, nos. 37 (28 September 1655) and XXXVIII (29 February 1656). Bonde told Cromwell that whereas in previous times it had been possible to hire foot for 6 *rdr.*, war was now so expensive that Philip IV had to pay 20 *rdr.* for men transferred from the imperial dominions: *infra*, no. XXXV (15 February 1656).

3. By August 1655 Charles had arranged with military enterprisers for 20,000 horse and 24,000 foot, *Carl X Gustafs armé*, pp. 128–9. Apart from the 2000 which Leven undertook to raise through his son-in-law Cranstoun, Charles hoped for permission to recruit some 5–6000 in Scotland: Carlbom, *Sverige och England*, p. 22. The Scottish levies seem to have been taken special care of and put in garrisons—presumably from a belief in their reliability: in July 1656 Cranstoun's regiment was in Elbing and Marienburg, and a year later there were still 600 of them in Thorn: *Carl Gustafs armé*, pp. 256, 265.

because there was keen competition from France;[1] but most of all because the musters contracted for could not be raised in time, since Charles lacked the money to settle accounts with the enterprisers. Reasons such as these made him eager to tap the unused resources of the Highlands; and it was reasonable to suppose that the protector would not be unwilling to permit such recruiting, as a vent for unruly or malignant spirits who might otherwise have provided backing for a Middleton or a Glencairn. And, not least important, the sort of alliance which Charles hoped to make would enable him to draw substantial assistance from the great navy of the English republic, should the Dutch take it into their heads to make trouble. There was good reason to think that they might: in the spring of 1654 disturbing news reached Sweden that a certain Nicholas de Bye, acting as the private agent of King John Casimir of Poland, had been trying to negotiate an agreement with the Dutch whereby they would provide him with twenty—or perhaps forty—units of their fleet.[2] Such a negotiation could have reference only to the possibility of a war with Sweden; and John Casimir had in fact come to the conclusion that he had better prepare for one. His prognosis was perfectly correct. The preparations which Charles was making were indeed designed for a descent on Polish Prussia.[3] By the end of 1654 the Swedish council of state—delicately manoeuvred by the chancellor, Erik Oxenstierna— had decided, after long debates, that the international situation required that Sweden should mobilize; they had agreed (less unanimously) that the mobilization should be directed—in the first instance, at all events—against the east; and in fact, though not in form, they had already accepted that mobilization must be followed by war.

By May 1655, accordingly, Charles was ordering Coyet to take soundings with the protector with a view to a stricter alliance between them. He found Cromwell very ready to be interested in such a proposal. Though the protector had as yet no knowledge of what Charles's plans might be, he could assure Coyet of his readiness to promote 'his laudable designs, as well by prayers to God as by all other positive means', since 'the liberty of the evangelical religion ... rested mainly on two columns, that is, England and Sweden'.[4] By

1. For Mazarin's recruiting-efforts see *Lettres du Cardinal Mazarin pendant son ministère*, edd. A. Chéruel, G. d'Avenel (Collection des documents inédits pour l'histoire de France, I Series) (9 vols., Paris 1872–1906), vii. 128, 177, 201–2. In March 1656 he was offering the Great Elector 15 *rdr.* for foot and 40 *rdr.* for cavalry.

2. Åke Lindqvist, 'Svenskarna och De Byes beskickningar 1654–1655', *Karolinska Förbundets Årsbok* (1941).

3. Birger Åsard, 'Upptakten till Karl X Gustavs anfall mot Polen 1655. Till frågan om krigets mål och medel', *Karolinska Förbundets Årsbok* (1970).

4. *Infra*, no. 15 (18 May 1655).

June Coyet could report Cromwell as saying that he and Charles 'could constrain the whole of Europe if there were a closer alliance between them'.[1] When the protector was officially notified of Charles's attack on Poland, he welcomed it as a blow for the Protestant Cause, and celebrated it with retrospective rhapsodies on Gustav Adolf. On the basis of a minimum of information he could as early as July speak of Charles with enthusiasm as 'your great and noble king'— a judgment which at that time was at least decidedly premature.[2] But for Cromwell, belief in Charles X as the Protestant Hero was almost a necessity: though God had chastened His people by the removal of Gustav Adolf, it was not to be thought of that He would leave them for ever comfortless, nor for ever deny to a godly England the chance to make atonement for the sin of Charles I's foreign policy.

All this might seem to indicate that Cromwell viewed a Swedish alliance in purely religious terms. And up to a point this is true. But it by no means follows that religious considerations were politically unrealistic. Among the statesmen of Europe, on either side of the religious divide, the idea that a new, general religious war was probable, imminent, perhaps inevitable, was indeed so far from being peculiar to the protector that it was almost a political commonplace.[3] From this point of view a Swedish alliance made sense, provided that it served to draw closer the bonds of protestant unity. But it did not make sense if its consequence should prove to be a loosening of those bonds; and this was one consideration—but not the only one—which in the end led Cromwell to decline it.[4]

There remains, however, the question—which cannot be avoided though it may be impossible to answer it—namely, how far we are justified in speaking of the foreign policy which England pursued during the protectorate as 'Cromwell's policy'? Judgments on that policy, whether adverse or favourable, have sometimes tended to assume, rather loosely, that it was. But this is to ignore that article in the Instrument of Government which laid it down that 'in all things concerning the keeping and holding of a good correspondency with foreign kings, princes and states . . .' the lord protector was bound to act 'by the advice aforesaid'—that is, by the advice of his council. S. R. Gardiner in his day, and Christopher Hill in our own, had apparently no doubt that he conformed to this restriction.[5] And indeed

1. *Infra*, no. 20 (8 June 1655).   2. *Infra*, no. 28 (11 July 1655).
3. Bonde, for one, was convinced of it; and so too were Schlezer and Sagredo.
4. See the perceptive and salutary essay by Roger Crabtree, 'The Idea of a Protestant Foreign Policy', in *Cromwell. A Profile*, ed. Ivan Roots (1973).
5. *The History of the Commonwealth and Protectorate 1649–1656* (new edn. 4 vols. 1903), iii. 334–7; idem, *Cromwell's Place in History* (1897), p. 86; Christopher Hill, *God's Englishman* (1970), p. 164.

there is plenty of evidence to suggest that it was no empty phrase: *ad hoc* sub-committees of the council were appointed to formulate policy on particular issues;[1] major decisions seem to have been taken by the council as a whole (Cromwell on one occasion told Nieupoort 'that he himself without the council did not use to dispose of such affairs');[2] Bordeaux clearly believed that policy-decisions were made in the council;[3] in September 1656 Barkman wrote to Charles X that 'all foreign affairs are at a stand, since *Concilium* does not sit'.[4] Its members were irremovable on all ordinary occasions; and in the fifteen nominated by the Instrument there seems to have been a reasonable balance between those who were predisposed towards Sweden, and those who (like the influential Strickland and Lawrence) were inclined to the Dutch: the council mirrored the conflicts in the protector's own mind.

Cromwell, after all, had no experience of foreign affairs, and (as Slingsby Bethel was later to put it, with unwonted moderation) 'I am apt to think, he was not guilty of too much knowledge of them'.[5] A few members of the council were rather better equipped;[6] and on occasion they had to intervene to remedy the protector's inexperience, or correct his *naiveté*. He came to the protectorate with certain strongly-held views of his own: the determination to see England pursue a foreign policy which bore witness to her religion; a conviction that it was his duty to deploy the arms which God had put in his hands—in the West Indies, perhaps, or it might be, in Flanders; and to these was added, after he had made peace with the Dutch, a firm resolve to remain on good terms with them, if possible—to the scandal of those Commonwealthsmen who in 1652–53 had been for a vigorous prosecution of the war and a Carthaginian peace. But there is no great reason to suppose that these ideals and ambitions, this mild intoxication of power, were not shared by at least some of his council. The fear of Orange and Stuart which had found expression in the Act of Seclusion, and which induced Oliver's ambivalent attitude towards Brandenburg (and Thurloe's too), must have been shared by his advisers. The refusal to accept preferential treatment for English

1. See e.g., *Calendar of State Papers (Domestic), 1657–8*, p. 27.
2. *A Collection of the State Papers of John Thurloe, Esq.*, ed. Thomas Birch (7 vols. 1742), iv. 653.
3. F. P. G. Guizot, *History of Oliver Cromwell and the English Commonwealth from the execution of Charles I to the death of Cromwell*, trans. Andrew R. Scoble (2nd edn. 2 vols. 1854), ii. 505, 517, 519–520, 550, 552.
4. BL Add. MS 38100, fo. 20.
5. [Slingsby Bethel], 'The World's Mistake in Oliver Cromwell', in *Harleian Miscellany; or a collection of scarce, curious and entertaining tracts . . . found in the late Earl of Oxford's library*, ed. W. Oldys (10 vols. 1808–1813), i. 289.
6. E.g. Fiennes, Lawrence, Strickland, Thurloe.

merchants at the hands of Charles X had solid backing in England, as Coyet perceived.[1] The Western Design, though it strikes us as peculiarly and personally Cromwell's, was apparently endorsed by the council after thorough debate; though once the enterprise against Hispaniola was seen to be a disastrous failure men were ready enough to put the whole blame on the protector.[2] The absence of any record of council debates on foreign policy, save in this instance, makes these contentions unprovable; but it does not make them improbable.

And they do in fact receive some support from these despatches. For while they make it possible for us to perceive Cromwell's personal reactions clearly, they also let us see that sometimes his opinions could be modified (and on one occasion overruled) by members of his council. Bonde seems to have been granted an exceptionally large number of private audiences, often with Thurloe as the only other person present; sometimes without even him: a total of fourteen in all, not counting two private talks in St James's Park. With the representatives of other countries the language employed at audiences had to be Latin, and it was convenient for the protector to have members of his council to assist him. With Bonde the conversation was in English, and we can hear the protector speaking: occasionally, it seems, to an already prepared brief, more often not; very frequently in a discursive, repetitious style. The results could on occasion be unfortunate, the expressions somewhat naive—as when he professed (to Coyet) to be unable to understand why the Dutch should think of sending a fleet to the Baltic 'since the driving of their usual trade thither was not refused to them'.[3] In his talks with Bonde he does not appear as a ready debater—as he does, for instance, when confronted with Commonwealthsmen and sectaries: when Bonde controverted the line which Cromwell and his advisers had agreed on beforehand, the protector was disconcerted, looked helplessly at Thurloe—and then simply reiterated what he had said before.[4] On occasion he seems to have accepted Bonde's arguments without giving the matter adequate consideration. One such incident occurred on 2 January 1656, at another private audience (without Thurloe, this time), when the question of the alliance was discussed between them, and the

---

1. *Infra*, no. 28 (11 July 1655), and no. 48 (7 December 1655).

2. On 28 September 1655 Coyet wrote: 'What weighs most heavily on the lord protector is that he knows that he urged and insisted on the American venture singly, against the desire and consent of the whole council, and so can blame no one but himself': *infra*, no. 37. Possibly he had this from a member of the council who took the opportunity of disavowing responsibility. Apart from Montagu's notes (*The Clarke Papers. Selections from the papers of William Clarke*, ed. C. H. Firth, (4 vols. Camden Society 1891–1901) iv. Appendix), the only other source is Thurloe, i. 759–63.

3. *Infra*, no. 28 (11 July 1655).

4. *Infra*, no. XXI (9 November 1655).

protector, who seems to have been fumbling for ideas, requested Bonde to give him his views as to what sort of alliance it ought to be. Bonde lacked precise instructions to guide him, and therefore played for time; but for the moment he committed himself to the opinion that it ought in the first instance to be defensive. And Oliver duly echoed him: 'we should think first of a defensive alliance'. When Bonde added that if such an alliance were concluded in the first instance between England and Sweden only, there was no real danger that the Dutch might take offence and seek the friendship of Spain, the protector 'skirted all round this with great caution', was 'somewhat taken aback' by Bonde's argument, 'spoke very slowly [and] wished it might be so'.[1] At the next audience, in the following week, it was a very different story. This time there was no faltering: the protector was as crisp and clear as his habitual style of conversation permitted; and roundly declared that nothing short of an offensive alliance against the House of Austria would serve.[2] Gardiner suggested that this declaration was prompted by his fear that the troubles between the protestant and catholic cantons in Switzerland might give an opportunity for intervention by the Habsburgs and by Bavaria.[3] But the protector had been fully apprised of the situation in Switzerland well before 2 January: in December he had offered to lend the protestant cantons £20,000.[4] One difference between the audience of 2 January and that which followed it is possibly not without significance: on the first occasion Cromwell was alone; on the second, Thurloe, Lambert and Fleetwood were with him. It seems not improbable that the change of attitude between 2 and 8 January was a consequence, not of the news from Switzerland, but of consultation with members of the council.

It seemed at first that Bonde's negotiations would follow the normal procedure: on 14 August Lisle, Pickering, Wolseley and Strickland were appointed commissioners to consider his proposals.[5] But everybody in the central government was at that time overwhelmed with pressing domestic business; the protector himself was ill that autumn, and Bonde found it difficult to obtain an audience; to his exasperation his commissioners did not meet him for business until 5 December; and meetings did not become regular until the following February.

1. *Infra*, no. XXIX (4 January 1656).
2. *Infra*, no. XXX (11 January 1656).
3. Gardiner, *Commonwealth and Protectorate*, iii. 443.
4. But when they made peace he cancelled the offer, Thurloe remarking that England could afford money only when protestantism was in danger—not when it made peace: Alfred Stern, 'Oliver Cromwell und die evangelische Kantone der Schweiz', *Sybels Historische Zeitschrift*, Bd. 40 (1878), p. 95.
5. *Infra*, no. VII (23 August 1655).

Though the evidence is a little confusing, it seems fairly clear that the intention was that the negotiations on recruiting, trade-privileges, contraband, and other minor issues which had been left unresolved by Whitelocke's treaty, should be dealt with by these commissioners; and it was appropriate that Whitelocke should be added to their number on 5 December.[1] The question of the alliance, however, seems early to have been placed upon a different footing. On 14 November 1655 Lambert, Fiennes and Strickland were appointed to be a committee to deal with those matters which the protector had communicated to council on 2 November as arising from an audience with Bonde (presumably that which had taken place on that day); and they were 'to meet daily until they have something to offer to the council'.[2] Whether in fact they met daily, as instructed, seems extremely doubtful, and of what they offered we have no record; but however that may be, the procedure which the protector was to use increasingly in the following months here has its beginning: consultation among, and advice from, a select group of council members. The original commissioners continued in a state of suspended animation until their composition was altered on 28 January 1656, when Lisle and Wolseley disappeared, and were replaced by Fiennes; but the nature of their concerns remained unchanged.[3]

Nevertheless, it seems that Cromwell could not make up his mind whether after all there should not also be commissioners to negotiate the alliance: on 8 January, after telling Bonde that he had much rather negotiate with him directly than by the usual device of commissioners, he had ended by promising that commissioners should meet him (inferentially, on the alliance) very shortly.[4] And the already existing commissioners were indeed appointed to meet him on that day. But with that their concern with the alliance came to an end before it had begun: Cromwell, after all, had made up his mind to do without them. Instead, he resurrected the idea which he had adumbrated on 8 January, and resolved to take the matter of the alliance entirely into his own hands. On 30 January he informed Bonde privately through Charles Fleetwood that in effect the commissioners would be restricted to treating only of minor details (by which he must have meant, the completion of Whitelocke's treaty: it would be difficult to say which items in Thurloe's draft could be considered 'minor'): the real negotiations would be carried on in

---

1. Whitelocke, *Memorials*, iv. 218; *cf. infra*, no. XXV (7 December 1655).
2. *CSP (Dom) 1655–56*, (1882), p. 20. The audience of 2 November had turned on Bonde's attempt to dissuade Cromwell from attempting mediation between Charles X and the Dutch.
3. Whitelocke, *Memorials*, iv. 221–2.
4. *Infra*, no. XXX (11 January 1656).

strict secrecy by private discussions between Bonde and himself.[1] The protector, it seemed, was to turn diplomat. It was not a part which natural genius or acquired experience fitted him to play. The decision no doubt proceeded from Oliver's extreme anxiety to conclude the alliance, and his feeling that he could get along with Bonde, on a personal level, better than an impersonal body of commissioners could do. And if the decision had been literally pursued, it must all too probably have landed him in difficulties. But already at the second secret audience after the inauguration of the new arrangement it became likely that in practice it might mean less than it had seemed to imply; for at that audience (15 February) Cromwell gave Bonde the confusing promise that he would *consider* the Swedish proposals in secret—but would *discuss* them with 'some members of the council'.[2] The wording might seem perplexing, but the protector as it turned out meant exactly what he said. Bonde might preen himself, as late as 11 April, on having 'conducted the entire negotiation with his highness personally, and without commissioners', and might regard that circumstance as eloquent of the unique confidence which existed between himself and the protector;[3] but though it was true that the commissioners, as a body, did not become involved, it is clear that some of them did. Pickering, for instance, was present at the audience of 6 March;[4] on 28 March Bonde had 'certain information that the alliance was being considered by the protector and council';[5] on 4 April, a week before Bonde made his self-satisfied report, it was resolved that 'The commissioners for the Swedish treaty ... meet the ambassador from Sweden this afternoon or to-morrow about business';[6] and on 11 April the protector somewhat belatedly informed him that the commissioners were to meet him shortly, though in fact they never seem to have done so.[7] All in all, we are left with the impression that the *secret du protecteur* was not so secret after all. Thurloe, Fleetwood, Pickering and Fiennes must have known all about it; the council itself seems to have been consulted: there was a limited spread of responsibility. But it was not sufficient to save Oliver from the kind of blunder which might have occurred more often if he

1. *Infra*, no. XXXIII (1 February 1656).
2. *Infra*, no. XXXV (15 February 1656). Whitelocke knew nothing of 'the most secret side of the business', and Bonde conjectured 'that his highness follows the maxim that the best way is to deceive such of his ministers as are to act in the affair': *infra*, no. XXXIII; and *cf.* Whitelocke, *Memorials*, iv. 222.
3. *Infra*, no. XLV (11 April 1656).
4. *Infra*, no. XXXIX (7 March 1656).
5. *Infra*, no. XLII (28 March 1656).
6. *CSP (Dom) 1655–56*, p. 256.
7. In regard to the alliance, that is: on other matters Bonde was meeting the commissioners regularly, and no special resolution was required.

had in fact kept the whole affair to himself. For in the course of a private audience on 11 April (without Thurloe) he made the astonishing declaration (if Bonde understood him correctly) that it was 'his absolute wish and determination to enter into a mutual defensive alliance *contra quoscunque*'.[1] Though Bonde's despatch expresses no surprise, this was in fact an astounding *volte-face*, a total reversal of the line to which he had been committed since the end of January, and at a most inappropriate moment. He was now accepting a defensive alliance (as he had done, to be sure, on 2 January, of which Bonde did not fail to remind him), instead of the offensive alliance demanded in Thurloe's terms; and by agreeing to *contra quoscunque* he was in fact excluding the Dutch from it. Whether his declaration is to be ascribed to inadvertence, or Bonde's pursuasions, or mental exhaustion accompanying bodily weariness, it was a major blunder; and it had to be quietly disavowed. It *was* disavowed, with little delay: on 21 April Thurloe and Fiennes informed Bonde that though the protector might perhaps be prepared to settle for a defensive alliance, he would certainly not swallow *contra quoscunque*.[2]

Whatever the explanation of this curious episode, it meant the end of Cromwell's venture into private diplomacy. Henceforward, the negotiations about the alliance proceeded—in so far as they proceeded at all—by way of private conversations with Thurloe (to whom, and not to the protector, Bonde first disclosed the full extent of Charles X's extravagant demands in his orders from Siedlice[2A]), and also with Fiennes and Fleetwood; and it is probably to them that Bonde alludes when he writes of dealings 'between me and the commissioners'.[3] After 11 April the protector resigned himself to leaving the negotiations to them, contenting himself with protestations of friendship, professions of personal regard for Bonde, anguished meditations about the Dutch, and rhetoric about the Protestant Cause.

When Charles X decided that he must seek an English alliance, it possibly occurred to him and his chancellor that the benefits to be expected from it—at least, if it were concluded on the terms that they had in mind—were more obvious from a Swedish than from an English angle. What indeed (he might think) had he to offer that England really needed? In a situation in which de Witt and Cromwell

1. *Infra*, no. XLVI (18 April 1656).
2. *Infra*, no. XLVII (25 April 1656).
2A. For those orders see p. 36, *infra*.
3. E.g. *infra*, nos. LII (30 May 1656), LIV (13 June 1656), LV (20 June 1656), LVII (27 June 1656) in all of which references to 'commissioners' turn out to mean talks with Thurloe or Fiennes. Bonde described Fiennes as 'the leading figure among my commissioners, and a very reasonable man': *infra*, no. LII (30 May 1656).

were linked together by common fear of Orange and Stuart, at a time when France and Spain were still competing for England's friendship, what need had the protector for an alliance with Sweden? In the Protestant Cause Charles never seems to have had more than a tepid interest: he had other, more pressing, more national, interests to take care of, and from these he was not to be diverted by the lamentations of oppressed protestants in Savoy, or Switzerland, or even nearer home in Silesia.[1] Any agreement for reciprocal military or naval aid, though it made good sense in Stockholm, could hardly be expected to have an equal appeal in London: the protector and his council might well ask themselves (though they do not seem to have asked Bonde) 'assistance against whom?' Until the outbreak of war with Spain the protectorate had no external enemy, despite the irritation of French privateering; and even after the Spanish war had begun, only misrepresentation—or misunderstanding—of Charles's activities in Poland could construe them as a useful diversion of Habsburg forces. It was perhaps a realization that this was so that led Bonde in the early months of his embassy to season his alliance-proposals with what he hoped might be tempting offers of trading advantages. Offers of this kind had indeed been made already by his predecessors in 1652 and 1653, and they came within the ambit of Coyet's and Bonde's instructions; but before 1655 they had been put forward, not with any alliance in view, but as equivalents for liberty of trade to America, or concessions in the herring-fishery off the British coasts, and had been designed simply to serve Swedish economic interests. These Swedish negotiators—Appelboom, Lagerfelt, Bonnel—had suggested, among other inducements, an English staple at Göteborg, or a preference for English merchants in the duties payable at harbours under Swedish control; and, not least, they had unrolled the grand prospect of a joint Anglo-Swedish effort to divert the Archangel trade to a port in Estonia, and in particular to Narva, Nyen or Reval.[2]

This last idea had a long history, and had for many years been a favourite pipe-dream of Swedish statesmen. As early as 1550 Gustav Vasa had had a plan for channelling the Russia trade through Swedish ports; but after the opening of the Archangel route John III had realized that no attempt to monopolize the trade to Muscovy could succeed as long as it was limited to the acquisition of ports on the

---

1. That is not to say, of course, that there was not plenty of zeal for the Protestant Cause among Swedish statesmen: Schering Rosehane was ranting about the danger from Roman catholicism in the approved style of puritan pulpit oratory: Artur Stille, *Schering Rosenhane som diplomat och ämbetsman* (Lund 1892), p. 111.
2. For Anglo-Swedish relations in the early fifties, A. Heimer, *De diplomatiska förbindelserna mellan Sverige och England 1633–1654* (Lund 1893) has now been supplanted by Sven Ingmar Olofsson, *Efter Westfaliska freden*.

southern Baltic shore and ignored the alternative outlet in the Arctic. In his reign, therefore, as in that of Charles IX, Sweden had attempted to conquer Archangel by expeditions moving overland across the Kola Peninsula. These efforts had had no success; and by the peace of Stolbova in 1617 this project was for the moment laid aside. But almost at once the Swedish council of state began to consider an alternative strategy: the diversion of the Archangel trade to Swedish harbours in Estonia or Livonia by the offer of inducements so attractive that the merchants who traded to Muscovy would find it in their interest to sail to Narva rather than to Archangel. If this could be accomplished, they believed, Sweden would be in fact in a position to control the Russia trade, in so far as it went by sea, and could expect a handsome revenue from the tolls which would be imposed upon it.[1] Reports on the feasibility of the scheme were commissioned by the Swedish government at frequent intervals: in 1633, 1634, 1643, 1653, and 1660—this last, incidentally, at the instigation of Coyet and Bonde. At the time of their mission to England, therefore, interest in the idea was running high in Swedish government circles: it was not until Pötter-Lillienhof's *Memorial* of 1674 that the council of state more or less resigned itself to a recognition of the fact that the plan was virtually impracticable.[2] There were many reasons for this negative conclusion, among the most important being the inadequacy of the harbour and port-facilities at Narva and the slender capital-resources of its inhabitants;[3] the fact that the tsars after the mid-century were themselves determined to promote an 'active' trade by their *gosti* through Baltic ports which they intended to conquer (though at the same time maintaining the Archangel trade under their own control, with attractive rates of toll);[4] the realization that the ruin of Archangel

1. For a useful short survey of the subject in English, see Artur Attman, *Swedish Aspirations and the Russian Market during the seventeenth Century* (Acta Regiae Societatis Scientiarum et Litterarum Gothoburgensis, Humaniora. 24). (Göteborg 1985).

2. The reports of these commissions are printed in the joint Swedish-Soviet *Ekonomiska förbindelser mellan Sverige och Ryssland under 1600-talet*, edd. A. Attman, A. L. Narotjintskij, *et al.*, (Stockholm 1978); and see Per Nyström, 'Mercatura Ruthenica', *Scandia* (1937), pp. 255–94. But already in 1643 Axel Oxenstierna had recognized that such a diversion was possible only if Sweden lowered duties at her Baltic ports, even if that meant cancelling their guest-right: K. R. Mellander, *Die Beziehungen Lübecks zu Schweden und Verhandlungen dieser beiden Staaten wegen des russischen Handels über Reval und Narva* (Helsingfors 1903), pp. 42, 50, 53, 58.

3. Shipping to and from Narva, according to the records of the Sound Tolls, dropped from 25 in 1654 to 15 in 1656 and 1 in 1657; partly, no doubt, owing to the Russian invasion of Estonia in 1656: Paul Bushkovitz, *The Merchants of Moscow* (Cambridge 1980), p. 76.

4. In the debate in the council on 11 December 1654 Bonde had spoken of the mercantile threat from the Russians and their desire for a Baltic harbour; though he had mistakenly supposed that their object was to replace the inconveniently located Archangel: *RRP*, xvi. 15.

could be achieved only by its conquest—an enterprise for which Sweden by then lacked the resources, and for which it would have been necessary to enlist naval aid from a foreign power—ideally, from England.[1] But until 1674 it remained an important objective of Swedish foreign and commercial policy; and to that objective the College of Commerce (of which, as we have seen, both Coyet and Bonde were assessors) was committed: hence its prominent place among the inducements with which Bonde sought to enhance the attractions of the alliance.

From the English point of view, the transference of the trade from Archangel to Narva might seem to have something to be said for it. The rigours of the Russian climate meant that an Archangel trader, if he was a Russian, got his turnover only in twelve months, and the foreign merchant in not less than five. A trade through the Baltic had thus advantages for westerners and Russians alike, as well as for the Swedish customs-revenues. Moreover, insurance would be cheaper, since the risk from piracy would be less; the cost of freight likewise. The Muscovy Company, which had enjoyed a uniquely privileged position in Russia since 1555, had had its privileges revoked in 1649 in consequence of the tsar's indignation at the execution of Charles I; and the mission of William Prideaux, sent in 1654 to endeavour to restore relations, had had only a limited success.[2] The Company, in whom the Archangel trade was vested, was in fact virtually moribund.[3] To shut down the Archangel trade, it appeared, would entail no great loss; the number of ships to visit the port had never been large; even the Dutch are estimated to have sent no more than twenty to thirty ships there each season; and as to the Company, it was never able (in Paul Bushkovitz's perplexing phrase) to despatch 'even a fraction' of that number to Archangel.[4] Nevertheless, the Archangel trade, such as it was, had advantages which made the

1. During the negotiations for an Anglo-Swedish alliance in 1665 the Swedes proposed an additional secret article providing for a joint Anglo-Swedish occupation of Archangel: the English rejected it: *Memoriën van den Zweedsche Resident Harald Appelboom*, ed. G. W. Kernkamp (Bijdr. en Mededeelingen van het Hist. Genootschap te Utrecht, vol. 26) (Amsterdam 1905), p. 366 n. 4. The last Swedish attempt to take Archangel was in 1701: see E. Holmberg, 'Sjöexpeditionen mot Arkangel 1701', *Karolinska Förbundet's Årsbok* (1918).

2. His report is printed in Thurloe, iii. 713 ff.

3. Though the Greenland whale-fishery was evidently still alive: in February and March 1656 the Muscovy Company successfully petitioned for freedom from impressment for the crews of five ships that were to sail there: *CSP (Dom) 1655–56*, pp. 183, 214.

4. Paul Bushkovitz, *The Merchants of Moscow, 1580–1650*, p. 44. And see Inna Lubimenko, 'The Anglo-Russian Relations during the first English Revolution', *TRHS*, 4th Series, xi (1928), pp. 39–60; and Maurice Ashley, *Financial and Commercial Policy under the Cromwellian Protectorate* (2nd edn. 1962), pp. 118–19.

Muscovy Company indisposed to lend an ear to Bonde's hints and persuasions. For despite the high cost of freight and insurance, trade to Archangel was still cheaper than trade to a Baltic port, for it escaped the Sound Dues, not to mention the tolls and harbour dues which could be imposed in the Baltic itself. It was also more certain, as being less liable to be dislocated by the dissensions of the Baltic powers. Moreover, after the new restrictions (from 1654) which forbade trading to the interior of Muscovy, it had the advantage of direct intercourse with Russian merchants, without the possible interposition of the guest-right which could obtain in some of the Baltic ports. It was probably these considerations which led the Muscovy Company to look coldly on Bonde's suggestions. As for the protector and his council of trade, there is no indication that either of them gave the idea much attention.[1] The Eastland Company, on the other hand, was ready and even anxious to come to an arrangement with Charles X: their trade was mainly to Danzig; and from Danzig they had experienced unkind treatment in the previous few years. They therefore looked forward to a Swedish occupation of that city, and counted on its being followed by the restoration of their old privileges—and, they hoped, by attractive new ones. But though the Committee of Trade received the petition which Bonde had instigated the Company to present, its only practical measure (nearly six months later) was to recommend the grant of a new charter which would have done something to liberalize the Company's constitution, and for the first time legitimized its trade to Narva.[2]

It does not appear that either the protector, or the commissioners with whom Bonde negotiated, ever seriously nibbled at the plan to give English merchants special privileges in Swedish-controlled ports.[3]

---

1. In August 1656 Barkman found that England would take no steps for any diversion against Russia (by which he probably meant, against Archangel), though Thurloe indicated that he had no objection to a purely private enterprise: BL Add. MS. 38100, fo. 405v.

2. R. W. K. Hinton, *The Eastland Trade and the Common Weal in the Seventeenth Century* (Cambridge 1959), pp. 124–9; Ashley, *Financial and Commercial Policy*, pp. 125–31; Report of the Committee of Trade and Plantations, 3 June 1656, in *CSP (Dom) 1655–56*, p. 346.

3. All that was conceded in the treaty of 1656 was the confirmation of former 'prerogatives', and most-favoured-nation treatment in future. Pufendorf (ii. 136) notes that Bonde's commissioners replied to his offers by remarking that they were valueless, since Denmark assured to the Dutch the same advantages at the Sound as Sweden could offer in Livonia and Prussia. This probably reflects Thurloe's suggestion (*infra*, no. IX, 31 August) that the Dutch might obtain advantages from Denmark in reply to Swedish advantages in Eastland. But the protectorate's peace with Denmark had guaranteed (art. VI) equality of treatment with the Dutch. One apparent exception to English indifference was the suggestion that a government company might be formed to buy up all Sweden's copper: this led to a preposterous proposal in 1657 (*infra*, p. 291

It was in vain that Bonde argued—correctly enough—that the interests of England and Sweden here ran parallel, in that both were concerned to lessen the commercial ascendancy of the Dutch. Swedish overseas trade in Swedish bottoms was in fact expanding; largely, it seems, as a result of their buying Dutch fly-boats. England, no doubt, bought them or captured them too: but it has been contended that these acquisitions were mainly employed in other trades (e.g. to the Levant) where the danger from privateers was less.[1] At all events Bonde's arguments seem to have made no impression, perhaps for that reason.[2] Swedish trading strategy had for the last two decades been directed to the maximization of revenue from customs and tolls: it had been Axel Oxenstierna's policy to give the utmost encouragement to traders of all nations, and to rely on the expansion of revenue which would result from keeping duties constant, and above all low. His famous *Instruction* to the College of Commerce, upon its creation in 1651, had had this clearly in mind:[3] only so, he believed, could his main objective be attained—the channelling of all the trade which flowed down the rivers of central and eastern Europe to Swedish-controlled ports. But this went hand in hand, from 1645 onwards, with a system of preferences for Swedish-owned and Swedish-manned merchantmen; and the rapid expansion of the Swedish mercantile marine during the years of the first Anglo-Dutch war had focused attention on this development.[4] With the coming of the war with Poland the situation was altered in another aspect also; for Charles X now needed a quick increase in customs revenue to help to pay for his armies. It is true that he assured Cromwell that tolls and duties would be kept at the old low level of 2%; but necessity forbade adherence to this principle: the tolls at Riga, for instance, were raised twice within three years; export duties on copper were quadrupled, to the dismay of English importers. The blockade of Danzig, as

---

n. 2); but the only trace of the idea in Bonde's treaty lay in an attached convention whereby a conference was suggested with a view to agreeing upon a price for those Swedish exports to England which were now to be deemed contraband if supplied to Spain.

1. Violet Barbour, 'Dutch–English Merchant Shipping in the Seventeenth Century', *Economic History Review*, I Series, ii (1929–30), pp. 272, 290.

2. But the petitions of merchants for convoys as far as Norway and the Sound suggest that fly-boats may well have been used in this trade, convoys being almost essential to the operation of the unarmed fly-boats: a standing convoy was in fact agreed to in June 1656: *CSP (Dom) 1655–56*, pp. 203, 222, 242, 304, 345.

3. Printed in A. A. von Stiernman, *Samling utaf kongl. bref, stadgar och förordningar etc. angående Sweriges rikes commerce, politie och oeconomie i gemen ifrån åhr 1523* (6 vols. Stockholm 1747–75), ii. 669–76.

4. See Birger Fahlborg, 'Ett blad ur den svenska handelsflottans historia, 1660–1675', *Historisk tidskrift* (1921), and Sven Grauers, 'Sverige och den första engelska navigationsakten', in *Historiska studier tillägnade Ludvig Stavenow* (Stockholm 1924), p. 57.

Charles smoothly explained it to other nations, was not to be considered as designed to produce extra revenue, but as a legitimate measure of economic warfare intended to damage the Polish economy and to prevent the import of strategic commodities which might assist the Polish war-effort. Though there was some truth in this, and although the record of the United Provinces in this regard left them in no position to cast a stone, behind this explanation lay a clear expectation—once Danzig had been brought to heel—of large fiscal gains: the Dutch could expect the episode of the *licenter* to be repeated.

As far as England was concerned the blockade of Danzig on 25 August, in itself, caused no great alarm: Danzig had imposed forced contributions on English merchants living there, it was reputed a centre of royalism, and relations with the protectorate were bad. But Danzig as a presage of what might happen if the whole Prussian coastline should pass into Swedish hands—that was, perhaps, another matter, despite the optimism of the Eastland Company. Though Charles might for the moment be offering England preferential treatment, his evident designs upon the Baltic littoral—'royal' Prussia first, Courland perhaps later (as actually happened in 1658)—threatened to produce a situation in which almost all the Baltic ports, with the possible exception of Königsberg, would be at his mercy. If that happened, the pledge of preference for English ships might indeed be honoured, but customs and dues might not improbably be raised at the good pleasure of the conqueror, as Christian IV in his day had raised them at the Sound. The protector and his council must have been alive to this possibility; the English mercantile community also. In the immediate future, whatever the short-term advantages to English traders might be, it was not difficult to foresee that sooner or later the Dutch would intervene, that a rupture between them and Charles X would follow, and that the unity of the protestant powers would be broken. If this were to occur, how valuable would any preferences accorded to England be likely to be? Even if England succeeded in avoiding involvement in such an imbroglio, the mere acceptance of Swedish preferences could not fail to be construed by the Dutch as a provocation. Bonde had no sooner made his offers—general at first, more precise very shortly—than he found that Coyet had been right when he advised that it would be wiser not to make them.

It could perhaps be argued that the protectorate could afford to take the risk of alienating the Dutch, in view of the immediate benefits which preferences might bring with them: the Dutch, after all, had just been soundly beaten, and their navy was in no state to resume the war. Or rather, it had been in no state to do so before the launching of the Western Design, and the outbreak of war with Spain which followed in November 1655. But thenceforward, as the protector complained, he found himself committed to maintaining three large fleets in widely-separated parts of the world: one in the West Indies, one in the Mediterranean, and one in home waters[1]—all of them largely dependent upon Dutch freighters for naval stores. The naval balance of power was no longer so obviously in England's favour as it had been. Henceforward the *régime* was under severe financial strain to keep the war going; and that meant that the monthly assessments must be increased again, after their temporary reduction in 1654. And it could never be forgotten that it was de Witt's own province of Holland—the province which had passed the Act of Seclusion—which was most concerned in the Baltic trade, and that Amsterdam, which was the nerve-centre of that trade, was bitterly hostile to Sweden. To quarrel with Holland over Baltic preferences risked subverting a main bastion of defence against Orange and Stuart. Quite apart from this, it was questionable whether the prospective gains from a preference in Swedish-controlled ports would, even in the short term, pay for the hazards of accepting it. As Bonde himself frankly pointed out, neither England nor Sweden possessed the tonnage of suitable ships necessary to compete with the Dutch in the Baltic trade: the Hollanders' spe-cially-designed 'fly-boats' could 'sail the English off the seas'.[2] Of this responsible statesmen in England must have been well aware. It was tacitly recognized that the Navigation Act was unenforceable in regard to the Baltic trade: its most perceptible effect in this region was to stimulate the carrying of Scandinavian exports in Swedish and Norwegian bottoms. England was in fact probably doing as much trade to the Baltic as she had the capacity to carry. Whereas the Eastland Company's petition of 1649 had included three paragraphs about the danger of Dutch competition, those paragraphs were omitted from their petition of 1656.[3] Bonde was quite right when, in rebutting the objection that preferences for the English would be damaging to the Dutch, he replied that whatever the situation, most goods from the Baltic would in any case have to be carried in Dutch vessels. Without the cargoes that they brought in the great Cromwell-ian navy could hardly be fitted out and maintained.[4]

At all events, Bonde's offers of commercial advantages met with a

---

1. *Infra*, no. LVII (4 July 1656). This dispersal of the fleets had been determined on as early as January 1656: *infra*, no. 52 (18 Jan. 1656).

2. *Infra*, nos. VII (23 August 1655) and XXXIII (1 February 1656).

3. Hinton, p. 127. The petition is printed in *CSP (Dom) 1655–56*, p. 97.

4. Compare Aitzema's argument disposing of the idea that Sweden could give, or England get, a monopoly of the Baltic trade: 'money is master of commerce ... and Amsterdam master of money': Thurloe, iv. 333.

cool reception, and that reaction was not peculiar to the protector. It may well be that Oliver was not well informed on mercantile matters, though it can hardly be maintained that he was uninterested in them. No doubt he made his personal position quite clear at the audience of 21 September, when he told Bonde that the *fundamenta* of his policies were 'freedom of religion and trade';[1] and if England's attitude on that point was to be considered as determined by the protector, that was answer enough. But the commissioners to whom Bonde expatiated on the opportunities he was offering showed no sign of appreciating them; and the negative attitude of some of them can be inferred from the fact (or what Bonde believed to be the fact) that they leaked the terms of his offers to the Dutch. If the Committee of Trade was of a different opinion, Bonde heard nothing of it, though his offers must have been discussed when they took the Eastland Company's petition into consideration. There have been widely differing views about English commercial policy during the protectorate; but the history of Bonde's negotiation seems at any rate to rule out, on the one hand, the suggestion that 'economic opposition to the Dutch was the funda-mental note of Cromwell's policy', and, on the other, the view that Cromwell sacrificed English commercial interests to the pursuit of a general protestant alliance.[2] In this matter Bonde and Nieupoort were in agreement: both report the protector as declaring unambiguously that he would entertain no proposal for privileges to the exclusion, or the prejudice, of the Dutch.[3] And it is difficult to resist the conclusion that in 1655–56 this was a sober and rational assessment of the situation, both economic and political.

Certainly it accorded well with the policy of de Witt, manifested repeatedly in the years from 1654 to 1658. In his first letter to Nieupoort in January 1655 he had declared his hope of increasing Dutch understanding for, and good-will to, the protector. He had promised to keep a sharp eye on the royalists; he had toyed with the idea of a union of the churches.[4] He was punctilious (as Thurloe was not) in observing his obligation under article XV of the treaty of Westminster to provide an opportunity for England's adhesion to any treaty the United Provinces might conclude, though by doing so he much dis-pleased the Great Elector.[5] In August 1655 he told Nieupoort that he hoped that each republic would agree in forswearing any trade

1. *Infra*, no. XIV (28 September 1655).
2. G. L. Beer, 'Cromwell's policy in its economic aspects', *Political Science Quarterly*, xlvii (1902), p. 47; Menna Prestwich, 'Diplomacy and Trade under the Protectorate', *Journal of Modern History* (1950), pp. 103–21.
3. *Infra*, no. XXIX (4 January 1656); Thurloe, iv. 389.
4. *Brieven geschreven ende gewisselt tusschen de Heer Johan de Witt . . . ende de gevolmaghtigden van de Staet der Verenigde Nederlanden* (6 vols.'s Gravenhage 1723–5), iii. 4, 14, 93, 96.
5. *Ibid.*, iii. 55; Thurloe, iii. 544.

preference at the expense of the other;[1] in March 1656 he instructed
his ambassadors in Denmark that in any alliance which might be
concluded between them, England must be included on terms which
gave the protectorate advantages equal to those which might be
accorded to the Dutch;[2] and, most notably, he secured that England
should obtain equal advantages from the treaty of Elbing. The seal
was set on this policy when, after a period of sharp tension and
mutual suspicion, the States-General in February 1658 acknowledged
Downing's offer to seek no special privileges for England in the Baltic
by giving reciprocal assurances on behalf of the United Provinces.[3] It
may be said that in matters of trade the Dutch could afford to be
generous; but there were many merchants in Amsterdam who did not
think so. What drew de Witt and Cromwell together, what restrained
them from pursuing policies likely to aggravate the underlying tension
between the republics, was a consciousness of the similarity of their
political positions. For de Witt, the overriding need was to defend the
True Freedom; for Cromwell, to safeguard the protectoral *régime*.
Each was confronted with a common enemy: Orange and Stuart.

It is of course obvious that Cromwell did not hesitate to pursue on
occasion an anti-Dutch policy in defence of English interests—a 'cold
war', as Hinton put it; but only in areas where he could risk it (as
Thurloe was later to say) 'without we doe provoke them beyond
measure'.[4] Dutch ships were taken at Barbados for violating the
Navigation Act; de Ruyter was humiliated in the Channel on suspicion
of convoying the supply of war-materials to Spain.[5] There was such
bitter indignation at the transport of Spanish silver to Amsterdam
under Dutch protection that Schlezer thought it might lead to war.[6]
Englishmen had a general disposition to regard the Dutch as careless
of higher obligations if only their profits were safeguarded: as Thurloe
wrote to Morland, 'the Hollanders had rather he [the protector]
should be alone in it [the common struggle against popery], than that
they should lose a tun of sack, or a frail of raisins'.[7] In March 1656
Nieupoort reported to de Witt that 'The jealousy and the hatred of
most merchants in the nation for us is incredible, and all the sectaries
seem also much animated against the United Netherlands—not for
any particular reason, but through an extraordinary urge and tur-
bulent spirit, which expresses itself in blood-thirstiness and confusion'.[8]

1. *Brieven*, iii. 110.   2. *Ibid.*, v. 434.
3. Thurloe, vi. 790–1, 818–19.
4. Thurloe, vi. 609: Thurloe to Henry Cromwell, 10 November 1657.
5. CSP (*Dom*) *1655–56*, p. 284.
6. *Urk. und Act.* vii. 744–5.
7. Robert Vaughan, *The Protectorate of Oliver Cromwell* (2 vols. 1839), i. 433–4,
Morland to Pell, 1 July 1656, quoting Thurloe to Morland.
8. *Brieven*, iii. 336–7.

But it seems to have been appreciated that there were limits beyond which unfriendly acts must not go; and the Baltic—perhaps uniquely—fell outside those limits. Thurloe's too well remembered sentence—'there were no greater considerations in England, in reference to forraigne affairs, than how to obviate the growing greatness of the Dutch'[1]—does not apply to Oliver at all: it refers to the special situation which arose after Charles X's second war with Denmark, and in particular to the early months of 1659. And the reason why the Baltic must be an exception was clear enough to the protector: more than once he pointed out to Bonde that the Baltic was 'the Dutchman's bread basket'.[2] The events of 1657–58 make it clear that Cromwell was not prepared to see the Baltic dominated by a single power, whether that power were Sweden or the Dutch.[3] This was a policy determined by economic considerations, and it cut across religious volitions. But unless the Dutch appeared to be meditating such a design, and once the suspicion that they were doing so proved to be groundless—when, in fact, Anglo-Dutch relations were as normal as Cromwell wished them to be—the protector and his advisers paid little attention to the clamours of those who lamented 'the lost trades': they sensibly accepted the fact that in so far as they *were* lost there was for the moment no help for it, no instant remedy; and they acquiesced in a situation which could not be mended by any immediate action of the state. It took Bonde some time before he grasped this. As late as the end of December 1655 he was still hoping that England would accept trade-concessions: the policies of the College of Commerce perhaps obscured the judgment of the

---

1. John Thurloe, 'Concerning the Forraigne Affairs in the Protector's Time', in *A Collection of scarce and valuable tracts ... extracted from public as well as private libraries, particularly that of the late Lord Somers*, ed. Sir W. Scott (2nd edn., 13 vols., 1809–15), vi. 331. His views are better reflected in his report on the negotiations with the Dutch for a Marine Treaty, printed in *EHR*, xxvi (1906), pp. 327 ff., in which he wrote 'And therefore though this state was very desirous of a neare and intimate conjunction with them, *as well for the support of things at home* [my italics], as for the managing of common designs abroad, yet it being evident that noe agreement could be made with them in these affairs without condescending to some things very prejuditiall to the kingdom in the great concernment of trade, the thoughts of such Allyances were even lay'd aside, and the considerations of preserving the Comers and navigation of this state ... were applyed to, least the English should be wholly eaten out by the people of the united Netherlands, but yet with a desire of holding a good Correspondence with them herein'.

2. *Infra*, nos. XXI (9 November 1655) and XXIX (4 January 1656).

3. See Michael Roberts, 'Cromwell and the Baltic', in Roberts, *Essays in Swedish History* (1967), pp. 159–70. Thurloe explained Cromwell's refusal of Charles X's offers in 1657 as being based on his fear that if Charles were to conquer Denmark 'he might engross the whole trade of the Baltic Sea wherein England is so much concerned': C. H. Firth, *The Last Years of the Protectorate* (2 vols. 1909) i. 321.

diplomat.[1] Charles X was quicker to appreciate the true position; and his orders from Schlippenbeil on 6 January forbade his ambassador to pursue the idea.

For the moment, Charles was much more concerned to obtain permission to raise recruits in Scotland than to pursue the long-term aims of the College of Commerce. Initially, it seemed that there would be no difficulty about it. But in this as in all other matters the protectorate deployed its well-tried tactics of procrastination. And this for two main reasons. The first was an intelligible nervousness that the highlanders recruited might sooner or later be available to the royalists; the second was that until news came of the fate of the attack on Hispaniola the protector could not be sure that they might not be needed as reinforcements for General Venables: Coyet's despatches reveal with what deep anxiety Cromwell waited for that information. But if there were difficulties on the English side, so there were also on the Swedish. For if the troops were to be recruited at all, those who raised them and shipped them over to Stade must be paid—and paid in advance. And if Charles X was short of troops, he was still shorter of money. The Scottish enterprisers raised their troops on credit; Charles duly authorized his commissioner in Hamburg to pay for them; but when Coyet or Bonde asked him for a draft it appeared that he had in the meantime received orders to apply the money to other urgent needs, with the result that the unfortunate Swedish diplomats had to dip into their own pockets, and gravely imperil their credit, in order to avert the scandal of a default, the damage to prestige, and the still more serious loss of the troops. In this, as in some other things, Charles did not measure his plans by his resources. Both Bonde and Coyet were soon more or less in financial difficulties (in Bonde's case, aggravated by an unreasonably large and expensive suite, designed to impress his colleagues and his host with a proper sense of his master's greatness), and both felt themselves obliged to lend substantial sums to Benjamin Bonnel to save him from a debtor's prison, and indeed from absolute starvation.[2] This, however, was of peripheral importance. Bonde's secret instruc-

1. Abbott's remark that Nieupoort prevailed over Bonde because he urged grounds of trade, but Bonde grounds of religion, is true neither for the one nor for the other: Abbott, iv. 78.
2. He put his claim for unpaid wages at 2580 rdr.: RA. Anglica 515 (unfoliated). His desperate letter to Thurloe appealing for help, as being an Englishman, is printed infra, p. 101, n 1. But this kind of thing was one of the normal hazards of the diplomatic life: Magnus Dureel in Copenhagen was in the same straits: C. C. Gjörwell, Nya svenska biblioteket, (2 vols. Stockholm 1762–3), ii. 177–9; so too was Harald Appelboom at The Hague: RRP. xvi. 334–5.

tions of 15 June 1655 had defined 'the real purpose' of his mission as being to obtain a closer alliance which should bind England to assist Sweden if any foreign power should try to send a fleet of war into the Baltic. And the *modus auxilij ferendi* which Charles was proposing was the putting of twenty English warships under his command, usable at his sole discretion, the expense of the enterprise being to be borne by England. Cromwell's instructions to Whitelocke in 1653 had clearly contemplated the sending of an English fleet to the Sound, if that should be necessary; and the treaty of Uppsala, concluded when the immediate danger from the Dutch was over, had declared the intention of the parties to safeguard freedom of navigation, not only at the Sound, but in the Baltic also, and indeed in all the seas of western Europe, not forgetting the Mediterranean. Charles X could cite this provision in asking for English assistance against any 'disturbers who would interrupt, prohibit, hinder, constrain, and force [trade] to their own will', within the Baltic. Any disturbance of this sort seemed likely to come from the Dutch, as their negotiations with de Bye had suggested. But two views were possible as to what really constituted disturbance. To Charles, it meant any attempt to constrain him to keep the ports open, and the duties at a level tolerable to those who paid them; to the Dutch, it meant the hindering of normal trade by blockade, or by exorbitant *licenter*. From the Swedish point of view, moreover, another long-established principle was involved: the doctrine of *dominium maris Baltici*,[1] which laid it down that no other power than the two Scandinavian monarchies was permitted to keep a fleet of war in the Baltic. That doctrine had most recently been violently asserted by Christian IV, when in 1637, without a declaration of war, he had annihilated the infant navy of Poland. And it was in line with the idea of *dominium maris* that Charles X did not now ask for an English *squadron* to be sent to the Baltic, but rather requested the loan of twenty individual ships from the English navy, which would merge with the Swedish fleet and lose their national identity in the process of patrolling the coasts of Prussia.

Between the arguments of Bonde and Nieupoort as to the nature of the threatened disturbance of trade the protector might well have difficulty in making up his mind; but one conclusion, at least, presented no problem: there seemed to be no good reason for agreeing to act as an auxiliary coastguard patrol in the Swedish service, especially as he was being asked to pay for that privilege. The suggestion that England should hand over a large number of ships to

1. See Nils Ahnlund, 'Dominium maris baltici', in his *Tradition och historia* (Stockholm 1956), and Fahlborg, *Sveriges yttre politik 1660–64*, pp. 25–32. Coyet and Bonde were not without nervousness lest England might by analogy raise similar claims in regard to the British seas.

Charles's absolute control, at a time when more ships were likely to be needed for the West Indies, when a war with Spain was at least possible, and peace with France not yet made—this was a singularly sanguine programme. Bonde's instructions had authorized him, in imprecise terms, to indicate that Charles might be willing to give some financial aid, if the protector found the burden too heavy;[1] but he was left uncertain about where it was intended that the ships should be used, about how much Charles would be prepared, if necessary, to contribute to their cost, and about any particular provisions that might be intended regarding their command. His enquiries on all these points elicited no answer from his sovereign—no doubt because Sweden's financial position in fact made any contribution impossible. All that he got was a letter from Koło of 22 August 1655, in which Charles suggested an agreement whereby he would assist Cromwell with as many ships in the Channel as England provided for him in the Baltic:[2] an exchange which made little sense, and was scarcely calculated to appeal to the protector, who would no doubt have much preferred to retain twenty of his own seasoned warships than to rely in an emergency upon aid from a Swedish fleet which was no longer the force that had shattered the navy of Christian IV at Femern in 1644. It is scarcely surprising that Bonde made no great effort to pursue the idea of an alliance on such terms.

About the time when Bonde's instructions were drawn up, the Dutch ambassador Nieupoort had put forward the idea of a triple alliance between England, Denmark and the United Provinces to safeguard commerce in the Baltic.[3] England had thus two options open; and the protector felt himself in a dilemma between them. The Dutch suggestion had obvious attractions, in contrast to the possible effect of accepting the Swedish proposals. For if England turned down the Dutch in favour of a Swedish alliance, that might endanger the great gain of 1654, when Denmark had conceded to England the same rate of toll at the Sound as that fixed for the Hollanders: in the very worst case, the protector might find himself confronted with another closure of the Sound to English shipping. It was certainly true (and was well understood in England, despite Bonde's propaganda) that the object of the Dutch was to settle the Baltic problem by peaceful negotiation: Nieupoort among other expedients spoke of an Anglo-Dutch mediation, on the model of that which had brought off the truce of Altmark in 1629.[4] Cromwell himself hoped for mediation by

1. Pufendorf, ii. 133.
2. *Infra*, no. XVI (12 October 1655).
3. *Brieven*, iii. 60–1 (7 May NS 1655), 62–3 (14 May NS 1655), 186–7 (25 February NS 1656).
4. *Brieven*, iii. 107 (20 August NS 1655).

England alone. But mediation by any power, or combination of powers, was in this early stage of the Polish war ruled out by Charles's absolute refusal to entertain it: he was in a position in which he could not afford to call off his war, if only because he lacked the money to pay off the forces he had raised to fight it.

Nevertheless, since Cromwell and his advisers had not yet appreciated Charles's determination to decline mediation, they might well have chosen the Dutch solution, had it not been for two things. First, the very real desire for a Swedish alliance—of which Whitelocke was the most vociferous, though not the most influential, representative—as part of a general protestant front: it was, after all, a moment when Englishmen were putting their hands in their pockets to succour the slaughtered saints of the Vaudois, and they looked to Charles to second their efforts. And secondly, because the Dutch seemed to be confusing the issue by their anti-Swedish treaty with Brandenburg—a measure which was ominously coincident with an upsurge of Orange feeling in the Netherlands, and was believed (mistakenly) to have been engineered by Amalia von Solms.[1] In these circumstances the protector and Thurloe were irresolute and more than ordinarily procrastinatory, to the exasperation equally of Bonde and of Nieupoort: Oliver was reported to be *en peine*. Even when the Brandenburg issue was resolved by Charles's imposition of his alliance upon the elector by the treaty of Königsberg, that did little—at first—to clarify the minds of those who directed policy in London: Thurloe's contradictory comments on that alliance make it plain that he could not make up his mind whether it represented a great gain for the Protestant Cause, or a defeat for the Dutch.

By the end of 1655, however, Cromwell and his advisers at last began to formulate a solution to their problem. Three developments forced them to it. One was the spectacular success of Charles's campaign in Poland; the second was the approach of civil strife in the Swiss cantons, which coming so soon after the Vaudois affair strengthened a feeling that Europe was on the brink of a general religious war; and the third was a change in Swedish diplomatic tactics designed to play upon that feeling. Bonde himself had at first been ready to think in terms of a protestant crusade: in one of his earlier despatches he had

---

1. Thurloe regarded the Dutch–Brandenburg alliance as 'an Orange triumph': see de Witt's denial, *Brieven*, iii. 69 (6 August NS 1655). For reports of the Orange revival, *ibid.*, iii. 125–6, 170–2; Thurloe, iv. 35, 203–4, 262–3, 312–13. *Cf.* Sir Henry de Vic to Nicholas, 1 November 1655: 'You heare how the old Princess Dowager of Orange is returnd, and how made much of by those in Amsterdam for having gotten the Elector of Brandenbourg to doe what they desird of. How doe you thinke Mr Cromwell will looke upon this, both as it referrs to the Suedes and the howse of Nassau?': *The Nicholas Papers: correspondence of Sir Edward Nicholas*, ed. Sir G. F. Warner (Camden Society, 4 vols. 1886–1920), iii. 103.

defined the object of the projected alliance as defence of protestantism against the catholic powers; in October he was writing of 'a terrible black cloud ... threatening us all with a great and violent tempest'.[1] In this matter the verbal instruction which he had received from Charles had ordered him to proceed '*caute*'; and though he twice enquired what Charles's views might be as to an alliance founded expressly upon religion, the only reply which he had hitherto received had reiterated that order.[2] But the protector's appeals on behalf of the Vaudois and the Swiss seem to have persuaded Charles that this might, after all, be the lever he needed in order to shift England in the direction which he required. His instructions from Proszowice of 25 October for the first time ordered Bonde to exploit the fear of a general catholic league as an argument for a Swedish alliance.[3] They reached Bonde on 30 November; and he lost no time in obeying them. In talks with Whitelocke on 14 December, in audiences with the protector on the same day and on 2 and 8 January, he beat the protestant drum with enthusiasm.

To English observers it was tempting, in the context of protestant fears, and of Charles's triumphant entry into Warsaw, to see him as the deliverer, the new 'Lion of the North'. The Swedish alliance became more attractive, and it seemed also more necessary. Bonde himself, expressing his private belief that the subjugation of Poland could hardly fail to be followed by a war with the Habsburgs, reported that 'some leading personages' were saying that if that should happen the English might be provided with a good opportunity for a descent on Flanders.[4] The enthusiastic Whitelocke was for an immediate offensive and defensive alliance which should destroy the papacy and put Charles on the imperial throne, while Cromwell, he thought, might then take 'places convenient to him'.[5] But though Bonde drily commented that he probably had not thought the matter through, his spontaneous reaction may have expressed a feeling shared by others. At all events, by the beginning of 1656 the months of havering between Sweden and the Dutch came to an end. The protector and his council, encouraged by Bonde's overtures, persuaded themselves that they could by a deft stroke of diplomacy reconcile the irreconcilables in an alliance which, in the name of protestant unity, should comprehend them both. The Swedish alliance was to be embraced in the context of a grand rally of protestant powers: it was to be part of

1. *Infra*, nos. VII (23 August), IX (31 August), XXI (9 November 1655).
2. *Infra*, nos. VII, IX, XXXVI (16 February 1656).
3. The instructions from Proszowice are summarized in Carlbom, *Sverige och England*, p. 47.
4. *Infra*, no. XXIV (30 November 1655).
5. *Infra*, no. XXVI (14 December 1655).

a general system. How far such a system could avail to defuse the smouldering situation in the Baltic, how far persuade the Dutch to suffer Charles's proceedings, they seem not to have paused to consider: the protector might lay it down that relations with the Dutch must be settled before the protestant union could take shape, but he offered no suggestions as to how that difficult feat was to be accomplished. For the moment his ideas were limited to a general alliance, offensive as well as defensive, against Roman catholics in general, and the Habsburgs in particular, and that alliance must include other protestant states, and perhaps France also. To which Bonde objected that he had no powers to conclude a general alliance (which was true); that it would be better first to conclude the Anglo-Swedish treaty, and then invite other states to adhere to it; that perhaps the League of Heilbronn was a useful model to follow (with, *impliciter*, a Swedish *direktorium* as in the time of Axel Oxenstierna?); and that he must take time to consider the proposal for an offensive alliance, not having hitherto supposed that the protector wished to go so far.[1]

He was not given much time for consideration. Already the difference had emerged which was to obstruct the implementation of the Proszowice strategy: the question, namely, whether the Anglo-Swedish alliance was to be concluded first, and the Dutch then to be invited to accede to it, or whether they (and other protestant states) were to be co-equal founder members of it. The draft terms with which Bonde was confronted on 26 January constituted a formidable statement of the English attitude. He was offered an offensive and defensive alliance to be directed against the House of Habsburg, 'whereof Poland is a chief branch' (an addition meant to be conciliatory). An army was to be raised to attack these enemies. The Dutch and other states were to be members of the alliance, and no peace was to be made without the consent of them all. If either party should be attacked in consequence of the alliance, the other was to give assistance 'regard being had to his circumstances'.[2] No rebels or fugitives were to be entertained by either, and royalist privateers were to be deemed pirates. There was to be no raising of tolls in either party's possessions, nor in possible conquests made by either.[3]

Such was the proposal. If Charles X's original terms for the alliance had shown little understanding of what England could reasonably be

---

1. And he could not help wondering whether the phrase 'the common cause' might not be a cloak to conceal the unacceptable idea of mediation: *infra*, no. XXXII (25 January 1656).

2. The formulation was borrowed from the final clause of art. XV of the treaty of Uppsala, and the English might therefore reasonably suppose that it was precise enough.

3. *Infra*, no. XXXIII (1 February 1656); Thurloe, iv. 486–7.

expected to do, England's terms for Charles showed an insensitivity to his probable reactions, and a misjudgment of political realities, which are astonishing. They would have committed him to attack Austria (which he had no desire whatever to do), and assumed that an assurance of the continuance of England's war with Spain balanced an obligation on Charles to involve himself in a new one; they left the matter of reciprocal aid decidedly dubious; they would have precluded him from making an advantageous peace (which at that time looked possible) unless England should also make peace with Spain (which was highly unlikely); they would have committed him to overt hostility to the Stuarts, which might have inconveniences later if there should be a new turn of the political wheel in England; they infringed his sovereignty in his own dominions by denying him the right to increase tolls if he thought proper, and barred the full exploitation of *licenter* in any ports he might conquer; and, finally, their inclusion of the Dutch settled the issues between Sweden and the United Provinces out of hand by virtually ignoring them. Eight months later, in very different circumstances, Charles would be glad enough to come to terms with the Dutch by the treaty of Elbing; but in January 1656, on the morrow of the treaty of Königsberg, at a moment when Swedish fortunes in Poland were at their zenith, the English proposals could hardly have been more ill-timed. All that Charles was being offered in return for this trampling on his most sensitive feelings was a liberty of recruiting—and that was but one more promise added to many ill-performed predecessors. Bonde was entitled to feel that the terms were almost an insult: he was neither empowered, nor did he desire, to have the Dutch included within the ambit of his negotiations in England. Thurloe and the commissioners seem to have been surprised by the vigour of his reaction. They fancied they had adroitly killed several birds with one stone: the terms safeguarded English commercial interests; they ensured England's continued good relations with the Dutch; they diverted Charles's energies to the quarter towards which most Englishmen who favoured the alliance wished to see them diverted; and they made such a diversion possible by bringing Swedes and Dutch together in a comprehensive system. What could be better? If Charles were really the Protestant Hero that the protector fancied him to be, how could he in conscience neglect such an opportunity?

It was not long before they were undeceived. The wreck of the Proszowice policy coincided, as it happened, with the abandonment of that policy by its originator. The conditions which Charles proposed in his orders from Schlippenbeil (which arrived on 8 February), and above all those from Siedlice (which arrived on 4 April) revealed how wide was the gap between his estimate of the situation and that which prevailed in London. The Schlippenbeil terms stipulated for a *defensive* alliance *contra quoscunque* (that is, even against the Dutch, should that prove necessary) and an English subsidy of 900,0000 *rdr.* a year, in return for which Charles would bind himself to provide 30,000 foot and 6000 horse *if* the emperor violated the treaty of Osnabrück sufficiently flagrantly to require the use of force against him. Bonde did his best to argue that the subsidy would pay for itself 'ten times over' through the effect of Charles's 'diversion';[1] but that argument made little impression. It was indeed disingenuous: Charles had no idea of making anything that England could consider as a diversion. Bonde took care, of course, to avoid saying that an attack on the emperor was unlikely, and from Charles's point of view would be untimely: he tried to convince the protector that a war with the emperor was for Charles an available option, though in reality it was no more than an unwelcome possibility. By the beginning of March Cromwell had firmly refused an alliance on the Schlippenbeil terms: the Spanish war made any payment of subsidies impossible; an alliance *contra quoscunque* might drive the Dutch to 'desperate courses'—that is, to an alliance with Spain. In the spring of 1656 it required all Oliver's self-control, all his determination to avoid a quarrel with the Dutch, to curb his irritation at de Ruyter's convoying of Spanish merchantmen, and his disquiet at what seemed to him to be the signs of an Orange revival. On 1 April he made Bonde wait an hour in his antechamber before giving him an audience; and when he did admit him was more than usually explicit in rejecting any alliance which did not include the Dutch.

The prospects were made worse by the terms of Charles's orders from Siedlice. Those orders disclosed, more frankly than ever before, his view of what he expected from the alliance. It must be pledged to conserve his Polish conquests; it must be defensive against all who would attack him for his actions in Poland and Prussia; it must provide a subsidy against the possibility that he might be attacked by the emperor; and it must be based on the treaty of Osnabrück. The accession of other powers might be considered once it had been concluded; and thus it would be, in effect, a protestant league under another name: to base it overtly on religion alone would be too '*éclatant*'.[2] The new terms came at the worst possible moment. Europe was filled with reports that the Swedish army had been totally defeated, and that Charles himself was not improbably dead. And if England needed any further disincentive on top of this disastrous news, it was provided by the infuriating tidings that the Spanish silver-fleet had come safe home. Such were the circumstances in which the

1. *Infra*, no. XLI (21 March 1656).
2. *Infra*, no. XLVI (18 April 1656).

protector, in the audience of 11 April, expressed his determination to conclude a defensive alliance *contra quoscunque*. Small wonder that members of his council found it necessary to intervene.

Bonde believed—and continued to believe—that if only the English navy had succeeded in capturing the silver-fleet, and so relieved the protector's straitened finances, the alliance would have been concluded. But he was egregiously mistaken. No English government could commit itself to guaranteeing Charles's conquests. England had not been a party to the treaty of Osnabrück; and though the Westphalian settlement did indeed bind the emperor not to give aid to Spain in her war with France (a provision which the emperor did not observe), it did not debar him from aiding Spain against England. And just as Thurloe had once warned Nieupoort that Charles would never tolerate being confronted with an Anglo-Dutch arrangement to which he was subsequently invited to adhere,[1] so neither would the Dutch be likely to accept an Anglo-Swedish alliance which they had had no hand in making. England was being invited to make heavy subsidies available to keep alive a struggle in Poland whose objectives were irrelevant to English interests, and now seemed in any case to be unattainable, and to participate in a war which at that moment looked as good as lost. Even if the money had been available, even if the Dutch could somehow have been persuaded to come in, it was an arrangement which had no attractions: a subsidy was to be paid, it appeared, even if the emperor should not attack; and England was given no promise of aid against Spain, since the alliance was to be defensive, and Cromwell was the aggressor. Already it was reported (prematurely) that a Dutch fleet was to sail for the Baltic. A week later came the news that Charles had extricated himself (though with heavy losses) from his apparently catastrophic situation; but it made no difference. On 24 April Bonde delivered a virtual ultimatum: England must accept the Siedlice terms, or he would take his departure. And on 7 May, having ostentatiously (and expensively) clothed his suite in new liveries by way of celebrating the better news from Poland, and proclaiming that he was not to be trifled with, he had a chilly audience which seemed to put an end to any hope of agreement: a verdict which Cromwell endorsed a fortnight later, when he told Bonde that 'we proceed upon principles so divergent that he did not see now we could negotiate with each other'.[2] Oliver declared his conscience to be involved; and the only result of the interview was an

---

1. *Brieven*, iii. 186–7: *Cf.* Nieupoort's own warning to de Witt that England would not agree to being tacked on to any existing alliance between Denmark, Brandenburg and the Dutch: *ibid.*, iii. 62–3.

2. *Infra*, nos. LI (23 May) and LII (30 May).

invitation to Bonde to come out to Hampton Court 'and kill a stag or two before his departure'. Nevertheless, this was not quite the end. The negotiations on the completion of Whitelocke's treaty, despite Cromwell's pessimism, were making progress, and would at last reach agreement. And on 11 June fresh orders arrived from Schneebloch which encouraged Bonde to try again. But in fact they offered little hope of success. Charles X, under the impression—which Bonde had encouraged—that the major obstacle to agreement was simply money, made what was no doubt intended to be a conciliatory gesture: he was now prepared to reduce the amount of the English subsidy by one-third. But since in all other respects the terms set out in his instructions from Siedlice still stood, and since Bonde took the line that they were an ultimatum, the offer had no chance of acceptance. Thurloe and Fiennes might indicate (on 21 April) that England would be ready to modify her terms so far as to be content with a merely defensive alliance; but this was a concession which did not remove the root of the difficulty. The obstacle to agreement lay not in 'offensive' or 'defensive': it lay, as it had always lain, in irreconcilable attitudes to the Dutch. At an interview on 17 June, in the hope of provoking Fiennes and Fleetwood into taking some positive steps (and also, it would seem, by way of venting his accumulated exasperation) Bonde affected a cold indifference as to whether the alliance was concluded or not, and told them that an Anglo-Dutch war appeared inevitable. And he went further: in a remarkable access of candour he asserted (what happened to be true) that the emperor was most unlikely to give any trouble, and that the Protestant Cause was in no sort of danger. After so many months during which the axiomatic basis of negotiations had been assumed to be the exact opposite, it was hardly surprising that the two commissioners were 'taken aback'.[1]

With Cromwell, good personal relations were soon restored; and with him Bonde had no scruple in reviving all his old arguments about the perilous predicament of the protestant community. The protector listened sympathetically; offered to refer the question of the alliance to commissioners; protested, quite in the old style, that if Bonde managed to bring off the alliance he would consider him as 'an angel from heaven'; and even meekly confessed that perhaps it would have been better after all if he had concluded the alliance some time ago, before his difficulties made it impossible.[2] It all meant very little: in effect, they had reached a stalemate; or so it seemed. By mid-July, however, the situation had altered. The news that reached Bonde from all quarters was very bad: the Swedish garrison in Warsaw had

1. *Infra*, no. LIV (13 June).   2. *Infra*, no. LVII (4 July).

capitulated to the Poles; the Russians had captured Nyen and seemed likely to capture Riga; the French had been defeated in Flanders and in Italy.[1] For Charles, the English alliance had become more necessary than ever before: his position had become—there was no disguising it—extremely critical; as Bonde realized. On 26 July, therefore—perhaps encouraged by the fact that Cromwell so far compromised with his principles as to drink a furtive health to Charles X—he used the Saturday afternoon of his last visit to Hampton Court to renew the subject with the protector. Once again he gave the now-familiar exposition of the dangers to the Protestant Cause, rendered more acute than ever by Charles's recent reverses; and he even ventured to disobey his sovereign's orders by reviving (somewhat tentatively) the idea of special privileges for English merchants. But his host, though as usual warmly benevolent, was studiously vague, and notably lacking in helpful suggestions.[2]

Charles, for his part, had not yet realized—and never was to realize—that Cromwell was not prepared to do what his critics have sometimes charged him with doing: that is, to sacrifice English interests for the sake of a Swedish alliance. As yet, Charles had no enemy in common with England, and he still had no intention of acquiring one if he could help it. But on 1 August, the day when Bonde wrote his account of his week-end at Hampton Court, there arrived orders from Nowy Dwór which for the first time gave some idea of the real measure of Charles's predicament. It was now as desirable to him as to Cromwell that the Dutch fleet should not precipitate a rupture. As the Dutch negotiators pursued their discussions with Erik Oxenstierna in Marienburg it became very clear that he was now desperate to avoid war with the United Provinces at almost any cost: on 24 August he was to write to Erik Oxenstierna 'I do not believe that our country has for many years been in such a dangerous situation: humanly speaking the only means of salvation is a quick settlement with the Dutch'.[3] The orders from Nowy Dwór were nothing less than an urgent cry for help: by a diversion against the Russians; by the loan of troops; by subsidies (at the very least, he must have money to pay for the 4000 men which George Fleetwood had been ordered to recruit): in the last resort he was now even ready to tolerate English mediation.[4] In the weeks before Erik Oxenstierna's death, the chancellor was advocating something like Cromwell's own solution: a European league of England, France and the Dutch against the

1. *Infra*, no. LIX (18 July).
2. *Infra*, no. LX (1 August); *Bondes Diarium*, p. 52.
3. F. F. Carlson, *Sveriges historia under konungarne af det Pfalziska huset* (2nd edn. 7 vols. Stockholm 1883–5), i. 316.
4. Carlbom, *Sverige och England*, pp. 117–18.

Habsburgs.[1] The great victory at the three-days' battle of Warsaw (news of which reached Bonde only on the eve of his departure), and the renewal—for the last time—of the alliance with Brandenburg, were transient gleams of success in what had now become a crumbling enterprise, which Charles would strive to prop up by hazardous expedients such as his alliance with George Rákóczy. The kind of alliance which had been propounded in the orders from Siedlice had been made hopelessly unrealistic by Charles's inability to cope with the Polish guerrillas.

To the anguished appeal from Nowy Dwór Bonde responded immediately. He at once sought an audience with the protector. In vain: Cromwell pleaded his *impuissance*.[2] He sounded Thurloe about a diversion against the Russians: he found him discouraging. He approached the Muscovy merchants as to the possibility of a purely private buccaneering enterprise against Archangel, and reported (improbably) that 'they seem very keen on it'. He toyed with the idea of sending 'a sharp young man' to the Netherlands to stir up discontent there and persuade the other provinces to adopt Holland's Act of Seclusion: he might have spared himself the trouble. Finally, at his special request, he secured the attendance of some members of the council at his farewell audience, and in their presence unkindly reminded the protector of all the salutary warnings to which he had paid no heed, with an alarming disquisition on the menace impending over England from the Dutch fleet. The protector, it seems, was 'deeply moved', even to the extent of cancelling a prayer-meeting;[3] but in the sequel he succeeded without difficulty in mastering his emotion. And when Bonde took his departure the only positive step which he had succeeded in inducing Cromwell to take was a decision to send an embassy to negotiate with Charles in person; and that was postponed and postponed until, more than a year later, Jephson was sent to Sweden, and Meadowe to Denmark, to try to compose the intractable troubles of the North. One other concession was indeed wrung from the protector by relentless soliciting: the despatch of a 'moving' letter of remonstrance to the States-General; but that was a measure which, on the morrow of the treaty of Elbing, was quite plainly superfluous. For as it turned out, the moderation of the Dutch negotiators at Marienburg, which made that treaty possible, did indeed relieve Charles of his most immediate danger—and also solved (for the present) the problem which had so long baffled the protector

---

1. Ellen Fries, *Erik Oxenstierna. Biografisk studie* (Stockholm 1889), p. 304. A vivid impression of the distracted counsels that prevailed in Charles's headquarters is afforded in the chaotic minutes of the discussions printed in *RRP* xvi. 730–42.

2. *Infra*, no. LXI (8 August 1656).

3. *Infra*, no. LXII (13 August 1656).

and his advisers—the problem of how to reconcile Sweden with the Dutch. It thus marked the end of a distinct period in the foreign policy of the protectorate; and that period was appropriately closed by Bonde's departure. As to Charles X, it does not appear that he took the failure to obtain an alliance too tragically. In 1656, in fact, the English alliance, though certainly desired, was not felt to be of the first importance: it is remarkable how little space Charles gave to commenting on it (just three lines) in the lengthy Proposition which on 20 February 1657 he sent home to the provincial diet in Stockholm.[1] By the time the autumn came, however, the Danish attack would alter his attitude to that of a solicitant, almost a suppliant; and in so far as the protector and Thurloe allowed themselves to respond to his entreaties they would be able to stipulate for so stiff a price (Bremen, for instance) that one may fairly doubt whether they seriously expected the price to be paid. Only the possibility that the Dutch by their aid to Denmark might threaten a return to the position of 1652–3 could again move them to think of a Swedish alliance; and once that threat proved to have no foundation they would be quick to renege on their promises,[2] however resonant the protestant rhetoric with which Oliver sought to animate his last parliament to the unloosening of their purse-strings.

It might seem, then, that the missions of Coyet and Bonde were barren of results. But this was not quite true. After hard bargaining and many delays something like a satisfactory settlement of the economic issues left open by Whitelocke's treaty was arrived at. The treaty which Bonde concluded on 17 July 1656 registered one considerable success for the Swedes: the concession of free fishing off the British coasts, with the necessary facilities for drying nets, and so forth, but without the payment of the tenth herring which had been stipulated for in Whitelocke's instructions of 1653. It also opened the possibility of trade to America by special permission in individual cases. On the other hand, article VIII promised to the English the restoration of all the old 'prerogatives . . . which they enjoyed heretofore, in preference to other nations' in their trade to Poland and Prussia, and assured them of most-favoured-nation treatment in any future alteration of tolls, or grant of further privileges.[3] De Witt, dissatisfied with Thurloe's

1. *Sveriges ridderskaps och adels riksdags-protokoll*, vii. 131–54: the reference to England is at p. 151.
2. Roberts, 'Cromwell and the Baltic', pp. 164–5.
3. This did not apply to ducal Prussia: by the treaty of Marienburg (15 June) Charles X agreed that the tolls in Prussian ports should be equal for all nations; and by the treaty of Labiau (10 November 1656) Sweden surrendered her share of the tolls in East Prussia for a lump sum of 120,000 *rdr.*: Georg Wittrock, 'Marienburg och Labiau', *Karolinska Förbundets Årsbok* (1922), p. 68.

explanation that the treaty was no more than an expansion and corollary of the treaty of Uppsala, and irritated by his failure to have a clause inserted providing for the possible adhesion of the Dutch in compliance with article XV of the treaty of Westminster, regarded this clause with a suspicion which scarcely seems justified.[1] It does not seem that any more was intended than the restoration of a situation which had earlier existed and had latterly been upset in—for instance—Danzig. On all other counts except one the treaty represented a compromise. That one was the question of the definition of contraband of war. In 1653 the negotiators of the commonwealth had drawn up a list of contraband from which some of the main exports of the Swedish dominions—tar, pitch, hemp, sailcloth—had been excluded, and Bonde fought hard to preserve that exclusion. But the situation had altered since 1653. England was now at war with Spain; and it was of vital importance to stop naval stores from reaching the enemy. The amount of trade to Spain in Swedish vessels was admittedly small; but the quantity of Swedish exports which might be carried there in Dutch bottoms was large. This question was therefore among the most intractable issues in Bonde's negotiations, precisely because it was also the main cause of disagreement in those negotiations for a Marine Treaty which Nieupoort was conducting simultaneously with those for which Bonde was responsible. Like Charles X before Danzig, the protectorate was seeking to deny the supply of strategic materials to its enemy. It was therefore essential to resist the Dutch doctrine of 'free ship makes free goods'; and it was impracticable on this point to yield to Bonde what they were not prepared to yield to Nieupoort. As regards Sweden, the solution eventually reached was based on the precedent of England's recent treaty with France, whereby such contraband of war was forbidden for four years, which was estimated to be the likely duration of France's war with Spain. Bonde's treaty therefore provided, in a separate convention, that Swedish naval stores should be deemed contraband for the duration of England's Spanish war, but only if Charles X consented to this arrangement when ratifying the treaty. He did so consent. For Sweden, the defeat was of no great consequence; for England, it was a success of some importance, since it helped to bar the making of any concession to the Dutch.

On the whole then, Bonde could claim a modest success for his commercial negotiations. The English commissioners, on their side, had likewise cause to be satisfied. They had obtained assurances which promised them all that it was realistic to hope for; and they had prudently abstained from seeking any preferences to which the Dutch might be expected to have strong objections. It was a judicious settle-

1. *Brieven*, iii. 260, v. 422.

ment which conformed well to the line which they had been pursuing during the period of Bonde's mission; and it implied a frank recognition of what was, and what was not, possible for English trade to the Baltic at that time.[1] One other of the unresolved matters from Whitelocke's treaty—the adjustment of claims for damages sustained by either side during the Anglo-Dutch war—did indeed remain for agreement, and the English negotiators seem to have been in no hurry to reach one: it was still dragging on when the protector died.

As to the political issues and the question of the alliance, Bonde at one time or another offered various explanations of the difficulty of coming to an agreement: the dubious stability of the protectoral *régime*; the press of urgent domestic business upon the protector and his council; the ill-success of the West India expedition; the chronic shortage of money, and the failure to capture the silver-fleet; the nefarious intrigues of the Dutch; the fact that there was no English diplomat in attendance upon Charles X, once Rolt had returned from his purely ceremonial mission; sabotage by the protector's domestic enemies. To these could be added the impact of the disastrous news from Poland in the middle of 1656, and the consequent growth of scepticism as to whether after all Charles would prove a useful ally. There were occasions, both at the start and towards the end of his mission, when Bonde for the moment wondered whether the English alliance was really what Sweden ought to be striving for, though the thought arose only to be rejected.[2] But in the good-will of the protector himself he never lost faith; and at the close of his mission he was confident that if the coming parliament should make the protector king, the conclusion of the alliance was sure.[3] In thus attributing consistency of purpose to the protector he was quite right; for (with one unfortunate lapse) Cromwell's attitude to the negotiations was indeed consistent. Where Bonde failed was in his lack of appreciation of the balance of considerations on which that consistency was based: considerations religious, political, personal. But he finally came to realize that the essential reason for his failure was the protectorate's steady refusal to pay for a Swedish alliance at the cost of alienating the Dutch: *quoscunque* marred all.[4]

---

1. Contrast, however, Firth's less favourable judgment: *Last Years*, i. 311–12.
2. *Infra*, nos. VII (23 August 1655), LI (23 May 1656), LIV (6 June 1656).
3. *Infra*, no. LVII (11 July 1656).
4. As Bonde confessed in a letter to Charles X of 1 October 1657: Carlbom, *Sverige och England*, p. 128. The explanation of the failure to conclude the alliance which is put forward in the instructions to Jephson of 22 August 1657 (Thurloe, vi. 478–9) is to the effect that Bonde, and after him Fleetwood, were not empowered to treat upon such terms as Cromwell thought necessary: i.e. they offered 'no places of safe retreat for our men', nor 'secure harbours for our ships', nor any understanding about payment of the cost by Charles X. This is a wholly fictitious construction, presumably designed to

But the lack of understanding was by no means all on one side. In the first place, Cromwell never seems to have grasped the real reason for Charles X's hostility to the Dutch: their intrigue with de Bye, and the threat of Dutch-Polish naval coöperation in the Baltic. In the second, his dream of a protestant alliance which should be *offensive*, and should include the Dutch, was from the beginning a delusion. If Charles X could not accept such a proposal, neither could Amsterdam or Holland: on 19 May 1656 de Witt informed Nieuwpoort that at a special meeting of the States of Holland they had resolved that they would not engage in any offensive alliance against Spain, nor in any way violate their peace with that country: their trade to Spain was too valuable to be sacrificed.[1] The Dutch might be zealous protestants, but their confessional zeal had its limits;[2] as Cromwell's also had. But *quoscunque* after all was only the sign of a more fundamental failure by each party to understand the policies and priorities of the other. Bonde may have been right when he thought that Cromwell's attitude to the Dutch was dictated by fear; but he erred in not seeing that that fear was a fear for the fate of the *régime*—in both countries. And the persistent Swedish inability to grasp this was balanced by a not less fatal misconception in England of the attitude of Charles X to Germany, and to the emperor in particular. The protector and his advisers never seem to have appreciated that in regard to the *Reich* the aim of Ferdinand III was to avoid awakening suspicion that he intended to violate the peace of Westphalia; that the need to cultivate German good-will in order to secure the election of Leopold as his successor, and the financial exhaustion of the hereditary lands in the post-war decade, forced him to pursue a policy that was essentially pacific and unprovocative; that except in the hereditary lands German protestants were really in no danger. Bonde had told them all this, on one memorable occasion; but they seem to have ignored his remarks as being a diplomatic feint, or a mere outburst of bad temper. Even as regards Poland, despite John Casimir's offer of the Polish crown, Ferdinand moved from a policy of mediation to one of intervention with characteristic Habsburg deliberation. The first step on that road—the Polish-Imperial alliance of 1 December 1656, which put 4000 men at John Casimir's disposal—not merely exempted the emperor from taking any action which should be contrary to the

---

influence Charles in regard to Cromwell's demand for Bremen. With Bonde's negotiation it had nothing whatever to do: with him, none of these issues was ever raised.

1. *Brieven*, iii. 227; and *cf. ibid.*, 216–19, and Thurloe, iv. 650, 712.

2. As Nieuwpoort frankly told Thurloe: 'We do indeed embrace the cause of religion, but we are also bound to have a regard to our temporal circumstances': *Brieven*, iii. 108.

Westphalian settlement (e.g. any attack on Sweden's German possessions), but also bound John Casimir to accept Ferdinand's sole mediation (i.e. not that of France) between Poland and Sweden.[1] At first, indeed, in the opening stages of the Polish war, Ferdinand almost hoped for a moderate Swedish success, since disaster might drive Charles X into the arms of France and into renewed Swedish meddling in Germany.[2]

So too with Charles X, who was at least as anxious to avoid a clash with the emperor as Ferdinand was to avoid embroilment with Sweden. Charles had no doubt dynastic interests in Germany—for instance, his contingent claim upon Jülich, which on occasion affected his relations with other German princes—but there is no reason to doubt him when he proclaimed his intention 'to preserve the peace, and religiously to adhere to what had been laid down at Osnabrück and Münster'.[3] As a member of the League of Hildesheim he might be ready to resist any blatant violation of Westphalia by the emperor, but he would not himself violate it; as was exemplified in 1657, when he was careful not to invade Denmark until Frederick III had broken the peace of the *Reich* by his incursion into Bremen. As late as October 1656 Charles wrote to the Swedish council of state that despite Habsburg intrigues in Poland, despite the fact that John Casimir had found refuge in Silesia, he had in his relations with Ferdinand 'shown goodwill and every confidence'.[4] In the elaborate explanations of his policy which Charles gave to the Swedish estates in 1658 he did indeed dilate at length upon the malign machinations of the Habsburgs, but that did not prevent him from making determined diplomatic attempts to come to an agreement with the emperor; for 'he well knew what an onerous and protracted war he might be involved in if it should again come to hostilities with the House of Austria'.[5] When on 27 March 1656 Per Brahe told the Swedish council that 'it is apparent that H.M.'s design is against the House of Austria, by reason that what was promised and granted in the treaty of Osnabrück has not yet come to any execution',[6] his observation reflects either Charles's notorious

1. Sten Bonnesen, *Karl X Gustav* (Malmö 1958), p. 176.
2. A. F. Pribram, *Franz Paul von Lisola, 1613–1674* (Leipzig 1894), p. 100; Ferdinand Hirsche, 'Der österreichische Diplomat Franz von Lisola und seine Thätigkeit während des nordischen Krieges in den Jahren 1655–1660', *Sybels Historische Zeitschrift*, p. 432. Gardiner understood this very well: *Commonwealth and Protectorate*, iii. 499.
3. J. Levin Carlbom, *Sveriges förhållande till Österrike under Ferdinand III:s sista regeringsår* (Göteborg 1898), pp. 7, 12, 16, 21; Hjalmar Crohns, *Sveriges politik i förhållande till de federativa rörelserna i Tyskland 1650–1658* (2 vols. Helsingfors 1901), i. 200, 221; Landberg, *Den svenska utrikespolitikens historia*, I: 3, 1648–1697 (Stockholm 1952) pp. 66, 85.
4. Crohns, *Sveriges politik*, i. 244 n.
5. *Sveriges ridderska-s och adels riksdags-protokoll*, vii. 322; and *cf. ibid.*, 323–9.
6. *RRP*, xvi, 425.

secretiveness about his plans, or the surviving influence of ideas (not peculiar to Per Brahe) inherited from the period of the Thirty Years War. No doubt it is true that Cromwell's delusions on these points were shared by Mazarin (though for very different reasons); but in each case they were delusions nourished by wishful thinking.

For whatever reason, the negative result of the negotiations for an alliance was no great disaster, for either party. Charles could console himself with the reflection that at least he had recruited some troops, if not so many nor so quickly as he could have wished; that he had escaped entanglement in a protestant front which had little relevance to his objectives; and that by escaping it his hands were freed, once he had cut his losses in Poland, for a settlement with the old enemy, protestant Denmark—a settlement which, if it gave him command of the Sound, would (he hoped) more than compensate for the lost *licenter* of Prussia.[1] And Cromwell, for his part, having providentially avoided involvement in Charles's unpredictable enterprises, had safeguarded that tie with de Witt which was basic to his policies; and so had made possible those Hague Concerts which in 1659 prepared the way for a peace in the North which would accord with the true interests of England.

1. See Birgitta Odén, 'Karl X Gustav och det andra danska kriget', *Scandia* (1961).

EDITORIAL NOTE

Coyet's letters are here numbered in Arabic, Bonde's in Roman, numerals. Foreign proper names and place names, after their first occurrence, are given their modern spelling, '*Ewre Köningl. Maij*', '*Es. Kl. M:tt*', are shortened to 'Y.M.', and some submissive and ceremonious adjectives and adverbs are occasionally omitted as superfluous.

Dating in the originals (which is here preserved) is Old Style; but New Style is standard for the de Witt-Nieupoort correspondence.

In BL Add. MS 38100 the letters of Coyet, in chronological order, are in fos. 58–183; those of Bonde, likewise in chronological order, are in fos. 221–412, except that where there is a gap in the RA *Anglica* series, or where a despatch has not been decyphered, the transcriber has supplied the want from Bonde's *Register*: these letters are in fos. 185–219. In the translation which follows, they are all ordered in one chronological series.

PETER JULIUS COYET, 1655–56

[Coyet's instruction for his mission to England was dated 25 November 1654.[1] The immediate cause which prompted his despatch was a rumour that Cromwell had expressed surprise that he had not been invited to mediate between Sweden and Poland—an idea which Charles X was anxious to scotch before it was formally raised.[2] His instruction ordered him to settle matters which had been left for future decision in Whitelocke's treaty of Uppsala of 1654: compensation for loss and damage at the hands of English privateers; the thorny questions of contraband and sea-passes. He was also to raise—but not to decide, pending the arrival of Christer Bonde as ambassador extraordinary—a number of additional points, most of which were not new: Swedish participation in the herring fishery off the English and Scottish coasts; a possible English staple somewhere in the Swedish dominions; the diversion of England's Russia trade to Swedish ports, where the duty was only 2%; and in addition the possibility of opening the trade to Barbados and America to Swedish vessels in exchange for a liberty to trade with Livonia and Ingria, with a hint that it might be to England's advantage if Sweden should obtain possession of Polish Prussia.

This instruction was supplemented by a further one from the College of Commerce dated 16 December 1654, and signed by Erik Oxenstierna (the Swedish chancellor) and Christer Bonde, the future ambassador: they ordered that in no case were iron, copper, grain, tar, or other commodities not expressly of a military nature, to be included among goods deemed to be contraband.[3]

On 8 February 1655 Charles X issued a further instruction: Coyet was to attempt, in collaboration with Alexander Leslie, earl of Leven, to arrange for the recruiting of six to eight regiments of Scots for the Swedish service.[4]]

---

1. Printed in full in Treffenberg, K. Carl X Gustafs instruction.
2. Pufendorf, i. 7–8.
3. The instruction from the College of Commerce is printed in Carlbom, Sverige och England, Appendix.
4. Carlbom, Sverige och England, p. 7. Leven had been released, and his estates had been restored to him, in April 1654, when Cromwell gave him a pass. He went to Sweden, where he arrived on 5 July, saying that his business was to thank Christina for interceding with Cromwell on his behalf: Abbott, iii. 268. While in Sweden he offered Charles X to raise 2000 men at his own charges. The six to eight regiments were intended to be in addition to these.

Envoyé Peter Julius Coyet's Letters to Charles X

1

Brussels, 6/16 March 1655

[Explanation of the delays on his journey from Sweden: called on Bradshaw, the English Resident at Hamburg; held up for nine days in Brussels by Queen Christina, who proposed plans for meeting Charles X in Wismar, preferably in July].[1]

2

London, 23 March 1655

[Account of his journey from Brussels to Gravesend, where he landed on 14 March].

And since it was getting towards evening, and I realized that on the following day, which was a Sunday [it was, in fact, a Thursday: Coyet, fresh from Brussels, was probably using NS; but even so he was one day out; according to NS next day was a Saturday], when there is no travelling in this country, Commissioner Bonnel could neither come to me, nor I to him, I made all speed the same day to London, that I might the more particularly inform myself of everything, and the more so since a house had been prepared for me and had for seven weeks been awaiting my arrival. I gave proper notice of my coming to the *Introducteur* Oliver Fleming, at the same time notifying him that I must remain at home some few days, until I was completely settled. Commissioner Bonnel came at once to see me, carrying Y.M.'s letters to me: namely that dated from Skenäs of 29 January, and that from Halmstad of 8 February; from which I received, with all due reverence, Y.M.'s commands, which shall ever be the rule of my conduct.

Commissioner Bonnel received Y.M.'s letter of recall, which I delivered to him, with much consternation: not, as he remarked, that he had any indisposition to comply with it with the utmost promptitude, but solely because, being in debt up to the ears, it is impossible for him to leave until he has paid his creditors, and fears that when they learn of his recall they will without scruple have him imprisoned. To avoid which disgrace he is forced to keep his recall

1. Coyet's leisurely progress provoked irritated reactions both from Charles X and from his chancellor, who were afraid that while he was lingering in Brussels the Polish agent, Nicolas de Bye, who was by now in London, might steal a march on him. For de Bye and his mission see Åke Lindqvist, 'Svenskarna och De Byes beskickningar 1654–1655', *Karolinska Förbundets Årsbok* (1941).

secret, not only from strangers but also from his own servants, who otherwise might easily spread the news; and to that end to continue his reports to Y.M. until he can obtain a draft for what is outstanding of his annual salary, and so satisfy his creditors here. All of which he humbly explains to Y.M. more at large in the enclosed letter.[1] It is true, most gracious sovereign, that his condition is most wretched, and if he does not soon receive some help from Y.M. he will not be able to avoid imprisonment, and must with disgrace waste away and die in misery. He has pressed me most urgently to lend him £70 sterling, partly to discharge some small debts, partly so that he may have the wherewithal to support himself from day to day; for he swore that he had not a halfpenny's worth of money at his command, and no credit to obtain any. And although I myself have need of money in this inordinately expensive place, yet in order to avert an affront which was hanging over the head of one of Y.M.'s ministers, and which might in future serve to discredit Y.M.'s servants in this country, I have put that sum at his disposal, in the certain trust that it will be remitted to me here.

Y.M.'s latest letter, dated from Göteborg on 13 February, came to me to-day by the ordinary post, and I shall accordingly use my utmost diligence to ascertain what may be the mission of the Polish envoy de Bye to this country, and will, under hand, countermine anything that he may attempt to the prejudice of Y.M. and our fatherland. When I have had my audience (which I gather will be at the beginning of next week), and when I have made the acquaintance of other foreign ministers at this court, I will send to Y.M. circumstantial reports of all that occurs here in the way of negotiations, in so far as it is possible to obtain them. But of other current affairs Commissioner Bonnel will be informing Y.M., and as he is better informed about them than I, I judge it unnecessary in this letter to repeat what he will have to say.

3

London, 30 March, 1655 [in German]

[De Bye, although eager for his *congé*, obtained it only yesterday afternoon: the delay probably due to the government's pre-occupation with the recent plot.[2] For at the time the plot was hatching the French ambassador repeatedly asked for his *congé* and threatened to break off negotiations and return home; no doubt with the idea of putting pressure on the government at a difficult moment, and so obtaining a settlement to his liking. But once the

1. Missing in transcript.
2. Penruddock's rising, and the events that preceded it.

risings were put down, and he was told he could have his audience, he began to regret his precipitancy; and to cover it alleged that he had received new instructions, by which he was to remain and bring the negotiations to a conclusion. Meanwhile he has been to Nieupoort[1] and solicited his assistance; which was so far effectual that the negotiations are in fair way, though this government still harbours resentments.

News meanwhile of the seizure of English ships and merchantmen in French waters. In retaliation the government has forbidden any vessel to leave any English port, and good watch is kept on the coasts. From which it looks as though they want a brisk naval war, and are providing for one. The embargo gives great anxiety to merchants with ships ready laden for the Indies or the Straits. It is still rumoured that the king somehow got into this country, and narrowly escaped capture. Reported also that Blake and his fleet may be recalled from the Mediterranean, in case of a breach with France.]

4

London, 30 March 1655

In respect that by reason of the sickness of some of my suite I am still in no condition to appear in audience before the lord protector, and in consideration that the many affairs which press upon him and the council, in order to prevent any recurrence of revolt against the present government, have caused him to postpone it for some days (as I have been reliably informed) I have been unwilling to solicit it, holding it more suitable to the high respect due to Y. M. to delay any request until I can be assured that I shall be admitted without delay, rather than to renew vain applications – as the Polish envoy de Bye did, and was for that reason derided in the English weekly newsletters. But since Mr [Sir] Oliver Fleming sent a message that my audience would take place next week, should I so desire, I have determined to solicit it at the earliest opportunity.

The lord protector's ratification of the alliance with Y. M.[2] is not yet sent off, and it is reported that it is intended to send it by express, as soon as the present troubles have a little abated. In the meantime I propose to withhold Y. M.'s ratification until such time as theirs is duly drawn and despatched. I have taken care (though without letting it be known) to obtain information that the protector has never agreed, nor will ever hereafter agree, that the title of the king of

1. The Dutch ambassador.
2. The treaty of Uppsala, negotiated by Bulstrode Whitelocke, dated 11 April 1654: text in Abbott, iii. 911–15.

France shall be placed first in any instrument that the protector is to sign. And should the king of France, on the resumption of negotiations, acquiesce in this (as to which, as also as to all else that passes here, I shall be able to obtain better information after the audience), then there is no doubt that Y. M. will not obtain it from the lord protector. Nevertheless I shall not fail, in accordance with Y. M.'s commands, to make suitable remonstrances with a view to disposing him thereto, in so far as it may in any degree be possible.

I have as yet had no opportunity to sound Mr Whitelocke as to whether Y. M. may be able, by a letter from the lord protector, to obtain permission to raise some regiments of foot in Scotland; the said Mr Whitelocke not being at present in town, but two days' journey away in the country, and expected home again within a fortnight. I will however not neglect, immediately after my audience, to make enquiries in the matter from others who may have some knowledge of his highness's opinion. And in order to save time, and the better to ensure Y. M. of his permission, it would in my humble opinion not be adverse to Y. M.'s service, nor contrary to his wishes, that I should first assure myself, through other persons, of the protector's inclination thereto, and then myself tactfully solicit permission from himself, though on the understanding that everything remain quite private until further orders. Alexander Leslie, earl of Leven, has visited me to congratulate me on my coming to this country, and said that he had experienced so many marks of favour from Y. M., and such handsome treatment from the Swedish nation, that he felt himself in the highest degree obligated to be of service to the meanest of Y. M.'s servants, and to pay a visit to him, that he might thereby in some measure manifest his gratitude. And when, among other things, he turned the conversation to Y. M.'s recruiting in Germany, he asked me if Y. M. was not in need of some Scottish soldiers. To which I answered, that that might well be, provided Y. M. first had assurance that recruiting in Scotland would be permitted. But Leslie said he had not the smallest doubt of it if the lord protector were now so minded, which he also believed to be the case, as it was when he (Leslie) went over to Y. M. last year. Adding, that there were many in Scotland who were willing, and brave fellows for Y. M.'s service, who were able in a short time to raise some regiments; as to which he had received repeated enquiries regarding Y. M.'s will in the matter. In particular he recommended to me his son-in-law, Baron Gladstone [sc. Cranstoun]; and asked me to write to Y. M. about him, since he had many children, and was capable to do Y. M. good service. I said that I was assured that Y. M. would be disposed to take his person into favour, if only recruiting in Scotland were permitted. Which he [Leslie] greatly desired, saying that we must talk of this another time at large. He then began to question me as to whether Y. M. had given me any commands in respect of a Scottish officer by the name of James Weems [Wemyss], of whom he had formerly spoken to Y. M. as one having useful inventions concerning artillery,[1] and especially its transport: as may be seen from enclosures A and B.[2] He added that up to the present he had encouraged the said Wemyss with promises, and had been the means of preventing him from entering the French service, to which he had been invited by Ambassador Bordeaux with a variety of inducements; and should there be much longer delay in obtaining some certainty from Y. M. as to whether Y. M. was pleased to look at these inventions, or not, then he would be forced to let the fellow go. And therefore urgently requested me to remind Y. M. of it, and humbly to entreat his answer.

5

London, 6/16 April 1655 [in German]

[Audience further delayed through press of business on the protector. Negotiations with France are moving again, thanks to the zealous efforts of Nieupoort: the government now appears to wish them to succeed, though some embittered and interested persons want a war. The arrest of English ships and merchants at Bordeaux confirmed; but said to be without the knowledge of the king of France, and on orders from the duc de Vendôme; though the fact that they are not yet released suggests that the orders came from a higher authority.

The newly-arrived Portuguese envoy is said to have brought only some additional points, and not a final ratification of those articles which had been dealt with already.

To clear up the remains of the late conspiracy a number of commissioners have been appointed to go round the country, equipped with full powers to try and imprison those implicated. Before the outbreak the protector took effectual measures to counteract it, by getting some of his men to pretend to be royalists; this encouraged the conspirators to rise, though when the government troops appeared these agents fled and left the royalists in the lurch. So when the appointed time for the rising arrived, other royalists became fearful and mistrustful, and did not rally to it. I learn from a well-informed source that among the measures taken by the protector to discover it was this:

a colonel of the army named Brown, a man of some £4000 a

---

1. One factor in the superiority of the Swedish armies in Poland lay in the excellence of their artillery: *Carl X Gustafs armé*, p. 277.

2. Missing in transcript.

year, suspected of royalism, received an anonymous letter through
a person (unknown to him) of small estate, urging him to signalize
his devotion to the cause, and avail himself of the favourable opportunity to collect friends on whom he could rely at a time and place
indicated in the letter, and the design would be communicated to
him. The colonel, in great perturbation, summoned the man who
had brought the letter and sharply questioned him as to who had
ordered him to bring it to him. He protesting that he did not know,
the colonel arrested him, and brought him and the letter to the
protector, who in great wrath caused the man to be imprisoned,
thanked the colonel, and exhorted him to continue in his good
affection to the state. But the next day the colonel, being on business
in the City, was surprised to encounter the same person who had
on the previous day been put in gaol; and supposing him to have
escaped from his captors, or broken out, arrested him, carried him
to the authorities, and demanded that he be kept in better custody
in future. But no one could have been more astonished when the
supposed miscreant mockingly cried: 'Sir, you are putting yourself
to trouble to no purpose. If you desire to know the author of the
letter you received, go to Whitehall and ask the protector, and he
will tell you'.][1]

6

London, 13 April 1655

The day before yesterday I was carried to my audience in the lord
protector's coach, drawn by six Oldenburg horses. After I had, in
Latin, made my Proposition, according to Y. M.'s commands, the lord
protector answered me in English (which the Master of Ceremonies[2]
interpreted into High German) to the effect that his highness was
rejoiced at my arrival at this place, and that he thanked Y. M., for
that he had not only sent his friendly greetings and congratulated him
on his assumption of the government, and had again notified him of
Y. M.'s accession, but had also (through me) evinced manifold signs
of his great affection and friendship for his highness, and for this
country. It was a matter of pleasure to him that Y. M.'s good inclination to this country and its welfare so well consisted with the esteem

1. This circumstantial story seems to be unsupported, and is improbable: none of
the Browns or Brownes listed in C. H. Firth and Godfrey Davies, *The Regimental History
of Cromwell's Army* (2 vols. Oxford 1940) seems a possible candidate; see Sir Charles
Firth's controversy with Reginald Palmer in *EHR* iii (1888), pp. 323–50, 521–9; and
iv (1889) pp. 313–38, 525–35.
2. Sir Oliver Fleming.

and good affection which he, on his side, had conceived for Y. M., his dominions, and his kingdom; assuring Y. M. of his readiness to give Y. M. true and effectual evidences thereof; and that in whatever Y.M. should require of him nothing should be wanting to be at his service, in such friendship and sincerity that Y. M. might count on finding his satisfaction in it, *etc.* And lastly the lord protector said that he would at the first opportunity appoint commissioners to enter into conference with me; and that in the meantime he would consider my person as that of a minister sent by his best friend.[1] There were present at the audience General Lambert, Pickering, Sydenham, Fiennes and Thurloe, all being members of his council, and the last his secretary of state. Mr Whitelocke had still not returned home; but two hours ago he sent to me to congratulate me on my happy arrival; adding, that he much regretted to have been away, and thus to have been unable to attend upon me or be of any service to me, but offering to call upon me to-morrow, if that suited my convenience. To which I replied with appropriate compliments. Wherefore I expect to have an opportunity to talk with him to-morrow: among other things, concerning the protector's intentions regarding permission [for recruiting].

The negotiations with France now make serious progress, with good hope of a successful issue, especially since in the last six days Messrs Pickering, Strickland and Sydenham, as commissioners, have twice been at the house of Ambassador Bordeaux for long conferences; not to mention the fact that tidings are come from France that the embargo upon all English ships has been lifted. Which is the more strongly confirmed by the fact that some merchants have informed me that those of them who drive a clandestine trade to Spain have been given a hint to beware of danger on that side.—A fleet of 60 ships is being fitted out, of which 25 are now ready in the Downs. For the rest I refer to the other letter which goes with this.[2]

7

London, 13 April 1655 [in German]

[Preparations for, and course of, his audience with the protector

---

1. Coyet's arrival probably prompted de Witt to instruct Nieupoort to take soundings as to Cromwell's attitude to Charles X. Among other things he was to enquire whether a Dutch–Brandenburg–Danish alliance, designed to put a curb upon Sweden, would 'shock him', or whether he would be disposed to join it. Thurloe's reaction was to ask whether in fact Danzig had made any appeal for assistance, and to remark that the elector of Brandenburg must be suspect, as being 'passionate in the interest of the prince of Orange': De Witt to Nieupoort, 23 April NS; Nieupoort to de Witt, 30 April NS; *Brieven*, iii. 47 *seqq.*, 62–3.

2. Presumably Bonnel's letter of 6 April, Add. MS. 38100 fo. 54.

(as in no. 6, above). Certain German noblemen, and some leading Austrian persons of estate, who happened to be in London, being eager to see the protector, attached themselves to Coyet's suite when he went for his audience. Two days previously he caused all the ambassadors and ministers of foreign powers residing here to be notified of his arrival; he was then complimented by their secretaries: visits from their principals are now to be expected, and must be returned. Thurloe informs him that he should have had his audience sooner if it had not been that his highness and the council were so occupied with business, often sitting until late at night. The outcome of the French negotiations still uncertain; though there are many, both within and outside the council of state, who wish them to succeed.

Various English merchants have serious complaints about their treatment by the king of Poland, such as arrests in Danzig, interference with their trade, and hostile proceedings against their co-religionists; so that de Bye is not likely to have the speedy assurances that he hoped for.

No further news of Penn's fleet. It is generally presumed that it has sailed for Hispaniola; though others say rather that it is destined for Brazil – possibly with a view to bringing the Portuguese to reason, and a ratification of the treaty. Blake and his squadron are at Tunis: to what end is unknown.]

8

London, 30 April 1655

On the 14th of this month Mr Whitelocke came to me; and after the usual compliments informed me that on the previous day, immediately after his arrival in town, he had spoken with the protector on Swedish affairs, and had found in him a great inclination towards Y. M. And that he had promised to dismiss me in a manner greatly to my satisfaction, though some time must first be allowed him to deal with important matters which required his attention; adding, that since the first sitting of the late parliament they have been so continually and fully occupied that they could not even think about the sending off the ratification to Y. M., nor deal with any foreign affairs. Among other matters, I asked him [Whitelocke] whether he thought that the lord protector would be willing to permit Y. M. to recruit some regiments of Scots, at need. To which he replied that he could see no reason why it should be refused; but that he would nevertheless speak to his highness about it at the first opportunity, and let me know the answer. I told him that Y. M. had not yet made up his mind in the matter, but that it might well be that Y. M. would make an approach to the lord protector on these lines, if only he were assured that his highness was not disinclined to it. From his [Whitelocke's] conversation and behaviour I perceived this state to be excellently well disposed to oblige Y. M. in all practicable affairs, and to grant things which they certainly would refuse and deny to any other friend. Some days later (in fact, on the 17th of this month) I was dining with Mr Whitelocke (whose son carried me thither in his coach, and treated me with every courtesy); and he then said that he had spoken with the lord protector concerning the recruiting of Scottish soldiers, and permission for it, and had then gathered that the lord protector was well disposed to oblige Y. M. therein. And he assured me that if in the conference [with the commissioners] I should wish to make such an application on Y. M.'s behalf, I could count upon receiving a good and agreeable answer. In his opinion the conference was fixed for the following week; at which I could bring foward the question of indemnity for the losses sustained by the Swedes at the hands of the English in the war between this country and the Netherlands, and could request an answer in writing; in which case he did not doubt that Y. M. and his Swedish subjects would obtain all that satisfaction which they could demand as a matter of right, in terms of their own [sc. English] law. In which also he promised all good offices, saying that he was Y. M.'s most faithful servant, who yielded to none of his loyal subjects in affection and good-will. And asked that I should assure Y. M. of his utmost zeal and readiness, and of his humble devotion.

From the reports of sundry reliable individuals I gather that the government of this country, and the generality of men also, are extraordinarily well-affected to Y. M., and entertain great hope of Y. M.'s arming and preparations for war, as being in the best interests of the protestant religion. And in particular that they would gladly see the Poles deprived of Prussia, and so be punished for the various indignities they have inflicted upon the English. For which reason the Polish envoy Monsr de Bye is not well seen here, and has small hope of being dismissed with satisfaction to himself. Which he confessed to me, saying *se nescire quo delicto meruerit in Insulam deportari*. For the rest, I gather that his mission consists in these two points: first, to incite the English against the Muscovites, with whom he believes there are matters of misunderstanding; and secondly, to agree with them upon an alliance tending to the defence of Prussia at sea, should it be attacked by any foreign potentate, and so to open a negotiation about trade to those parts. Among the reasons why he is of no consideration here—apart from the complaints of various merchants as to the loss they have sustained at the king of Poland's hands (among whom is one Smart, who alleges he lost 70,000 florins merely because he was more inclined to parliament than to the king of England), which grievances were partly detailed in my last—are the insults offered to some English ministers; as Y. M. may see from a schedule drawn by one [?Thomas] Fowler as admiralty solicitor, and delivered to the lord protector. And in order that his highness may the longer detain him here, or absolutely decline to have any dealings with de Bye, he demands that the envoy obtain credentials and full powers from the Polish republic, without which he will have nothing to do with him.[1] I gather also that the Dutch ambassador Heer Nieupoort, for his part, is disposed to support Monsr de Bye's mission here, especially in regard to the defence of Prussia at sea, raising great alarms at Y. M.'s armaments, and at the danger which the English, and all other nations, would run if the trade to Prussia should be stopped in the event of Y. M.'s overrunning Prussia in the course of a war with Poland. But the English believe that without engaging themselves with any power other than Y. M. they are well able in such a case to obtain acceptable terms for themselves. In which opinion, as occasion offers, I endeavour to confirm them.

9

London, 20/30 April 1655 [in German]

[Visits of compliment received from the Portuguese and Polish ministers, and from Whitelocke; who invited Coyet to his house at Chelsea. Coyet had asked him to treat him on a more familiar and less ceremonious footing, but Whitelocke replied that his respect for Charles X and for Sweden would not permit him to abstain from showing it. And explained that the recent constitutional changes had hitherto prevented the ratification of the treaty; but now that the worst and most troublesome parts of the business were over, it was intended to send the ratification very shortly, entrusted to a 'public person' the choice of whom was still under discussion.

The French negotiation still ambiguous: what diminishes the hope of success is the information that 6000 French horse (among them, in particular, Cardinal Mazarin's regiment) were intended to be landed under the command of the duke of York when the rising had begun and looked like succeeding; and to seize some places in Kent and Essex while the protector was busy quelling it in the northern counties. The lord protector is said to have had an inkling of this design for some time; but because he was not able to sift it to the bottom he employed the artifices mentioned in Coyet's previous letter, and so forced the plot to an untimely and precipitate outbreak. And the last parliament was dissolved principally because

1. De Bye was acting simply as agent of King John Casimir.

many of its members had knowledge of the project. The talk now is that an extraordinary courier is hourly expected from France, and that there are better appearances of a peaceful settlement. No certain news of Penn's fleet, nor of his real objective, though it is now seven months since he sailed. About a fortnight ago there was a rumour that he had met with a severe storm; but no particulars are available. Blake's fleet is said to have left Tunis for Malta, to exact satisfaction from the Knights for piracy committed against English merchantmen.[1]

Execution of conspirators in Salisbury; and a similar fate is intended for others involved in the plot.

A few days ago arrived an ambassador from Siebenbürgen, reported recently to have been in Sweden: the purpose of his mission unknown.[2] He has let me know that he will shortly take occasion to speak with me, when the object of his negotiation may emerge. A Muscovite delegate and a Turkish Chiau are also expected. The Polish envoy, de Bye, has still had no conference; and the prospects look very bad, for reasons mentioned in the previous letter. Divers opinions here of the great war-preparations Charles X is making. It is believed that they are intended for Prussia, which leads men to hope that the protestants in that country may obtain better terms than they have hitherto enjoyed.]

10

London, 27 April 1655 [in German]

[No conference yet: the French negotiations probably deferring it. Half-hour visit from Whitelocke, who brought renewed assurances. The ratification of Whitelocke's treaty to be sent by express: Whitelocke promises Coyet a copy.

Spoke with the earl of Leslie [*sc.* Leven] concerning recruiting in Scotland: who said he had been previously informed by the [Swedish] Master of the Horse, Robert Douglas, that such a commission had been given to him [Douglas]; which Leslie much approved of, not doubting that Douglas would acquit himself well

---

1. Blake destroyed nine ships of the Tunis fleet at Porto Farina on 4 April: there was no truth in the story that he designed to attack the Knights of Malta: Julian S. Corbett, *England in the Mediterranean*, (2 vols. 1904), i. 306–12.

2. The envoy was Constantine Schaum: his speech to the protector is in Thurloe, iii. 422–3. He urged an Anglo–Dutch–Swedish league, and asked for Cromwell's attitude to the approaching crisis: *ibid.*, 438–9. Paulucci wrote to Sagredo (7 May NS) that Schaum was seconding de Bye's pleas for aid against Russia, but was unlikely to succeed: *CSP (Ven) 1655–56*, p. 54.

of it.[1] Leslie confessed that by reason of his advanced years he was in shaky health, suffering much from gout and catarrh. I detect in him a genuine affection to Y. M. and an inclination to raise a regiment at his own expense if only he could obtain full recovery of the lands in Scotland of which this government has deprived him, to the extent of 2000 *Reichsthaler* a year in rents. He observed that though, out of gratitude for the favours conferred on him by the Swedish crown, he had never asked for payment of arrears of his pension, if they were to be paid he would undertake to use the money for the advantage of the Swedish crown, and not for his own.

The Portuguese resident, Don Antonio Ferrara Raballa, observed that the recovery of Brazil seemed to him a divine manifestation, since humanly speaking they could not have expected so great a success, the Dutch in Recife being as strong as the Portuguese outside it, and well provided with arms and provisions; and it was for some time not credited even at the Portuguese court: the garrison must probably have been bribed.

No progress in the French negotiations. Much resentment on the English side that the previous French Minister, La Basse [*sc.* de Baas] soon after his arrival engaged in plots against the protector and the government.[2] If he had been dealt with after his deserts he would have been sent back to France in the expectation that his sovereign would, by inflicting appropriate punishment, manifest his abhorrence of the enormity he had committed. But de Baas was not only not brought to justice, but was actually promoted; whence it was obvious that the king of France knew of the plot and would have been glad of its success. The attitude of Bordeaux, on the occasion of the late rising, the collecting of some thousands of troops to be brought over by the duke of York, and Bordeaux's procrastination over the negotiations on the pretext that France must await the election of a new pope, sufficiently demonstrate the same attitude. To which the French answer that the English similarly had leagued with Spain against them, helped to cause the loss

1. Leslie had been prominent in the Swedish armies during the Thirty Years War; Douglas was equally so in the wars of Charles X: C. Sanford Terry, *The Life and Campaigns of Alexander Leslie, first Earl of Leven* (1899); Archibald Douglas, *Robert Douglas, en krigaregestalt från vår storhetstid* (Stockholm 1957). Douglas was in fact no longer Master of the Horse: one of Christina's last acts before her abdication had been to replace him in that office by her favourite Clas Tott: Douglas, pp. 168, 205.

2. Thurloe, iii. 309, 351–3, 412, 437. Mazarin had in fact instructed de Baas *either* to try to obtain an alliance with England *or* to stir up trouble for Cromwell to keep him from making mischief; though he subsequently indignantly repudiated allegations of complicity in the Gerard–Vowell plot; *Lettres du Cardinal Mazarin*, vi. 157 and *n.* 2, Mazarin to de Baas, 8 May NS 1655.

of Dunkirk, had hindered (by Blake's fleet) the French attack on Naples, had taken some French forts in Canada, and by their privateers inflicted irreparable damage on French merchants. The English retorted that they did what they did, against a declared enemy of the crown of France, at a time when there was no negotiation, nor any thought of peace, between France and this country. For the rest, it was a question of justifiable retaliation; while the French had had secret intelligence with disaffected elements plotting to overthrow a republic which France had recognized, and with which public negotiations were being carried on.

A strong rumour among merchants that Charles X is besieging Danzig with 140 ships and 15,000 men; which tends to confirm the opinion of some that his armaments were intended to be used against Prussia.[1]

The arrival of the marquis de Leyde [Leda] as ambassador extraordinary of the crown of Spain is daily expected: it is supposed he has secret instructions to prevent the conclusion of a treaty between this state and France. This expectation, and the hope of news of the success of Penn's fleet, are probably the reasons why they drag out the negotiations of the French treaty.]

11

London, 4/14 May 1655 [in German]

[Conversation with Paulucci [the Venetian envoy], who announced that Venice had nominated an ambassador extraordinary to this country.

A conference appointed for next Tuesday, the English commissioners being Fiennes, Strickland and Jones, all three of the council of state. But as a preliminary Coyet had demanded a copy of the preamble and conclusion of [Whitelocke's] treaty, so that he might scrutinize it. This was provided, and the conference postponed until Wednesday. It actually took place on the evening of Thursday the 3rd [OS]. Thurloe was also present: Coyet was given precedence. He had made some amendments to the text, which they promised to incorporate; whereupon he delivered the Swedish [i.e. Christina's] ratification.

The latest news of Penn's fleet reports him still, on 29 March, at Barbados, in pretty good shape: he had taken the 18 to 19 Dutch ships which he captured (and some French) with him to his objective.

In the last few days troops, both horse and foot, have arrived in London from the country, which gives cause to wonder whether the

1. The rumour was premature, but it alarmed the Dutch: *Brieven*, iii. 60–1.

whole army is approaching, and whether the protector is minded to have himself crowned king, or emperor—the latter being the more likely, since the kingship has been abolished by Act of Parliament.]

12

London, 4 May 1655

It is my duty to inform Y. M. that in my last conversation with Mr Whitelocke I perceived him to be not well content with the present government. For he laid great stress upon the danger he ran, as Keeper of the Seal; in that, for his own protection, he was sometimes obliged to disapprove in silence when he was called upon to affix the seal to things which were against their law, from which he had no disposition to diverge, nor could he excuse it to himself on the ground that he had done so at the order of the protector. But in the parliament's time a man could discharge the duties of that office with safety. Wherefore he told me that he was desirous of divesting himself of that appointment at the first opportunity;[1] adding, with a woeful countenance, that he was confident that others than himself might well be found more capable of doing Y. M. good service, but none to surpass him in devotion.

The conversation then turning upon the lord protector, he said that his highness would yield place to no king, being that he had a greater power and might in his hand than any king of England before him: yea, that he was *re vera Anglorum Imperator*, in whom alone rested *jus belli et pacis*. Since when I have been reliably informed that the lord protector a few days since had a sharp passage with *Custodibus Sigilli*, because they had refused to seal a special Act which they held to be contrary to the liberties of the country, saying that if the protector was minded to take from them by force the seal with which parliament had entrusted them they must suffer it, but they could not acquiesce in it of their own free will, since it touched their honour and honesty. It is said that the lord protector has caused another seal to be prepared, in which appear the arms of Scotland, and those *familae suae, sc. Cromwellianae*: the truth of which time will show.[2] This only is certain, that at present Whitelocke, *Custos Sigilli*, is not as well seen by Cromwell as had been supposed. Some add, that one of the council, Fiennes by name, is designed to supply his place. However that may

---

1. For Whitelocke's dissatisfaction see his *Memorials*, iv. 191–201.
2. *Cf. The Clarke Papers*, iii. 38. Nieupoort noted (7 May NS), as a sign of Cromwell's possible assumption of the crown, that the lawyers lately called in to aid in the administration of justice had declared that the laws of England would only square ('*quadreren*') with a monarchical form of government: *Brieven*, iii. 60.

be, it seems at least that this government is not yet on a footing of stability, but that other great alterations may be impending.

The government is pretty frequently in council, sometimes from 8 in the morning until 4 in the afternoon without food or drink; and is so much preoccupied that all foreign affairs go extremely slowly here, and at present little can be done. Nevertheless, after I had several times, through Mr Whitelocke and Sir Oliver Fleming, reminded the lord protector of my conference, I was at last called to it about 6 yesterday evening, with an excuse that the commissioners (namely Fiennes, Strickland, Jones and Thurloe) had been the whole day taken up with business in council, and had thus been unable (as they intended) to arrange a meeting with me. And since I had learned from them and others that his highness's ratification was ready, and in a condition to be despatched immediately by express to Y. M.; and since also the copy of the preamble and conclusion of the ratification which was sent to me had nothing objectionable *in essentialibus*, but only some words omitted which they promised to insert in the text of article 17, and which seemed necessary for greater security (namely: that the lord protector shall ratify *non tantum suo, verum et reipublicae nomine*)—which last had been omitted, I was prepared, in order to expedite my mission, to use the occasion to deliver her majesty the queen's ratification to the commissioners, with appropriate expressions of good-will; but at the same time pressed for compensation to Y. M.'s subjects for the damage suffered at the hands of the English, and urged that a list specifying contraband goods, and a definite form of sea-pass, be drawn up and put into effect with the minimum of delay, in order to rule out every pretext for further molestation on the high seas. To which they answered with many assurances of the lord protector's friendship and good affections towards Y. M., and how that on their side the alliance would be adhered to in every particular; adding that the English ratification had long since been ready, in the form in which it now lay on the table, and that it should be sent off immediately to Y. M., as an express to be carried by a member of the nobility.

Since Mr Whitelocke had assured me that his highness the lord protector would not refuse to permit Y. M. to recruit some Scottish regiments, and had advised me to make application on Y. M.'s behalf at my first conference, I considered that it would not be inadvisable, for Y. M.'s service, to broach the subject in the following manner: that should Y. M. be in need of some Scottish regiments for the service of himself and the country, he felt assured that the lord protector's friendship would not in that event refuse to Y. M. permission to raise some regiments in Scotland by proper means; and for that reason, in order that Y. M. might have the more certainty in the matter, and the better avail himself of the opportunity, that Y. M. had desired me to ascertain the lord protector's wishes. All of which I have been the more desirous not to neglect bringing forward, since the earl of Leven informed me that Earl Douglas, Master of the Horse, had written to him that Y. M. had made an agreement with him for the raising of soldiers. For the rest I refer to my other letter which accompanies this [no. 11, *supra*].

13

London, 11/21 May 1655

Since my last letter I have made every effort to press for an answer to the points I raised at my last conference; and to that end thought it expedient to take the opportunity to visit Viscount Lisle, the eldest son of the earl of Leicester, who is still one of the lord protector's council, and well affected to the crown of Sweden. And though it is forbidden to all who serve the state here to hold any communication with the public ministers of foreign powers, or to receive visits from them, I nevertheless contrived, by the instrumentality of one of his close friends, that he should make no difficulty about my visiting him at his estate at Richmond, 8 English miles away. And after making the compliments which are customary on such occasions, and other general conversation, he assured me of this country's great disposition in favour of Y. M. and the crown of Sweden, promising with many words to do all in his power to speed my return. Speaking of the raising of some Scottish regiments for Y. M.'s service, he said that it would certainly not be easy for anyone to obtain such permission; but that he did not doubt that Y. M. might very well obtain it, from the particular regard which the lord protector and this country had for him. Subsequently the earl of Leslie [*sc.* Leven] has been with the lord protector, who told him, among other things, that Y. M. was minded to recruit some Scottish regiments, and that he, the protector, would not only gladly give permission for it, but would in other respects do his best to serve Y. M. in everything he might ask of him. The earl of Leven answered, as he later informed me, that the lord protector could by doing so gratify no one more [than Y. M.], since Y. M. had not only the highest regard for his person, but was also much disposed to hold a good relationship and a sincere friendship with his highness. Which the lord protector, with great professions of his particular inclination and affection towards Y. M., showed himself pleased to hear.

I was yesterday with Mr Whitelocke, who asked me if I had not heard of the *rencontre* which he and his colleagues had had with the lord protector; and when I said that I had heard something of the matter, he said '*Nos Angli sumus, nec possumus ferre ut aliquod contra privilegia nostra fiat*'; adding that it was his intention to resign at the first opportunity, since he never could consent to anything which he could not in the future justify to himself. For I see very well, he said, that though his highness, now that he understands that we neither will nor can by any means approve of his proceedings, feigns therewith to be satisfied, as though it was not his purpose to undertake anything contrary to the liberties of the country; yet we nevertheless suspect that he is trying under hand by every means to subvert us. And when I complained that I had still received no answer, and that all business here proceeded so slowly, he observed that I must not think it strange at this time, especially when they are burdened with so many affairs upon which their whole welfare depends; but that he did not in the least doubt that his highness would attend to Swedish matters as soon as possible, and speed their despatch.

The Spanish ambassador, the marquis de Leda, out of apprehension that the treaty with France might be concluded, this morning sought and obtained a private audience with his highness, in order to prevent it; alleging that his business could brook no delay. The lord protector is said to be greatly disturbed that Penn's fleet has not yet carried out its mission, and I am informed by a trustworthy source that the only reason is that by a particular accident all, or the greater part, of their powder was spoiled, and that therefore a great quantity of powder (among other things) is despatched by the last ship sent out to him, and until its arrival his objective cannot be pursued. To all appearances the treaty with France will be fully concluded within a fortnight, or it will not this time be concluded at all.

The Polish envoy has still not had his conference, and for many reasons I scarcely think that he will obtain it. It is at all events certain that he will not be able to effect anything here to Y. M.'s prejudice; to prevent which I have used, and shall continue to use, my best endeavours. The Dutch ambassador Heer Nieupoort does his best to alarm them here concerning Y. M.'s great armaments; but I hope (and have been told so much by a certain person) that he will thereby rather impel this country to embrace Y. M.'s friendship than to undertake the defence of Prussia;[1] and I shall not fail to traverse Nieupoort's intrigues with certain persons, and by appropriate means to countermine them.

---

1. Boreel, the Dutch ambassador in Paris, warned de Witt (21 May NS) that if the States General were to commit themselves in the Baltic, they might find Cromwell backing Sweden: *Brieven*, i. 208. And on 26 May NS he wrote that France was not privy to Swedish armaments, and would have preferred Poland not to be harassed, as being a bulwark against the Turk 'and other powerful eastern powers': *ibid.*, i. 209. This was true: Mazarin to d'Avaugour, 14 May NS: *Lettres du Cardinal Mazarin*, vi. 473.

As I write this, the Latin secretary has come to me with the answer to the points I raised at my last conference: I find it to be expressed only *in generalibus terminis*, and the last point (concerning permission for recruiting) to be framed in somewhat dubitative terms. But I am confident that his highness has done so only that he may the more clearly demonstrate that when he allows the recruiting (as I believe he will) he gratifies Y. M. by a concession which is not without risk to him, and so wishes to emphasize its magnitude *quasi beneficii*; especially when to what Mr Whitelocke, Viscount Lisle and others have said to me is added what the lord protector himself said about it to the earl of Leven. Early next week, before I have another conference with the commissioners, I will try to obtain a private audience with the lord protector himself, in order to persuade him to a course of action consonant with Y. M.'s wishes.

14

London, 11/21 May 1655 [in German]

[The French treaty drawn up, and ready for signing; but violent disputes arose on some of its terms, and Bordeaux, despairing of success, again asked for his dismissal, which was at once accorded him.[1] But Dutch intervention succeeded in calming the disputants, and the treaty is said to have been accepted *in integro*. It is generally thought that Bordeaux had long ago been fully empowered to sign the treaty as it now stands, but deliberately concealed the fact, with the idea of extorting this or that concession by his tergiversation. On the other hand, this government was equally dilatory, and showed no great desire to conclude, being anxious to learn what proposals de Leda brought with him. De Leda arrived last Saturday [5 May]; account of his entry: his audience on the 8th; absented himself from the dinner prepared for him afterwards, which gave offence.

No certain news of Blake's or Penn's fleets.

The emissary from Siebenbürgen has had his audience, and is expected to leave soon: his mission a secret.

Last week the protector issued an edict ordering all Jesuits or mass-priests in the country to leave it by a certain date, under heavy penalties; and another confiscating two-thirds of all the property of papists over the age of twenty-one who do not renounce their faith and accept the reformed religion. This prompted by a

1. For Anglo–French relations under the commonwealth and protectorate, see most recently Charles P. Korr, *Cromwell and the New Model Foreign Policy* (Berkeley, Calif., 1975).

great fire which ravaged London some weeks ago; and the lord major and aldermen caused a solemn day of repentance and prayer to be held yesterday, to avert further disasters.

Alexander Leslie leaves to-morrow for Scotland. He dined with me yesterday, protesting his devotion to Sweden.

Has just heard that de Leda to-day had a private audience with the protector in an attempt to hinder the conclusion of the French treaty; in which it is thought that he will not succeed.]

15

London, 18 May 1655

Since I considered it necessary, or at least useful, in order to forward Y. M.'s commission to me, and also to strengthen the impression that Y. M. was well with this country and that those here were disposed to support his plans, and thereby also to frustrate the hopes of the Dutch ambassador Heer Nieupoort (and others) of being able to do Y. M. a disservice with this government, I have requested a private audience; which after the utmost diligence and daily reminders was granted me by the lord protector, and took place yesterday afternoon. In which, after protestations of Y. M.'s great inclination to hold a good and confidential correspondence with his highness, and of Y. M.'s confidence that the lord protector on his side would similarly manifest all friendship (to which the common welfare and interest of both states not only gives great cause, but to a great degree obliges them), I said that in the answer sent to me on 11 March [*sc.* May] by the commissioners it had among other things appeared that (against all expectation) it was formulated in somewhat dubitative terms in regard to whether Y. M.'s recruiting of some Scottish regiments could be permitted at this time; although I was well assured that Y. M. had no intention of asking it save in such a form as would cause no prejudice to his highness and this republic, and that his highness need expect no inconvenience from such a recruiting, since thereby the country would be quit of many unruly persons disposed to war and disturbances. To which the lord protector answered, that he had not definitely rejected Y. M.'s request for recruits: it was only that since he was not informed of their numbers, the method of recruiting and transporting them, or the purpose for which Y. M. required them, he had deferred taking a resolution upon it; assuring me that he would deny to Y. M. nothing that was feasible without danger to this state, since he desired Y. M.'s friendship above all things. As to the number of soldiers and the method of shipping them abroad I answered that Y. M. could well use 6000 or 8000 men, it being understood that they would not be armed in Scotland, or gathered into large bodies there, but that some hundreds would be successively recruited, taken to their ships, and sent off. But for what purpose in particular Y. M. wished to use them I was at present ignorant, though I was nevertheless assured that Y. M.'s plans could not be reasonably objected to, since Y. M. sought by his arms only to advance the common weal and to defend his rights by appropriate means; and that should I receive no commands in regard to these matters, at the very latest Y. M.'s ambassador extraordinary (who is to be despatched by Y. M. to his highness and this republic as soon as possible) would be able to give the relevant information as to Y. M.'s designs, upon his arrival.

The lord protector answered that he would speedily let me know what he was able to determine regarding permission for recruiting, promising to comport himself therein in such a manner as to demonstrate not only with words but with deeds that he sought the friendship of Y. M. and the Swedish crown. Adding also—*ipsissima ejus formalia sunt*—'that he would seek to promote Y. M.'s laudable designs, as well by prayers to God, as by all other positive means, in the sure belief that Y. M. on his side, as he on his, would always seek to uphold the honour of God's name and the liberty of the evangelical religion, which (humanly speaking) reposed mainly on two columns, that is, on England and Sweden'; and for that reason enquired whether Herr Christer Bonde as ambassador extraordinary had it in command to treat of such things with this state. I then gave him to understand that the ambassador undoubtedly would treat with his highness about such matters as might not only conduce to the maintenance of existing amity, but to a closer alliance between our two countries; and that I supposed that he would arrive within four to six weeks, if his coming were not deferred for want of his highness's ratification. To which the lord protector replied that as soon as he had had a little time to think about it he would without delay send a distinguished person with the ratification. The conversation now turning to the satisfaction which is claimed by Y. M.'s faithful subjects, he said that he was not aware that they had any [ground for complaint],[1] and that the judges would deal with Swedish cases with the utmost expedition; and when I insisted, and complained most urgently that some of Y. M.'s subjects had lain here a long time,[2] and still could not get their cases heard;

1. On 11 May Strickland and Jones, on behalf of the council, had replied to Coyet's remonstrances by denying any refusal of justice to Swedish subjects; had intimated that they would be ready to confer on the matters of contraband and sea-passes; and had informed him that the protector, though willing to oblige about recruiting, doubted whether permission could be granted at present without prejudice to their affairs: Carlbom, *Sverige och England*, p. 14 n.

2. Abbott (iii. 718) translates: 'that some Swedish subjects had hired legal aid'—an error presumably arising from his confusion of the past participles of the verbs *ligga* (to lie) and *lega* (to hire).

adding that I did indeed believe that his highness out of his love of just dealing must have ordered prompt justice to be done to Y. M.'s subjects, but that the judges—against his will, and against all equity and reason—were oppressing Swedish subjects; and therefore begged his highness, out of concern for justice, to consider taking other means and giving other orders, so that every one of them might be given his right according to the nature of the case, and none might have cause to complain of a denial of justice—he answered, that if anything contrary to the law of England had been done to Y. M.'s subjects, and no satisfaction obtained, it was not only absolutely without his knowledge, but a matter for his displeasure; and therefore he would instruct the commissioners to confer further with me about it. At the conclusion of the audience the lord protector expatiated at some length on his desire to enter into a closer alliance with Y. M.

As far as I can see from all these circumstances, this government looks forward to a somewhat stricter alliance, once the ambassador arrives; an alliance which will extend to the safeguarding of the Protestant Cause. To this they seem excellently well disposed; or at least they would be glad to be thought so, and to be seen to be in negotiation with Y. M. on such matters, in order to the better promoting their policies towards other powers. The fact that *papa romanus* is now making every effort to unite all catholic potentates causes them to fear that on his incitement they may undertake measures most oppressive to the protestants; especially since, as *nuncius apostolicus* and mediator, he protested against the German peace [of Westphalia]; and this [danger] might be prevented by an alliance between Sweden and England. However that may be, I believe that at least they would be glad of a general rumour of such an alliance, even if it never came to any actuality. Whether this is acceptable to Y. M. and his realms is now a matter for Y. M.'s consideration. This at least is certain, that if Herr Christer Bonde were on his arrival to propose anything of this nature, it would be very well taken here, and facilitate all other business.[1] A trustworthy person has informed me that [the government] here would like, through Y. M., to prevent any catholic hereafter from being elected [emperor: undeciphered]; and in such a case would be disposed to aid Y. M. not only with men but with subsidies. From a reliable source I learn that the lord protector's only anxiety about the recruiting of Scottish regiments, as requested by Y. M., is

1. On 24 May Coyet wrote to Erik Oxenstierna asking him to inform Christer Bonde of the protector's inclination to form a protestant league with Sweden, adding 'for though I believe that members of the government here, and especially some of them— General Lambert, Viscount Lisle, and others—have pretty well no religion, they nevertheless wish to appear as men of great piety, and as very anxious for the liberty of religion against the papists': Carlbom, *Sverige och England*, p. 19 n. 1.

that Y. M. might within a short time conclude peace, and when the Scottish men were paid off they might attach themselves to the king of Scotland, to the great prejudice of this government. For their thoughts here are that Y. M.'s war with the Pole cannot be of long duration, by reason of his [the Pole's] miserable condition.[1] Not the least of the reasons (among many others) why I am pressing for permission to raise troops, is that thereby I may better discover their attitude to Y. M.'s designs. Since it is probable that if, on the incitement of the Dutch, or of others, they were disposed to thwart them, then they would by no means be ready to give permission to raise troops in Scotland.

Yesterday evening, after I had been at my audience, yet another plot was discovered, and three of the conspirators put in prison in the Tower: their intention, as I am just now informed, is said to have been to murder the lord protector and the leading personages of his council. For the rest, I refer Y. M. to my letter which goes with this.

16

London, 18/28 May 1655 [in German]

[The day before yesterday Bordeaux met Strickland and Fiennes and settled the outstanding points of difficulty: the French treaty now seems virtually assured.

No news of Penn; but Blake is reported to have landed a thousand men at Tunis, driven off 3000 Moors in flight, killing 1500 of them, and destroying nine of their best pirate-ships in the harbour. But this is a report which is not at the moment credited.[2]

Penn's force considered now to be 6000 soldiers, 5000 sailors, and two companies of horse.[3]

Ceremonial connected with his audience. Leslie has left by sea for Scotland.]

17

London, 25 May 1655 [in German]

[Blake's attack on Tunis made more credible by his letters recently arrived. The reason for the enterprise was that the Barbary pirates refused to restore captured English ships and liberate slaves: they relied on their strong fortifications. The nine ships which Blake

1. This was Mazarin's opinion also: *Lettres du Cardinal Mazarin*, vii. 78. Hostilities did not actually begin till July; but it was evident that war was impending.
2. The report of the destruction of the ships was true; all the rest was fabulous.
3. The total force probably did not exceed 8000–9000: *The Narrative of General Venables* (ed. C. H. Firth), (Camden Society 1900), p. xxv.

burnt were destined for the Turks, for service against Venice. As a consequence of Blake's success Algiers is said immediately to have offered to release English ships and captives.[1]

Much discourse here for the last few days concerning Cony's refusal to pay the usual duties. The circumstances are as follows: about six or seven years ago parliament passed an Act imposing an extraordinary levy on saleable goods, which has been operative uncontested since then. But the Act was for six years only; has now expired; and was not renewed by the late parliament. Some weeks ago the protector tried by various means to persuade Cony to pay the arrears of duty (amounting to about £500), but he would not listen to reason, began to dispute the protector's authority, and told him that no king in former times would have presumed to require it of him without the consent of parliament, and has appealed to the laws of the land; and has especially chosen for his counsel Maynard, Twisden and Windham, as three of the ablest available. They charged the protector with openly violating the law of the land, and pressed the case so hard against him that he was forced to secure their persons, and a week ago put them in the Tower. If Cony remains obstinate a verdict in the protector's favour may be expected.

Last Monday all the Scottish gentlemen imprisoned in the Tower for suspected involvement in the late plot were transported into the country to other secure places; among them the earl of Lauderdale was taken to Portland. General David Leslie and Mr Ken, however, remain in the Tower.

England refuses to ratify the treaty with Portugal, because the Portuguese have made alterations in several articles: the Portuguese envoy may soon return to Lisbon with his mission unfulfilled.

The persecution of the Piedmontese by Savoy has much moved the protector, who has contributed £2000 for their relief from his own means, and intends shortly to impose a tax through the entire kingdom for that purpose; and to write to the duke of Savoy urging him to milder measures, and to making a safer place of refuge for them within his country.

Those taken up for evil designs against the protector's person have been arrested at night and imprisoned: among them, I learn, Lord Byron and other persons of quality.

Has just learned that the protector's younger son Henry has been made Deputy in Ireland, and Fleetwood has been summoned home; and his eldest son Richard is named Deputy for Scotland, which like Ireland is to be ruled, as is usual, by an appointed council. Richard however has declined; but Henry is making ready to start.

1. This was correct: Corbett, *England in the Mediterranean*, i. 312.

P. S. Was about to close this letter when the Latin secretary came asking me not to do so until he had delivered a letter from the lord protector for inclusion in the packet, promising a copy of it tomorrow. He said its contents solely concerned the duke of Savoy's tyranny against the protestants.[1]]

18

London, 1 June 1655 [in German]

[Refers to his last letter concerning the transference of Scottish prisoners from the Tower. Since then, General [David] Leslie has been transferred to Plymouth.

Cony's case still undecided, and postponed to the next court-day some three weeks hence. to give time for the preparation of further argument.

The persecution of the protestants in Piedmont causes increasing resentment, as more particulars come in of the atrocities. A fortnight ago a general day of prayer and fasting for them was ordered, and is to be followed by a general subscription, which seems likely to bring in a considerable sum; and at the beginning of this week Mr Murland [*sc.* Morland], who accompanied Whitelocke to Sweden, is sent with 6 persons to Turin to complain to the duke of the cruelties there practised, and to demand reparation. A similar mission to Paris, since these murders, which amount to 26,000 persons, were mostly committed by French troops.

No progress with the French treaty: it seems that the persecution in Piedmont has raised an obstacle.[2] One other reason for the delay is doubts of French sincerity, on account of the various intrigues fomented by them, and because Bordeaux, in conversation with his staff and others, indiscreetly gave it to be understood that he would indeed conclude and sign the treaty, but that it was not his crown's intention to observe it longer than it was to its advantage, and to the advantage of the republic. All of which has come to the ears of the protector.

The merchants of this country trading to Spain have recently handed to the protector a petition, in which they allege that the Castile trade is much more advantageous to this country than the

1. See no. 19, *infra.*
2. Intelligence from The Hague, 29 May NS, reported that 'many here will not be sorry' for the hitch in the negotiations, 'for they do imagine, that France and Sweden are agreed to prejudice the House of Austria, and that the chiefest design of the Swedish preparations is against Austria': Thurloe, iii. 473. Bordeaux wrote to Brienne, 3 June NS, 'I know not to what I shall attribute this proceeding, so contrary to all expectations. The zeal of religion is certainly not able to shake the design of the lord protector': *ibid.,* iii. 470.

trade to France, and that the latter could be sacrificed with only moderate loss. It is thought that this was a manoeuvre by the Spanish minister.

A private conference yesterday with Thurloe, and once more pressed the case of the imprisoned earl of Lauderdale; but was answered that though the protector would gladly defer to Y. M., could he do so without danger to the state, if Y. M. knew of the earl's practices against the government he would not meddle in the matter.

I was also assured by Thurloe that the emissary who is to go to Sweden on behalf of this government would be not only nominated but despatched, within a week, with the ratification.]

19

London, 1 June 1655

Since the lord protector's letter to Y. M. concerning the Savoyard persecutions came to me eight days ago, very late, shortage of time on that occasion prevented me from properly reporting that when Secretary Meadowe brought me the letter I took the opportunity to speak of errors in the chancery here as to Y. M.'s titles: namely, that Y. M.'s full title was not set out in the superscription, though he must well know that Y. M. describes himself as of other lands and principalities also; and further, that the predicate *domino* had similarly been forgotten. To which he answered, that it was not by intention, but solely *per incuriam scribe* [*sic*], and that such a thing should not occur again. And professed that he would have been ready and willing to have the letter re-written, and corrected as I requested, had it not been that it was impossible to do it that evening for lack of time— especially since the lord protector, who must sign it, had that afternoon gone to Hampton Court. At the same time he promised that any defects in courtesy or form of address which had appeared in letters of congratulation to Y. M. from the lord protector, as also in this letter recently despatched, would hereafter be avoided. Subsequently, perceiving that my commissioners were very occupied with business, I sought an opportunity to talk with the secretary of state himself, Mr Thurloe; who told me that the lord protector would within a week not only nominate a nobleman, but also despatch him to Y. M. with his highness's ratification, duly amended as I had demanded; and that he would take with him the authorization which Mr Whitelocke had pledged himself to obtain within three months. He said that he had learned from Secretary Meadowe that there was some defect of title noted in the lord protector's letter to Y. M., which happened solely *per inadvertentiam scribarum*, and which should be taken care of in future, since his highness had no intention to act contrary to Y. M. either in that or any other matter.

Speaking of permission to recruit in Scotland, he asked me whether Y. M. would not just as lief have Irish as Scots; but I answered that I did not think so: first, since Y. M. had not mentioned anything of them; 2°, Y. M. could best come to terms about recruiting with Scottish officers, since that nation was used to being in Sweden; and 3° that the Scots were protestants, but the Irish were papists, upon whom Y. M. could not place equal reliance if they should be engaged in a war with *principe pontificio*. He acknowledged that this last reason was of importance, and promised to manage his highness's consent as quickly as possible. From this, and from several other circumstances, it may fairly be deduced that the last paragraph of the lord protector's recently despatched letter to Y. M. expresses their serious intention, namely that he would be *paratissimum eacum Regia Vestra Majestate communicare consilio, quod ad rem Protestantium toto terrarum orbe sustinendam atque firmandam maxime pertinuerint.*[1] Mr Thurloe also told me that next week the commissioners would be conferring with me concerning the claims for restitution and compensation for damage, since explicit orders had been given them to discuss with me how this matter was to be adjusted.

The Polish envoy de Bye has still not had his conference, although he does his utmost to obtain it; but instead he has been presented with the complaints of some English merchants, with a request that he will first give a satisfactory answer to them. He said himself, when he met me the other day in St James's Park, that he was resolved to go to Holland and fetch his family thence, because he perceived that he would be obliged to remain here a good while longer, all business here going on so cruelly slowly.

The longer the lord protector sits in the saddle, the securer his seat in it; so that there is every likelihood that his government may last for the remainder of his life: indeed, all circumstances lead me to believe that he will either try to get the law altered by consent, or (which seems more probable) that he will very shortly assume the title of king. There are indeed reasons which might seem to hinder such a step. First, if he took it, he would to a great extent alienate himself from the militia, and among them some high officers—such as General Lambert and others like him—who may well have *spem successionis in dignitatem protectoris* once he is dead; of which hope the protector would deprive them, *assumpto regio titulo*; to say nothing of all the anabaptists, who can neither wish nor suffer that the government remain in one

1. Cromwell's letter of 25 May 1655, of which Abbott (iii. 726) prints an English version only, seems the only one for which the date, and the general drift, fit this quotation, though the precise wording by no means squares with it.

family. 2°. The struggle between the nation on the one hand and the royal family of Stuart on the other would thereby be transformed into a private quarrel between the Houses of Cromwell and Stuart; and in that quarrel many would defect from the protector. 3°. It would conflict with an Act of Parliament which lays it down that all kingly power in one person is *in perpetuum* abrogated for ever in England.

But on the other hand there are other and more powerful reasons to persuade him to the assumption of the royal title. First, that this country has always been accustomed to be ruled by a king, and all their English statutes and ancient laws are founded on that: a situation which cannot be altered without great disorder. 2°. It can be seen from the difficulties now daily advanced by the lawyers that the law and the present government are not in accord; and therefore it would be best to undertake a change in the constitution to prevent such difficulties for the future. 3°. It is easier for the protector to make himself king now that it was to become protector. 4°. The nobility in the country would be better satisfied; their pre-eminence and preservation, as experience has taught, consisting solely in a kingly government. 5°. General Lambert and his followers could in such a case be given such favours as to content him, and that immediately, in the present protector's lifetime, the more especially since it is doubtful whether he would ever succeed to the dignity of the protectorship, not being accounted as religious, and unable on that ground to oppose what the present protector has done, and is doing. 6°. The anabaptists and their leader Harrison were not able to prevent the protector from attaining to his present exalted position, though it conflicts with their maxims no less than does the royal style and dignity. 7°. In a quarrel between the Cromwellian and Stuart families the protector's power will be able to maintain himself and his followers hereafter as hitherto, not least because through his conduct this country has acquired a greater reputation abroad than ever was the case under all previous monarchs. 8°. The greater part of the country would be obliged in their own interests to stand by him—that is, all those who are in possession of crown or church lands (which amount to about a third of the country), besides those to whom confiscated estates have passed either by donation or by purchase, of whom there are a great number who would risk losing their property if the House of Stuart were not excluded from the government. 9°. All those in this country who have either supported the parliament against the king, or been neutral, have nothing to look for from a Stuart restoration, since in that case the king would be bound to promote and reward those who have lost everything because of their loyalty to him, rather than those who later take his side simply out of hatred for Cromwell and his party. 10°. Such a restitution could not take place without great tumults and disturbances in the country; and this is a danger to which they will not willingly expose themselves, feeling it to be a matter of indifference to them by whom they are ruled, if only they be preserved in the free enjoyment of their law and religion. 11°. The Act of Parliament would no more hinder the taking of the name of king than it was able to prevent the exercise of royal authority under the title of protector; for this was something which did not come to pass with their [*sc.* parliament's] good-will: it was the work of the army alone, as everybody knows; apart from the fact that it was only the House of Stuart and all who may claim the crown *ejus jure niti* whom the Act excluded from the exercise of royal power. 12°. Parliament at first always resolved that it had no intention of abolishing the authority, dignity or name of king of England; and if they afterwards in fact did so, *rebus eorum sic exigentibus*, in contravention of their fundamental law, so now they can the better and the more easily restore it *secundum antiquorum legum prescriptum*.

However that may be, time will soon reveal what can be determined on. Meanwhile the army is in this neighbourhood, and orders have been issued to raise a company of horse in every county, in such wise as appears more at large from the attached translation of an order, which, though it is not yet promulgated, is to be made public immediately, and of which the English draft was made available to me by my correspondent.[1] The companies will together make 6000 horse.

In Scotland order has been fully restored, since all malignants (as they are termed here) have presented themselves and reconciled themselves to the government. James Wemyss has determined to go to Y. M. and present his inventions as soon as he has recovered his health, which has suffered under a long illness. I received Y. M.'s gracious letter of 28 April by the ordinary post, and shall conduct myself in accordance with it.

20

London, 8 June 1655

Your Majesty's most gracious letters from Stockholm, both of 12 May, were received by me yesterday with all due reverence; and from them I have gathered what Y. M. is pleased to command: namely, the consent in writing to the recruiting of men in Scotland;[2] the agreement

---

1. The translation of the order is missing in the transcript.
2. They brought orders to ask leave to raise 5–6000 men in Scotland, in addition to the regiment of 2000 which Leven had already promised. George Fleetwood, whose arrival was expected shortly, was to take charge of their forwarding. Leven's 2000 must

with Count Leslie [*sc.* Leven]; the notification of the expected embassy; the utilization of the generality's ill-affection towards Poland and the consequences that flow from it, as also the purchase of some horses: all of which shall have my obedient attention. And for that reason I wrote yesterday to the earl of Leven, who is now in Scotland: I expect his answer shortly. Although Secretary Thurloe at our last meeting assured me of the lord protector's written consent to the raising of troops in Scotland, I have nevertheless still not been able to obtain it. To-day I spoke with the Latin Secretary, Meadowe, who assured me *juramento* that at this time everyone connected with the court was so burdened and distracted by other important affairs of a domestic nature, that it had been impossible for them to do anything in the matter, but nevertheless promised that it should be attended to immediately; though he considered that permission could be given only for 5 to 6000 men at the most, since the lord protector must send over numbers of Scots to Ireland and to America.

In the course of the next week I shall attempt to obtain an opportunity once again to speak with the lord protector himself, as well of this as of other matters which may conduce to the realization of Y. M.'s wishes. From my former reports I have no doubt that Y. M. will have gathered the disposition that exists here to enter into a closer alliance with Y. M. And I certainly believe—in so far as may be judged from the language of leading personages, and indeed of the lord protector's own words as reported to me by reliable persons— that they are excellently well disposed to it. For he said on one occasion 'that Y. M. and he could constrain the whole of Europe if there were a closer alliance between them; since Y. M. on land, and he at sea, were mighty considerable'; adding, that he did not believe that Y. M. would soon lay down his arms, in consideration of the great advantages Y. M. could look forward to. A nobleman by the name of Rolt, a Lord in Waiting to his highness, and as I am informed a near kinsman of his, has been nominated to carry the ratification to Y. M., and is to set off within eight days.[1] But in my opinion he will defer his departure until the alteration in the government is completed: it is to be put into effect shortly, and at all events before this month of June runs to its end. Whether the lord protector will take the *titulum regium* or *imperatorium* is still uncertain, though by the most part the latter is thought the more

be trained men, furnished with clothes, and delivered at Stade, at Leven's expense. Coyet was to sound Cromwell on the prospects of an alliance; to justify Charles X's reasons for war with Poland; and to hint that he was disposed to give English traders privileges better than those enjoyed by the Dutch: Carlbom, *Sverige och England*, p. 22.

1. Rolt's instructions, and the ratification of Whitelocke's treaty, are printed in Thurloe, iii. 418–9; *cf. CSP (Dom) 1655–56*, p. 235: he did not leave, however, until 30 July: *CSP (Ven) 1655–56*, p. 94.

appropriate, since the lord protector will take the legislative power to himself, which the kings of England have never before possessed separately from parliament. It seems also that the signature of the French treaty is postponed until that event. It is certain that with *custodibus magni sigilli* and with *supremis angliae judicibus* there is to be a great reformation. Cony and his counsel, whom in my former reports I mentioned as having been imprisoned, are now unexpectedly let out, and given their former liberty again. Many are inclined to interpret this as a collusion, as though the lord protector wished in this matter to seek a pretext to hasten, and indeed to necessitate, his design to assume the legislative power, and for that reason suborned the one to refuse the payment of duty, and the others to dispute the protector's authority.[1]

The Portuguese resident is not departing, as I stated in my last letter: he remains here awaiting fresh orders from his king; to which end he recently despatched his secretary to Portugal. On his last visit to me he informed me that he still hoped to bring his affair here to a good conclusion, since the matters still at issue were of no great moment.

Every day some persons are put in prison, as participants in the plot which Lord Byron and several others are said to have been hatching. The plan is said to have been to shoot the protector with a steel bow.

The horses which Y. M. ordered me to purchase here are readily available, and I shall accordingly buy them without delay and forward them to Resident Möller in Hamburg, drawing a bill upon him to correspond with the purchase-price.

Count Pontus de la Gardie arrived here in London from Paris a few days ago, but to-day sets out again for Dunkirk, and thence to Hamburg.

21

London, 15 June 1655 [in German]

[General day of prayer yesterday, and a general collection for the suffering protestants of Savoy.

Some days ago the Spanish ambassador was admitted to an audience and requested his dismissal: the general opinion is that he has not effected very much.

The day of prayer, and the preoccupation of the protector and

---

1. *Cf.* Ludlow's comment: 'The new Chief Justice [Glynn] before he came to sit on the bench, took care to have this business accommodated with Cony': *The Memoirs of Edmund Ludlow*, ed. C. H. Firth, (2 vols. Oxford 1894), i. 413.

council in establishing this government, prevented Coyet from obtaining an audience: promised one for to-day.

The emissary from Siebenbürgen, who originally intended to be no more than 9–10 days in this country, has obtained his dismissal after a lapse of nine weeks: he professes to be satisfied, and intends to take Pomerania on his way home. De Bye has asked the protector for leave to visit his family in Holland, and promised to return after a short interval.

The regiment of 1500 men ordered to proceed to America in a fleet of about 19 ships arrived at its port [of embarkation] this week.[1] By the same fleet many of those imprisoned, as involved in the late plot, are being sent to the West Indian colonies, among them a Lord Grandison, who stabbed himself to death on board ship.[2] The frequent conspiracies against the republic have led to increased care for security, and throughout England all the magnates who are suspected of disaffection have either been secured or forced to give security not to undertake any hostile actions, to the number of at least 600, or as some assert not less than 1000, among them the earl of [sc. Lord] Newport and his brother, Lords Lindsey, Willoughby and Lovelace. On the other hand Commissary-General Reinhold [sc. Sir John Reynolds] and the presiding judge at Salisbury have been knighted, the latter obtaining the special favour of being allowed to retain the sword with which the protector knighted him.

The protector has taken the Great Seal into his own hands: it is not known to whom he will give it; some say, to a chancellor who is to be appointed.[3] The small seal is given to Colonel Fiennes. The old Great Seal has been destroyed, and a new seal made, which includes the arms of the Cromwell family, as well as those of England, Scotland and Ireland.[4]

I am certainly informed that the protector's eldest son Richard is appointed High Admiral;[5] his younger son Henry is to be Deputy in Ireland, and to leave next week. The former Deputy, his son-in-law [Charles] Fleetwood, is to be Treasurer.[6] And General Lambert is to be Governor of the Cinq Ports.

---

1. Cf. *The Narrative of General Venables*, pp. 171–2.

2. He was still alive in December 1655, when the protector authorized a grant of money to him to enable him to leave England: Abbott, iv. 59; cf. Gardiner, *Commonwealth and Protectorate*, iii. 310 *n*. 1.

3. Whitelocke was deprived of the Great Seal on 6 June; on the 15th it was given to Fiennes and Lisle: Whitelocke, *Memorials*, iv. 205–6.

4. Cf. *The Clarke Papers*, Newsletter, 8 May 1655, iii. 38.

5. Coyet was misinformed.

6. And on this point also.

Commissioner Bonnel has presented his letters of recall to the protector and obtained his leave to depart: he is now preparing to leave as soon as possible for Hamburg, and thence to Charles X.[1]]

P. S. [in Swedish]
Since it was late in the evening when I had my audience with the lord protector I have not been able to give an account of how it fared. I am therefore obliged to postpone it to the next post. In the meantime—if any trust is to be put in words, assurances, and demeanour—I cannot gather from the lord protector's remarks any other impression than that he desires to favour Y. M.'s designs in every way, and that the Dutch will effect little here.

22

London, 22 June 1655 [in German]

[Little to report: the council of state is engaged on business said to be of importance, but kept secret. Additional names of suspects imprisoned: the earls of Northampton, Peterborough, Devonshire; the marquis of Hertford; Colonel Long, Eyres, Panton, Griffin, 'Wedfort' [*sic*: qy. Bedford? see *infra*, p. 89].

Yesterday was the state funeral of William Constable, late governor of Gloucester.

The Great Seal of England has been given to Lord Fiennes and Lord Lisle, as commissioners, who shortly afterwards in the Court of Appeal delivered to Glynn a sealed patent, in the name of the protector, appointing him Chief Justice in the place of Mr Rolle, resigned; upon which he delivered a handsome sermon demonstrating the happy constitution of the present government, and how far it excelled the achievements of former kings and princes.

No progress with the French treaty. De Bye left for Holland to-day as wise as he came, after staying four months.]

23

London, 22 June 1655

Y. M.'s letter of 19 May from Stockholm reached me by the ordinary post a week ago;[2] and in accordance with Y. M.'s earlier instructions

1. Bonnel received his recredentials on 20 June: Abbott, iii. 573–4.
2. It ordered Coyet to try to divert the Dutch from taking action against Charles in Poland, it having been reported that they were attempting to form an alliance with Poland, Danzig and Brandenburg, and had determined to send a convoy-fleet to the Sound, with the intention of getting a foothold there and in the Baltic: he was to point out to Cromwell the danger of such proceedings: Carlbom, *Sverige och England*, p. 23.

I have made every effort to speak with the lord protector; for which I did not receive permission till last Friday, the 15th, and that late in the afternoon.[1] I did not get home from his highness until almost 8 o'clock, and was therefore unable at once to report the course of the interview. When I came to him I told him, after the proper courtesies, that Y. M.'s confidence in the lord protector was so great that he had not wished to conceal from him his intention of making war on Poland, but that he had given me proper notification of it, and of its causes, in order that his highness might judge for himself how justified Y. M.'s arms were. Coming then to the grounds for war, I detailed them almost in the same order as in the short extract that was sent to me; with an appropriate conclusion to the effect that Y. M. was well assured that his highness would not *in specie* disapprove them, and that he therefore would be the more inclined to take such counsel with Y. M. as might best tend to the fortunate issue of Y. M.'s designs, the averting of any obstacle that might be raised by others, and the welfare of the general Protestant Cause.

To this he answered that it was a matter dear to his heart that Y. M. had conceived such confidence in him personally, which he would endeavour to preserve in every way and by all suitable means; and he acknowledged it to be a signal act of friendship that Y. M. should not only have communicated to him *decretum de bello Polonis inferendo* (which he might almost have inferred from the circumstances of the case) but had also been willing to disclose the weighty reasons for it; which he admitted to be valid and sufficient grounds for declaring war. He therefore wished Y. M. all good fortune in his undertaking and God's blessing, which Y. M., he presumed, might in his righteous and justified war expect from the hand of the Almighty; and among the reasons for it enumerated one that had been mentioned already, namely, that he did not doubt that Y. M. would thereby

---

De Witt had been projecting an alliance with Brandenburg since the beginning of May, and hoped that Cromwell would adhere to it; though Nieupoort warned him that the protector was unlikely to agree to being included in a system he had had no hand in framing. De Witt however hoped that the offer would persuade Cromwell that Brandenburg was not an Orange partisan; but in fact the suggestion gave great offence to the elector. The Dutch then tried another approach: on 10 June NS the States of Holland ordered Nieupoort to propose a Dutch–Spanish–English alliance to preserve freedom of commerce in the Baltic: *Brieven*, iii. 55, 62–3, 67, 69; Thurloe, iii. 544. The English reaction was cool: Thurloe did indeed assure Nieupoort that the protector considered a Dutch alliance as the basis of his policy, but he thought the proposed triple alliance with Denmark premature, and hoped that Brandenburg would never be included in it: Nieupoort to de Witt, 30 July NS, *Brieven*, iii. 92; and same to same, 9 July NS, *ibid.*, 78–9, for the protector's doubts about Denmark.

1. The granting of audiences in the late afternoon of Fridays (which was post-day) was a characteristic (and for foreign diplomats frustrating) habit of the protector.

have an opportunity subsequently to advance the general welfare of the Protestant Cause. He spoke much of the high esteem he had for Y. M.'s person, and of how it was not only this personal respect (very great though it was, and one that strongly influenced him), but the common interest, and the welfare of the whole of protestantism, that obliged him to do all in his power to forward Y. M.'s laudable designs.

When I afterwards raised the point of a written consent to the recruiting of Scottish soldiers, he said that it was a matter of much dissatisfaction to him that he must still withhold permission to recruit for a little while longer; not that he refused it to Y. M., but that being still not on quite clear terms with his powerful neighbours, his situation did not yet allow him to declare himself in writing.[1] And when, with many long remonstrances, I put him in mind of the hopes he had given me by those who first spoke with his highness of the matter, and how his highness himself at my last audiences had given me assurances, [and pointed out] the arrangements and agreements Y. M. had in consequence made, and the possible advantage which Y. M.'s enemies might derive from this delay, he answered at last, after a long discursive speech,[2] with many asseverations of his great inclination to oblige Y. M. in all matters, that he was unwilling to believe that Y. M. would take this delay otherwise than as it ought to be taken, or ascribe it to any failure of good will on his part, since he was prepared to give Y. M. such proofs of his affection that Y. M.'s friends would rejoice thereat, and all his enemies be confounded. And that you may know (he said, and I translate his own expressions into Swedish) 'what it sticks on, it is that I am expecting within a fortnight or three weeks at the latest, tidings from the fleet in America; and I shall be forced to take my measures accordingly. I hope at all events that they may be such that I am able to oblige your great king in all—indeed, I hope in more than all—that he asks of me; for the granting of recruiting I hold for only the slightest token of my friendship for the crown of Sweden, while I hope that we may have the opportunity to shake hands with each other, which *Anglorum more et lingua* implies great intimacy, and the maintenance of particular friendship'. He spoke much also of his late majesty King Gustav the Second and Great, of glorious memory; saying among other things that, being then a private

1. But on 8/18 June 1655 Nieupoort reported to de Witt that Thurloe had explained to Coyet that the levy had been refused merely to please the Dutch, though it was to the protector's interest to clear the Highlands of every single highlander: *Brieven*, iii. 71.

2. Abbott translates 'he answered me as before, but only after an arrogant speech': here and elsewhere he takes '*wijdlöfftigh*' to mean 'arrogant', though the real sense is simply 'diffuse, discursive, prolix'.

person, he nevertheless had always followed his great campaigns with the greatest pleasure, had many times thanked God, with tears of joy in his eyes, for His gracious mercies, and when the tidings came of his death, had so mourned it that he could scarcely believe that any Swede could mourn it more bitterly; for he saw that a great instrument to quell the power of the papists had been taken away. But he hoped now that Y. M. would repair that loss, and follow the late King Gustav's laudable example; and that with all the more fruit and benefit to the common cause, since he made no doubt that on his side there was a readiness to contribute all possible means to the seconding of the work; which before had not been properly attended to by this state, and much good thereby neglected.

I answered, in general, that Y. M. also had a great wish to be more closely united with his highness; since he perceived how advantageous such an alliance would be, not only to these two states, but also to the whole Evangelical Cause, especially since other states who (either from private jealousy, or from selfishness and wilfulness) attempt to obstruct Y. M.'s plans for the common weal, might thereby be brought to reason and be refrained within their own limits. But I did not, on this occasion, think that I could with advantage propound a definite plan, or say anything of a closer alliance designed to prevent the Dutch from making themselves masters of the Baltic and using it to their sole advantage, even though Y. M. in his letter ordered me to do so; and this for the following reasons:

1, because I was afraid that the English would conclude that it was fear alone that made Y.M. seek their friendship; which would lessen such respect as they have for the might of Swedish arms;

2, since they might perhaps take the opportunity to stipulate for good terms in the Baltic, which might in course of time prejudice Y.M.'s revenues, and Sweden's trading preferences;

3, because I perceive that they sufficiently favour Y.M.'s designs already, and are so far content with [the assurance] on Y.M.'s behalf that the trade of the English to the Baltic shall remain unmolested; and for that reason will not be prepared to hinder those designs at the solicitation of the Pole, or of the Dutch;

4, I do not think that the Dutch, realising the lord protector's unwillingness to go along with them, would venture to undertake anything in the Baltic to obstruct Y.M., since they fear that in such a case Y.M. would enter into a closer alliance with England, to their exclusion. This last prospect would, I think, effectively intimidate them, if it were held out to them as a warning by Herr Appelboom at The Hague; for they know very well the disposition of the English everywhere to gain some advantage in trade over them. To this end I have written these my humble thoughts to Herr Appelboom for his guidance, so that he can avail himself of them on the spot, as may be appropriate to the situation. I shall nevertheless, if I detect any danger of Dutch intrigues being afoot, or of the English showing approval of Dutch proceedings, do my utmost on all occasions to make the aforesaid alliance for the defence of the Baltic go down with them here, trusting that Y.M. will not take it ill that I have not so far been ready to mention it *in specie*, for the above-mentioned, and for other, reasons. It is certainly true that Heer Nieupoort attempts by every means to depreciate Y.M.'s power at sea, alleging that Sweden has no more than 15 warships in service,[1] and that he seeks to make Y.M.'s laudable designs odious. But if it is possible to put one's trust in good words, assurances, and benevolent attitudes, I do not perceive that he effects anything by it, but rather prostitutes himself and his principals. However that may be, I shall always make use of every opportunity, and of the utmost vigilance, to countermine everything that he may adduce to Y.M.'s prejudice.

The Polish envoy de Bye has had no better success, as far as I can gather, but this morning goes off to Holland on the pretext of a wish to visit his children and take order for his family there; after which he is to return to pursue his business here; for he has not taken leave of the lord protector, but has simply obtained a passport to travel. I am confident that in the present circumstances he has more chance of doing Poland some good in Holland than he has been able to do here. He told me himself that he had expected to remain here for only 4 to 5 weeks, but against all expectation has been kept waiting for 15 weeks, and departs as wise as he came, but in worse spirits and with less hope.

I have not yet delivered Y.M.'s ratification of [Whitelocke's] alliance with this country, or mentioned anything of the matter, particularly since they have never made any enquiry about it, but are

---

1. This was a considerable underestimate: at the beginning of the war Sweden had 36 ships: see the list in Finn Askgaard, *Kampen om Östersjön på Carl X Gustafs tid. Ett bidrag till nordisk sjökrigshistoria* (Carl X Gustaf-studier, 6) (Stockholm 1974), pp. 28–9. Despite the fact that in 1647 Christina sold four ships to France, and a further nine to Louis de Geer, Sweden maintained a (varying) superiority over Denmark's navy: see the diagram in *Från Femern och Jankow till Westfaliska freden. Minnesskrift utarbetad och utgiven av Försvarsstabens krigshistoriska avdelning* (Stockholm 1948), pp. 47, 50. In December 1654, nevertheless, Bonde had asserted that the Swedish fleet was not capable of dealing with the Dutch and Danes in conjunction: RRP., xvi. 18. But on this point Thurloe was accurately informed: he wrote to Henry Cromwell on 15 May 1655 that Charles X, if he took Danzig, 'will by this have the command of all the trade in the Baltique sea, haveing besides a good fleete of 36 men of warre, with which to beseidge the sayd town at sea': Thurloe, iii. 440. Nieupoort had also told Thurloe that the Swedish navy could not dispense with Dutch commanders and boatswains: *Brieven*, iii. 63. There was more truth in this: the Swedish navy had numbers of foreign officers— English as well as Dutch.

content with Queen Christina's ratification. I therefore await Y.M.'s further orders as to how I am to deal with this question. As I write this, Y.M.'s letter of 26 May has been delivered to me: it came with the ordinary post, having taken longer than usual.

24

London, 29 June 1655

I beg leave to inform Y.M. herewith that the Polish envoy, de Bye, left for Holland on the 23rd. Shortly before his departure he paid me a valedictory visit, during which he said, among other things, that he was sure that on the Polish side they were well inclined to give Y.M. and the Swedish crown every satisfaction; and therefore hoped that the war which to all appearance was hanging over them from Sweden might be averted; since both their ambassadors were by this time without doubt on their way to Y.M.,[1] and Prince Charles being now dead, who in his lifetime was a great obstacle to peace-negotiations.[2]

I answered that it was desirable that Y.M. should come to a settlement with the crown of Poland without bloodshed, and be given proper assurances *de servandis promissis* in all eventualities. 'Yes', he replied, 'but is it not security enough that the king of Poland should renounce *juri et praetentioni suae* to Sweden and Livonia?'. To which I answered, 'As to Sweden, and the greater part of Livonia, they were no longer in the king of Poland's possession, and he would therefore be giving nothing that was his own; besides that Y.M. in that case would be no more secure that peace would be kept by the Poles any more inviolably than the truce was now'; and rehearsed cases in which they had broken their agreements. He denied that the incursions of Boot and Crakow had had the approval of the king or diet;[3] of

1. The ambassadors (who were sent by the diet, not by the king) had nothing new to offer, and did not arrive until Charles X was actually embarking for Pomerania.

2. Charles Ferdinand, brother of King John Casimir. He died '*vario morborum genere vexatus*', on 9 May 1655. At the election of 1648 Sweden had maintained neutrality as between John Casimir and Charles Ferdinand, though conscious that Charles Ferdinand would make the better king. John Casimir being childless, Charles Ferdinand offered the best hope of keeping alive the claims of the Polish Vasas to the throne of Sweden; but the precise bearing of de Bye's remark is not clear: see Olof Jägerskiöld, 'Karl Ferdinand Vasa och det polska konungavalet 1648', *Historisk tidskrift* (1948), pp. 213–28.

3. Herman Bothe had made a raid into Swedish Livonia in 1639; J. Ernst Crachow had made an incursion in 1643. The Swedes believed—or affected to believe—that both events had the connivance of the Polish authorities. This was a grievance which the Swedish government kept warm, for propaganda purposes: see, e.g., *RRP*. xvi. 9, 100; and *Sveriges ridderskaps och adels riksdagsprotokoll*, V₂, 212–13, 216, 220.

the other points he knew nothing, and in particular disclaimed all knowledge that the Cossacks had been incited to fall upon Livonia: in regard to these it could not be asked of him that he should *praestare alterius factum*, or make any answer to them. He asked also 'what security it was that Sweden required'?. In reply I expatiated at some length upon the actions of the Poles and their breaches of the truce, in so far as their [domestic] circumstances made it possible for me to have any knowledge of them; and as to security I remarked that I did not really know what Y.M. might require, but this I would say, that if anybody were to consider this as though it were a private quarrel, and were to pronounce a judgment on it, he could not in justice do otherwise than judge that the injured party must receive damages and all costs of the case, and that what the other party had taken from him *sub conditionis pacis habendae* must be restored to him again. And that therefore since [royal] Prussia *ex natura contractus*[1] was by the crown of Sweden handed over to Poland solely *ea conditione* that the truce should be inviolably maintained by them—and, as had been shown, it had not been duly observed—then Y.M. could *optimo jure condiere Borussiam quasi causa cessam vel datam causa vero non secuta*, as the lawyers put it. 'And so I understand' (said he) 'that you are demanding the retrocession of Prussia, which is a matter of concern to all states; for if Sweden had it, it would become more powerful than all other nations, [which] in such a case must live at Sweden's mercy, and so to say receive their sustenance at her hands'. To which I retorted, 1. That the crown of Sweden in such a case would be no more powerful than it was when Prussia was formerly in its possession. 2. When Prussia was Swedish, the Swedish crown had not forbidden trade thither to any, and still less would it hereafter prohibit or harass the trade of its friends. 3. Without Y.M.'s friendship, nobody could safely trade to Prussia, even though it should never become Swedish, *ratione dominij Maris Baltici.* 'And how', he enquired, 'can Sweden *ratione dominij Maris Baltici* forbid the trade to Prussia to any who may not be its friends, seeing that Poland also has a share in that [*dominium*], having land and ports upon the Baltic coast?'. I answered that the king of Poland might indeed for the moment have a Baltic coastline, but he was not for that reason entitled to have the smallest concern with *Mari Balthico*, as can be sufficiently deduced when (comparing *privata publicis*) [we see] that many persons are owners of estates which run down to a lake or a river, but it does not follow that all who live on the shores are entitled to fish, or to build mills, without the permission of whoever has, either *per conventionem* or *praescriptionem*, the

---

1. The truce of Stuhmsdorff, 1635: its duration was to be twenty-six years, so that it was not due to expire until 1661.

jus piscandi et molendi, as *juris est notissimi*. And therefore it was much to Y.M.'s prejudice that the said king of Poland should have sought, by the terms of the treaties he had proposed,[1] to bring foreign warships into the Baltic, though he himself has no *jus classis habendae in Mari Balthico*, and is therefore in no position to confer it upon anybody else, since no one may transfer *plus juris in alium* than he himself possesses: as I demonstrated more at large by various reasons *ex jure communi*, and from the papers published at the time of the dispute with the town of Danzig some years ago; adding that Y.M. recognized no *jus classis habendae in Mari Balthico* to pertain to any, save to himself and Denmark; and was consequently not only entitled, but necessitated (*evitandae* [*sic*] *praejudicii causa*) to prevent, *vi armata*, any other power than Sweden and Denmark, no matter who it might be, from having *praeter morem et consuetudinem, tanquam in mari re vera clauso*, any *bellicam classem*: any more than the States of Holland would permit the crown of Sweden to assert *jus classis bellicae* in the Zuyder Zee. But this is not to be understood to apply to merchant fleets or ships, which may drive their trade without disturbance.

When after these exchanges de Bye at length took a courteous leave, he said that he hoped that the dispute between our countries might be settled amicably; but if not, he commended his cause to the righteous judgment of God. That I thus spoke somewhat strongly *de peregrina classe bellica in Mari Balthico* was only for the reason that (as I reported in my last letter) I did not doubt that he would retail it all to the Dutch ambassador; and I trust that these and other observations *de cautione praestanda servandae pacis* may be graciously approved by Y.M.

Y.M.'s letter of 2 June arrived yesterday by the ordinary post, with its orders tactfully to keep the lord protector from committing himself to anybody to undertake a mediation before the arrival of Y.M.'s ambassador. This, in all submission, I will do, and likewise take order for all the other matters which Y.M. was pleased to enumerate. I have so far, indeed, not heard either from the lord protector or his council anything which could be interpreted as tending that way; but if an opportunity should present itself to speak of mediation (if in fact they have any idea of it) then I have on a number of occasions told them that Y.M. was not bound by any *pacta, ad reassumendos tractatus* more often than has happened already; and I have often on suitable occasions reiterated this, by way of taking from them any *spem mediationis*; especially in view of the fact that the English were not prepared to admit the mediation of her majesty Queen Christina

---

1. De Bye's efforts to obtain an alliance with the United Provinces which would have bound them to send a fleet of warships to the Baltic.

between themselves and the Dutch.[1] But I shall immediately inform myself how the land lies, and take tactful precautions. For the rest, I refer to my letter which accompanies this.

25

London, 29 June 1655 [in German]

[Letters from St Kitts of 9 May, and others from Spain, report that Penn sailed directly from Barbados to Hispaniola, landed his men, and took St Domingo. Great rejoicings here: more of this later. News also that Algiers and Tripoli treat Blake with great respect and have liberated all English slaves. The Dutch slaves sought refuge on the English ships; but to avoid prejudice this was notified to Algiers, and ransom-money paid for them. A Dutchman of quality then offered a bill of exchange in settlement of the ransom paid, but the English declined it, alleging that they acted from Christian charity and courtesy.

In Scotland the war is completely over; after Middleton's departure the others (Glencairn being the last), submitted on terms, and no more trouble to be expected on that side for the present.

Before leaving the Barbary coast, Blake left a consul, to maintain good relations; has been off Cadiz, to their great alarm, since the silver-fleet is daily expected.

More gentlemen arrested: the earls of Bedford and Northumberland, Lord St John, Lord Maynard, Lord Lucas, Lord Coventry, Lord Peters [Petre] and many others; the reason being that after the protector and council had considered the reasons for the many late plots, he thought it advisable to assure himself of all persons of quality and wealth throughout the country, and to force them to give security to abjure the king of Scotland and support the government. The total number involved said to be as much as 2200. The former President Bradshaw is deprived of the chancellorship of the duchy of Lancaster for failing to appear before Cromwell when summoned; one Warburton appointed in his place. Whitelocke, having been deprived of his place as Commissioner of the Great Seal, comes less often to court.

A general rumour that the Swedes have attacked Wesel; no doubt

---

1. Charles X, having mobilized on credit, could not afford a quick settlement, which would have left an unpaid army on his hands. As the French ambassador in Stockholm remarked, if a peace were somehow patched up, 'it will turn this great army both by sea and land another way: it being certain, that Sweden will not rest with these considerable forces on foot': d'Avaugour to Bordeaux, 10 July 1655: Thurloe, iii. 598.

spread by the Dutch in order to make Sweden odious: story also that the Swedes have demanded, and been refused, a passage through Holland; and 'similar futilities'.[1]

This is not a good moment for reaching a settlement on Swedish claims for compensation for losses by English privateers: better deferred.]

26

London, 6 July 1655

I beg to inform Y.M. that I have to-day *had another private audience with the lord protector.*[2] The reasons for it, and what led up to it, I cannot relate at length at the moment, time being short, and I having returned home late, so that I must defer it until the next post. I must only give a brief report, setting out the lord protector's declaration, which was: *that he would not only do his best to forward Y.M.'s design by all means, but would prevent the Dutch from being in a position to block it by sending their fleet into the Baltic; to which end he promised all his good offices, since he could not see what advantage it would be to the Dutch to do so. And said that he attached great importance to the successful issue of Y.M.'s design.*

As to recruiting of Scottish soldiers he gave me good hopes, only that I must still wait a little, since he was every day expecting an opportunity to give Y.M. full satisfaction, and thought that it would arise within 8 or 14 days.

English privateers have intercepted some Dutch, or rather Zeeland, ships, which has caused the States of Zeeland to write a pretty strong letter to the lord protector in their favour, though it contains some polite expressions also: a copy is attached, marked A.[3] A ballad on the accident which befel his highness when he insisted on driving his Oldenburg horses himself has also appeared, and since it is an entertaining piece, and expresses esteem both for Y.M. and the Swedish alliance, it is attached, marked B.[3] What a certain Count Ludowicus Gustavus of Hohenlohe handed in to the lord protector may be seen from the copy of it, here marked C.[3] And with that I close this letter, referring Y.M. to my other letter that goes with it.

P.S. Y.M.'s letter of the 9th instant came safely to hand by the ordinary post yesterday. The letter which accompanies this ought to

---

1. Manning reported to Thurloe, 28 June OS 'Charles Stuart hopes much to have foreign forces from the King of Sweden': *CSP (Dom) 1655–6*, p. 220; and *CSP (Ven)* 1655–56, p. 91, where Sagredo conjectures (8 August NS) that English fears on this head may lie behind the recent wave of arrests.

2. The italicized passages presumably in cypher in the original.

3. Missing in the transcript.

have been forwarded 8 days ago, but by an unpardonable error was left out of the packet: I now send them to Y.M.

27

London, 6 July 1655 [in German]

[Continued reports of Penn's success in Hispaniola; Sedgwick's fleet, with a regiment of soldiers under Colonel Humphries, sailed from Dover on 29 June.

The Spanish silver-fleet has not yet arrived: Blake is still off Cadiz lying in wait for it. A recent rumour that after Blake's expedition to the Barbary coast the English resident in Constantinople, together with all other Englishmen, was strangled, and their ships and property confiscated; but as letters from Italy say nothing of it men are inclined to believe that it is put about by the Venetians in the hope of involving this country in their war. A Venetian ambassador extraordinary, one Sagredo, is on his way here, hoping to obtain an alliance against the Turks.

It is thought that all the complaints by this state against the Dutch will shortly be withdrawn, the negotiations with France being now promising.

Louis XIV's recent letter to the protector concerning Savoy is not deemed satisfactory, on grounds of defective stylization.

Nieupoort has recently had a private audience: its purpose unknown; but on various previous occasions he put it about that Charles X was on good terms with the Great Elector, and under the pretext of pursuing territorial claims would try to take possession of the Rhine fortresses with a view to helping the prince of Orange to power, to the great prejudice of this country. No doubt he hopes thereby to make Sweden's arming odious here.[1]

Serious fire recently on the riverside.

Continued stringent measures against the royalists.

The protector has not yet used the new Great Seal; but is expected to do so once the mustering of the militia on the 12th of this month is over.]

---

1. Nieupoort was invited to Hampton Court on 30 June. He informed Cromwell that Frederick William of Brandenburg had arranged to hand over Pillau to Charles X (in which he was mistaken); spoke of persecution in the Habsburg lands as being worse than that of the Vaudois; and wondered whether Charles X might not be prepared to attend to it. To which Cromwell replied that he only hoped that he would. Cromwell invited him to play bowls; but (unlike Bonde later), he declined the invitation, excusing himself on the ground of his ignorance of the game: Nieupoort to de Witt, 9 July NS 1655, *Brieven*, iii. 78–9.

28

London, 13 July 1655

Since Heer Nieupoort had a secret audience with the lord protector on the 4th, I thought it the more necessary to ask for one also, so that I might have a good opportunity to do away with any suspicions of Y.M.'s laudable design that he might have aroused, and to counteract anything he might have brought forward to Y.M.'s disadvantage. Especially so, since I knew that he put the worst construction upon Y.M.'s armaments on all occasions. At last, a week ago, I obtained my audience, when we spoke of the benefit that might be expected from a closer alliance between Y.M. and the lord protector. I expatiated on this at length, enforcing it with all the arguments that occurred to me as serviceable, not forgetting to point out how useful to England it would have been in the last Dutch war if Sweden, as an ally, had been available to prevent Denmark from meddling in it; and concluded by saying that Y.M.'s *extraordinarius legatus* was by now undoubtedly on his way hither, and might be expected shortly; that he was instructed by Y.M. to treat for a closer alliance; but that with a view to bringing the negotiations to a speedier conclusion it might not be unserviceable if the lord protector on his side were pleased to make some overture now, indicating how far he was disposed to go towards it—particularly if there were any points to be borne in mind, so that I could notify Y.M. of them in good time, and the ambassador might the sooner obtain Y.M.'s instructions as to how far he might go.

To which he replied that he was fully aware of the value of a confidential friendship and closer union between our two states, and knew of none between whom (for reasons he mentioned) a more confidential friendship could subsist; wherefore he not only received the news of Y.M.'s good intentions with pleasure, but would with all his heart conform to them; and that in order to evidence his inclination to forward a stricter alliance with Y.M. he would bethink himself of some particulars to which consideration should be given, and cause them to be presented to me for transmission to Y.M. The conversation then turning to the rumour that was going about that Y.M. had some design against the Dutch, he said he wondered at such talk, since he well knew that Y.M. had a greater design in hand, and one more serviceable to the common cause; in which he wished Y.M. all good fortune.

I answered that I did not know why such rumours were spread, first in Holland and then here, if not solely to make Y.M.'s arming appear generally invidious; also, that they had let it be known that they were willing to send a fleet to the Baltic; which had come to

Y.M.'s ears.[1] Now Y.M. certainly could not believe that the States would do it, since they could well imagine that Y.M., *evitandi praejudicij causa*, would in such a case be obliged to prevent it, *vi armata*, which would lead to far-reaching consequences. Nevertheless, in consideration of what crazy *consilia* the Dutch had been pursuing for some time past, Y.M. was not entirely assured that they might not possibly, out of mere jealousy of the happy success of Y.M.'s designs (of which they have given evidence many times in the past as well against Sweden as against other allies of theirs), undertake something of the sort, to the great injury of themselves and the common cause. For Y.M. could by no means suffer any power, other than himself and Denmark, to keep *in Mari Balthico classem bellicam*. The importance of which could easily be deduced from the fact that among the causes of the German war against the emperor was this: that the duke of Friedland [*sc.* Wallenstein] built a war-fleet in the Baltic for the emperor's service. If then the interest of the crown of Sweden could not permit the emperor—who nevertheless possessed a coastline and harbours on the Baltic—to fit out a *classem bellicam* there, how much less was it to be suffered from the Dutch, who ought always to be accounted there as foreigners. And therefore, to prevent anything of that nature, and—even more—all misunderstanding and controversies between protestants, Y.M., out of the friendly confidence which he entertains for his highness [hopes] that he, like Y.M., will discountenance such procedures and malevolent practices, which may be the cause of many troubles; and that if an amicable request was made to him, his highness would interpose his weighty authority to dissuade them from such notions, which can only conduce to the ruin of the Protestant Cause; neither the Dutch nor any other nation having any reason to fear that their trade to the Baltic would be disturbed by Y.M., provided they confine themselves within the limits to which they are entitled.

To this the lord protector returned a lengthy reply; of which the substance was that he would not only favour Y.M.'s laudable designs, but would use all good offices with the Dutch to restrain them from

---

1. Rumours that the Dutch were thinking of sending a fleet to the Baltic had reached Charles X as early as May. In June the States-General decided to send 10–12 ships to the Sound, as convoy. The Dutch–Danish 'Redemption' treaty of 1649 permitted up to five Dutch warships to pass the Sound without prior notification, and more than five on three weeks' prior notice. However, the 'Rescission' treaty of 1653 abrogated this concession, and forbade Dutch warships to proceed beyond Helsingör: the Swedes seem at this time not to have appreciated the change: J. Levin Carlbom, *Magnus Dureels negotiation i Köpenhamn 1655–57* (Göteborg 1901), pp. 12–14, 27–37. The provisions of the truce of Stuhmsdorf (1635) prohibited the Poles from maintaining warships in the Baltic, and also made it clear that no other state than Sweden and Denmark would be permitted to do so.

doing anything which might in any way hinder Y.M., or give any offence. And in particular that he would demonstrate, in this as in all other ways, that he is Y.M.'s hearty friend; adding that he could not see for what purpose they needed to send a fleet to the Baltic, especially since the driving of their usual trade thither was not refused to them. And when at the end I again alluded to the recruitment of the Scottish soldiers, and showed with many reasons that since the summer was already passing the affair was now in such a state that a decision could not well be postponed much longer without disadvantage to Y.M., the lord protector answered me that he expected every hour to be in a position to give his consent to it—within a week, he believed, and perhaps even earlier—as soon, in fact, as he had certain news about the West Indies fleet; and when I urged that in the first instance permission to raise 2000 men be given now, to gain time, the lord protector answered that that would take a day or two, and by that time he hoped to be in a position to give Y.M. full satisfaction. And he asked that the delay should not be taken for a refusal, or any bad construction put upon it, since in truth he would refuse neither that, nor any other thing of importance, to 'Your Great and Noble King' (as he termed Y.M.). His language was always excellent, and I do not doubt that its effects will be answerable thereto. And though it will appear from what I have written that I brought the business before him in another way than that which Y.M. was pleased to order, I can assure Y.M. that the state of affairs here would not have admitted its being raised in any other manner so as to serve Y.M.; as I in part explained to Y.M. in my previous letters, and as I can explain at large by word of mouth when I have the honour to lay myself at Y.M.'s feet. Above all, I spoke about *dominium maris Balthici* with such circumspection, and in such terms, as may avoid exciting any jealousy in this country, or give them any ground *ex ijsdem principijs* for maintaining their pretended *dominium maris Britannici* in the future, to the exclusion of Swedish convoys, or the prohibition of the herring-fishery.

Two days before I had my private audience with the lord protector I was permitted to pay a private visit to Mr Lawrence, the president of the council of state, with whom I went over the same ground. Among other things, by way of showing how unreliable the Hollanders were as allies, and how they laid themselves out to desert old friends for their supposed private interests, I rehearsed *ex historijs* how they had leagued themselves against the Rochellois, and in particular I adduced the secret articles of the treaty concluded with France by their ambassador Heer Boetselaer, *anno* 27;[1] to say nothing of what

1. Gideon van den Boetzelaer was ambassador to France from 1614. By the treaty of 1625 Dutch warships were to serve against Soubise. Coyet was possibly confusing

they did to others, by mutually contradictory treaties. All of which was designed to exhibit them in an odious light, and to make the English disinclined for their alliance, should they propose concluding one to the prejudice of Y.M. I considered it the more necessary to inform this Mr Lawrence of all these circumstances because he is said (notwithstanding that he is one of the ablest in the whole council) to be somewhat inclined to the Dutch, since while the civil war was being fought in this country he remained for many years in Holland, and was not well informed about Swedish affairs, or Swedish interests.

Some days ago, in the course of a visit, I had a conversation with the Dutch ambassador Heer Nieupoort, and found him unusually courteous. In particular he protested at length his principals' sincere intention to live in good confidence and correspondence with Y.M., as is becoming and proper for old allies to do; and at last came out with the remark that he had been given to understand that some misunderstanding had arisen between the crown of Sweden and the United Provinces, he knew not for what reason, but which he attributed to a false rumour which seemed to suggest that the Dutch designed to offend Y.M. But in the space of 20 years in which he had been employed in public affairs he had never, either in the assembly of the States, or in the case of any person, perceived any ill-will towards Sweden, much less had any resolution been taken to give the smallest offence to the Swedish crown. That they had fitted out 5 warships to convoy their merchant fleet to the Baltic was a thing no one could take ill, since they had always done it before without giving umbrage to any of their friends.

To this after a suitable compliment I answered, among other things, that although Y.M., of his own inclination, and in accordance with the praiseworthy example of his predecessor, had always sought to preserve a firm friendship with the States-General, Y.M. had been the more surprised at the general report that the States-General had determined to send a considerable number of warships into the Baltic; a measure which would not only tend greatly to Y.M.'s prejudice, but also necessitate him to prevent it by force; from which another great crisis must necessarily follow. He asked why Y.M. should wish to molest the convoys of his friends, they not being *naves bellicae, sed praesidiariae*, which meant no harm to anyone but were designed only to defend the merchantmen. I replied that no convoys were needed

him with van Sommelsdijk, who in 1626 agreed to make 25 ships available at need for service against Louis XIII's subjects. For the Dutch and La Rochelle, see G. W. Vreede, *Inleiding tot eene Geschiedenis der Nederlandsche Diplomatie*, (2 vols. Utrecht 1856–65), ii₂. 50–1, 100–2.

in the Baltic, since in that sea there was no danger of pirates;[1] and
further, that he, as a man learned in the laws, knew very well how *jus
conducendi* is *in jure* limited, so that no one may convoy or *conducere*
anyone through *alterius territorium*, but *dominus territorij* alone has *jus
conducendi*; and that since Y.M. claims *dominium Maris Balthici*, therefore
no one could assume to himself any right to convoy there, which I
explained at some length with many parallels and reasons, with the
object of frightening them off it—being sufficiently assured that the
lord protector (as I mentioned before) did not approve the Hollanders'
proceedings. At last he said that he was well assured that the States
could never have wished to send convoys further than to the Sound;
which I believe, now that they perceive they have no support here.
It seemed to me, from his speech and behaviour, that he must have
been spoken to, either by the lord protector himself, or on his behalf,
and that he was therefore very willing that it should appear as though
the Hollanders themselves entertained similar peaceable ideas on their
own account.

In his last audience with the lord protector Heer Nieupoort complained most strongly of the English privateers, who every day capture
and intercept many Dutchmen, on the pretext of their being, or their
cargo's being, French; so that some of them have been intercepted
five times within a few months, to the great dereliction and destruction
of their trade.[2] As a result, the lord protector has determined to
withdraw, by proclamation, all commissions or letters of marque
issued against France; but with this condition, that since they are
revoked as a concession to the Dutch and other traders, but without
prejudice to those English who have claims for compensation upon
France, all such claims are to be notified to the States, or to their
Admiralties, and satisfaction is to be sought from them in the form of
such prizes as the States' warships may take from the French, until
the treaty with the said crown is fully concluded.[3] To-day, between
10 and 11, the French ambassador, Monsr. Bordeaux, had likewise a
private audience with the lord protector: his mission is still secret, but
I shall make efforts to discover it.

1. The reservation of the right to maintain ships of war in the Baltic as exclusive to
Sweden and Denmark was always justified on the ground that they kept the sea clear
of pirates and maintained navigation-lights. Convoys, however, were nearly essential
to the safety of the unarmed Dutch *fluits*, and were requested (and provided) even for
the protection of the heavier, armed, English ships as far as the Sound: see *CSP* (*Dom*)
1655–6, pp. 203, 222, 242, 304, 345.

2. On 18 June NS 1655 Nieupoort wrote to Ruysch to the effect that the Dutch
desired an Anglo–French alliance because of the 'intolerable injuries' to Dutch skippers
under the guise of reprisals on France: Thurloe, iii. 528.

3. A proclamation revoking all letters of marque as from 1 August was issued on 12
July: *CSP* (*Dom*) *1655–56*, p. 240.

General [George] Fleetwood arrived here some days ago, and showed me the instruction which Y.M. had given him.[1] As I found that it contained some mention of the preference in trade and treatment which Y.M. might be prepared to grant to the English, as against the Dutch, my strong wish to avoid the jealousy which this might arouse in other nations, and also not to give the English a chance thereby to make exorbitant demands, [led me] to beg him to leave that topic absolutely alone, and allow it to await the arrival of Herr Christer Bonde;[2] the more so since I am sufficiently informed that there is no longer any danger to be expected from the Dutch in the Baltic, and since the lord protector is certainly disposed to favour Y.M.'s design, even without such advantages: which Herr Fleetwood promised to do. Baron Cranstoun has still not arrived, but it is reported from Hull that he (and the lord protector's horses likewise) were driven there by stress of weather; however, he is daily expected here.

The day before yesterday Secretary Meadowe called on me with the lord protector's ratification, which he showed to me, saying that since Mr Rolt was to leave with it within the next 2 or 3 days on his way to Y.M. he had been ordered to let me see it so that they could be assured, before his departure, that it was properly drawn; they having altered some things in it at my request. When I looked it over, it was in the same terms as when I was shown it at our first conference, and the alterations which I thought ought to be made in it in various places simply added *inter lineas*, but the whole not altered and corrected as it ought to have been. I accordingly said that Y.M. might have great hesitation in accepting an instrument of such importance, thus amended, and that therefore I neither could nor ought to consent to transmit it. He said that their only purpose in showing it to me had been that I should give my opinion of it, and that they would certainly have the one page fair-copied if I really insisted on it. He asked also where I [thought] the intended envoy would be able to find Y.M.,

1. Major-General George Fleetwood had had a distinguished career in the Swedish service. At the battle of Lützen he had played an important part in saving the day at a critical moment: his narrative of the action is in *Arkiv till upplysning om svenska krigens och krigsinrättningarnes historia* (3 vols. Stockholm 1854–61), ii. 643–4. Fleetwood was to act purely in a private capacity. He was to make contact with the protector, and express his hope, as a native Englishman, for an alliance between the two countries: Charles X, for his part, would prefer an offensive and defensive alliance *contra quemcunque*, Sweden taking care of the Baltic, and England of the North Sea. In such a case Sweden would be willing to grant English merchants preferential treatment as against the Dutch and other foreigners. In the meantime Charles would take care that his approaching war with Poland entailed no disadvantage to English merchants trading to the Baltic: summary of his instructions dated 15 May, in Carlbom, *Sverige och England*, pp. 35–6.

2. In this he correctly judged Charles X's intentions, as would appear from the orders of 23 June, which must have reached him shortly afterwards: Carlbom, *Sverige och England*, p. 34 n. 1.

whether in Sweden or in Germany. I said that if the envoy went directly to Hamburg he could there get the best information from Y.M.'s resident[1] as to where Y.M. and his army might be, and that he must take his road accordingly. For the rest, I refer to the letter which goes with this.

29

London, 20 July 1655

Some time ago I may have reported to Y.M. that it was quite apparent that the lord protector would take another title—whether of king or of emperor—and the reasons that might persuade him to this step. But now I learn that by reason of the opposition of the principal officers, who will by no means have a *hereditarium imperium*, the lord protector has been forced to change his purpose. For it is certain that upon one side of the new Great Seal his title has long ago been made to run *Olivarius Dei Gr. Angliae, Scotiae et Hyberniae*, but it has been left open whether he shall be designated *Rex* or *Imperator*. Deliberations about this having continued for some time, many reasons *pro et contra* being urged, it was nevertheless at last resolved to adhere to the title of protector; and some time ago the vacant space on the Great Seal was filled up. As far as I have been able to find out, there were numerous debates about it in the council; and, in particular, those who were backed by the leading officers in the army used these arguments, among others: that neither *regius titulus* nor *imperatorius* could be made to agree with the intention of the present constitution; which was, no doubt, to establish a sovereign power in a single person, with some few others conjoined with him, who were to exercise the legislative power; but not to restrict that power by heredity to one family. 1. Because the authority of the king, though in England it had never been as great as this, being confined within limits by the parliaments, yet *quo ad transmissionem juris in heredes* it was greater. 2. *Imperatoris titulus*, in the sense in which it is now commonly used, no doubt agrees well enough with their intention if we have regard only to the manner of election; but in authority, particularly with respect to the legislative power (which the emperors of to-day do not possess) there is a wide difference. 3. And former emperors, such as Augustus, Tiberius and others, who had *potestates condendae legis per L. Regiam*, could not be reconciled with this constitution, since they could of their own will, and without seeking the opinion of any, make laws *pro arbitrio*, and hence could transmit the same power to their heirs. 4. All nations, and especially the Romans, have always used a new name when establishing a new authority, both to dissociate themselves from

1. Vincent Möller.

what had been odious in the previous authority, and also to avoid all other problems of disobedience and sedition which might follow [if they did not]; as may be seen from the examples of dictators, tribunes and emperors. 5. The title of protector was an agreeable title; it was bound by no rules which might in the future limit its power; it was already by all kings admitted to stand on a footing of equality with them, and for that reason could not well be altered. For if they now took *regium titulum tamquam superiorem protectoris titulo*, kings would be troubled as to what the equating of the protectoral title with that of the royal title in written communications might [then] imply. Similarly, *imperatorius titulus*, as kings would see it, would seem to imply a claim to precedence, which at this time they would never concede, although they are accustomed to grant it to *imperatori Romano*. And as the former protectors, who represented the government during royal minorities, had not the power which the present lord protector has, there is nothing therefore to prevent him *sub eodem titulo* from getting a still greater authority hereafter; for it is not the title which commands respect, but force and *potestatis exercitium*.[1] And so the highest power here in England can be exercised under the name and title of protector; just as in the time of the Romans *tribunitia et dictatoria potestas, quae erat absoluta, sub imperatoris titulo*; the word 'dictator' signifying originally no more than an army commander, and the first emperors exercising dictatorial power; so that the title which was in the beginning *officij* became *dignitatis plusquam regiae designatio*. I have it from a confidential quarter that the lord protector was anxious to have in his own hands *legislativam potestatem* in order to avoid *necessitatem convocandi parliamentum*, but was not able to obtain it because of the many objections that were raised (for the English are by no means willing that it shall rest in one person alone), but at last they hit on an expedient agreed upon by the council, the high officers of the army and the lord mayor of London, namely that the lord protector, the council, the leading officers of the army, together with twelve moderate men learned in the law, to be selected by the lord protector and council, should exercise the legislative power absolutely, and that what they resolve shall have *vim actus parliamentarij*. Whether this is in fact the case,[2] time

---

1. Compare the view of the Venetian ambassador: 'The best way would be to raise the protectorate to the dignity of emperor of the three kingdoms. This conspicuous title is not ill adapted to the might and power of this state. The emperor would be elected by the army, in imitation of the ancient Romans, elevated to the throne by the legions and exalted by arms. Cromwell has the courage, character and authority to uphold this high dignity with honour': Sagredo to Doge, 5 November (NS) 1655: *CSP (Ven) 1655–6*, p. 132.

2. If the 'confidential quarter' was correct in the report, the plan was not pursued and has left no trace.

will very soon show, and in particular when use begins to be made of the new Great Seal. With the small seal a beginning was made a week ago.

What the lord protector recently wrote to the king of Denmark in reference to an English ship which went ashore off Mön, Y.M. may gather from the attached copy, marked A.[1] And from B, the tenour of the credentials with which the lord protector's envoy is provided, who is to leave immediately on his way to Y.M. with the lord protector's ratification: it will be seen that the lord protector further protests his friendship for Y.M., and also that the former errors in style and title have been for the most part corrected.[2] From Resident Appelboom's letters from The Hague I gather that de Bye is alleged to have said that the Swedes were more angry with Holland than with Poland—which (among other things) he is supposed to have learnt from me, as also that I had still not visited the Dutch ambassador. This language seems to me strange, because the contrary is in fact the case; and de Bye seems to have invented it for no other purpose than to incite the Dutch still more against Y.M. and Sweden. I therefore entreat Y.M., if this or anything like it should be told to him, to give no credit to it, nor to visit me with his displeasure; since I have never so far forgotten myself as to imagine that at present it was not more useful to emphasize Y.M.'s good inclination to remain friends with Holland. But what I did say to de Bye—and indeed to the Dutch ambassador himself—was that Y.M. could not suffer that the Dutch should come with a fleet of war into the Baltic; and I do not believe that this could be taken and interpreted in such a sense, nor do I expect that what I said should be without effect.

Y.M.'s extraordinary *legatus*, Herr Christer Bonde, arrived here safely at Gravesend the day before yesterday, and thither I betook myself yesterday to pay my respects, and also to learn how Y.M. may have disposed of my person: whether I am to remain here longer, or am now summoned home at once. But to my great disappointment I have heard nothing of the sort; and what is still worse from my point of view is that his excellency tells me that he has no orders to make money available to me to live on, though I have not only long since exhausted, in this expensive place, the amount assigned to me for this mission, but have also advanced to Commissioner Bonnel, on my credit, a considerable sum, in order to save him from indignity and imprisonment.[3] Wherefore it is my humble petition that Y.M. may

1. Missing in the transcript, but printed in Abbott, iii. 785.

2. Rolt's instructions, but not his credentials, are printed in Abbott, iii. 774–5.

3. On 5 June 1655 Bonnel made a request for a private audience with the protector: Thurloe, iii. 517. If he obtained it, it must have been unsuccessful, for on 17 July he wrote to Thurloe:

be pleased to cause orders to be issued that I have my subsistence here, and later go to Y.M., according to his gracious commands; particularly since (apart from what is due here) my means, and my family's means, consist in debts owed by the crown, and for the rest I am in no position to extract even a trifling sum from my other debtors.

30

Gravesend, 27 July 1655

Some days after my last report I betook myself to London, and having been granted an audience on the 24th delivered Y.M.'s letter to the lord protector in person, with an appropriate compliment; which he received with the greatest courtesy and signs of especial pleasure. He did not, however, open it in my presence, saying that he would do so with due ceremony, not doubting that God will use Y.M. as a special instrument, to the welfare of the common Protestant Cause. For the rest I entered into no extended discourse upon it, Y.M. having in his letter forbidden me to do so. The conversation finally turning to Y.M.'s ambassador's arrival at Gravesend, he said that his heart

---

Paper cannot blush. It is my unhappiness, and not my sin, that makes me to suffer; and most of my suffering is for being an Englishman, and for having been ever true and faithful to my native country; the which hath bred me many enemies in Swedland, who would be very glad to see me forsaken here, and to fall into some inconvenience; not that they or any of them can accuse me of having been any way wanting in the service I owe to the king my master, who I have now a long time served with as much fidelity as any man could have done. I have now a long time been promised and kept up with hopes from time to time, that my sallary should be sent to me by exchange, else I would have provided myselfe of mine owne means, which, thanks be to God, are able yet to maintaine me; but being frustrated of my long hopes, and the necessity of my pressing departure not giving me time to send into Sweadland for my owne money, which would take above two months time, I have been necessitated to addresse myselfe to your honour to move his serenissime highnesse, that in case his highness would be pleased to vouchsafe to gratify me, his most humble servant, with what I made bold to speak [of] with your honour lately, assoone as ever I come over, I will be ready to lay the same downe at his highness's command and pleasure. Sir, a thing soone done is double done; and therefore I am the more pressing, my necessity forcing me to it. And in what place or quality I am, or hereafter shall be, I shall assure your honour that I am and will ever be till death, his serenissime highness's most humble, true, faithfull, and obliged servant, which I will endeavour to shew with deeds and effects, and will always approove myselfe
Your honour's most humble
and faithful servant.
I shall expect and hope a favourable answer from your honour: Thurloe, iii. 655.
As appears from what follows, the application must have been unsuccessful, and long after the 'two months', his 'owne money' had not arrived from Sweden.

rejoiced at this happy landing, and that he had that same day sent some noblemen to congratulate him upon it. Of the recruiting of Scottish regiments I on this occasion said nothing, General [George] Fleetwood having spoken to the lord protector of it some days ago, and at that time I knew nothing of what answer he had received, since on my return to London Fleetwood was away, having taken another road to Gravesend. But subsequently I learned from him that his highness had assured him that he would see to it that it was treated as a matter of urgency, and would give his final resolution upon it within a few days: as Fleetwood himself will have informed Y.M. more at large.

As to the situation in other respects, his excellency the ambassador has undertaken to inform Y.M. of it, to whose report I refer Y.M. The day before yesterday Ambassador Nieupoort had a conference with Secretary Thurloe: what passed upon the occasion I have not been able to learn;[1] but in view of all the circumstances I can only conclude that if he adduced anything to Y.M.'s prejudice (as Resident Appelboom's letters suggest) it is not likely to have had any effect here. And I fancy that the Dutch themselves make more noise in Holland about their sea-armament, and their efforts to conclude an alliance with England and Denmark, than they seriously intend, thinking by such means the better to move Y.M. not to levy tolls in Prussia, since they persuade themselves on the basis of Heinsius's[2] reports that they can deter Y.M. from doing so on the simple rumour of their arming.

In accordance with Y.M.'s commands I have bought four horses, and the remainder I shall obtain as soon as possible, if I can find any particularly good ones. As soon as I get the pass which the lord protector has promised me I will forward the four to Hamburg. For

1. What passed was influenced by Thurloe's knowledge of the Dutch hope of an alliance with Denmark in which England might be included: and by the news, lately arrived, of the conclusion on 7/17 July of an alliance between the United Provinces and Brandenburg. On 20/30 June Thurloe had told Nieupoort that 'the protector holds the alliance with our state for the ground and foundation, on which he is resolved for the future to base all treaties and alliances'; but that though he approved the idea of a Dutch–Danish alliance in principle he thought it unnecessary at the moment; that it would be better to wait until they heard what Bonde might have to say; and that the protector still hoped that Charles X might be diverted to attack the emperor. He had added that he trusted that Brandenburg would never be included in the Dutch–Danish alliance, since the elector had shown such 'passion' against the protector. The news of the Dutch alliance with Brandenburg therefore came as a severe shock: on 27 July/6 August he told Nieupoort that he regarded it as an Orange triumph: *Brieven*, iii. 87, 92, 96–9. For Dutch feelers in Denmark see Carlbom, *Magnus Dureel*, pp. 28–36, 44–46; Thurloe, iii. 588–9, 633, 667–8. For the Dutch–Brandenburg alliance, W.J. Kolkert, *Nederland en het Zweedsche Imperialisme* (Deventer 1908), pp. 79, 93–102, 116–18, 152–6.

2. Nicolaus Heinsius was the Dutch resident in Stockholm.

the rest, Y.M. will gather from the attached report what goes forward here.

P.S. Y.M.'s draft for 12,000 *riksdaler* which was directed to Resident [Vincent] Möller [in Hamburg] has reached me safely, and shall be applied in accordance with Y.M.'s commands. I have had a letter from Earl Leslie,[1] in which he promises to stand surety for his son-in-law.[2]

31

Gravesend, 27 July 1655 [in German]

[News that Henry Cromwell has been received with acclamation in Dublin. The transplantations into Connaught not yet completed: in various places the Irish say they would rather die than move; but the government sticks to its policy.

Penn and Venables reported to have landed 9000 men in Hispaniola, but have no design (as earlier rumoured) to take St Domingo. Major-General Heans [*sc.* Colonel Heane] and a small detachment ambushed and beaten by the Spaniards: a man of good reputation, the event much lamented. Particulars expected when letters arrive from the fleet.

Blake reported still cruising off the Straits; Spain has ordered 30 ships to be fitted out, to protect the silver-fleet. English merchants in Spain live in fear of attack, of which they have been warned, and have put their goods aboard ship with a view to clearing out of the country: the presence of the English fleet makes this possible.

The Portuguese minister recently told me that he learned a week ago of the despatch hence of an emissary to Portugal: it was done without his knowledge or notification, and he can get no further information about it: he thinks it may be in order to arrange the junction of the English and Portuguese fleets. This seems doubtful: it must be something which the government does not wish the Portuguese minister to know.

The protector and council recently held a private day of prayer and fasting: whether because some important business is pending, whether it has to do with Hispaniola, or whether it is simply *in genere* for the welfare of the nation, cannot yet be decided.]

1. Alexander Leslie, earl of Leven.
2. Lord Cranstoun.

AMBASSADOR CHRISTER BONDE

[Bonde's instructions are dated 14 June 1655, and were supplemented by secret instructions dated 15 June.[1]

By the former, he was ordered, in general, to complete what had been left unsettled in Whitelocke's treaty of 1654; was to do everything possible to ensure that commerce should be free from interruption; to draw up a list of contraband goods which should exclude copper, iron, tar, grain and timber, but should include all weapons of war, soldiers, horses and cloth; to reach agreement on a form of sea-pass; to seek access to English possessions in America, and to the herring and cod fisheries. He was further to try to divert English trade to Russia from Archangel to the Baltic harbours under Swedish control, the duties on such trade not to exceed 2%; to offer permission for customs-free deposit of Russian goods in Ingria or Livonia, with the right to sell them retail; and to emphasize England's obligation, in terms of the Whitelocke treaty, to assist Charles X against any disturbers of the trade in the Baltic or North Sea, in view of the fact that war with Poland was imminent.

By the secret instructions the 'real intention' of his mission was defined as being to seek a closer alliance than that established by Whitelocke's treaty, and to reach agreement on *modus auxilii ferendi*; and especially to persuade the protector to agree to come to Sweden's assistance if any foreign power should attempt to send a fleet of war into the Baltic: the assistance to take the form of twenty war-ships, properly manned, commanded by officers appointed by Charles X, and to be used at his discretion, the cost being borne by England; though in the event of an English refusal of these terms Bonde might offer to bear some part of it. Further, England was to engage to keep the North Sea and the Channel open to Swedish ships, as in the event of war Sweden would keep the Sound and the Baltic open to English ships; each party recognizing the *dominium maris* of the other in the Baltic and the Channel, respectively. And finally Sweden was to have full liberty of recruiting soldiers and ships in the territory of the English republic. The alliance should be for ten years. But Bonde was to proceed cautiously about disclosing these terms.

On 14 June an instruction for Johan Barkman appointed him commissioner in England in the room of Benjamin Bonnel.]

---

1. A full summary of both instructions is printed in Carlbom, *Sverige och England*, pp. 43–5: that in Pufendorf, ii. 132–3, is less satisfactory.

LETTERS OF CHRISTER BONDE AND PETER JULIUS COYET TO CHARLES X

Bonde to Charles X

I

Gravesend, 20 July 1655

I have thought it unnecessary to trouble Y.M. with any letters from the places which I have been forced to touch at in the course of my journey, since they afforded nothing worth communicating to Y.M., other than to report what might have been obstacles to it; and of this I have written to the chancellor,[1] presuming that he will have given the information to Y.M.

I have, I thank God, had a pretty fortunate journey, and with my whole household arrived here at Gravesend in good health on the 18th of this month. And though it yesterday was five weeks since I left Stockholm, it is only four since I put out from Landsort. I reached the Sound on 29 June, the wind being then favourable; but the following day it was against us, and continued so for so long, that I could not pass the Sound until the morning of Wednesday, 4 July. After that we made pretty good progress for three days; but on the 6th, about noon, it blew a violent storm, which drove us up to Norway. On the following day we were forced—partly because the storm continued, and was dead against us; partly because the ship sprung a leak—to put in at a Norwegian harbour called Öster Risöör, where we were held up by adverse weather until the morning of Wednesday the 11th. We then put to sea and made good progress before a welcome favouring wind, until on the early morning of the 16th we had sight of a point on the English coast named Olferness [Orford Ness], to which we directed our course, and so happily arrived here on the above date. But we were twice in great danger: the first time at Öster Risöör, when the sailor who had the rudder—either from carelessness or from fright—put it over to the wrong side, contrary to orders; so that the ship, in that narrow inlet, was within a few yards of the rocks. Thanks be to God, we escaped; for the helmsman, who is an intrepid sailor, rushed forward, and thrusting aside the other sailor put the helm over: the ship answered, and was put on course again. The second time, we were in equal danger when entering the estuary here.

1. Erik Oxenstierna.

The skipper took on an English pilot in the narrows, who boasted that he was perfectly acquainted with the right course and knew all the sand-banks; but when he came aboard he proved to have no idea, but sailed us straight for a sand-bank, and the rudder had already touched bottom; but by the special providence of God we got off directly and cast anchor until we could get another pilot, who came to us when he heard us shooting, and brought us safely here. On my arrival I saluted the Castle, or Blockhouse, with sixteen rounds, struck the flag on the mainmast and then hoisted it again, before sending a gentleman, Mr Baretz, to inform the governor of my arrival. He was himself ill, but made me very welcome through his lieutenant and when I shot [my salute] caused all the guns on the Blockhouse to reply: an honour which they are not wont to pay to everyone. To-day I am sending the secretary with one of my Gentlemen to notify my coming to the secretary of state, Thurloe; having been informed by Herr Coyet (who came to me yesterday) that it was considered polite here for foreign ministers to do so; besides which Lord Whitelocke is in deep disfavour, and has lost both his position as Lord Keeper and his office as Treasurer,[1] so that I think it questionable whether I ought to address myself to him on such a public occasion, especially in this country, which is exceptionally touchy and suspicious. Nevertheless, I am arranging, as a matter of politeness, for Secretary Barkman to make an unostentatious visit to him at his home three English miles from London, to present my compliments to him; since if I did not he would undoubtedly take it very ill, and that might later on prove a disservice to Y.M.; for being one of the ablest men the protector has, he may easily be restored to favour, and probably will be so, if he accommodates himself to the protector's policies.

I have had bad luck with the horses which were shipped from Göteborg, as I gather may already have been reported by Cranstoun, who sailed in the same ship with them. It was forced by a violent storm (no doubt the same that drove us to Norway) to put in to Hull; and the partitions which had been constructed between the horses were smashed: one of the horses is dead, and some others trampled on, lacerated and injured. I expect news of them every hour. When the protector heard of their arrival he was good enough to send orders to his governor [at Hull] to get them here in the best way he could manage.

In regard to other matters concerning my mission, I cannot at present have anything particular to communicate, since I have not spoken to anyone from whom I can gather what their intentions may be. I only rejoice with all my heart to learn from Herr Coyet that

---

1. Bonde was mistaken, as he later realized: Whitelocke retained his post as a Commissioner of the Treasury.

there is not much danger that Y.M.'s designs will be obstructed at sea this year; and that the protector expressed himself to him in very satisfactory and confiding terms: as no doubt he has already written to Y.M. And I hope too that one effect of the news of this embassy may be to hinder any such attempts. For which reason I shall be the more watchful in taking care of Y.M.'s interests.

II

Gravesend, 27 July 1655

The narrative of my journey, and the news of my safe arrival here at Gravesend, together with such details as seemed worth retailing, have presumably reached Y.M. through my letter of a week ago from hence. Although since then I have used all diligence, it has proved impossible for me to come up to London before (if God will) to-morrow, when I have made all arrangements (and the protector's order has been given) for my entry. Of this I hope to advise Y.M. by the next post, together with any steps which I may then have taken in regard to the real objects of my commission. What has most delayed me has been my horses and carriages. The horses must have some time to recover after being exposed to a trying journey across the sea, as I mentioned to Y.M. in my former letter. The carriages I have caused to be upholstered in black,[1] and this, with other alterations, had to be ordered. I have encountered here some distinguished young Swedish cavaliers, who will help to expand my suite, so that I now have seventeen noblemen; and I trust that this mission will present itself in such honourable style as Y.M.'s illustrious reputation here demands, and as can on this occasion be achieved in black clothes.

As I may have informed Y.M. in my last letter, I sent my secretary and one of my Gentlemen to Secretary Thurloe to announce my arrival. In return (in the absence of the protector, who ordinarily goes to Hampton Court on Fridays, and returns on Mondays) he sent one of his subordinates by the name of Mr Meadowe, together with six other young noblemen, to congratulate me on his behalf, and to excuse the fact that the protector, by reason of his absence, could not do the like: the day before yesterday the protector sent a captain and six noblemen to me, to compliment me on his behalf.

I gather from reliable persons that this embassy is highly appreci-ated here, especially by the protector; who alone fully realizes how great an advantage it is for him that Y.M. gives assurances of his friendship; and so when talking to General [George] Fleetwood (who

1. In mourning for Maria Eleonora, widow of Gustavus Adolphus, who had died on 18 March [OS] 1655.

is in high favour with him) he always alludes to Y.M. as 'your great and noble king' [English in orig.]. And this great esteem I shall endeavour to cultivate, by the most appropriate means, and as far as lies in my power, to the advantage of Y.M.'s service.

But in order that I may not in any way run contrary to Y.M.'s intentions, I have thought it necessary in all submission to ask some questions about certain matters, humbly entreating Y.M. graciously to receive them, and graciously to reply to them. But first I think it most necessary to note down my impressions of the government in this country, in so far as I have been able to collect it from the conversation of the governor [of Gravesend] and of various other noblemen. And I think the state to be in an extremely uncertain condition, since it appears to be based solely on force and on the army, and it is more than probable that there is very little support in the country for this government. The army itself consists mainly of a collection of officers who as to a great part of them have been drawn from the common people (the colonel who is governor of this place is by trade a goldsmith, and most of the others are of the same sort). The protector's maxim in this regard seems to be that such people must stick to him in their own interest, since any change of *régime* can be expected to cause their inevitable ruin and downfall. The common soldiers he binds to himself by the high pay that he gives them, the like of which is almost unheard-of; so that a lieutenant of foot has 36 pence a day, an ensign 24, a sergeant 20, a corporal 14, a *captain [d']* *armes* 12, a private 10, and a cavalryman 30 pence; so that it is possible to maintain such strict discipline that the country scarcely knows that there is an army in it.

But this device breeds exceeding bad blood between all the inhabitants; since the common people resent being ruled and commanded by their equals, and the better sort despise them in their hearts; and it is easy to imagine with what sentiments they must see themselves placed at their mercy, put in prison by them, and suffer harder or easier conditions by their favour. But on the other hand it is his [the protector's] strongest support that the greatest part of the country is discontented, and that now the question *An habebunt Regem* seems to have been changed to *Quem habebunt Regem*, and consequently that the quarrel which before was between the House of Stuart and the whole population of England has been transformed into one between the House of Stuart and Cromwell only. For these reasons the protector seems now to have taken the decision that since he is not able, with the connivance[1] [of the generals and] other officers, to turn the hearts

---

1. At this point the MS has an asterisk referring to a note at the bottom of the page. The note is almost undecipherable, but may be in English, and could read '? of the generals and'.

of the population towards him, nor induce it to be quiet and make no trouble, still less to accept him as good coin and accord him the honour which his eminence demands, he has therefore clapped into prison, in London and other parts of the country, some 10,000 persons (or so I am informed by one trustworthy nobleman), most of them of the leading families in the country; and has in addition issued an order that anyone who has at any time been of the king's party shall quit the City of London within six days and retire to his home in the country, and shall not, on pain of loss of life and property, come within twenty English miles of the City. As a result of this order all who have been on the king's side are totally crushed; since anyone who departs from the City thereby confesses himself guilty and is arrested in the provinces, while if he remains, and is known to have favoured that party in any way, it is easy to fix a charge upon him. And thus a great part of those who are of any consequence are accordingly arrested, and stand in danger of losing life and livelihood, even though they may have compounded with the parliament some years ago. Some indeed think that his plan may be to let them all loose again, in the hope of winning their affection by that means; they having been held in terms of a general order of imprisonment, and then liberated individually as a special *beneficium*: the idea being that they will thus on the one hand be frightened off from causing any more trouble in the future, and on the other that each one *in particulari* will feel himself obliged by such an act of clemency. At all events those who in general refuse to recognize his government, or speak ill of his person in their cups or on other occasions, will be compelled to sue for his grace. It appears in fact that he has already set free some who have been willing to ask for it through some of his friends. It seems to me that as things now are it is a deplorable situation, both for him as ruler, and for them as subjects; which is why when in London he always keeps himself close, as Y.M. has no doubt been informed by Coyet. He himself is said to be personally a very capable, wise and intelligent man, very *doux* in his manners, and *obligeant*; so that in spite of everything it is thought that he will be able to maintain this government during his lifetime, being excessively careful in his appointments. But none the less that life is in great danger among so many who wish him ill. For these reasons I should much wish to be informed

1. how far Y.M. may consider it advisable to engage with him. Hitherto we have mostly negotiated with him *nomine protectoris et reip[ublic]ae. anglicanae.* But it seems that he wishes to change this, and conclude in his own name alone; as he is already said to have altered the Great Seal, eliminating both '*reip.*' and 'the commonwealth of England', and substituting his own name and arms. Hitherto, all

foreign potentates in their dealings with the country have had in mind England itself, without especially concerning themselves with what sort of a government there was here, which they considered to be a private controversy in which they did not meddle, as was the case in Sweden in the time of King Charles [IX] and King Sigismund; so that no blame attached to them, whatever the issue of the quarrel. But if any agreement is concluded with him [the protector] singly, it will seem that at last we are *taking his side*[1] in their domestic differences. I write at some length on this point, for I learn that there has been some uneasiness here because some ill-disposed persons have spread the story that Y.M. was minded to join with the elector Brandenburg, attack Holland, restore the prince [of Orange] to his former dignity, and then help the king of Scotland (or the *king of Cologne,*[1] as he is called here) to recover his realm of England.[2] Although this can hardly be believed by the protector, who has been fully informed of Y.M.'s friendship by Herr Coyet, others give a good deal of weight to it, thinking Y.M.'s forces to be so redoubtable that there is no enterprise Y.M. could not carry through, if he were so minded. In this situation it could happen that the protector might seek to link himself to Y.M., not so much *nomine regni anglicani* but *suo*; and he might be disposed to a mutual alliance which would oblige him to take Y.M.'s part against Y.M.'s enemies, but also commit Y.M. to defend his personal *interest against all*[1] royalists and others who may wish to subvert *statum regiminis*. And this, in my view, would be a very questionable arrangement for Y.M., though a very satisfactory one for the protector. It is true that by the treaty already made Y.M. has promised not to give assistance to anyone in attacks on this state; but neither has he bound himself to come to the aid of the protector in his private quarrels: the words [of the treaty], *dominum protectorem et remp. angliae* constitute an inseparable expression. I have therefore determined, pending Y.M.'s further orders, to take the line of never neglecting to protest Y.M.'s earnest wish for the welfare of the lord protector and England; and I mean always to link that last word [England] with 'the protector', since my instructions always refer to them *conjunctim* and all the points in which according to my orders I can oblige them are directed solely to England and its inhabitants, and not to the protector's private

---

1. Underlined in original.

2. De Witt himself was for a moment almost inclined to suspect that the elector was secretly in league with Charles X: de Witt to Nieupoort, 2 July NS 1655, *Brieven,* iii. 77: *cf.* the comment of one of Thurloe's agents in Holland, to the effect that a Dutch–Brandenburg alliance would be 'a trick put upon the States of Holland, in regard that alliance is more Orangeist and royalist than any one in the world. And the States of Holland making profession to esteem the amity of the protector, ought not to make amity with men so violently royalist': Thurloe, iii. 525–6.

interests. I intend none the less also to speak handsomely of the protector personally, and thereby (if possible) to find out what he has in mind, so that I do not spoil any acceptable opportunity to give some support to his interests: as the French seem to have been careful to avoid doing, since they have drawn up in common a list of the persons whose presence in either country shall not be tolerated.

2. Next, I shall be very glad to know whether I am to say anything as to whether the 20 warships for which Y.M. is asking are to be used in the North Sea to prevent other fleets of war from entering [the Baltic], or both in the North Sea and the Baltic; or whether I shall rather try to frame the request in words which specify neither sea, but are capable of later being interpreted according to the situation that arises, so that I may know what line to take if any such difficulty presents itself. And although, according to my instructions, I shall make every effort to get what Y.M. wants without the payment of any sum of money, it may nevertheless happen that they not only ask for money, but also

3. some other *beneficium* in return for their undertaking to assist Y.M. at need, even though they be paid for doing so. I therefore ask, in all submission, that Y.M. will be graciously pleased to let me know the utmost advantage that he would be willing to concede to them in such a case. In the meantime I shall take care that they do not obtain too much.

4. Nor is it specified what is the maximum sum per month which Y.M. is prepared to pay for each ship. And although Y.M. may wish first to know what they are demanding, I nevertheless humbly beg to be informed how much Y.M. is prepared to agree to, and this especially because we are so placed that it takes not less than seven weeks to receive an answer to a letter, and should Y.M. be in Germany or Prussia the post could well be slower and more uncertain.

5. In point 4 of my secret instuctions it is mentioned that Y.M. asks leave to recruit soldiers and hire merchantmen and warships in the land and provinces of this state; but no mention is made as to whether Y.M. may be willing to grant the same to the lord protector in regard to his own kingdom and its subordinate provinces, and so establish a reciprocity. And although I fancy that Y.M. will have little hesitation in conceding this, I should nevertheless be glad of express orders.

6. It could also happen that the protector, in return for the ships, might ask Y.M. for soldiers to employ against his enemies overseas, either against Spain or some other country. [I should be glad to know] what, in such a case, Y.M. would wish me to answer—always provided that it was a question of himself and England *conjunctim*, and not one which concerned his [the protector's] private interest only.

From Appelboom's letters I learn that the Dutch are said to be once again very hot against Y.M., particularly in regard to any levying of tolls in Prussia, and were near to concluding a treaty with the elector of Brandenburg.[1] And because it is extremely important for me to know how Y.M. stands with the elector, since in this country he is reckoned, as guardian of the young prince in Holland, to be the head of the royalist party, I humbly beg Y.M. to give me that information. I have still had no letter from Y.M. since that of 23 June from Stockholm, and I have no doubt that Y.M. is now either in Germany or Prussia, and his affairs in good order.

III

London, 29 July 1655

I could not neglect to wait upon Y.M. with this letter, since it is to be carried by one who is a close relation of the lord protector, and one of the Gentlemen of his Chamber: a Mr Rolt, whose person and services are highly esteemed here, and who has asked that he may be the bearer of my letter on his way to Y.M.

Since my last of the 27th instant the only occurrence has been that I was yesterday brought to London, which happened in this wise: *Le Maistre de Ceremonies* Sir Oliver Fleming, together with a large number of young gentlemen, came out to me at Gravesend in the morning; and after I had given them as good a meal as this place afforded, we boarded the lord protector's yacht (which he had brought with him for that purpose) and sailed up the river: we had an unusually strong wind against us, which dispersed our company, and caused us to come late to the City. All went well, however, and my Lord Whitelocke and my Lord Strickland met me at the Tower and accompanied me in the lord protector's coach (with a great many others: twelve of them, which is said to be more than for any other ambassador) to the house opposite to Westminster Hall where ambassadors extraordinary are used to be entertained. I take it as a great thing that Whitelocke was appointed to meet and entertain me; since although he is not of the council, and is considered to be in some disfavour, nevertheless (I understand) he still retains his post as Treasurer, has resigned only his office of *Custodia Magni Sigilli*,[2] and has precedence over Strickland, who is a member of the council. He is, moreover, very well disposed, and has a good grasp of the major interests that both countries have

1. A defensive alliance was signed on 7/17 July 1655, the Dutch taking care to insist on the provision of the treaty of Westminster (art. xv), that England was to be free to join it.
2. Whitelocke was deprived of the Great Seal on 6 June; on the 15th it was given to Fiennes and Lisle.

in common. He manifested—as did Strickland and Fleming—both verbally and by their entertainment extraordinary great respect and affection to Y.M. I hope very much that I may get Whitelocke as one of my commissioners: if so, I hope that I may be able to do some good.

I was yesterday exposed to some impertinence from the French ambassador's people, and his coach. It happened that by reason of a great block in the traffic, my coachman stopped in the middle of the road in a place called Tower Hill, immediately opposite the landing-place [Tower Wharf]; and when he attempted to take his proper place next after the protector's coach in which I was riding, the French ambassador's coachmen and lackeys began to draw their swords to try to prevent it, but were nevertheless forced, when my servants and the protector's people intervened, to give my coach right of way. This unfriendly and uncivil act annoyed me greatly, since I have every reason to consider Y.M. as being as great and noble a potentate as any in the world, and for as long as I bear my present character I will yield to no other ambassador, from wherever he may come. But as soon as I had returned home his secretary and Gentlemen, who had been present, called on me on his behalf and apologized profusely, saying that their lackeys had been drinking while they were waiting; that the incivility had been committed against their will; that they had got out of their coaches in a hurry in order to set it right again; and that the cause of the disorder was that they had leapt to the conclusion that it was the coach of the Spanish ambassador (who was not there); to which I answered courteously that it was a matter of great concern to me, and that I was unwilling to believe that what had passed was done with their consent, much less with that of their principal.[1] I shall take care to obtain further satisfaction from the ambassador himself. The gentlemen who had been sent to convey me were extremely angry, and zealously ordered the Guard and the lackeys to drive off the others; which they duly did.

The Dutch ambassador's representative came to me immediately to congratulate me on my arrival; to whom I returned a compliment.

Of the protector's intentions I can as yet say little; but so much I can perceive: that there will certainly be war between Spain and England; and for that reason they would be very glad to bind Y.M. to them, so that there may be a mutual defensive arrangement for the Evangelical Cause. I should therefore be very glad to have information of Y.M.'s will in regard to this, and to my former questions; and I am emboldened to write this, having been assured that this gentleman [Rolt] will faithfully deliver my letter, and since Whitelocke insists

1. *Cf. The Clarke Papers*, iii. 46. A similar brawl about precedence (this time between the French and Portuguese ambassadors, with swords drawn) had occurred in March 1654: Roy Sherwood, *The Court of Oliver Cromwell* (1977), p. 92.

that it is a sign of the high esteem the lord protector has for Y.M.'s person, and for the crown of Sweden, that he sends such a distinguished person as envoy. I hope on Tuesday to obtain an audience, and so to be able by the next post to report to Y.M. anything that may be worth the writing.

IV

London, 3 August 1655

Y.M. will be pleased to gather, from the attached relation,[1] what has passed here since I last wrote from Gravesend on 27 July. But I have not ventured to entrust to the post the full particulars of what was said in my private audience with the lord protector. I have therefore determined to send off, by express, one of the young cavaliers I have here with me; and in the meantime I can only say that I was exceedingly well entertained and distinguished by the lord protector and his ministers, so that it is said here that in respect of ceremonial matters no ambassador has had an equal reception. It was also a very great thing that no sooner had I sought a private audience with the lord protector, so that I might by this post acquaint Y.M. with the details of my arrival, than Sir Oliver Fleming came to me and invited me to a private conversation with him [the protector] that same day (which was the day after I had had my public audience), and came, as arranged, between 4 and 5 o'clock, and carried me in the protector's own barge to Whitehall. At our conference he ordered all who were present to withdraw—Secretary Thurloe with the others; which has never happened before, for the secretary is his *intimus*.[2] I must admit that my English comes in extremely handy, and the protector is very glad of it: when I excused myself in case I should not be able to express myself as I ought, he answered that it was a matter of grief to him that he had been so ill educated that he scarcely ventured to speak any other language than English, and that he was therefore the happier that he could speak to me in confidence without an interpreter or other assistance. Since I knew for certain in advance that some who begrudge Y.M. his good fortune have attempted, by arguments which they knew would have most weight with them [the English], to make Y.M.'s actions and intention so suspect that all former assurances were scarcely able to bring them to another way of thinking, I sought by all appropriate means to persuade him of the contrary;

1. The original transcriber has here inserted: 'This appendix is annexed to the letter, but I have not transcribed it'. It probably contained an account of the ceremonial connected with Bonde's formal entry.

2. Bonde's *Diarium* for 1 August notes that the audience lasted an hour and three quarters, '*cum tamen nunquam id voluerit facere, nisi ad minimum in praesentia Secretarii Thurloe*'.

which I know he was well content with. He gave the most emphatic assurances of friendship that could be imagined; and since he piques himself on his eloquence, he cast about for the most expressive English words wherein to emphasize his intention to maintain a faithful friendship. Of Y.M.'s person he spoke in terms of extreme laudation, and always referred to Y.M. with the epithet 'your great and noble king'; could not wonder at the resolution taken by Y.M. to ensure his safety; and wished Y.M. success and many blessings on his design, as I hope to inform Y.M. more at large by the express which I have alluded to already.

The post did not arrive until to-day at midday; and though it was late, it was the more welcome as bringing tidings of Y.M.'s fortunate crossing, and in addition of Field-Marshal Wittenberg's inimitable great progress in Poland, beyond all expectation;[1] which was a splendid welcome. This signal blessing of God at the start of Y.M.'s campaign gives indubitable hopes of its further success, and is indeed a matter for rendering devout thanks to Almighty God, and for praying with all our hearts that He may continue His grace to Y.M.[2] I hope, indeed, that by these first great achievements Y.M.'s designs may everywhere be made easy, and that those who are shamelessly jealous of Y.M.'s success may be refrained within their proper limits.

That a negotiation has been begun between the elector of Brandenburg and this country, and that the lord protector has promised him assistance, is what I attach no importance to. It is true that every effort has been made to obtain it, and not only by him [the elector]; but I hope that I am in a position to assure Y.M. that nothing has been done in the matter so far, nor do I expect that anything will be done in it hereafter.[3] I am rather of opinion that such projects will presently come to nothing of their own accord, since they have been forestalled by Y.M.'s might and successes; but I shall nonetheless keep them under observation and act as I know may be most for Y.M.'s service. Herr Coyet believes, and I would assure Y.M., that there is

1. The encounter at Ujście, which resulted in the capitulation of Opaliński's forces.
2. Paulucci, in his despatch to Sagredo on 22 August (NS), reported a conversation with Bonde in which, on receiving congratulations on the initial victories in Poland, Bonde is reported to have said that 'the Swedes mean to press their good fortune against Poland, but with their eyes fixed on the empire, since this minister went on to say that if his king should happen some day to envision a protestant emperor, the present state of the world would be changed indeed, and the Ottoman empire would certainly be subdued. This is looking far ahead, and it will stir all Christendom with a terror like that caused many years ago by King Gustavus': CSP (Ven) 1655–56, p. 97.
3. The Dutch–Brandenburg alliance of 7/17 July was known to Thurloe on 27 July/6 August. By it the elector promised not to allow any foreign power into his harbours, and the Dutch promised 4000 men to assist in repelling any attack in the Baltic or in Cleves: Georg Wittrock, 'Fördraget i Königsberg och dess förhistoria', Karolinska Förbundets Årsbok (1921), p. 21.

no danger to be feared from that quarter. As to what Y.M. mentions regarding ratification of the late alliance, that has already been taken care of, and Mr Rolt, the lord protector's kinsman, and a Gentleman of his Chamber, left last Monday by ship for Hamburg, and thence to Y.M. He had some splendid horses with him which the lord protector gave to him: whether he intends to make Y.M. a present of them I cannot say with any certainty; but I understand that the protector himself thinks to make Y.M. a present of horses on some suitable occasion. I understand that the lord protector has not yet received Y.M.'s ratification of the treaty, but only that of H.M. Queen Christina; of which circumstances I intend now to take advantage. Nor shall I neglect to remove all unfavourable reactions to [the activities of] Y.M.'s fleet; and to prevent as best I can any such reactions in the future.

As to the recruiting, that depends solely on the lord protector's permission, about which General [George] Fleetwood spoke to him again this evening; and I hope to be able to send Y.M. more precise information about it by this post.

P.S. After I had finished this letter the Latin secretary Mr Meadowe came to me bearing a copy of a letter written by the lord protector to Y.M. on a private matter. A copy of it goes by this to Y.M. And although the murder did not take place on Y.M.'s territory, but in Pskov, I hope that Y.M., by way of attracting the English to the Russia trade, will give him assistance as far as the law allows.[1]

Coyet to Charles X

32

London, 3 August 1655 [in German]

[After receiving congratulations on the 22nd, Bonde was brought with his suite on the 28th, by Sir Oliver Fleming and others, in ten galleys, to Tower Wharf, received there by Whitelocke and Strickland, driven through the City in the protector's coach to Westminster, and lodged in the house of D. Johnstone in Palace Garden: great crowds along his route. Bonde and his suite treated with great magnificence in his house for three days: Whitelocke and Strickland (the commissioners with whom he is to treat) called at dinner-time; Fleming and others also. On 31 July Bonde was carried in the protector's coach, many other coaches following, to Whitehall

1. The allusion is to a brawl between one Richard Broke and some 'Belgians' in Pskov, in which one of Broke's assailants was killed: the protector's letter to Charles X is printed in Abbott, iii. 798.

for a solemn audience.[1] He has now moved to his appointed lodging, Salisbury Court, formerly the house of the earl of Dorset; but the same day was summoned to a second audience in private, which is a great rarity and signal distinction.

No news of Penn's fleet; but Blake has moved from the Straits to refresh and re-provision, and is now off the Portuguese coast near Faro Bay, where the king of Portugal sent to compliment him, and supplied him with provisions. The protector has recalled six of his frigates, which have arrived in England: Blake's further orders will soon be known.

A French ship of 24 guns, with linen and other commodities to a value of £80,000, has been taken up, without resistance, and also seven other ships laden with salt.]

P.S. [in Swedish]. I can assure Y.M. that the elector of Brandenburg has neither sought, nor intimated to the lord protector a design, to conclude an alliance: it is a mere rumour.

Bonde to Charles X

V

London, 10 August 1655

In my last letter, which went by the next post, I may have informed Y.M. that in the interests of greater security I have resolved to send one of the Gentlemen I have with me to Y.M. with a detailed account of everything of which I think it necessary to apprise Y.M. at present. I shall despatch him from this place within a few days, and the principal reason why I have delayed sending him is for the purpose of obtaining another opportunity to talk with the lord protector, so that I might be in a position to send Y.M. a fuller account. I accordingly had an audience yesterday at 5 o'clock; but I am not just so satisfied with it as I was with the former, for on this occasion he was not absolutely alone, the audience-chamber being full of members of his council; and for that reason I said little or nothing to him, apart from communicating to him the news of Y.M.'s happy successes; after which I did my best (according to Y.M.'s orders) to rid him of any jealousies arising from Y.M.'s fleet;[2] which, as I explained, stood off

1. *Cf.* Whitelocke's account: 'There were of his company five Swedish barons and about thirty other gentlemen of quality, about four pages, and ten lackeys; his other servants made up the number of two hundred persons; generally proper handsome men, and fair-faced; they were all in mourning (very genteel), as the ambassador himself was': Whitelocke, *Memorials*, iv. 209.

2. The Swedish fleet (of 14 ships, to which 5 were added later), took station in Danzig Roads on 25 August. The decision to blockade Danzig had been taken on 28 July, after the arrival of the news of the Dutch–Brandenburg alliance. The admiral was to take toll of all ships entering or leaving the port *except* English ships. The

that coast only to give Y.M. security on that side, and to ensure that no contraband goods should be carried in to reinforce Y.M.'s enemy: as Y.M., by his letter from Wolgast of 21 July, commanded me to do. I then asked him whether he would do me the friendly office of communicating to me his thoughts on a possible closer alliance, which he had lately given me hopes of, so that if there was any point upon which I needed Y.M.'s instructions I might the sooner write to Y.M. about it and await his answer; which would be some saving of time. As to Y.M.'s campaign he answered very well, saying that he rejoiced at it and thanked me for my news of it. As to Y.M.'s fleet he made no answer at all, either because it slipped his memory, or that he (like myself) was not happy about the presence of all those who were standing and listening, and consequently was not willing to discuss it, but remitted that point to his commissioners, who are to start negotiating with me next Tuesday. I confess that I should have much preferred to discuss it with himself before it came to the commissioners; for Nieupoort is doing everything he can to countermine my proceedings in the minds of those who are of the council of state, some of whom are good Dutchmen. But though I saw that by such a postponement I should do little except waste time, I accepted the arrangement as being something to begin with, and we must see how it turns out. I also reminded him about the recruiting, and pointed out that the season was nearing its end; adding that Y.M. would be very glad to have that token of friendship on his part so that the world might see that the lord protector acts the part of a friend *realiter*. He apologized for the delay and said that the same commissioners would be giving me an answer. Cranstoun comes to me every day, and has his caution-money ready, besides the names of officers and a crowd of privates, and he waits only for permission in order to start his levies.

I had previously permitted myself to remark on the fact that I was forced to live here as *retenu* with the lord protector as were the other ministers; and that I should not be averse to visiting him at Hampton Court when he went out there, so that I might be able to use the

---

blockade became fully effective on 10 September, and continued for the remainder of the trading season until 25 November. Danzig's reply was simply to close the port entirely, thus denying to the Swedes any financial advantage: see Finn Askgaard, pp. 31–5. Abbott is in error when he writes (iv. 71) 'the English merchants in Danzig wrote to ask protection against the Swedish king who had been hindering their trade': on the contrary, as the letter from them to Thurloe (iv. 404)—to which he refers— makes clear, their complaint was against Danzig's imposition of head-money, and the city's refusal to accept English goods which had been re-routed through Pillau to avoid the blockade: cf. *ibid*, iv. 368–70, 490, v. 88. For varying Danish reactions to the blockade, see P. W. Becker, *Samlinger til Danmarks Historie under Kong Fredrik den Tredies Regering af udenriges Archiver* (2 vols. Copenhagen 1847), i. 74, 77–8.

opportunity to get upon more familiar terms with him; by which I should be able to effect more on a single occasion than I could do in a long time, through commissioners. I have the impression that this came to his ears. For among other courtesies he politely gave me to understand that he would be very glad to see me there occasionally so that I might enjoy the fresh air. I lost no time in gratefully accepting, and am accordingly to go there next Saturday, which is to-morrow, together with my Lord Whitelocke, whom he suggested as a person to accompany me. It has never before happened that a public minister has been able to visit him in the country;[1] but I rather think that among other things the chance to talk to me in the language he understands has a great deal to do with it. I shall do my utmost to advance Y.M.'s service in every possible way, and to see whether this occasion may not give me an opportunity to lay in his mind the foundations upon which I may later be able to build something. Y.M.'s letter of 28 July, from Stettin, duly came to hand yesterday, after my return from the lord protector; from which I learn that all is well with Y.M., and that Y.M. thinks of following up the great successes which he has so happily obtained: in which I wish Y.M. all the good fortune he could desire, and the blessing of Almighty God. Y.M. mentions also that he is minded to station his ships off Danzig to levy toll, and asks my advice as to how I think I may best reconcile the English to this. As this seems to be a matter of great concernment, and may undoubtedly alter their opinions here if it is not tactfully handled, and as I find it difficult to give my opinion of it at short notice, I entreat Y.M. not to take it ill if I defer my answer to the next post. I am fairly confident that before then I may be able to effect something, and so be in a position to express my thoughts to Y.M. after more mature consideration.

Herr Appelboom wrote to me that the Dutchmen appear to be serious about their intention of sending a fleet of warships to the Baltic.[2] I cannot believe that they will venture upon such a folly, and I am confident that Y.M. will give himself no great trouble about them, now that he has got a foothold in Poland. I shall make every effort to excite opposition to the plan here and at least to arrange

1. Bonde was mistaken: Nieupoort had been invited out to Hampton Court on 30 June, and Bordeaux received a general invitation on 8 May: Guizot, *History of Oliver Cromwell*, ii. 560.

2. The Dutch had already decided to send a fleet to the Sound (but not to the Baltic). De Witt defined its object as being to protect Denmark from attack. It had been decided also to send a deputation to Denmark to find out what Frederick III's attitude would be if the Swedes were to disturb trade to the Baltic by imposing new tolls, or otherwise harassing shipping: De Witt to Nieupoort, 13 August NS 1655: *Brieven*, iii. 101.

matters so that [the English] do not meddle with it.[1] I think it is expedient to deliver to them Y.M.'s own ratification of the alliance that has been concluded, and so deprive ill-wishers of a great argument which they could use against Y.M. If it is not displeasing to Y.M., I would gladly recommend [to Y.M. the case of] Mr Bonnel, who is a burden to Y.M., and can do no service: he remains fixed here, to his own ruin, because he has no money, and he awaits with the greatest impatience to receive his salary and obtain his deliverance.

VI

London, 17 August 1655

From the attached report Y.M. will be good enough to gather what has passed here in regard to public affairs since last I wrote. Although I had intended to have some talk with the lord protector at Hampton Court, no opportunity for it presented itself, my visit being short, and night approaching; [but] he made every effort to show me all courtesy and provide me with entertainment:[2] a thing he has never done before for any foreign minister. Last Wednesday after dinner I had my first conference with my commissioners: I send Y.M. their names, and fuller particulars about them, at the first opportunity by Per Bonde, who is to leave for Hamburg. The sum of what I proposed is what Y.M. commanded in his secret instruction. On this occasion I spoke mostly *in generalibus terminis* both in regard to what Y.M. was asking and what he intended to offer; and this for particular reasons, and especially with a view to sounding their inclinations before I exposed

1. On 3 September (NS) Nieupoort reported to de Witt that Thurloe stressed his fear of involvement in a war with Sweden, and England's inability to bear another war, as the protector's main reason for disliking de Witt's alliance-policy: *Brieven*, iii. 114. De Witt on 30 September NS informed Nieupoort that the States of Holland had decided to send embassies to Sweden and to Denmark in the hope of composing the Swedish–Polish quarrel, and that he hoped for England's collaboration in obtaining a settlement: Thurloe, iv. 45.

2. Bonde's *Diarium* for 11 August gives a rather different account: '... heard music; walked in the park, killed a stag; then to bowling-green and played bowls; then kissed the hand of Cromwell's wife, and his daughter's cheek; then drank a glass of Spanish wine, and returned to London' (p. 50). Ekeblad adds that after playing bowls with Cromwell, Fleetwood and Whitelocke, Bonde was conducted to Cromwell's wife and daughters, 'three of them, and ugly they were': Ekeblad, *Brev.* i. 415. Bonde seems to have been invited to Hampton Court only once again, on 25 July 1656, when he was on the eve of departure. It is conceivable that Cromwell preferred to have his week-ends unspoiled by business. But a royalist observer could already report '[Cromwell] is exceedingly intimate with the Swedish ambassador ...; they drive, sup and hunt and play at bowls together. Cromwell never caressed any man so much, nor sought the friendship of any so much as the king of Sweden': Nicholas to Jos. Jane, 4/14 September 1655: *CSP (Dom) 1655–56*, p. 135.

myself by entering into details. But I made every effort to remove any
suspicion at Y.M.'s expedition, and likewise to find out whether in
the present situation Y.M. has anything to fear from this country. I
was assured in the plainest possible terms that Y.M. was by his
highness and by this country held in the highest esteem and regard,
and in particular because they are certainly hoping that Y.M. may
be disposed to reanimate the cause of protestantism in general; to
which they would lend all the assistance in their power. Other points
they took *ad referendum*, and I must await their answer. I shall spare
no pains, and take every available opportunity, to forward Y.M.'s
service as it may require.

To Y.M.'s letter concerning proceedings in regard to Danzig, which
reached me by the last post, I asked Y.M.'s leave to postpone an
answer till this post; but by this post there came to me a letter of 31
July from Damm dealing with the same matter. I have been turning
it over carefully in my mind. It seems to me to be a somewhat dubious
action at this time, since it will provide the Dutch with more solid
and stronger reasons to act against me here, and so make my negotiation more difficult. They will now argue the more forcibly that
what they call the disturbance of trade, and the burdens upon it, can
be seen to have become a fact, and that things have turned out as
they predicted and feared; so that I shall have the greater difficulty
in justifying that action and in controverting their arguments. Moreover it would seem to be now so late in the season that all the
commodities that were in Danzig have been already shipped off.[1] The
war with the Muscovites has meant that the country has little to
export; the price of corn, which is the principal item of their trade, is
everywhere low; so that I am afraid that this year the toll will not
repay the cost of collecting it.[2]

It is probable that it would be easier for me to bring this country
round to Y.M.'s plans if I were able more clearly to demonstrate the
unjustifiable nature of the arguments and fears of others. Nevertheless
I have no doubt that Y.M. has weightier reasons of his own than I
have any knowledge of at present. And if this action is to be taken—
as it undoubtedly has already been begun—I think it would be very
good policy to levy toll without exception for any, so that this country
is not in a position to claim a preference before it has settled its

1. On the contrary, the arrival of the Swedish fleet coincided with the climax of
Danzig's trading season: the busiest day of the year was St Dominic's Day, the day of
the opening of the August fair: Norman Davies, *God's Playground. A History of Poland*, i
(Oxford 1982), p. 258.
2. In a letter to Bonde of 30 September Charles X asserted that the blockade had
not been imposed for the sake of revenue, but as a measure of economic warfare:
Carlbom, *Sverige och England*, p. 45 n.

122 SWEDISH DIPLOMATS AT CROMWELL'S COURT

business, and has given the undertaking which Y.M. wishes to obtain from it in exchange.[1] Otherwise, if they have previously gained a point, they will be able to negotiate *tanquam ex possessorio*, and their courage will rise higher because they will in that case judge that Y.M. has too great consideration for them, and is afraid of them. I must consider what reasons I can hit upon to justify the action, and to show that Y.M. is putting no obstacles in the way of trade, but allows it to all nations, now as before; and that if a toll is imposed upon goods it is permitted *ex jure gentium* to inflict every type of damage upon one's enemy—which must undoubtedly result from the fact that by reason of the toll he must pay dearer for what he buys, and get less for what he sells; and further that it is important for Y.M. to take measures to prevent any contraband goods from coming into his enemy's possession.[2] I shall make every effort to conduct myself in this matter as I may judge for the best advantage of Y.M.

I enclose a copy of a letter of a particular friend of Prince Radziwiłł to one of his intimates here, which sufficiently indicates how discontented he is, and that it seems not improbable that he might be brought to seek Y.M.'s protection, always supposing that he has not done so already, which I hope may be the case.[3]

The attached copy of a petition has been printed here in English, and I caused this German translation of it to be made: Y.M. will be pleased to observe to what end it is directed.[4] It would seem that the people are not averse to the idea of having a king again; but there are things in the petition which do not please the more prudent and sensible sort, as appearing to confer upon him greater power than any king of England ever had before, in direct violation of their fundamental law. It is said that the petition is to be banned by public proclamation; but it is nevertheless impossible not to believe that it is a deliberate manoeuvre by themselves.

It would be of the greatest possible service to my negotiations here to know what Y.M. means to do about Russia, for they [the English]

1. Charles accepted this suggestion, deciding on reflection that a preference for English merchants would be too provocative to the Dutch: Pufendorf, ii. 70–1.

2. The blockade ended in November 1655, and was briefly renewed in the following spring. The economic effects on Danzig were perceptible, but much more important was the effect of Charles X's campaigns, which ruined the countryside and prevented commodities from reaching Danzig down the Vistula: Edmund Cieślak, 'Gdansks militär-politiska och ekonomiska betydelse under det polsk-svenska kriget 1655–1659', in *Polens krig med Sverige 1655–1660* (Carl X Gustaf-studier, 5) (Stockholm 1973), pp. 145–7.

3. He had already turned traitor to the Polish republic and concluded a treaty with Charles X.

4. Missing in transcript, but *cf. The Clarke Papers*, Newsletter, 11 August 1655, iii. 48.

are concerned about the Russia trade through the Baltic, and how they may get it into their hands; and the only means to that end that I can suggest for the moment is that Y.M. should allow himself to act as mediator between them and the Muscovite, and so by persuasion and commercial advantages win him over to the idea. I therefore beg Y.M. to let me know his thoughts on that matter.

A Swedish *boijort*[1] arrived in London yesterday with four elks—two oxen and two cows—addressed to General [George] Fleetwood: he presented them to his highness the protector, who was very pleased to receive them. They report that they encountered a fearful storm, to which two of the elks succumbed: the report of the storm is confirmed, and many other ships sustained great damage. Although Coyet has agreed with a ship from Hamburg [to transport] to Y.M. the horses he has bought here, I fancy that he intends to send them by Y.M.'s own *boijort* to Stade, as the Master of the Horse requested. If no earlier opportunity offers, Pär Bonde will sail by the same *boijort*, and continue day and night to Y.M., since it is of the highest importance to me to know Y.M.'s resolution upon the various questions which he carries with him. I hope that he may find Y.M. at the very least in Warsaw, if not beyond; and from a humble and faithful heart I wish Y.M. all good fortune and many blessings on his happy successes.

I venture to put in a humble plea for Bonnel's recall: he cannot be sure from hour to hour that he will not be put in prison; and people here—especially foreigners who wish us ill—speak in very contumelious terms of the fact that Y.M. has now three ministers here at one time (with General [George] Fleetwood making a fourth), and that though they are recalled they cannot leave the country for lack of money. Coyet is still here also, and it does not seem that he can perform any service while I am here, and so is not particularly useful; for Secretary Johan Barkman was already (after I left for this country) ordered to come here as commissary, and he could perfectly well discharge any duties that I did not do myself. Bonnel has at last been asking assistance from me; but God knows that my suite here is forty persons more numerous than was intended; and apart from that this place is excessively expensive. Nor am I certain how soon I shall be able to get away, and it is an extremely slow business to obtain any further help from home, since two months must elapse between writing and receiving an answer. I therefore humbly entreat Y.M. not to take it ill that I am not able to facilitate his departure.

This week—either to-day or to-morrow—I shall be sending Herr Olivecrantz to Brabant to offer my humble duty to H.M. Queen Christina.

1. A *boijort* was a light craft equipped with both sails and oars.

VII

London, 23 August 1655

As it has been my earnest wish to discharge Y.M.'s commission to this country with fidelity and zeal, I have been worried as to how the secrecy which is requisite in matters of such high importance may be properly taken care of. And as I have had experience from time to time of the post's being stopped on one pretext or another, and the contents of the letters scrutinized, I have not ventured to confide all *specialia* to Y.M.; and have therefore determined to send this my humble relation to Y.M. by the hand of this young nobleman: he is my cousin Pär Bonde; has for some years travelled in foreign countries; has applied himself with some diligence to the study of fortification and to other subjects which may be of use to a soldier; and is firmly resolved to embrace the profession of arms. I leave it to Y.M.'s gracious pleasure whether to send him back to me with an answer, or whether Y.M. may be pleased to keep him so that he may make a start with his career either about Y.M.'s person, or with the army.

The manner of my introduction here, how I have been caressed and entertained, and what has passed of a public nature, I have from time to time reported through the post, and these matters I now omit, referring to my former despatches. After being conducted to my public audience I made a short speech to the protector in terms which Y.M. will be pleased to see from the attached copy, and which was interpreted into Latin by Secretary Barkman as in the annexure.[1] In it I for the most part followed the lines laid down in my instruction, though for particular reasons I touched, as it were *en passant*, on religion, and that a reciprocal friendship between Y.M. and this state was to the honour of God; which I did mostly because, even though this be really the case, they would take it very well, and it would be a means of attaching them from the beginning. The protector answered in a good speech; but, as I perceived, he did not wholly understand the Latin, which was pronounced in our fashion (though Barkman spoke loudly and very distinctly), and so he confined himself mainly to *generalibus*, reiterating the pleasure it had been to him that H.M. Queen Christina had evidenced such great affection to this state; but adding that that pleasure had been greatly augmented by the knowledge that the existing friendship was by Y.M. maintained and strengthened, in particular by the sending of this considerable embassy; adding some words of compliment to myself, and apologizing for the reception offered to me. He continued by saying that Y.M.'s name and great reputation had already been well known to him before his accession to the Swedish throne. He therefore rejoiced in

1. Missing in transcript.

his heart that God had given to Christendom such a notable [accession of] power, and congratulated himself that it had been vouchsafed to him to be a friend of such a 'king of men' (as he expressed it, laying especial emphasis on the words); and so protested eloquently his inclination to be a faithful friend of Y.M. With that the conference ended: the large suite I have here made a notable impression, for all members of it paid their respects to him. On taking leave I made him a compliment in English, and said that if he would grant me a private audience I hoped to give him such proofs of Y.M.'s friendship as would give him cause to make a suitable acknowledgement, and such as might be communicated to Y.M. On my own account I thanked him for the honour and civility which had been shown to me since my arrival; and added that since I believed that (without infringing my fidelity to Y.M.) I might be in a position to do him some service (a thing which I hoped the interests of both countries rather demanded than prohibited) I should be most happy if in return for the manner in which he had received me I might do anything agreeable to him. To which he replied with a *riante mine* which sufficiently indicated his satisfaction. And with that I took my departure, and was escorted home in state to the same house from which I had been accompanied. The audience took place in the great chamber which is here called the Banqueting House, having been built by the late king for banquets and ballets. From the outside it is so arranged that it looks as though it was of two storeys, but inside there is a narrow gallery running round the walls at the level which would have separated the two floors, and there were assembled a great number of distinguished ladies, and the hall itself was crowded with people. I confess that when, on my withdrawal, I reflected that this place, which had been built for the king's pleasure, and later had been the place from whose windows he went out to be beheaded, was now hung with the most costly tapestries (*prioris regis spolia*) and was now the scene of the splendid triumph of one who (to put it *mitissime*) had been a main agent in that deed, I could not look on it without emotion and compassion for the mutabilities of this world. His guard was drawn up outside in the square and on both sides of the street for the whole route: pretty handsome young men; but they were not in livery: each was clad in his particular colour, mostly grey; and when I observed the manner in which they handled their muskets they did not seem to me to be more than moderately well drilled.[1]

---

1. In Ekeblad's opinion 'they had not nearly so good an appearance as our soldiers, and kept pretty indifferent order on the march, but their cavalry is well mounted': Ekeblad, i. 421. But Sagredo observed that 'The troops are paid punctually and marvellously appointed, so that a private soldier is as well equipped as an officer in Italy': Sagredo to Doge, 24 September NS 1655: *CSP* (*Ven*) *1655–56*, p. 112.

When I got home that evening I indicated to Strickland and Fleming that I should be glad to have a private audience on Thursday, since I wished to inform Y.M. of my doings by the next post. They seized eagerly on the idea; and on Wednesday morning Sir Oliver Fleming came to me in my own house (to which I had by then removed), and that same day presented me for an audience: this particular mark of favour has never before been accorded to any public minister (most of them have to wait a week for an audience): it makes a great sensation, and is much to Y.M.'s service, since by such outward complaisances it deprives the Dutchmen of any hope of inducing this country to engage against Y.M.

In the afternoon, between 4 and 5 o'clock, Sir Oliver Fleming took me to Whitehall in one of the lord protector's own barges. I had polite conversation with Fleming while we were being rowed; which he began by saying that I should do well to speak quite confidently to the lord protector, and need have no difficulty about what title I ought to give him: I might sometimes call him 'his highness', and sometimes 'Sir', as I pleased. I at once discerned his intention, 'Sir', being the form of address usually given to a knight, and much below what was suited to the lord protector. He admitted that this was the case, but that nevertheless it was closely related to 'Sire', which is the title of the king of France, and said that they of the council of state commonly called him so. I replied that I should take very good care that the question of his title should not distract me from what I had it in mind to say; that I was not nice about titles; but that I intended to address him as his highness, as I had been ordered to do. From this Y.M. can easily perceive that he did not speak as from himself; but thought by these means to put me, as the public minister of so great a king, in the position of giving him the royal title, which he is certainly ambitious to obtain. When in this manner we had come to Whitehall, Strickland met me in the courtyard, with courtesies on the lord protector's behalf, and carried me up to a small room, where I waited a little time, as the custom is here; which they excuse as being designed to provide an opportunity for getting one's breath after going up the stairs. When I entered the lord protector's chamber, immediately afterwards, he gave me a friendly greeting, and at once signed to those noblemen who were with him to retire. This they did, and there remained no one except Strickland and Secretary Thurloe; but when I began my remarks by first begging to be excused if I were not able to express myself in English as I could wish, they too went out through another door into a neighbouring room which I had noticed upon a previous occasion.[1] [The reason] why I was especially anxious to

---

1. There being no reason for them to remain, since Bonde was not going to speak Latin, with which Cromwell might have needed some assistance. For the ceremonial

speak with him alone was because some of his council are good Dutchmen; particularly Strickland, who was formerly ambassador in Holland, and has in other respects special interests in that country.[1] But Thurloe is a pretty good Swede, and is the protector's right-hand man. I had been told some days before by a particular friend, who in this was very well informed, that the Dutch had employed all the means they could lay their hands on to arouse the protector's suspicion of Y.M.'s friendship, and to draw him into the alliance which they design to form between this country, Denmark, Poland, Brandenburg and themselves; as Y.M. will already have been informed by Herr Appelboom's reports. To this end they first made use of the most telling argument, and the one most calculated to alarm this government by reason of the fear and suspicion of the king's party which prevails here, and have put it about that Y.M.'s design, whatever might be pretended in regard to Poland, was certainly to assist the king's party; and that [the elector of] Brandenburg, who is the guardian of the prince [of Orange], would join with Y.M. to instal the prince in Holland and the royal family here.[2] However gross this fabrication, it has nevertheless caused great perturbation here, since any touching of that string arouses suspicion, the country being still full of royalists. I am not able to judge whether this impression may not have been reinforced by the fact that Y.M.'s own ratification [of Whitelocke's treaty] was not handed over by Herr Coyet, but only Queen Christina's; on the ground that they did not ask him for it, and he had express orders not to let it out of his hands unless they made a point of it. But as everything is suspect to the suspicious, it is possible that it may have caused some doubts in their minds as to Y.M.'s armaments.

It seemed to me that the first necessity was to get this idea out of their heads. I therefore began my speech by reminding him that it was a matter of experience that some who could not suffer Y.M.'s welfare and prosperity have wished to make him suspicious of Y.M.'s friendship; and I wanted, as a *praeparatorium* to all the rest that I had

---

at Cromwell's court see, in general, Sherwood, *Court of Oliver Cromwell*; and Stern, 'Oliver Cromwell und die evangelische kantone der Schweiz', p. 58.

1. He had relatives in the Dutch forces, whose promotion was a matter of concern to him.

2. When in October 1654 the French minister to Sweden had presented Charles II's compliments to Charles X, the acknowledgement had been in terms of studiously vague good-will: d'Avaugour to Charles II, PRO. SP 95/5B/130–1. A letter of intelligence of 14 September NS 1655 from Cologne informed Thurloe that royalists there believed that Charles X was double-crossing them. There seems no reason, in fact, for supposing that Bonde's apprehensions were well-grounded, though de Witt for a moment seems to have suspected it: *cf.* Coyet's letter no. 27 *supra*, p. 91 and *n.* 1.

to communicate to him, to clear his mind, as far as possible, of any such notions. And I could therefore give him an assurance that Y.M. had never had, nor did he now have, any other thought than to preserve a good friendship and understanding with him, and that he would in the future experience Y.M.'s sincerity towards him. I accordingly began to expand on this point; and by way of strengthening his appreciation, both of Y.M. and of our Swedish *façon* of acting (though it was already highly esteemed here in comparison with that of the French, Danes, and others), I demonstrated to him how from former times to the present we have pursued *reale consilia*: if he would look into it, he would find that the common factor in them was caution, and that hardly anything had been done by us *temere*. If he would consider how we have behaved towards England, he would find that we have always preserved a firm friendship with them, and that not only in words, but had indeed—even before we were bound to them by any specific alliance—done them such services that I felt that they ought to be suitably appreciated. When they were engaged in an onerous war with Holland, and Denmark had intervened in it at the solicitation of the Dutch (and what reason they had to do so I was in no position to know, nor was it incumbent upon me, as a matter outside my competence, to pronounce a judgment), they [the Dutch] did not fail to use all the persuasions they could think of in an attempt to draw us into the same game on their side. But we took a totally different line, and not only declined to be of their party, but did England and this government a very great service by restraining Denmark so that it did not venture to conjoin its forces with the Dutch. From this his highness might judge of our intentions towards England and whether our aim was to be their friend or their enemy; and it might easily occur to him that if we had any grudge against the lord protector or this government, that then would have been the time to give vent to it, and not now when he has thus established himself, and the Dutch are to all appearances his friends, and no internal or external enemy hampers him. Besides, we have since been bound to them in an alliance; and our forefathers have always been very jealous (as we are too) to keep our faith and promises. That reputation it is our intention to preserve above all other things; and we shall not molest our enemies—and still less our friends—unless they have given us such great cause to do so that we may, before God and in our conscience, have sufficient and just reason to be able to expect God's blessing. But as a means of wholly eradicating such prejudicial ideas from his mind I was disposed, in accordance with Y.M.'s orders, to reveal to him the real purpose of Y.M.'s armament, which [I said] Y.M. was desirous of disclosing to him as a close friend with whom it was his intention to live in amity, to the great benefit of both countries, and which Y.M. had not hitherto communicated to any other potentate so explicitly and expressly. I therefore told him that Y.M.'s principal purpose at this time was to make war on Poland; and in order that he might believe this and approve it I expounded at some length the reasons and grounds which had mainly obliged Y.M. to do so. First, the importance and magnitude of the issues which divided Sweden from Poland: that their pretension to the crown of Sweden was unreasonable and intolerable, since that family had been deposed and renounced once and for all by an *actu publico* at [the diet of] Norrköping [1604], and that our dear fatherland had since that time been happily ruled and led, first by King Charles [IX] of famous memory; then by King Gustavus, who was held in the highest praise not only in our country but by the whole world, and especially by the evangelical part of it, and who shed his blood gloriously for the sake of God's people and the defence of his country. Thereafter by that great king's daughter; during the twelve years of her minority through regents drawn from the Swedish nobility, and thereafter in Queen Christina's own person. During which time we manfully defended our country, vindicated our emancipation from the papacy, and consequently considered ourselves neither bound to, nor desirous of, any other king than one of that family. But when there was a default [of heirs], the great God in His mercy richly provided for it; in that now, when Queen Christina of her own volition has renounced crown and country, and rather preferred a quiet life, He has vouchsafed to us a king in Y.M.'s person, who is not only on his mother's side the grandson of King Charles of famous memory, but is also the best king in the world by reason of his incomparable virtues, great ability and experience; who has thus richly supplied and compensated that deficiency in the succession, and whom we are all heartily resolved to give our life and goods [to defend], if necessity should so demand.

I then touched a little on Livonia, dwelling principally on how the twenty-five [*recté* twenty-six] years' truce with Poland had in many ways been violated, so that it was insupportable for Y.M. and his faithful subjects to suffer it any longer; and explained how at various times and in various places they have contravened agreements by the attacks upon Y.M.'s territories (undertaken with their permission) by Boot and Cracou—and this at a time when we were engaged in a troublesome war with the House of Austria and the popish league; and not only that, but when the intolerable actions which the crown of Denmark took against us compelled us to take measures of defence on that side [in 1643], they lost no opportunity of giving our enemies all possible aid and comfort. But God of His grace not only protected us against two such mighty open enemies (and one secret one), but by His mercy granted that by our victorious arms we obtained from

Denmark a secure and honourable peace, and afterwards brought the German war to an end with a good reputation, to our great content. At that time he [the Pole], by negotiations in Lübeck [in 1651–53] (*semel iterumque*, as provided for in the treaty) made a show of treating for peace, until our armies in Germany had been paid off, and he had nothing more to fear; at which point he broke them off, having by these great appearances done no more than deceive us and all the world. Since then he has constantly laboured for our destruction, and by negotiations intolerable to the crown of Sweden sought to introduce a foreign fleet into the Baltic:[1] a thing of which the crown of Sweden is more jealous than of any other, and which it cannot possibly tolerate. Against all this we have taken no advantage of the precarious situation of the crown of Poland in its difficulties with the Cossacks and the Muscovites until now, when we have been so harassed that we were forced to take thought for our safety. On all this, and more, I laid the greatest emphasis; and especially upon the last treaty concerning a fleet in the Baltic,[2] since it gave me an opportunity to contrive that he [the protector] might thus *in tertia persona* be notified that Y.M. will by no means suffer a foreign fleet to come there. Of his [the Pole's] intrigues and plans to stir up the Cossacks against Sweden I said nothing, partly because I was not fully informed about them, partly because it seemed that what had been said already was sufficient. But I presented him with a copy of the letter from the Swedish council of state to the council of state in Poland, and promised that as soon as I had a copy of the manifesto which is preparing, I would gladly communicate it to him.

But since the Dutch have been trying to give the greater plausibility to their insinuation that Y.M.'s armament against Poland by its very dimensions greatly exceeds the measures which might seem to be necessary in the case, and that Y.M. could well obtain what he wanted with half as many, I told him plainly that I knew such stories were put about, and that if therefore Y.M.'s armament should give him any cause for disquiet, I was ready for that reason to give him the satisfaction of imparting to him the reasons which moved Y.M. to it. First, that Y.M. and his faithful council and subjects always accounted it for an excellent maxim never to do anything *à demi*, and have therefore always been careful not to proceed in any degree *mediocriter*, but rather in any just cause to avail themselves *realiter* and with all proper seriousness of the means which God has graciously granted them for their defence. Next, that our quarrel with Poland is of long

1. A reference to de Bye's negotiations of 1653–4.
2. Whitelocke's treaty of 1654 laid it down that England and Sweden would coöperate to prevent disturbance of trade in 'the Baltic, Sound, Northern, Western and British Seas, Mediterranean, Channel and other Seas in Europe': Abbott, iii. 914.

standing; and we should count our trouble and expense well bestowed if thereby we were able to obtain a settlement which gave us what we desired. Nor could Y.M. be certain at the start of a war what emergencies might arise from it, and therefore considered it most necessary for his safety so to arrange his affairs that he was in a position (under God) to rely upon himself, and not be placed at the mercy of anyone else. These reasons he [the protector] grasped very well, and by his particular expression of countenance seemed highly to approve of— no doubt because he knows that they are identical with the basis upon which his own *régime* rests.

I proceeded by saying that I knew also that those who wished to give the lord protector an unfavourable impression of Y.M.'s armament have employed the argument that because Y.M. wanted to begin a war against Poland, and because his fleet lay off Prussia, that therefore trade in the Baltic would be very seriously affected; and that it was of great importance for England, no less than for Holland, to prevent this, since the interests of both were involved in the matter. I admitted that they had neglected no opportunity of adducing anything that they knew would forward their intentions, and that they used this as an argument so fundamental that it could not be controverted; but that in this case, as in the former, I was ready to remove any scruples he might have, since it gave me a chance to let him understand what Y.M.'s intention was. I began by dwelling upon the fact that he was well aware that last year a treaty was concluded between England and Sweden in which we bound ourselves on both sides to maintain *libertatem commerciorum in Mari Balthico*, as well as in other specified waters—an obligation which Y.M. was resolved to comply with; and I was ready to assure his highness that whatever advantage over his enemies God might be pleased to grant him, he was minded to grant that liberty, and especially to the English. And since in article 15 of the same treaty it stands that should it be necessary there shall be special discussions on *modus subsidij et auxilij*; and since the rumour runs that at this time a fleet of war is to be introduced into the Baltic by certain ill-disposed parties (which undoubtedly must lead to disturbance of the trade), Y.M. would therefore be glad to know the lord protector's attitude in such a case in terms of that clause in the alliance, and his view on how it was to be prevented, and how the aforesaid *modus subsidij ferendi* was to be obtained. If Y.M. perceived that the lord protector was serious about preserving the aforesaid liberty, he would be disposed not only to obtain liberty of commerce for England, but to give such advantages in the Baltic trade (on whose importance it was unnecessary for me to dilate) that they would, for their common interest, have the greater cause to take steps to secure its safety, and hence to judge of Y.M.'s real wish to maintain good relations with his highness and with England, and so *junctis viribus* to coerce and restrain any third party who sought, unbidden, to meddle in an affair which did not concern him.

I then began to enlarge upon how impertinent it was of the Dutch to intervene in a situation in which we had deserved better of them. At the time when they were engaged in an arduous war with Spain they could hardly have carried it on if our campaigns in Germany had not diverted their enemy; and we had besides given them aid at need with men, and in other ways. But their good disposition lasted no longer than as they found our aid necessary to them; and they had now turned against us for two reasons: one was that we had been unwilling to join our arms with them against England [in 1652–3]; the other, that for some years we have been striving in some measure to improve our commerce and navigation. The lord protector, I fancied, knew more of this than he relished: how with their light ships they had sailed England—and all others—off the seas, and that they accordingly considered trade to be their property, pertaining to them by hereditary right, and therefore could not suffer that any others applied themselves to it. And that I said this to him, not because Y.M. or the Swedes entertained any jealousy or enmity towards the Dutch: we were rather minded to do them all good offices, if only they would not meddle in matters which were none of their business, and would be friends with us again; but that I put the point to him because the English and the Swedes were at one in regard to navigation, both having big ships, carrying guns, which were on that account expensive to build. And it was not in the nature of either of us to be so envious as not to be able to endure the rise of another power alongside us. It was true that England was now at peace with Holland; but that peace had been extorted by victorious war; and he well knew with what feelings they regarded him and England, especially at a time when his highness and England were doing all they could to recover their former trade. This common commercial interest obliged us both to a mutual good understanding, and would be sufficient to preserve it undisturbed once the world realised how we were bound together; and there would be no one with courage enough to make an attempt upon our union.

My speech thus sufficiently conveyed my meaning, and at the same time gave him an occasion to think about the Baltic trade. In conclusion I emphasised that Y.M. was pacifically inclined, and would willingly accept a sound and secure peace, but that a righteous war was better than an uncertain peace, or one which touched the reputation of Y.M. and his country. Of this the case of Bremen was a clear example: Y.M. could easily have taken it if he had chosen to do so, but all that Y.M. wanted was to bring them to reason and make them acknowledge their obligations: beyond that he had no demands to make.[1]

And since I knew that talk of religion was very acceptable to him—and, I hope, in no way prejudicial to Y.M., since I touched on it only lightly *in generalissimis terminis* and as from myself—I said that personally I considered that Christendom (of the true evangelical religion) had no greater support to rely upon at this time, than Y.M. and England; and that consequently I thought it above all things necessary that there should be a good understanding between them, and that they should not allow this or that [power]—even though of the same religion, and hence having a duty to help Y.M. against a catholic enemy rather than to hinder him—to stir up discord between them for what they supposed to be their own advantage. I wished that God might prevent all disunion and bloodshed, but the posture of affairs at present suggested to me that we had little good to expect from the papists. When the present pope was *nuntius apostolicus* at [the congress in] Münster, he solemnly protested against the peace there concluded; and the pope who was living at that time annulled it in the strongest possible terms. The religious changes in Germany, and other proceedings of theirs, sufficiently declared their intentions; and it was therefore needful that we should be good and constant friends in all cases, whatever might happen.

With this I ended my speech; and the protector, after he had considered a little, thus began his reply: that all the days of his life, even when he was still a young man, he had been devoted to King Gustavus the Great, of glorious memory, and that he had mourned his death more than could have been expected from one of his age and station. He had always lamented that at that period English policy had been so ill directed that his late majesty (and after his death, the crown of Sweden) had been given no help or comfort—though every honest Englishman at that time was disposed to give it—but had been left to meet danger unassisted and alone. However that might have been, a like affection had been awoken in him towards Y.M. He set the highest estimation upon the friendship of that great and noble king; he rejoiced that Y.M., through me, had shown his confidence by revealing to him his intentions; and from all Y.M.'s actions he could judge that he wished well to himself and this country; as he had shown by the great favour and honour which he had manifested to his ambassador in Sweden. Though he freely acknow-

1. After 1648 the city of Bremen had claimed to be immediate to the emperor and had refused to acknowledge Swedish overlordship. Christina had declared war; Bremen had successfully defended itself; Charles X on his accession had forced it to accept a compromise peace which conceded the Swedish demand but left the question of immediacy open.

ledged that his [Whitelocke's] conduct in some measure might have moved Y.M. thereto, he could not help feeling that those honours were granted to him mainly on account of his principal. Coming then a little nearer to the point, he said that he must confess that Y.M.'s armaments had raised a great alarm in this part of the world and all round about, it appearing to everyone that Y.M. had no need to arm on such a scale against Poland. But he found that there was solid reasoning in what I had said, thanked me for expounding the matter so thoroughly, and added that for his part he could only say that he was not connected with Poland by any ties whatever, but Y.M. was his faithful ally; and that therefore he wished Y.M. all good fortune and many blessings in this as in all his other generous enterprises.

As to the Dutch, it was true that they had fought a bitter war against himself and England; but that was now by God's grace decided, and a good peace between them established; and since they were of the same religion, and had with great courage, prudence and resolution cast off the popish yoke, he could not hate them after all. And he took note of my assurance that Y.M. equally bore them no ill will provided they would keep quiet and do Y.M. no ill offices. He must confess that as trade had been the sole basis for the rise of the Dutch, so also they were very jealous of it, and wished to keep it wholly in their hands; and he could not approve of the envy they showed to others who busied themselves in it (I could see that on this point he meant more than he said, but spoke very deliberately and *caute*, lest he should say too much). He said furthermore that he had cause to praise Y.M.'s very different policy, as evidenced by the fact that he was ready to share with him any advantage which—it might be—he should obtain for himself. That what I had said as to the similarity of the trading interests of England and Sweden was certainly true, and he hoped, indeed, that they could live side by side without jealousy. He expressed himself highly obliged for [Y.M.'s] offer; and assured me that he would give consideration to how he could do Y.M. all possible services, though he hoped that for the moment I would not ask him to say more on the subject. What he could say was that he had the highest respect for Y.M., and was disposed to link himself to him as closely as any two powers could be allied.

He then fell into a discourse on religion, speaking once again of the danger which our religion had to fear from the papists; and remarked that I had done well to recall the protest of this pope [at Münster], as being a thing of enormous importance; and that he could tell me this, that he had good information that this pope is making every effort to arrange a peace between the catholic monarchs, and then to turn their united forces against us. His [the pope's] actions, and those of the catholics—in Germany and against the poor protestants in

Savoy, who have practised their religion there for over a century undisturbed—sufficiently manifested their intentions. He had also great reason to rejoice at the excellent answer which Y.M. had sent him on the Savoy affair;[1] which led him once again to wish Y.M. all good fortune. And he said that he certainly believed that Y.M. would not limit himself to his present plans, but rather hoped that the beneficent design whose execution in Germany Almighty God had seemed to destine to the hand of King Gustavus (of illustrious memory), but by him could be no more than begun, might by the great King Charles be completed, and achieve its ends to the glory of God; and to this he was ready to contribute what he could.

He then spoke politely of myself, particularly since I had begged to be excused for not having sufficient command of the English tongue to be able to express myself as properly as I could wish, saying that he wished to deal frankly with me, setting all ceremony aside, and upon a basis of mutual trust; and that he was ready to appoint commissioners who could discuss matters with me more at large. I had deliberately refrained from saying anything about commissioners, for I wished rather to speak with himself a time or two, and was beside apprehensive that he might, on the spur of the moment, before I had been able to take steps somehow to have men who understand matters of trade—it is in any case nothing but a prostitution of precious things [to open them] to those who do not understand their value—appoint some whom I would rather not deal with; and I wanted, besides, to have men who were good Swedes. However, I immediately answered that in this, as in all other things, his politeness anticipated my wishes. I had therefore great cause to be grateful to him; hoping only that I might have another opportunity to talk with him, at which we might reach a closer agreement on these matters. On this he called to the secretary and Strickland, who came out; and with that I took my leave. After which I was rowed home to my house again, accompanied by Fleming; who rejoiced at the happy expression on both our faces, saying that thereby he could confidently predict that our great king and the protector would one day be linked in closer union, and be in a condition to do great things.

From all this Y.M. may gather how far I got at this first conference, and what reception I met with at the start of my mission. I might well have touched on some other points, but I thought that this was sufficient for the present. I humbly beg that Y.M. will not be displeased that I spoke something of the papists, for I did it only with the aim of finding out what the protector's dispositions were. And I have not committed Y.M. or myself in the smallest degree.

1. The Vaudois massacres: the protector's appeal to Charles X is printed in Abbott, iii. 968.

All this discourse has made me ponder as to what it would be advisable to say at this juncture (and how far it would be advisable for me personally to say it) by way of turning the feelings of the protector and his government towards a strict alliance, to their own advantage. On the one hand there seem to be strong reasons against it: first, the uncertain position of the present government: I may have written to Y.M. about that from Gravesend, and described the present situation in this country. Since then I have made diligent enquiry; and though I now judge that the protector has firmly established himself, so that he can venture to aim at a higher station, and in consequence seems (humanly speaking) able at the least to maintain his position during his lifetime; nevertheless not only is the country full of malcontents, but he might personally fall victim to some sudden accident—either by violence or illness—and so this government be involved in disturbances once again. If the king's party were to come in, it would be difficult to avoid their hostility to any who had maintained so close a correspondence with their adversaries. Next, it would seem that the danger which principally obliged Y.M. to seek assistance from this country at sea is for the time over, since Y.M. and his army are safely across the water and have already established so firm a foothold in Poland that with the help of God the enterprise must be going well; and even if the Dutch should presently think of sending a fleet there (as they are considering doing at this moment) I hope that before they get there the season will be so far advanced that they will not be able to effect anything. Since, therefore, all the reasons which moved Y.M. to seek a closer alliance with this country seem for the moment to have fallen away, it becomes a matter for consideration whether it would not be better, instead of pressing on with it, to keep our hands free and content ourselves with the alliance we have already, which (moreover) pledges them to liberty of commerce and forbids them to oppose Y.M.'s plans by word or deed. And it might well not fit in with Y.M.'s purposes just now, at a time when Y.M. has made such progress in Poland and has promised them [the Poles] freedom of religion, to proclaim to the world the establishment of a closer alliance based on religious considerations. And this might make them reluctant [to engage], and perhaps give them cause to suspect Y.M. of propounding something new to them; with the consequence that the trust and affection which they have conceived for Y.M.'s person might be subverted by those who wish him ill.

But as all this, and other reasons too, are matters for consideration on that side of the question, so on the other hand there are excessively great reasons which seem to demand and require a strict alliance at this time. It seems to me that the first thing that we have to consider is that such an alliance with England is useful not only to Y.M. in the present circumstances (when there is reason to fear the actions of the Dutch), but equally so in the future; for the jealousy of our neighbours and of the Dutch is hardly likely to cease, but will rather always be on the increase, especially if God should bless Y.M.'s arms and grant him success. And so to forestall all their plots and intrigues a special relationship with England is of the highest importance, as providing a possible balance in all emergencies. The great new successes in Poland, moreover, suggest to me that they may inevitably involve Y.M. in a new war. If it should be a war with Russia, no power can do Y.M. greater service than this one; for I imagine that they would make every effort (as, indeed, they seem very much disposed to do)[1] to make the Archangel trade so difficult for the Russians that not a single cargo could be exported; and perhaps might easily be brought to declare them open enemies, block the entry to the port of Archangel, and then (in conjunction with Y.M.'s arms, or through his mediation) seek to divert all the Russia trade through Y.M.'s harbours in the Baltic, where they might be granted a staple and a liberty of trade along the lines of Y.M.'s former plan and his instruction to me, in exchange for such aid and support as might be obtained from them when the time comes.

And if Y.M. were not able to avoid a war with the emperor—which might easily happen now that Y.M. is so close to the hereditary lands—and if perhaps the emperor were to give some aid to the king of Poland, and if (as is reported here) he is energetically recruiting, and continues his religious reforms more vigorously than ever—if [I say] Y.M. should be drawn into a war with him, then likewise he gives the best possible support to Y.M.'s plans in regard to this country, which is most eager for such a war, as Y.M. will have gathered from what I have said already. They freely confess that it is England alone who betrayed the general cause of protestantism at La Rochelle, and again in Germany, where they allowed them [the protestants] to face danger without assistance; but now they seem anxious to repair that error. They say King Gustavus, of glorious memory, longed for nothing so much as that England might be in the situation in which it ought to be in regard to the evangelical cause; but although his hope remained unfulfilled then, the state of affairs here is now such that they are ready to embrace the common cause, and that therefore no opportunity ought to be missed, but should rather be exploited, in an attempt to safeguard the Protestant Cause, so that it might not every day be in fear of danger from the catholics. In such a case they would not only do everything in their power to

---

1. For the Muscovy Company's grievances against the Russians, see *CSP* (*Dom*) *1653–4*, p. 340, and *1655–56*, p. 189.

aid Y.M. at sea, but perhaps might be persuaded to come to Y.M.'s assistance with a considerable sum of money.

As to the argument arising from the uncertainty of affairs in this country, that too does not seem to give grounds for apprehension, for in the first place the protector seems in various ways to have firmly established himself, so that it is hardly likely that the king's party will ever get the upper hand here; one decisive reason for which is that all those in this country who have the power and the money are for the most part of his [the protector's] faction, while all the royalists are impoverished and indigent. They see very clearly that if the king were to come to power again he would be bound on all accounts to favour and assist those who had remained faithful to him and lost their property for his sake; and the country would not have resources enough unless he followed the same tactics as the protector has used, and deprived those who have been his adversaries; and such rewards as might be available would all go to his adherents, leaving the rest with no hope of improving their situations in any way. There are many other reasons which might be adduced to demonstrate the stability of this government, with which I am unwilling to trouble Y.M. Even if the king's party should get the upper hand, that could not hurt Y.M.; for our alliances are not with the protector personally, or with his family, but with the English nation, and if the king rightly understood his own advantage he would take good care of the nation's interests, which are not to be changed by any alteration in the persons who govern it. Nothing, moreover, is more usual when such great alterations occur than the issue of a general amnesty for what has passed, and he would be glad to forget all the wrongs he may suppose himself to have suffered, if only he could bring Y.M. and the crown of Sweden over to his side. Besides which, all the commercial privileges which Y.M. has it in mind to grant them (which are the most effectual means to bind them to him) affect the inhabitants and residents of England, and the protector and his family have no private interest in them.

There is something to be said for the consideration as to [Y.M.'s] policy towards the [catholic] religion in Poland;[1] but the point could with prudence be blunted by the treaty itself. For the end and object of that treaty, it seems to me, must be (i) the defence of the [protestant] religion in case its adherents be attacked or injured by the catholics; and it cannot be desired, if God should give His blessing to our arms, that we should then, by a sort of protestant inquisition of the kind the catholics employ, either persecute the catholics or convert them, but rather that we should grant them the free exercise of their religion for

1. Charles X at the beginning of his Polish campaigns found it expedient to adopt a relatively tolerant attitude, since he relied on the support of the Polish nobility.

as long as they made no trouble, and seek only to bring them into the right way by fair means, and *insensibiliter*. The second object of the treaty, it seems to me, must be *libertas commerciorum*, to which end Y.M. and England would bind themselves to join their forces to prevent those who wish to disturb it, and to ensure that Holland and Denmark do not combine for the destruction of the trade of others, nor allow any foreign fleet of war to enter the Baltic: in which event the 20 warships mentioned in Y.M.'s instructions to me could come in very useful.

I humbly entreat Y.M.'s pardon that I presume to set down my thoughts at such length. I take God to witness that all I write comes from a loyal heart. I desire only to know Y.M.'s pleasure, which shall then always be the rule of my conduct; and I have thought it better to importune Y.M. with a lengthy despatch and many questions, than to do anything which might be contrary to Y.M.'s pleasure and intentions. In the meantime, while I perforce await an answer, I have resolved so to comport myself that I give them no occasion to grow cool in their inclination to a strict alliance, but to respond to it with courtesy, and always to give them cause for hope. For it could happen that *rerum facies* might in some degree alter, and that [though] Y.M. might then be very glad to have [a treaty?] it might not then be possible to obtain one: as a good friend has already hinted to me, by way of a warning. In the meantime I am working to make the Russia trade by way of the Baltic attractive to them, and I shall do all I can to see whether it is possible to obtain what Y.M. desires, in exchange for the minimum possible grant of liberties. And I hope (if it can be managed) that Y.M.'s advantage and theirs may be firmly united, and that for the sake of their own interests they may find it necessary to accept [the principle of] the freedom of the Baltic, which I firmly maintain can never be secure if any fleet of war which is not either Y.M.'s or the king of Denmark's were to come there, since it is a thing that can never be suffered by Y.M.; and no other power, town or republic is entitled or empowered to keep a fleet of war there, other than Sweden and Denmark only.

After my first conference I had another private audience on the 9th of this month; but since there were others present the only business of any consequence that I could transact was to have commissioners appointed to meet me on the following Tuesday; as I may have informed Y.M. by the last post. Last Saturday, a week ago, I was at Hampton Court: as to how I was entertained there I gave Y.M. an account by the post. On the 15th of this month I had my first conference with the commissioners. Those who are deputed to negotiate with me are Viscount Lisle, Mr Pickering, and [Sir Charles] Wolseley; but since Lisle was ill, Strickland came in his place, who has the reputation of having formerly been a good Dutchman. They are however pretty reserved, for it is as much as their lives are worth to do anything [except] *caute*. After the usual courtesies I emphasized that Y.M.'s behaviour towards England should easily allow them to judge of his sincere affection to the lord protector and this country. And I begged them, if any had sought to make Y.M.'s armament in any degree suspect here, that they would give no credence to it; adding that those who would be glad to see that Y.M. and this country were not good friends had in like manner wished to arouse Y.M.'s suspicions of the lord protector, and had spread the rumour that his highness aimed at a union with Denmark, Holland and Brandenburg which should unite to oppose Y.M.'s laudable and necessary intentions;[1] but that Y.M. was not capable of believing that his good friend and ally would without any reason act contrary to the alliance which had been concluded, and to the general interest of protestantism, which must find its strongest support in the friendship of our two countries and their common interest.

I then adverted to what I conceived to be the question we were to negotiate, namely, the establishment of a hearty, unclouded and sincere confidence and friendship. To this Mr Pickering made a very handsome reply. After compliments reciprocating mine, he said that he and his colleagues did not use to give any answer at the conference before discussing among themselves the proposals before them; but that in this case he considered it unnecessary to confer with them, since the faithful friendship which his highness and this country felt for Y.M. was so sincere, and so well-known, that he could avow that in no case had he heard less of anything which might, on the one side or the other, conflict with it. It might well be, when that warlike nation which had for many years so valiantly waged its victorious campaigns once more armed itself on such a scale (especially under a king so noble and so valiant), that this should provoke reflections among all its neighbours; but he could assure me of all faithful friendship on this side, and that it had never entered their thoughts to interpose an obstacle to Y.M.'s fortunate enterprises: on the contrary, they wished them all good success, and desired by all means to assist and forward them.

To which I answered that to receive such satisfaction on the part of his highness and those good gentlemen was no more than I had

---

1. Something like this emerged as one improbable solution to the protector's perplexities a month or so later, when Nieupoort reports Thurloe as suggesting that the best solution to their difficulties might be a defensive alliance of England, the Dutch, Denmark, Sweden—and Brandenburg. Nieupoort to de Witt, 9 October NS: *Brieven*, iii. 218–19. On which Nieupoort drily commented that it might be worth while to take him at his word: *ibid.*, 130.

expected; and for that reason I intended the more confidently to communicate my thoughts to them. I then began to expound at some length how Y.M. had sent me to England to discuss, together with them, what might be most expedient for both countries to do in the present circumstances, as also to complete whatever had been postponed at the time of the conclusion of the former treaty. I enlarged upon the danger threatening the common cause of protestantism, which seemed to be little less than what the catholics at this moment were inflicting upon the protestants of Savoy. However, there was still peace; and as the question did not appear to be immediately pressing, I left it for the moment, only asking his highness and these good gentlemen to think about it and turn it over in their minds, so that they might give me their views about it: I would then gladly do everything in my power; and for the rest did not doubt that Y.M. would be very ready to concur in whatever might conduce to the common welfare of both nations.[1] But as it was provided in the recent treaty that an agreement should be concluded *de modo subsidii et auxilij ferendi* if any danger seemed to be imminent which might infringe *libertatem navigationis et commerciorum*, it was now necessary to discuss how such a danger might be averted, since there was a general report that a foreign fleet of war was to be expected in the Baltic. Y.M. believed and desired that the two allies should concert measures, *unitis viribus,* to prevent it in this and similar cases. I then explained how impossible it was for a foreign fleet to be brought in without causing a disturbance of trade; and how his highness and the republic of England—not only in terms of the said treaty, but in general— have a great interest in preserving liberty of commerce for the sake of the Baltic trade at this time, and indeed that this was an interest which might come to be still more important to them; and that therefore Y.M., in order to make them the more ready to enter into his wishes, was disposed to accord various favours to their Baltic trade, which I depicted to them in the most glowing colours. I also mentioned the Russia trade; showing them how in place of the trade to Archangel (which was now destroyed) they might have the same trade, with various greater facilities, by way of the Baltic; to which Y.M. would help them by giving them staple-rights, and by favouring them in other ways: instancing in this connexion the trade to Estonia and

---

1. There seems no justification for Guernsey Jones's suggestion that Bonde at this conference committed a diplomatic blunder by dismissing 'the Protestant Cause'- argument as of little importance: Guernsey Jones, p. 35. He probably got this idea from Pehr Kalling, *Om Riks-Rådet Frik. Christer Bondes. Ambassad.*, p. 17, who paraphrases Bonde as saying 'For the protestant religion nothing was now to be feared. The catholics had made no attacks, except against the protestants in Savoy, but this was an affair which seemed of small importance'.

Livonia, and especially to Riga. And added that if God of His goodness should be pleased to bless Y.M.'s arms and grant him such successes that he was in a position to exercise control of the trade to the harbours now in his enemies' hands (either by burdening it or by facilitating it)—not only strengthening his forces thereby, but also inflicting all sorts of damage on his foes—in such a case he would be no less disposed to give his highness and the inhabitants of England such advantages that they might take into their hands the trade of the Baltic—if not entirely, then at least a great part of it. And so, spinning it out by circumlocutions and superfluities, I explained to them how important it was for England that their neighbours and ours (and they very well knew what reliance we could place on either of them) should be kept under close watch by means of a good cooperation between us; to which end it was necessary that our united forces should hinder the Baltic from being disturbed by a foreign fleet, or their [sc. our neighbours'] trade from growing too great.

The main reason why I was not anxious on this occasion to open myself further as to Y.M.'s demands was that Strickland, who had come in Lisle's place (he being ill) is attached to the Dutch party; but I also wished only to give them an opportunity to think about what I wanted to find out—that is, how far they might be prepared to accept them. Still less was I anxious to be explicit about how and in what way Y.M. was prepared to give them preferences, or to make any mention of Sweden, Finland and Pomerania, which I shall try to reserve, if possible, to Y.M.'s subjects: rather Pomerania than Livonia; for the Russia trade is all-important in Estonia and Livonia, and I am most anxious, with their [England's] help, to channel it through Y.M.'s dominions. I am always free to make some concessions; but it is not so easy to revoke a promise. I expect very shortly to be able to judge from their answer what their feeling is, and I shall then give Y.M. a faithful account of it. But first I ask Y.M. in all humility, to let me know if [the idea of] a strict alliance to strengthen the common cause of religion commends itself to him. If they insist on it, I shall answer as seems unexceptionable; and I have from time to time felt compelled to allude to it, because that is the only way to get anywhere here, and to conciliate them. The common people, on the Exchange and in the streets, say openly that all the learned men have shown, from the prophecies of Daniel and by other reasons, that a king of Sweden, with England, shall overthrow the seat of the pope, and give to the service of God its right prosperity and use again; which time is now at hand, and the occasion necessary to be embraced.[1] I must also

1. Some fervent protestant syncretists were attracted by an apocalypticism which promised that the Latter Days would probably start in 1654 or 1655; and to some of them Charles X's attack on Poland seemed to be the signal for their beginning. Samuel

know Y.M.'s intention with regard to the Russians, and the means Y.M. envisages for diverting that trade to the Baltic, with the help of England: of which I may have made some mention in my last despatch by the post.

My instruction touches only a little, and *en passant*, on the terms to be arranged between Y.M. and England as to the command of the fleet which Y.M. is to obtain from them as a reinforcement; and I therefore humbly ask that if it is Y.M.'s pleasure that additional conditions, other than those already specified, are to be borne in mind, they may be such as are acceptable to Y.M. [*sic:sc.* and that I may be informed of them]. It is a somewhat slow business to negotiate with these people: the French ambassador has been doing it for three years. Nevertheless, I shall use every effort to hasten it, as far as I possibly can. I hope at least that I have already ensured that this country will not be a nuisance to Y.M.; and this for the present I think is sufficient, even if it means that I must procrastinate until I obtain Y.M.'s answer to this letter. Y.M. may perhaps by that time have resolved to frame the treaty in quite other terms, and to transform it from a particular to a general defensive system; but this I respectfully refer to Y.M., and await his orders, which I shall apply myself to carrying out as far as may be possible *etc. etc.*

The enclosed letter and proposal have come to me through a Greek, one Leonard Philaras, or as he is called in French De Villère, with an earnest request that they may be forwarded in all submission to Y.M. He gives as his referees Mr Radzievski [*sc.* Radziejowski] and l'Abbé Daniel,[1] who was sent to Y.M. by Mr Chmielnicki. He is himself a

---

Hartlib, John Durie, Drabik and Comenius were of this persuasion, and looked forward to a godly coalition between Charles X, Cromwell, and George II Rákóczy of Transylvania. Durie and Hartlib were in close touch with Cromwell, though it does not appear that they succeeded in seriously interesting him in their ideas: see Sven Göransson, *Den europeiska konfessionspolitikens upplösning 1654–1660* (Uppsala 1955), especially pp. 44–5, and Folke Dahl, 'King Charles Gustavus of Sweden and the English astrologers William Lilly and John Gadbury', *Lychnos* (Uppsala 1937), ii. pp. 161–86. For Durie, see J. M. Batten, *John Durie. Advocate of Christian Reunion* (Chicago 1944). He had been a member of Lisle's embassy to Sweden in 1652. It was probably one of Lilly's enthusiastic predictions that Bonde took home with him to Sweden: Ekeblad, *Brev*, ii. 61.

1. Vice-Chancellor Hieronymus Radziejowski was a rebel and fugitive from Poland, who fled to Sweden in 1652. He entered into (possibly unauthorized) communications with Chmielnicki, who had just concluded the treaty of Pereyaslavl, which transferred the allegiance of the Cossacks to Russia. When his intrigue with the Cossacks leaked out he was sent to England with Christina's recommendation, and was well received. Thence he went to France, where he involved himself in efforts to organize a coalition against the Turks, with the object of liberating Greece. Exiled Greek patriots, anxious to obtain the aid of Chmielnicki, sent the Abbot Daniel to the Ukraine, with proposals for an alliance. Thence he went to Stockholm, arriving in September 1654, with an

handsome and capable man, who can talk very well on the affairs of the Turks, the Cossacks and Tartars, and the Muscovites. What Y.M. may make of his proposal I leave to Y.M.'s dijudication.

VIII

London, 24 August 1655

This is a copy of a petition[1] which a great part of the inhabitants here had intended to present to his highness, expressing their desire that he assume the royal style and dignities. I had meant to send it to Y.M. by the last post, but it was impossible to finish it in time, mostly because on that day I preoccupied with some celebration which I had arranged by way of demonstrating my joy at Y.M.'s happy progress. I send it herewith, humbly entreating that Y.M. may be willing not to mark his displeasure at my inability to send it before. Since then his highness has been doing his best to suppress it, although it has been both printed and disseminated among the populace, and the news-sheets now print that he is trying to hush it up; but this is certainly all a device, whose purpose will in time appear.

In the last week it has not been possible for me to effect much, for I have not been able to bring my commissioners to a discussion. They are now extremely preoccupied, and yesterday a day of prayer and fasting was secretly arranged at Whitehall; which suggests that something of importance is in hand. Last week also I despatched Per Bonde to Y.M.: I hope he may arrive shortly. I was told in confidence by a person who has reliable information that the king of Spain has secretly sent to Lisbon to treat for peace, and that the opinion is that [the negotiations] are likely to be successful. It is reported here (and by the French themselves) that there is to be a peace between them and Spain, and that it is to include provisions of great consideration for them; from which it seems that by all appearances this pope is labouring hard to reconcile the catholic monarchs, and what his further intentions may be is easy to judge.

I have also had a letter from Duraeus [i.e. Durie], at Hanau: this is the same person who has so long been labouring to effect a syncretism

---

offer of an alliance *contra quemcunque*—including, therefore, Russia. Philaras was another Greek with the same objectives. The Swedish council debated Daniel's offers in January 1655, but considered that though Chmielnicki's revolt against Poland was to be encouraged, they would for the moment await developments: for all this, see Bohdan Kentrschyńskyj, 'Ukrainska revolutionen och Rysslands angrepp mot Sverige 1656', *Karolinska Förbundets Årsbok*, (1956), pp. 28–37. Daniel continued to act as an intermediary between Chmielnicki and Charles X in 1655–56: Carl Wibling, *Carl X Gustaf och Georg Råkóczy* (Lund 1891), pp. 10, 28.

1. Missing in transcript.

between lutherans and calvinists (Y.M. will no doubt have heard of him); and since [the letter] seems to be very remarkable I have caused it to be translated into German, and transmit a copy of it herewith.[1]

I shall do my utmost to meet with my commissioners next week, and expect to be able by the next post to give some account of the progress of my negotiations in this place.

Ever since I arrived here there has been almost continual rain, and all the seed in the ground has been ruined, and is rotting away; to the great distress of the people.

The post has in fact arrived a moment ago; but since I may not by this letter delay the delivery of other letters, I must postpone to the next post my answer to what is in it. May God grant me good news of Y.M., and keep watch over Y.M.'s person, and bring success to all his noble enterprises, so that all men of good will may have cause to rejoice at it.

Coyet to Charles X

33

London, 24 August 1655 [in German]

[The English have conquered Jamaica, and are expanding their quarters there; the main concern is for the danger to the fleet from the autumn hurricanes.

Blake again off Cadiz, and cruising in the Straits. Report that before the emissary from Tunis could arrive at Constantinople with complaints of Blake's proceedings, the English ambassador Thomas Bendyshe forestalled him, and justified Blake. And when the emissary complained that Blake had destroyed ships which were to join the Turkish fleet, Bendyshe asked for another audience, and contrived to conciliate the Grand Vizier, pointing out that the people of Tunis gave the Turks a bad reputation, and so hindered their trade; that they were insubordinate subjects; that they enslaved Englishmen and refused their release to Blake; and if on account of Blake's proceedings anything unpleasant were to happen to Englishmen in Turkey it was as well to remember that Blake's powerful fleet was not far off, and he might seek revenge on Turkish trade, their harbours being open to him. At which the Grand Vizier informed the Tunisian envoy that he could do nothing in the matter at present.

Letters from Spain report that another embassy may shortly be expected here, and that an agent has gone to the king of Portugal to try to arrange a peace on the basis of a marriage between the

1. Missing in transcript.

infanta and a son of the king of Portugal: its effect considered very doubtful here.

Yesterday his highness and his court, with the whole council, observed another private day of prayer, with four sermons one after the other.]

Bonde to Charles X

IX

London, 31 August 1655

Since my last letter I have done my best to advance my business here; and to that end have demanded of Thurloe that my commissioners should have another meeting with me so that we can get to grips with things. Besides, I wanted a chance to talk for once with Thurloe alone. I had previously indicated my wish for such an interview,[1] for it is principally he who transacts all business with the protector; and he is besides a pretty intelligent man, and well disposed to Y.M. He therefore met me last Tuesday in St James's Park at 4 o'clock in the afternoon. I then spoke to him more openly than to any of the others, laying much stress on the common interests of Y.M. and the protector, [explaining them] clearly and at length; and offered him, by way of binding this country still closer to Y.M., to give all the advantages which Y.M.'s half-free ships[2] enjoy above others in the Baltic trade, and particularly in the traffic of Russia, Livonia, Poland and Prussia; and of all these I gave him exact particulars (exaggerating the value of the concessions). [I said] it provided a means whereby that large and important trade could, for the most part, be diverted into their hands; in return for which all that Y.M. asked of the protector was that he should come to Y.M.'s assistance with a number of ships in the event of the Baltic's being disturbed by anyone else.

He took all this well enough, and gave me the strongest assurances of the constant and sincere friendship of his highness towards Y.M.; and [said that] since I had spoken so openly to him he would do the same by me. He described how many advantageous alliances had been offered to his highness, and how he had been unwilling to accept

1. Bonde's letter is in Thurloe, iii. 736. Abbott (iii. 814) links it to Charles X's proposal that England should lend him twenty warships; but this does not appear from the text.

2. By an Ordinance of 1645 Swedish merchantmen, if adequately armed, and manned by Swedish crews, were to be 'wholly free'; others who did not quite come up to this standard were to be 'half-free': i.e., the former to enjoy a reduction of one-third, and the latter of one-sixth, of the ordinary duties payable: text in Stiernman, *Samling utaf ... stadgar ... aug ... Sweriger ... commerca*, ii. 400 ff. Bonde's offer probably went beyond the terms of his instructions.

them lest they might prejudice Y.M. in any way; and he was prepared to tell me that Mr Whitelocke's embassy to Sweden had been intended to lead to a very strict alliance, which this country was more inclined to conclude with Y.M. than with any other ruler. As to the proposal I had made to him, he seemed to set a high value upon it, though he raised several difficulties: first, how one was to deal with the Dutch, who would undoubtedly resent it above all things, and might make a bargain with Denmark which would give them the same advantages over England as we were granting them over Holland; so that our design would fail of its object, for both of us. To this I answered that I could hardly think that the king of Denmark, in the existing state of affairs, would presume so openly to offend England, in violation of the treaties between them; and that even if it meant that it might cost England a war with Denmark, Y.M. would in that case intervene to secure their freedom of navigation. He then remarked that it was nevertheless a matter for consideration that if the Dutch, for whom this proposal would be a great blow to their trade, saw that they could not rely on England and Sweden, they would look for other expedients and ally with other potentates (and by this, as I could see, he meant France, with whom they are still on an extremely bad footing by reason of the persecution of the protestants in Savoy, and of the Huguenots in France) and so take some kind of hostile action against us. In such a case what was to be done if we did not cooperate more closely, and provide for all such eventualities? I replied that what he had said was of great importance; but since Y.M. at the time of my departure could not be sure (in view of the stories that were being put about) what the attitude here might be, he could not give me orders which extended further than I had detailed them; but that I was desirous of knowing what his highness's intentions might be, and when I knew that I would do my best to see that Y.M. took such further action as he might find conducive to the general interest.

He then changed the subject, and told me in confidence that North Holland, as well as Zeeland, had protested to the States-General against the fitting out of a fleet to go to the Baltic, and that therefore Y.M. for this year had hardly any ground for apprehension.[1] He promised to convey all this to his highness, and especially the idea of a general defensive alliance of protestants, and to let me know his highness's reaction, either himself, or through my commissioners. Moreover he talked a good deal of the designs of the catholics, and of the present pope, and said that his highness was well informed about

---

1. Thurloe's information was correct, as far as it went; and in the end the convoy-fleet sailed only as the result of a compromise, designed to appease the opposition in Zeeland, by which it was to have no official character: Kolkert, *Nederland en het Zweedsche Imperialisme*, pp. 26–8, 159–64.

their activities, and was moreover dissatisfied with the disadvantageous peace which the protestants of Savoy had been forced to agree to.

I then raised the question of recruiting, and [urged] that at the least Cranstoun might have leave to raise 2000 men, so that the world might see that his highness was giving real evidence of his friendship for Y.M., and might consequently frighten [Y.M's enemies] off from their evil proceedings. He promised to let me know how the matter stood; and with that we separated. I now await his answer every day.

Yesterday I visited Mr Whitelocke at Chelsea, and with him also I spoke very frankly. I learned that his highness had refused him leave to go into the country, since his presence here is necessarily required for the business with Sweden. He tried his best to convince me of England's friendship, and demonstrated how on the contrary no dependence could be placed on the Dutch; for they were mere merchants who attached little importance to generosity and honour, but allowed their interest and profit to draw them on—contrary to *datam fidem*—to offend their friends; of which we had had sufficient experience. But England, on the other hand, was—like Sweden—ruled by a king: although [the office] had not yet that name, yet it was a kingship *in re vera,* and soon would be so in fact. For only a king can rule England; and [Englishmen] could well see how ill their affairs went during the little time that they were a republic. Moreover, both countries had a splendid and honourable nobility, many even of their merchants being sometimes noblemen, and therefore both could rely with confidence on any promise once given.

From this I brought him to a conversation on the Russia trade, showed him the situation on the map, and pointed out its value to us both. He received this information, with other things I was able to tell him about the trade, with considerable attention. Although I have as yet had no categorical declaration of the protector's attitude, it seems to me that things have nearly reached the point when I need to be instructed on these matters by Y.M.; for what I most deplore is that I cannot be sure what line to take on this subject. On the one hand I am led, by what my small understanding of the matter leads me to judge to be the interest of Y.M. in the friendship of this country, to take care that their inclinations in that direction be not allowed to grow cold, and perhaps take an unfavourable turn; on the other I lack accurate information as to Y.M.'s wishes—especially now, when the welcome successes with which God has blessed Y.M. may possibly give Y.M. occasion in some measure to amplify his designs. I entreat Y.M. to look with indulgence upon my efforts: I shall manage the matter with all possible caution, and with the greatest fidelity, to the best purpose I am able; and if I should either write with too much presumption, or happen not to shape my actions as Y.M. could wish, Y.M. may be assured that I shall never do so deliberately, and that my only intention and desire is to execute Y.M.'s gracious commands, and to serve him as faithfully as I can.

First: I ask to be informed of Y.M.'s attitude to the defence of the cause of religion in general; and if it should be that Y.M. is in any way inclined to it, to receive full instructions as to what Y.M. wishes to demand of this country, how far Y.M. is willing to oblige them, and any other point on which Y.M. may find it necessary to command me. (2) Y.M.'s attitude to an offensive and defensive alliance, not only concerning religion, but in regard to Holland, Denmark, Germany, France etc. (for I find that here they are much disposed to it), and what conditions Y.M. would be stipulating for, in such a case. (3) Should Y.M. not be pleased to go so far, if any complications should arise with Holland and Denmark (or those who might ally with them) as a consequence of my negotiations here, what attitude I am to take, and what answer I am to make to their observations. (4) As far as I can see, this seems to be the best moment to attempt to draw in the Russia trade through the Baltic, whose value Y.M. well knows to be of such dimensions that scarcely any other trade is to be compared to it. The facilities Y.M. can offer this country to get the greater part of that trade into their hands, as also the injury they consider themselves to have suffered from the Russians, have an inspiriting effect upon them, and make me think that it might be extremely useful if I were to stimulate the protector to send an embassy to Russia, and by the interposition of a mediator as powerful (and at the moment as redoubtable) as Y.M., to force them to agree to the following terms: (i) that both the English and the Swedes be given unhampered liberty of trade in and through Russia according to the tenour of the old agreements; (ii) that they may have their free houses and market-places in Moscow, Jaroslav, Novgorod and Pskov; (iii) that the Russians may of course not prohibit the export of goods to the Baltic; (iv) that if a fixed duty be agreed upon, to be paid in Novgorod and Pskov, the Great Prince be not permitted to increase it, to the burdening of commodities; with a threat that if they are unwilling to agree, then the Englishmen will harass Archangel by sea (in which case Y.M. might have something to say to the question, and I fear that the great progress the Russians have made in Lithuania, and their approach to the Baltic, may well provide the occasion for it);[1] but if these terms were to be accepted, I fancy that the Archangel trade would shortly wither away, and the whole trade be drawn to Y.M.'s harbours in the Baltic, to the very great advantage of Y.M. and his subjects.

1. The Russians had invaded Poland in 1654, had overrun Lithuania, and in the spring of 1655 had entered Polish Livonia, and were in alarming proximity to Riga.

I really cannot see that any danger to Y.M. would follow if I urged this with discretion, especially through exaggerating the value of the staple-rights which Y.M. would then grant to England; but I shall not, in this matter or in any other, express myself too unreservedly before Y.M.'s orders can reach me. I see that in the letters which Y.M. sent to me from Alt-Stettin on the 28th, and from Damm on the 31st of July, some words on the importance of England's friendship are included, from which I judge that my ideas are not altogether different from those of Y.M.

Last Tuesday I sent off Per Bonde with a letter to Y.M. and a full account of everything; since then he has had a good wind, and I hope will soon be in Hamburg. From there he will make all speed by day and night to Y.M., since I am exceedingly anxious for an answer. He has with him in the same ship some horses from Herr Coyet for Y.M.: I hope they travel well. The *boijort* which brought the elks here[1] could no doubt have taken the horses over, but the skipper had already been paid for them, and was not to be persuaded to hand them over. The last two posts have brought me no letters from Y.M., nor any news that my letters have reached him.

X

London, 7 September 1655 [from Bonde's *Register*]

Since my last of 31 August nothing of consequence has taken place in regard to my negotiation, his highness having been this week so out of sorts that he is said to have been unable to attend to any business.[2] I have let Thurloe know, through General [George] Fleetwood, and also through my secretary, that I am somewhat dissatisfied that my negotiation makes such slow progress, it being now a fortnight since the commissioners were with me; though [in fact] I am not sorry that there is some delay, since it gives me a chance to receive Y.M.'s answer to my letter before I get very far with them. Yesterday his highness sent Fleming to me with apologies for the delay: it had no other cause than his highness's illness; and since it is now to be expected that he is upon the mending hand my business is to be given serious attention. I wish that the letter which I wrote by the last post may come safely to Y.M.: in it I dealt with matters in some detail, in consequence of a conversation which I had had with Secretary Thurloe some days before. In the meantime General Fleetwood has spoken of the

1. Presents of elks and reindeer frequently occur in Swedish diplomacy: they were curiosities from a country not over-endowed with such things.

2. Bonde's *Diarium* notes, under 29 August, 'Cromwell unwell', and under 1–3 September, 'protector very ill'.

recruiting, and other concerns of ours, in various quarters—among others, to Sir Henry, the Protector's eldest son [*sic*], to General Lambert, and to Thurloe, and told them some home truths; but it seems that the Dutch lay themselves out to put obstacles in our way, as Thurloe frankly confessed to him. They have a strong party here, and in the council there are many who are good Dutchmen and do all they can to hinder Y.M.'s service in this place.[1] Among other things they argue that they have recently had an expensive and difficult war with the Dutch, that there is now peace between them, and that therefore it would be extremely ill-advised to provoke them again, they lying so close at hand and able to be very troublesome at sea.

I think that there can scarcely be any place where it is more difficult for a great minister to act than here; for he is cut off from all contact with those whose word carries weight in the government. And to call on Thurloe at his house, as the Dutch ambassador does, like any other private solicitant, I account as an indignity to Y.M.'s honour and reputation. However, it must soon become clear what their intentions are: I fancy that they have still not made up their minds as to what they want to do; for though the protector himself, and some others who are good patriots, and have some grasp of affairs, place the highest value upon Y.M.'s friendship and the great advantages which would accrue to England in terms of the proposals I made to them, the Dutch party oppose it tooth and nail: I hope to be able to give Y.M. a better account by the next post. The Dutch here also made a great pother [*exaggererat*] about Y.M.'s proclamation on religion;[2] but both Fleetwood and I have taken every opportunity to remove any scruples on that score from their minds. Four days ago Whitelocke was called up to the council to give his opinion on these matters; but since I had briefed him beforehand on all of them he argued for England's interest in Y.M.'s friendship as well as possible: time will show with what effect. As soon as the protector is admitting visitors

---

1. In conversations with Thurloe on 20 and 27 August NS Nieupoort argued that Bonde was simply trying to gain time; suggested that England, France and Holland might jointly intervene to end the Polish war, as they had done in Altmark in 1629; and urged a quick and secret alliance with Denmark. Thurloe asked why England should engage in an alliance which might easily lead to a war to defend the elector of Brandenburg, 'who hates us, and has recently offered Charles II 3000 men if he can provide a landing-place'?: would it not be better first to try persuasion with Charles X, get him to agree to a treaty pledging him not to disturb trade, and then, perhaps, a quadruple alliance with Denmark, Sweden and the Dutch? To which Nieupoort replied that Denmark must be 'animated' in the meantime. And Thurloe conceded (or professed to concede) that Sweden was only 'amusing' England: *Brieven*, iii. 107, 112.

2. See *infra*, p. 152, *n* 1.

I shall see if I cannot come to him myself, and will use my best efforts to bring him over to Y.M. as far as possible.

Y.M.'s letter of 13 August, from Gnesen, came safe to me by this post, and I shall take care to comply precisely with Y.M.'s commands contained in it: God be praised, who sustains Y.M. and daily blesses his noble plans: may He continue so to do, and to grant them His constant grace and benediction.

Should the protector or his commissioners suggest to me any substantial proposal, of a nature that demands Y.M.'s resolution upon it, I was thinking of allowing Herr Coyet to take it to Y.M. in person: now that I am here he has no useful function to perform, but lies here as a burden upon Y.M.; and it gives our ill-wishers cause for *médisance* that we have four different ministers from Y.M. in this place [simultaneously]. I have no means of knowing whether my letters have yet reached Y.M.

XI

London, 13 September 1655

Although this time I have nothing particular to tell Y.M. beyond what I previously intimated, I could not neglect writing something to accompany the messenger, Mr James Wemyss, who carries this letter at his earnest request. He was formerly the [late] king's general of artillery, and before that was employed for a good while in the service of the Swedish crown; but—like all others that served the king—has been much persecuted; and he therefore intends to make his way to Y.M., in accordance with Y.M.'s gracious commands in his letter to Herr Coyet.

In my business here I make mighty little progress; and since my talk with Secretary Thurloe I have not been able to get speech with any of this government. His highness, through Sir Oliver Fleming and Secretary Thurloe, has made many apologies to my secretary on his behalf, assuring him that the delay has no other cause than the indisposition which has been troubling him for the last fortnight. And since I see that the Dutch try *directe* and *indirecte* to denigrate all Y.M.'s actions and make a great business of the Ordinance on religion which Y.M. has issued in Sweden;[1] and spread a story of how harshly Y.M.

---

1. Nieupoort to de Witt, 20 August NS 1655: *Brieven*, iii. 107. In June 1655 Charles X, anxious to rally the clergy to the support of his war, issued a Statute of Religion which would have prohibited calvinist religious services. The Swedish council of state decided on 22 November to postpone its publication: as Per Brahe remarked, 'Herr Christer Bonde is already in England, negotiating with the protector; and if news of this got about ... that would undoubtedly greatly hamper the aforesaid ambassador in his negotiations, so that he might not be able to obtain from the protector what he otherwise might have had good hopes of; for in this connexion it is well known how

has treated the protestants in Poland; and since moreover they [the Dutch] have many in the council who favour their cause, and counter-mine *quibuscunque artibus* anything that tends to Y.M.'s service; I have therefore determined to seek an interview with the lord protector himself, and put the case to him as well and as plainly as I can: which I feel confident will not fail to bear good fruit. I have been promised that I may go to him before this post leaves, provided his state of health can bear it.

XII

London, 14 September 1655

Although I have not failed, with all possible courtesy, to request a private audience with the protector, and he has not only granted it but indicated that he would himself be very glad to talk with me, nothing so far has come of it. He pleads his indisposition, and on his behalf both Fleming and Secretary Thurloe strongly affirm that this is the only reason why it has not taken place so far. With that I must be satisfied; though I believe that his sickness lies mostly in the ill success of most of his enterprises. From what I have been able to learn, I judge that his plans have been based on the following ideas: that since the English nation has always been accustomed to contribute very little or nothing to the public service, and the revenues of former kings have come from royal estates scattered here and there through-out the country, together with the Great Customs, and the Wardships of the minor children of the nobility which were in the king's hands (apart from subsidies, which were rarely granted, and only in case of urgent need, and whose yield did not go very far); and since these means proved inadequate during the last troubles, a great excise was laid upon the country, and in addition a tax which all inhabitants— earls, knights, noblemen, burghers, peasants and officials alike—are forced to pay; it being levied on their estates and all movable and immovable property according to an estimate and valuation made by persons deputed for that purpose, or by the owners themselves. And he sees very well that these great extraordinary impositions cannot possibly continue for very long, since everybody, whether in town or country, finds himself oppressed by them, especially now that the country is not engaged in any open war. In order, therefore, to strengthen his own position and that of the public finances, he has

---

much the aforesaid protector took to heart the persecuting of the Waldensians by the duke of Savoy ...': *RRP.*, xvi. 278. But on 1 May 1656, in consequence of orders from Charles dated 7 March, the council ordered the immediate publication of the Statute: *ibid.*, 455.

been anxiously considering how to augment the revenues of the crown without burdening the people of England. He has therefore used every effort to increase the population of Ireland, and to organize and regulate its government in the best way; since as a result of the late troubles the majority of those who owned land are driven off it, or slaughtered, and their lands in consequence have passed to the hands of the government, under the name of confiscation; and these he is trying to develop to yield the maximum yearly income. For some years his [Lord Deputy] was Sir Charles Fleetwood, brother to General Fleetwood, who is accounted here to be one of the ablest men England has; and now he has sent his own son, Sir Henry Cromwell, to be there as Vice Roy [*sic*].

These plans lay behind Penn's fleet also, which was an enterprise to capture Hispaniola, and so make that country a source of revenue to the crown. So too the purpose of Blake's [fleet] was to surprise the silver-fleet, and by that means to pay off the debts of the state, which are said by some to be very great. These two last projects are now thought not to have been fortunate for him. For Penn and Venables have come back home; and though it is given out among the populace that Jamaica is of great value, the reverse appears to be true; and those that have returned from that expedition speak very ill of the protector, and of the great sufferings they were exposed to. So that this great expedition is considered to have been as good as a failure; and despite the fact that reinforcements have been sent out, there are said to be not more than 4000 men there, in a wretched condition, incapable of withstanding Spanish forces from Hispaniola, Cuba and Nova Hispania, or the *flota* which has been assembled in Spain and is despatched against them. With Blake things are not much better. The silver-fleet has not yet arrived, and the king of Spain has meanwhile fitted out a strong fleet to defend the silver-ships; so that it is feared that very little will come of this grand design. Both these misfortunes are the more sensibly felt because they do incalculable damage to the reputation of the protector, who had hitherto been considered so prudent and fortunate that no disaster could occur which he could not provide against, nor any enterprise so great that he could not bring it to a fortunate issue. And so, the whole country being discontented, they reproach him with [these failures] and complain loudly that he oppresses the country with the aforesaid great taxes and excise, applies them to such useless expenditures, and does not pay the country's debts. From all of which I judge that the position of his government is much worse than it appears to be; and though they can see very well that Y.M.'s friendship would be to their interest and advantage, and may wish for it, they nevertheless do not venture to do anything to offend their closest neighbour the Dutch. And if, in desperation at the danger which they [*sc.* the Dutch] apprehend in the Baltic and at the fact that they have little good to expect of England, they should once again seriously espouse the king of Scotland's party, it is feared that this country, which is not well content with the present government, might adhere to them, and thereby new and greater conflicts be provoked. No doubt Y.M. will have learned from Herr Appelboom's letters how the Dutchmen view the protector's declining fortunes.

In these circumstances it seems that my best course for the present is to give them occasional encouragement, so that they do not conclude that I have altered my opinions, and indeed I do not mind the fact that things go on somewhat slowly: it enables me to see how matters may develop here, and also how far God may be pleased to bless Y.M.'s arms—which will undoubtedly be decisive for determining policy both here and in Holland. In the meantime I hope to receive an answer from Y.M. to the letters I sent over with Per Bonde (I see that he arrived in Hamburg on the 4th of this month); and for the present be satisfied with having [prevented them from aligning themselves with] Holland and Denmark *etc.* And since as a result the Dutch have been deprived of any hope of that, it is clear that they must alter their policies and reconcile themselves with Y.M.; for I find it difficult to believe that they would venture to engage in any overt action if the people here were not at one with them in it: already they are beginning to take a lower tone, and to say that they did not really mean it in regard to the fleet for the Sound, but will let things take their course for this year. As far as I can judge, from one thing and another, the best thing the Dutch can do is to seek such advantage for their country as they can get, in friendship with Y.M.; and as I am afraid that Y.M. will not be able to avoid fresh complications in other quarters, I think it would be useful that they, at least, should not be our enemies.

As I write this, Sir Oliver Fleming comes to me and tells me he is sent by his highness to say that although he feels very unwell, and is unable to stand, or to talk much about business, his respect for Y.M., and his affection to my person are so great, that if I pressed the point he was willing to allow me to come to him this afternoon; with many other compliments. To which I answered that I was far from being so discourteous as to wish to incommode his highness in any way; but that I very much wished to put my thoughts before his highness with all clarity and sincerity; and as I had gathered from Secretary Thurloe that he was disposed to receive them, I had requested that it might be done before this post went off, but only on the understanding that our meeting took place at a time that suited him; and I therefore asked him to make this clear to his highness, and to tell him that it was for him to select such time and hour as might best suit him, for that would always be convenient to me. This he took with great satisfaction; and all our conversations confirm me in what I have previously written to Y.M. And in particular that they seem well disposed to a general religious system; of which I have already written to Y.M. at some length.

Coyet to Charles X

34

London, 14 September 1655 [in German]

[Penn's return to England with sixteen ships. He recently appeared before the protector at Whitehall and gave an account of his actions in the West Indies: in what state he left Jamaica, the condition of the men and ships there, the fact that he had delegated the command of the ships remaining to Vice-Admiral Goodson, and the command of the 6000 troops which still survived to Colonel Fortescue, though many doubt this last particular. A ship, *Paragon*, caught fire through carelessness while lying off Cuba, and was abandoned, with 100 men on board.[1] General Venables also arrived here on 9 September, very ill: Penn and Venables are said to be on bad terms.

The 27 Spanish warships ordered to protect the silver-fleet keep Blake under observation: according to reports here they are a strong force. Their admiral is Don Paulus de Contereda, and the vice-admiral the duke of Medina. The fleet carries 11,400 men and almost 1000 guns, more than 500 of them brass; and has ten fireships.

The long-expected Venetian embassy has arrived; and the ambassador, Sagredo, is now in London, but incognito pending his finding a house to suit him: when he has done so he will make the usual ceremonial entry.

Major-General [Charles] Fleetwood is on his way here from Ireland; his brother, Major-General [George] Fleetwood (who is in the Swedish service) has left in order to meet him.

Unusually rainy weather, which has done much damage to hay and corn: prices may be expected to rise shortly, and a year of scarcity to follow.]

---

1. *Cf. The Narrative of General Venables*, p. 167.

Bonde to Charles X

XIII

London, 21 September 1655[1]

Since my last there has arrived news of the greatest consequence: namely, that the king of Spain has taken action against all the English merchants and their property, as Y.M. will see from the attached *Relation*.[2] This will mean open war between this country and Spain, and will undoubtedly entail a great change in their policies: among other things it will oblige them to caress Y.M. more than they have done hitherto, especially since they might thereby be able to draw Y.M. into a war with the emperor, and consequently to embrace, *unitis viribus*, the cause of protestantism generally—not to that cause's advantage only, but also to them in their private war with Spain, should Y.M. engage a considerable portion of the forces of the House of Austria by a diversion in Germany. They talk here, moreover, of what a great service they did to Y.M. this year by retarding the silver-fleet; as a result of which Spain could send no money to help the emperor, and the emperor in turn had neither the forces nor the means to help the king of Poland against Y.M., as they maintain he would assuredly have done if the money had arrived from Spain. However that may be, and whatever effect it may have had, it can hardly be reckoned as an instance of good-will; for the object of [Blake's] fleet was not Y.M.'s service but their own profit—though the two powerful fleets which they have kept at sea all this summer have in fact brought them not profit but damage and disgrace. Which particularly rejoices the malignants in this country, who say that the glory of the protector has now attained its apogee, and expect that his fortune is now upon the decline. I learnt to-day that Generals Penn and Venables are said to have been sent prisoners to the Tower, and some think that they stand in great danger of their lives.

His highness has just now, at 4 o'clock, informed me I might have a private audience. I have been asking for one for some time; but now, it seems, they wish in some degree to caress me, for the reasons I mentioned above. I have resolved to tell the truth pretty plainly: that I am afraid that Y.M.'s inclination to their friendship may be

---

1. On 30 September (NS) de Witt informed Nieupoort that the States-General had decided to send embassies to Sweden and to Denmark: the purpose of the latter being to invite the aid of Frederick III in restoring good relations between Sweden and Poland. De Witt feared that otherwise Denmark might be driven into alliance with Sweden: Thurloe, iv. 45; J. A. Fridericia, *Adelsvaeldens sidste Dage. Danmarks Historia fra Christian IVs Død Till Enevaeldens Indførelse* (Copenhagen 1894), pp. 222–3.
   2. Missing in transcript.

cooling, since they have not effectually obliged him either in the matter of the recruiting, or in any other way. By the last post I sent Y.M., in considerable detail, an account of the state of affairs in this country. I rather doubt whether they will risk accepting my proposals for fear of the Dutch, to whom they are certainly a matter of concern; but at the very least I hope to be able to ensure that they may sit still and give no support to those who do not wish well to Y.M.

In the meantime I hope that God may bless Y.M.'s arms, so that he may be master of Poland and Prussia and *ex consequenti* of Danzig. And if Y.M. has Holland's bread-basket, necessity will no doubt force them to give Y.M. good words and come to an amicable understanding with him. In which case it may perhaps be better that they [the English] should have obtained no favours from Y.M., but that he should have his hands free, and then be able to take such measures in that matter as he may find most advisable. It is now a long time since I had any letters from Y.M. or from the chancellor. I shall therefore try as far as possible to keep the protector aware of what Y.M. has been intending in his regard. And if so great an opportunity is missed, he may blame himself and those about him, and need not expect to have the chance of it a second time.

Coyet to Charles X

35

London, 21 September 1655 [in German]

[A lieutenant newly arrived from Blake's fleet reports that the two fleets are keeping each other under observation, but no hostilities yet. A Spanish captain went to Blake to inform him that their only object was to defend the silver-fleet: he was courteously received.[1] The lieutenant reported that the English fleet was in great need of provisioning, and might therefore be forced to return to England. Unconfirmed reports of the arrest of all English merchants in Spain: a general rupture to be presumed, if true.

Penn and Venables, after appearing before the protector to give an account of their actions, are both sent to the Tower (each blaming the other) for not obeying orders.

Reported to-day that the protector has shut all the ports: no entry without pass, especially from Holland; quarantine for fourteen days, for fear of the plague.]

1. *Cf.* Corbett, *England in the Mediterranean*, i. 316.

P.S. [in Swedish]
I humbly beg Y.M. that I may have an answer to my letter, so that I may know what Y.M. wishes—in particular, whether I am to remain here longer, or not; and likewise from what source I am to obtain money, both for my maintenance and for payment of the sum I lent to Commissioner Bonnel, and for which I have pledged my credit to others; for living in this uncertainty will be ruinous to me. I learn that G. Drakenhielm is not paying the amount assigned to me by Y.M.'s Exchequer Chamber, as he undertook to do, and his acquittance for it properly given, but is paying his own debts with it. This leaves me totally stranded; and I beg Y.M. most humbly that I may be provided with a bill drawn on Resident Möller, or someone else in Hamburg, irrespective of whether Y.M.'s orders are to stay longer, or to go to him with a report on the state of affairs here. I await, with submission, Y.M.'s reply. As to the situation in this country, and the policies they pursue, his excellency the ambassador will be writing at length, and I therefore humbly refer Y.M. to his letter.

Bonde to Charles X

XIV

London, 28 September 1655

Last Friday, which was post-day, I had a private audience with his highness, and since I could not manage on that day to let Y.M. know how it went I was obliged to defer an account of it until this post. The audience went well, as I hoped that it might; not least because his highness caused all the rest of those members of the council who were with him to retire, and spoke to me with only Thurloe present. I had asked for this beforehand, for their presence on the previous occasion had restrained me from expressing my thoughts to him as I had intended.

After congratulating him on his restoration to health, and other courtesies, we both sat down, and I began (covered) to expatiate on Y.M.'s constant desire for a friendly relationship with his highness and the English nation, and how that he was minded, through me, to concede to them very substantial commercial advantages. I then proceeded to specify them, and mentioned that they were to be enjoyed in Livonia and Prussia; and I pitched their value very high (which is indeed the truth), and depicted the indubitable effects which would follow, as proved by our own experience. I then went in some detail into the value of the trade to those parts, how that value to them would increase, and how as a result the strength of our ill-wishers would diminish. I turned next to the Russia trade, and presented Y.M.'s offer of a free staple in Narva, taking occasion (as of myself) to remind them that now would be the best time to settle their controversies with the Russians, since Y.M. was now in negotiation with them,[1] and would be in a position to use his weight as a mediator in such a way as to be of great assistance to England; and I pointed out what I thought it was necessary that they should demand of the Russians in regard to the channelling of trade to the Baltic; as I believe I mentioned to Y.M. some time ago. From that, I began to dilate on the persistent efforts of the Dutch to sow ill-will between Y.M. and him, with the object of depriving us of that intimate and confidential intercourse and friendship which constitutes the strength of both of us, and subsequently of seizing any opportunity that may offer to ruin us, one after the other; so that if things went as badly [as they desire] England's main advantage would perhaps be what Polyphemus promised Ulysses: *ut ultimus comederetur*. And since among other things they had adduced the proclamation on religion which Y.M. caused to be issued before he left Sweden, I thought it necessary to remove any scruples he might have felt on that score; and did so, at some length: which I think it necessary to retail to Y.M. Among other things I laid particular stress on the happiness Y.M. and his realms enjoy in virtue of their religious unity, which so binds the hearts of Y.M.'s subjects together that they work together in harmony in the service of the common cause; and in a few words hinted at the troubles other countries could avoid if that *vinculum* were firm and enduring: a point which might tell the more with him since he knows that one of the greatest sources of England's miseries is the confusion that has arisen from having so many religions; from which *fonte dissidiorum* all the rest has followed, and which is still the greatest source of difficulty to the government. I likewise removed any scruple that they [the Dutch] might have fabricated as to Y.M.'s ill-treatment of those of the reformed religion in Poland, which I demonstrated to be a blatant *mensonge*.

I then came a little nearer home, and showed him what dangers England might have to expect if a powerful Dutch fleet, in union with Denmark, were to enter the Baltic;[2] and how in such a case their main object would be to obtain a harbour in the Baltic through a treaty

---

1. A large embassy, headed by Gustaf Bielke, had been sent to Russia in July with secret instructions to 'amuse' the tsar with plans for a partition of Poland, but on no account to conclude any binding engagement: Sten Bonnesen, *Karl X Gustaf*, pp. 78–9. So far from being 'amused' the tsar very soon imprisoned them.

2. On 10 September NS Nieupoort reported that Thurloe had told him that he had heard that Denmark had promised that no warships would be permitted to pass the Sound. De Witt's reply (17 September NS) was silent on this point: *Brieven*, iii. 118–19.

with Brandenburg; and that if it came about that they established themselves firmly there, though Sweden could hold its own, having formerly been able to manage without such places, England would not only lose the advantages which were now available to them, but her whole trade to the Baltic would be endangered; and if (as I could not doubt) the expansion and enterprise of Holland would be a formidable thing for them [the English], I could assure him that the conquest of the entire East Indies would not be of more use to them [the Dutch] than a position of this sort in the Baltic.

Apart from this, and other reasons which I advanced in support of [the proposal], I bore testimony in warm terms (*medh mouvante ordh*) to my affection to his highness and this country; and I frankly confessed that I was afraid that the industrious attempts of the Dutch to make the protector and his actions suspect to Y.M. might be so far effective as to cool Y.M.'s desire for their friendship. I pointed out also that they write quite openly that they have taken such measures to prevent the success of Y.M.'s recruiting here that his highness had said that he would wait seven or eight years before coming to a decision, since he did not need to make one in order to have regard to Y.M.'s actions; that I knew quite well that this was not the truth, but merely their *artificia*; but all the same, since their words agreed with their actions, I feared that they might be able to make some impression on Y.M.'s mind; especially now, when God had so signally blessed his arms and enterprises. I mentioned too that the rumour was in circulation that Brandenburg hoped for some assistance from him [the protector]; and I therefore begged his highness to turn over all this in his mind and adopt such policies as he might find necessary to the strength and welfare of us both.

To this he answered, at some length, that it was with much gratification that he had received Y.M.'s offers, which he felt were so great, and of such importance, that they valued them most highly; and so began to protest his affection to Y.M. and his earnest desire for his friendship. He then laid bare, in the greatest confidence, the *fundamenta* of all his policies; which were directed to no other ends that *libertatem religionis* and freedom of trade. He spoke first of Spain, and how he could have come to an understanding with them on all other points, if only the English in that country could have been safe from the Inquisition; but upon this it had been impossible to reach agreement. It was the same with Portugal, with whom an alliance had indeed been concluded; but *ecclesiastici* in that country had afterwards made alterations in the terms which he had been unable to accept; though he thought that they would nevertheless come round to [his] terms. As to France, the situation had been such that neither Tunis nor Algiers had done as much damage to English merchants in the Mediterranean as they have, so that he was bound to take strong action against them in that quarter; and he confessed that although both the one and the other have for a long time as good as begged peace of him, he was not prepared to accept it without regard to the two fundamentals to which he had alluded. He went on to say that the protestant powers were a mere handful in comparison with the catholics; and if God had not miraculously sown discord between the catholics themselves, he could not see how the protestants would have been able to defend themselves against them. He then recapitulated my proposal regarding trade in the Baltic; said that he was extremely appreciative of it and greatly obliged to Y.M.; and that he would give it the careful consideration which it warranted. As to the Dutch, he said that if Y.M. pleased he was willing to intervene with Ambassador Nieupoort to hinder their design and to resolve, in a spirit of amity, any difference that might have arisen. As to what Nieupoort had reported to the effect that he was suspicious and envious of Y.M.'s successes, and also in regard to contacts with Brandenburg, he could assure me that nothing of the kind had ever been the case, and he took Secretary Thurloe to witness—as 'a man as well acquainted with all my affairs as I am myself'—that he had never so far forgotten himself; for he had always desired, and would desire, that God would always bless Y.M., as one of the greatest supports of the Protestant Cause; and so far from being chagrined, he would rather wish that Y.M.'s armies should be so successful in that quarter that their limits might reach to the Caspian Sea, or beyond it. And so ended with professions of respect and friendship for Y.M.; adding that he was now better able to give me assurances on all these matters, since he had in the meantime pondered them and consulted about them; and finally expressed a particular regard for myself.

To this I responded with profuse expressions of gratitude for his agreeable answer. In regard to the common cause of religion, I had previously gone so far as to express to Secretary Thurloe how anxious I was to know his highness's intention therein (as I previously wrote to Y.M. at some length), and would therefore trouble his highness with that no longer; but this only I would say, that the catholics could never obtain a greater advantage than by inciting the protestants against each other. I was in some doubt about giving a categorical answer to his offer of interposition, mainly because I was afraid that it was designed to put him in the position of a mediator of some kind between Y.M. and the Dutch. I was afraid that this might not be acceptable to Y.M., since the Dutch might be glad of it in the hope of obtaining terms (relative to England) in the trade to Prussia which they would hardly get otherwise. Moreover, I have no instructions from Y.M. in the matter. However, since Y.M. in his orders to Herr

Coyet expressed a wish that the protector should try to divert the Dutch designs in the Baltic, I answered that as far as Y.M. was aware he had no quarrel with them, much less any hostile intentions towards them, that he would undoubtedly be very glad that his highness should attempt to divert them, and that I did not doubt that Y.M. would wish it and would take it well. And so we ended, with mutual compliments on both sides, among which he said that as I had manifested my personal attachment to him and the English nation, and had been willing to deal with him as honestly as if I were an Englishman myself, he was minded in the like manner to treat me as a Swede rather than as an Englishman. And finally, I recommended to him the cases of Cranstoun and of the Irish bishop;[1] and so took my leave, for I perceived that he was not strong enough to talk further with me. Though he had previously given some hope about the recruiting, I was unwilling to touch on that question further than I had done already, since he was sufficiently aware of my views; but postponed it to a conversation which I had to-day with Secretary Thurloe. To whom (after some compliments—of which the chief was that he had condescended to visit me at my house, which is something he would hardly do for anyone else) I said that the main reason why I desired to talk with him was that there was something in the protector's last remarks that I could not understand as well as I could wish, and would be glad if he would explain to me. First, how far, and by what means, his highness thought he might intervene to prevent Holland's designs in the Baltic; and next, how—in regard to recruiting or any other matter—I was to take his highness's words 'that he was now in a position to give me a better answer than before, since he had carefully pondered and deliberated about it'. To which he replied that as to the first point he had not discussed it with his highness since our previous conference, but that his highness had then thought that I would have broached the subject, and that he was minded to exchange views with me on the best way of doing it. As to the second point, he said that his highness's meaning had been to make it clear to me that he was now disposed to permit Cranstoun's recruiting in accordance with our last request, pending an agreement on further recruiting on such terms and conditions as we might propose.[2] To this I answered that on that occasion I did not immediately understand his highness's intention, and therefore could not answer him otherwise than I did; but I could now tell him that as Y.M. had never given any offence to the Dutch, and did not intend to do so in the future, he was not conscious of any points of difference

1. I have not been able to identify the Irish bishop.
2. Bonde's *Diarium* for 28 September reads: 'Talked with Secretary Thurloe; *et veniam largitus est de conducendis militibus in Scotia*'.

with them. But since the rumour which had recently been circulating (that they wished to send a fleet of war to the Baltic) seemed to be a matter of great concern to his highness, both because of the great harm it would do to the protestant interest from the disunion which would inevitably follow from the despatch of such a fleet, and also because of the disturbance of trade which would be its consequence, [I said] that his highness was bound *vi pactorum* to help to prevent it by such means as could be agreed upon between us. If his highness, therefore, should be pleased to indicate to Ambassador Nieupoort that such an expedition was not agreeable to him, and should by that means attempt to prevent it, I was certain that Y.M. would not only take it for a friendly action, but would in return demonstrate by all practicable and possible means that the policy of the Dutch was completely unjust; and that it would be better for them if, as our old allies, they put whatever request they might have to make to Y.M., and then sought to get what they wanted by amicable agreement, rather than by proceeding to a rupture, which is usually regarded as an extreme measure, to be taken only when all other means have been tried. For the permission to recruit I gave him very many thanks, and hoped that all might conduce to the honour of God and the welfare of both our countries: as to the detailed arrangements I would refer them to General [George] Fleetwood, who would put him in mind of what was still to be done. He answered that he would convey to his highness my views on what might be said [to Nieupoort], and had no doubt that he would come to a satisfactory resolution upon them. We had, in fact, a long discussion on these matters; and I hope that all will go smoothly.

We then spoke of their trade with the Muscovites, and how this was a moment at which they might consider Y.M.'s mediation. He assured me that this, like my other proposals, was now under consideration in the council, and that I would soon be dealing with my commissioners: I pressed this last point a little, saying however that I did not wish to be importunate, but referred it to their convenience, not least because I might in the meantime have a letter from Y.M. At this we rose; and after I had reminded him of some particular points—as for instance of Cranstoun and the English [*sic*] bishop— he began to talk of the news which had arrived by this post of Wittenberg's great victory over the Poles, saying that Field-Marshal Count Wittenberg and Königsmarck's son were now *qwätze*.[1] He then

---

1. *Svenska Akademiens Ordbok* gives the meaning of this word as (i) injure, wound, hurt; (ii) oppress, repress, humiliate. Neither seems appropriate here. Neither Wittenberg nor Königsmarck was wounded at Ujście, which was a short encounter which terminated in the capitulation of the Poles. It might apply if Thurloe was speaking ironically; but that does not seem likely. Johan Ekeblad (*Brev*, i. 428.) uses the word to describe how

told me, as it were in confidence, that the pope in Rome had had various meetings with the cardinals expressly [on account of] Y.M.'s great successes, which they felt to be of the greatest importance and danger to them. He told me too that not much trust could be placed in the French, who were full of jealousy of Y.M.; and that their defeat in Italy, and the raising of a citizen force at its own charges in the Spanish Netherlands, would force them to think about peace with Spain, and consequently to espouse the general interests of catholicism. Also, that Poland had offered to be a hereditary kingdom under the emperor if only he would assist them against Y.M.[1] As far as he [Thurloe] was concerned, he was delighted at the success of Y.M.'s arms; though he could assure me that this was not the view of everybody.[2] I thanked him warmly for his great confidence; told him what I had heard of Wittenberg's engagement; and, for the rest, that there could be no doubt that this Polish war could easily lead to some new confrontation, for great characters and good fortune are never without their *invidiosis*, which however was better than being an object of pity; and that God would bring all things to a good and happy ending. And with that we parted. I have been turning over in my mind this offer of the protector to intervene with the Dutch, and I cannot decide whether they may not be behind it. Now that they realize that no fleet can be fitted out, nor anything effected, this year, they see no more honourable way of abandoning a project which they have been

---

he felt *smothered* in the enormous English beds; but regularly uses it to mean 'wounded'. It seems likely that what Thurloe said was 'quits', and that Bonde's secretary mistook it for '*qwätze*'. Hans Christopher von Königsmarck had captured—on the very eve of peace—the 'New Town' of Prague, with immense booty. Wittenberg's bloodless victory at Ujście could be compared to this achievement only by way of flattery, and it leaves unexplained the reference to Königsmarck's son, who in 1648 was only 19.

1. After Wittenberg's victory at Ujście John Casimir on 22 July/1 August offered the Polish crown to Ferdinand III.

2. On 1 October (NS) Thurloe informed Nieupoort that Cromwell had been consulting 'with a few gentlemen who take part in the most secret and important deliberations' on the Baltic question. They found three difficulties: uncertainty as to Denmark's intentions; the elector of Brandenburg's dislike of England; the uncertain political situation in the United Provinces, where the Orange party appeared to be gaining strength. Cromwell wondered if the other provinces would not be prepared to follow Holland's example and pass an Act of Seclusion: which Nieupoort declared to be impossible. De Witt explained that as to Denmark, Frederick III wanted no more than 'an opportunity to obtain reparation for the damage and disasters sustained in the last war with Sweden', but would not give provocation 'unless and until the occasion should clearly arise': *Brieven*, iii. 125–30. Strickland subsequently informed Nieupoort that the 'few gentlemen' comprised himself, Lambert, Fiennes and Lawrence: *ibid.*, iii. 146. Thurloe was still brooding on the effectiveness of the Act of Seclusion as regarded Brandenburg in June 1656: Schlezer to elector, 13 June 1656, *Urk. und Act.*, vii. 752.

trumpeting for the whole year than by availing themselves of the pretext that they have changed their minds as a result of the protector's interposition; and thus (they reckon) they oblige him, and he in turn obliges Y.M. Whether this is the case, or whether it represents the protector's real thoughts, grounded upon the reasons which he has given, it comes to this: that this year there is no question of their expedition, and I hope that before the end of winter their former enthusiasm for it may have cooled, and that in the meantime Y.M. will have put himself in such a position in Poland that their policies will be forced to conform to the situation.

Coyet to Charles X

36

London, 28 September 1655 [in German]

[Thirty new warships fitted out, and to put to sea shortly: half to reinforce and revictual Blake; half to Sedgwick in the West Indies. Report that Monck is to be appointed admiral to succeed Penn; but it is doubted if he will accept, and Ayscue's appointment more likely. Penn and Venables were taken to the Tower through Traitor's Gate: an ominous sign.

English merchants to Spain have petitioned the protector, by reason of the arrest of their goods there: the protector said that he did not doubt that they would shortly recover their trade to Spain.

Again talk of a new parliament in the New Year. More proclamations against royalists and malcontents.

A petition on behalf of Biddle offered to the protector, citing the article in the Instrument of Government concerning freedom of conscience. The protector discussed it with the petitioners, and in the end declared that this article in the constitution should never be interpreted to cover the denial of the divinity of our Saviour, or other opinions irreconcilable with the fundamentals of Christianity.]

37

London, 28 September 1655 [in Swedish]

That the West Indies expedition, against the lord protector's expectation, turned out badly, and that Admiral Penn and General Venables, with the greater part of the fleet, returned home without orders, has caused great consternation here; particularly since it means that the plan which the lord protector has had in mind for some time—that is, to take the legislative power to himself, and so escape the need to summon parliament if he is in need of money—seems now to be badly out of joint, and postponed. What weighs most heavily on the lord protector is that he knows that he urged and insisted on this American venture singly, against the desire and consent of his whole council, and so can blame no one but himself. The soldiers and the sailors who hoped to better themselves by it, but endured great hardships and sufferings on the expedition, are very discontented, and frighten others from engaging in another voyage of this kind; and others who would be glad to see some alteration in the constitution take courage, and hope that the protector's luck is changing. The expenditure upon the fleet has been extraordinarily great; and to prosecute the design (which they have finally resolved to do) will cost still more; and for this the ordinary revenues are insufficient. I have been informed from a reliable source that the lord protector will therefore be forced to call a parliament to supply him with money. But to prevent any from obtaining a seat in parliament who may entertain any views opposed to his, the lord protector has this week caused a proclamation to be issued, in terms of which he and the council order that no one who has previously been punished, imprisoned or arrested by the government, or has otherwise adhered to the king, or engaged against the government in any way, shall be deemed capable of election, or be eligible for any office or public appointment.[1] And in addition, that the officers of the county militia which was first set up last June shall take especial care that in every county only those shall be returned for that county whom the lord protector would wish to see in parliament, and of whose fidelity he can be well assured.

There recently arrived in this country Johann Friedrich Schlezer, brother to the Brandenburg resident in Sweden, to sound the lord protector, *tamquam alium agendo*, as to whether an envoy from Brandenburg would be well received, and whether this country would in all circumstances be disposed to deny assistance to the elector; with orders in case of a [favourable] response to assume the character of a public minister.[2] But in view of all the circumstances I can come to no other conclusion than that he will not be able in the slightest degree to effect anything to Y.M.'s prejudice.

In the meantime, General Fleetwood having left some days ago to meet his brother the Lord Deputy of Ireland (who has now arrived

1. The proclamation prolonged the Act of 1652, disabling royalists from election to corporations and other offices: Gardiner, *Commonwealth and Protectorate*, iii. 324, though he does not associate it with any plan to hold parliamentary elections.

2. His instructions are printed in *Urk. und Act.*, vii. 721–4. They included a request to the protector to send a special envoy to the Baltic to try to mediate peace, and suggestions for trading privileges for English merchants in Prussia. Schlezer was not granted an audience until 4 December: *ibid.*, p. 729.

here) I have had a number of talks with Secretary Thurloe, by way of hastening a decision on the granting of a written consent to the recruiting of at least 2000 men for Y.M.'s service, in terms of Y.M.'s agreement with Baron Cranstoun, and urged, with many arguments, that this business might be brought to a satisfactory conclusion, especially in view of the many promises which have previously been given. At last he told me yesterday that the lord protector has for the present determined that Baron Cranstoun shall raise the 2000 immediately, and that he [Thurloe] was instructed to inform his excellency the ambassador of it; which he has in fact done, and Y.M.'s ambassador will be duly informing Y.M. of it.

As it is now necessary that Resident Möller accept the bill for 12,000 *riksdaler* which Baron Cranstoun is to have as muster-money, I not only notified him of it a week ago, so that he might have time to provide himself with the money if he happened not to have it in hand, but am also informing Y.M. of it, not doubting that Möller will have the 12,000 *rdr*: if not, it will be an occasion of great scandal and disgrace. And since it is uncertain how many men Colonel Cranstoun may be able to bring up to town this autumn, I have thought it best for Y.M.'s service not to give him Y.M.'s bill immediately, but that I should myself send the bill to the resident in the form of instalments of 3000 or 4000 *rdr*. at a time, depending upon the progress of Cranstoun's recruiting, until the whole amount is taken up; so that if he sends only a thousand foot this autumn he gets from me no more than 6000 *rdr*. As this is solely designed to advance Y.M.'s service, I humbly rely upon Y.M.'s gracious approval of it, and that he will sanction the arrangement beyond the possibility of doubt, so that my credit and my worldly welfare are not jeopardised; which would inevitably be the case if Y.M.'s bill were not duly honoured. On this I humbly await Y.M.'s answer, as also his gracious permission to proceed to Y.M., that I may give a circumstantial account of the course of affairs in this country. I hereby beg also that Y.M. may be pleased to give orders that I may be allowed to draw bills on Resident Möller to the amount which Y.M. in his instruction appointed to be granted to me, and to cover what I have in addition advanced to Commissioner Bonnel.

Bonde to Charles X

XV

London, 5 October 1655

Nothing worth mentioning in regard to my negotiation has occurred since my last letter; but (as Thurloe assures me) there has been much debate in the council on my proposals, and I hope that some action will shortly be taken in regard to them. The protector's illness is made an excuse for the long delay; but as far as I can gather it is clear that the unfortunate expedition against Hispaniola has upset all the protector's plans, and it is firmly believed that if the project had succeeded as he had hoped, he would have taken the title of king, and would have made no bones about entering into a closer alliance with Y.M., since he and Secretary Thurloe (who are both strong supporters of Y.M.) are much inclined to it. But this unfortunate expedition has put a stop to all that, not least because they are now involved in hostilities with Spain, and are for that reason afraid to take any action against the Dutch. I have with due reverence received Y.M.'s letter of 22 August from Colo [Koło], which arrived yesterday, and in which Y.M. was graciously pleased to reply to the letter which I wrote from Gravesend: I shall give careful attention to its contents, and conduct myself as may best suit with Y.M.'s service. Since I learn that Per Bonde left Stettin for Y.M. on the 16th I hope that he may already be with Y.M., and so no doubt I may expect to learn what Y.M. wishes in regard to the business which is committed to me. As to the alleged passages between the elector of Brandenburg and this country, I hope that I am in a position to assure Y.M. that there is nothing in it, as appears from my last letter and the protector's own verbal assurances. Some days ago there arrived here a minister from the elector, one Johann Friedrich Schlezer, together with his brother, who was the elector's resident in Sweden: he has no public character, and was sent only to sound out what the feeling was in this country; but I hope and think that I can assure Y.M. that he will not be able to effect anything here to Y.M.'s prejudice.

For lack of time I was forced to cut short my letter by the last post, in which I intended to include something on how France and this country stood towards one another. It had been spread abroad that the treaty between them was already concluded; but the contrary is now said to be the fact, and there is much talk of the eagerness of the catholics to make a peace between France and Spain. The merchants here who trade to Prussia give hints to me that they would be very glad of good terms for their trade to Danzig. I give them good hopes, and incite them to urge the protector to ask me for them—all with the idea of increasing their [the government's] appreciation of the value of the Baltic trade. I do the same with the Muscovy merchants, and shall do so also about the means to channel the trade from Russia to this country through the Baltic: in these things, as in all others, with my utmost diligence. Last Wednesday the Venetian ambassador[1] made his *entrée*: I was in great doubt whether I should allow my

1. Sagredo.

carriage to accompany him, or not; but at last I determined to go out of town for a time, and so be in a position to make a polite excuse. If I had sent the carriage I should have had to decide either to take precedence of the French ambassador by force, or to give place to him; and as I was by no means prepared to do the latter, so I thought the former might be an awkward matter; for however it went it would certainly have led to ill-will between the French ambassador and myself. This I was not anxious for, since we now live on terms of good friendship and confidence; and it might have given occasion for those who wish us no good to interpret it as a particular presumption, springing from Y.M.'s victorious campaigns, to venture to claim precedence over the king of France, which no one has ever done before. There could be no question of equality, for the streets are too narrow for the carriages to go side by side; and even if they had not been, there must still have been disputes as to which took the right-hand side. And if as a result there had been an accident, in this country one could hardly expect to come off without very serious repercussions, as the tragic case of the brother of the Portuguese ambassador sufficiently proves.[1] I had also the example of the late Päder Sparre, who was ambassador to Denmark on the occasion of the marriage of Prince Christian, and who absented himself on the wedding-day in order to avoid a clash with other ambassadors. I hope and trust that Y.M. may be pleased to approve my conduct in this affair. Tidings of Y.M.'s great and fortunate progress in Poland, and of his remarkable victories, arrived here yesterday, to the great joy of us all.[2] I hope that they will do much to aid the course of my negotiation; for a great many here, misled by the bad news fabricated by the Dutch, had already judged Y.M.'s campaign in Poland to be a disaster: thanks be to God, who has confounded their malevolence.

XVI

London, 12 October 1655

Since my last I have made no progress with my negotiation. Though I use all diligence to bring my commissioners to discussing a treaty, they continue to put me off with promises; saying that my proposals are to be debated in the council, and that as soon as some deter-mination is come to about them they will proceed to negotiate. It would seem that the great alterations in the world which have followed

1. The case of Dom Pantaleon Sá, who in 1654 killed a man in a brawl, and was tried and executed by the English courts.
2. After the encounter at Ujście on 14/24 July a section of the Polish nobility recognized Charles X as king on 7/17 August.

so hard upon each other—Y.M.'s great successes in Poland on the one hand, and their unfortunate naval exploits on the other, to say nothing of the talk which comes from all quarters of the *rapprochement* between the catholics, and their designs against the protestants—still keep them in a state of suspense, so that they prefer to procrastinate until they see whither affairs are tending, rather than to engage themselves in any way. I am more and more confirmed in the view which I earlier put forward, that although they understand well enough that the conditions I have propounded might be of great advantage to this country, and though they would undoubtedly accept them if their affairs were in such a state that they could risk offending the Dutch, their rupture with Spain—and also *res angusta domi*—make it impossible for them; apart from the fact that *status regiminis* itself (as far as I can discover) is very sick and in poor condition, and can hardly be remedied without firm action by the protector.

Mr [*sc.* General George] Fleetwood, who sees his brother every day, and has opportunities to speak of affairs of state with various persons, tells me that if Y.M. were prepared to conclude with this country an alliance in which the Dutch might be included, it would pass immediately and without difficulty; but hitherto Y.M.'s purpose and interests have forbidden that, and since God has been pleased so far to bless Y.M.'s arms—which (with God's help) I take to be the case, and Y.M.'s great victory at Opoczno has confirmed it[1]—then Y.M. should be finished with Poland before any other power can come to its aid. And since the Dutch (as is now reported and asserted) are accordingly to send an embassy to Y.M., it may be that (under God) all *causa dissidiorum* may therefore be removed, and a firm friendship with them be once again established: a thing which this country seems greatly to wish for.

When I consider the state of affairs in the world at this moment, and examine the reports that come in from various quarters, I am increasingly confirmed in the opinion which I have held from the beginning, ever since Field-Marshal Wittenberg's successful invasion of Poland; namely, that it may come to a war with the emperor, and *ex consequenti* grow into a general war of religion. I have sent Y.M. my humble but honest thoughts on this topic at various times, and particularly by Per Bonde. I am confirmed in them by Herr Dureel's negotiation for a closer alliance with Denmark;[2] which, though it

---

1. On 6/16 September 1655.

2. From mid-May Charles X had been sending repeated orders to Magnus Dureel in Copenhagen to try to obtain an alliance with Denmark; but the first exchange of proposals did not come till the beginning of November: J. Levin Carlbom, *Magnus Dureels negotiation*, pp. 27, 51, 55–60. The proposals were for an alliance against all powers attempting to intervene in the Baltic: *cf.* Thurloe, iv. 149–50.

would be a great stroke to weaken the Dutchmen's party (and might indeed bring them to see reason) seems to me no less useful on the assumption that the catholics are successful in their plotting. I see this last as a terrible black cloud gathering in those quarters, and threatening us all with a great and violent tempest.

The enclosed letter[1] was communicated to me by a particular friend. It is written by a well-informed man who has a large correspondence in Holland, Flanders, and especially with the court of the king of Scotland. I do not know his name, for he did not sign the letter, and there is no other address than an inn, where the letter is to be collected secretly by whom it concerns. Among the rest what seems to me to be worthy of notice is what he writes about Cardinal Mazarin; and I could not refrain from communicating the proposal to Y.M.

From Y.M.'s gracious letter from Koło of 22 August I judge Y.M.'s plan to be to assist this country in the Channel with as many ships as Y.M. is asking of them for the Baltic, and thus arrange for a reciprocal assistance. So far I have not ventured to make any such proposal, having received no instruction to that effect; and as things are here at present I have some hesitation in doing so, since I doubt whether anything is to be got from them by such an offer, and fear that it might make them more arrogant if they perceive that we so earnestly seek to oblige them. I doubt too whether they would consider it sufficient; and consequently I think it to be more advisable to await Y.M.'s answer to the letter which Per Bonde carries with him: I hope before it arrives that Y.M.'s progress in Poland, and other similar factors, may effect a change in their attitude, and perhaps so direct the course of events that all the protestants may seek by their united forces to hinder the designs of the papists. To which end this country seems much disposed, apart from the fact that their difference with Spain seems to oblige them to it.

I feel my stay here to be very long: I am virtually a hermit, excluded from all association with those who conduct the business of the state;[2] and moreover there is now no more than a month left of the period for which means were appointed for my maintenance—which in this expensive place, and because of the considerable state which for Y.M.'s reputation I am bound to keep up, can be made to suffice only with great difficulty. Nevertheless I shall consider no trouble too great if thereby I can do Y.M. acceptable service. For which I wish with all my heart that the good God may of His grace grant me under-

1. Missing in transcript.
2. By the rule that foreign ministers might not visit or be visited by members of the council of state: hence the recurrent references to apparently casual meetings in St James's Park. Nieupoort was provided with a key to the Park (Abbott, iv. 24), and Bonde must have had one also, though he makes no mention of it.

standing: my desire, and my loyal and sincere intention thereto, being always unalterable; in the sure confidence that should Y.M. deem my presence in this place necessary, he will then graciously cause such measures to be taken as may enable me to uphold the dignity which [his service] demands.

Bonnel is fallen into a miserable condition: melancholy and other afflictions have brought a sickness upon him, and he has not even so much as can buy him a bit of bread; and though I have myself nothing to spare, I must in some measure help him, lest he die of hunger here, to the great prejudice of that respect which is due to Y.M. If I might venture to intercede for him with Y.M., I would humbly ask that he might be delivered from hence.

Coyet to Charles X

38

London, 12 October 1655 [in German]

[Fifteen warships have left to reinforce Blake's fleet; but that fleet, being ignorant of this, and being short of provisions, has just arrived in England, the reinforcements having missed him. Great consternation at court about this,[1] though some new ships are being fitted out to prosecute Blake's design: whether they will arrive in time to intercept the silver-fleet remains to be seen.

The Spanish ambassador, Don Alonzo de Cardenas, has received orders of recall, and says he will leave next week. Letters by yesterday's post brought news that all English merchants in the Spanish Netherlands, and their property, are under arrest: a rupture between the two countries is not now to be doubted. On the other hand, after long negotiations the peace with France is already engrossed on parchment, and there is reliable information that the *instrumentum pacis* will be signed shortly.

The new Venetian ambassador had his audience with the protector on the 9th: compliments and protestations of Venice's desire for continued friendship.

A proclamation recently issued by the council in Scotland directed at ministers who pray openly for the king, to the effect that although this had been long forbidden, the government had decided to have patience with them, and would suspend punishment until 5 November, after which they would no longer be permitted to

---

1. This can hardly be true, for the protector gave him leave to stay out or come home, as he pleased: he anchored in the Downs on 6 October, 'with his fleet as worn and strained as himself': Corbett, *England in the Mediterranean*, i. 317.

flout God's special dispensation, to the prejudice of the peace of both countries.

Yet another fire in London last night: several houses in Holborn destroyed, and the fire not yet extinguished.]

P.S. [in Swedish]
I yesterday had a letter from Resident Möller informing me that he had no orders to pay any money for Cranstoun's recruiting, Y.M. having otherwise disposed of the moneys destined for that purpose, and that he therefore could not accept my bills. I am now in acute embarrassment, and do not know what I shall do. It is impossible to wait for Y.M.'s answer before drawing a bill. Where the money is to come from, if this autumn any men are to be sent from hence to Germany (as Y.M.'s service seems to require) [is a problem], and if I draw bills in the meantime I risk my credit here, which might easily be ruined if the bills were not accepted, and hence an opportunity be given to Y.M.'s ill-wishers to discredit Y.M. in this country, should the business stick this year for lack of funds. It would also have exceedingly unpleasant consequences for Colonel Cranstoun, who—relying upon the assurances given to him here that it would be permitted—has disbursed various sums to advance the project, which in such a case he would lose, and his friends be ruined. On top of all this, I am in an extremely awkward position, since I have partly pledged myself that the money will be paid to Y.M. here; never thinking that Resident Möller would have had no orders to accept Y.M.'s draft upon him, or a bill for some part of it, and to provide means to meet it when it should fall due. I therefore most humbly beg Y.M. that orders may be sent to him regarding this matter, so that I may not lose all my credit and be utterly ruined, for I will neglect no occasion, in so far as it is at all possible, to do Y.M.'s service, even at the utmost hazard of my welfare.

Bonde to Charles X

XVII

London, 19 October 1655

Last Friday, the 12th of this month, Mr [George] Fleetwood obtained the written permission of his highness for Lord Cranstoun to raise recruits in Scotland. The order is directed to General Monck, who commands the militia in Scotland. Though it mentions only 1000 men, Lieutenant-General Lord Charles Fleetwood (who is the protector's son-in-law) has not only promised to give Cranstoun good recommendations in Scotland, but has said that in the event of his being able to collect more than 1000 men before spring he will get him permission for an extra thousand. I think it advisable to content ourselves with the first 1000, both because Cranstoun will hardly be able to ship over more than 500 at this season of the year, and also because I hope that before the rest follow I shall be in a better position to know what Y.M. has to expect of this country. Having thus, with no little difficulty, got this matter settled, another obstacle has presented itself; for Möller writes from Hamburg that he cannot accept Y.M.'s bill since Y.M. is said to have cancelled the recruiting here. I must confess that this surprised me exceedingly, in view of the fact that both I and Fleetwood have made such a point of it—not only in regard to the service Y.M. can obtain from the men recruited, but even more in order to stop the mouths of all malevolent persons who sow suspicion between Y.M. and this country, and so to deprive them of any hope of being able to draw him [i.e. the protector] over to their side. Moreover, Y.M. has not yet countermanded his order to me in this matter, but mentioned in his letter to Herr Coyet that in the event of Y.M.'s making any other disposition of the money designed for the purpose Y.M. would nevertheless arrange to make other funds available in its place as soon as the matter was brought to his notice. If now, when recruiting is beginning, we are to delay until Y.M.'s answer to our enquiry reaches us, so much time will elapse that it will be impossible to do anything this year; which will provoke enormous *médisance*, since for mere lack of money we shall have been forced to leave undone something which we have made such efforts to obtain. Cranstoun's father-in-law, Lord Leven, and his officers, have already collected a large number of men in Scotland whom they find it a great burden to maintain; and if they were to disband them, or to keep them on foot till spring, it could not be without great damage to themselves.

In this extremity I saw no other resource but to write to Resident Möller and Commissioner Hoffstetter and exhort them to accept the bill, it being a question of Y.M.'s reputation and interests—always supposing that my urging and entreaties had not [in the meantime] persuaded Herr Coyet to pledge his credit to raise money here on condition that if Möller or Hoffstetter did not accept Y.M.'s bill they would accept Coyet's instead, and reimburse him. He [Coyet] depicted his lamentable situation in the strongest terms, saying that the welfare of himself, his wife and his father-in-law now depends upon the crown; that he has advanced ready money, in good faith, out of devotion to Y.M.'s service; that he has never received a penny of capital or interest; that when he leaves this country he will be in no position to pay off his debts in the event of deaths in his family; that at the request of the chancellor [Erik Oxenstierna] he has lent

Bonnel 1000 *riksdaler* to save him from imprisonment, but has since not heard a word of the matter; that of the money for which Drakenhielm accepted a bill, 800 *riksdaler* are still outstanding, of which his wife has received absolutely nothing; not to mention the fact that he has been forced to continue here for long over his time, and the resulting expense has drained all his resources, exposing his wife and children to great hazard if anything should happen to him. In spite of all this I have persuaded him to do Y.M. this service yet again, employing as my main argument that by doing so he will lay a still greater obligation upon Y.M. to take his former just claims into consideration. I have had to give him a written assurance that his action constitutes a signal service to Y.M., and to bind myself to assist him, his wife and children, to the utmost of my power, to extricate them from their predicament. I would not have taken this grave step if I had not seen that if this recruiting came to a halt for lack of money I should have exposed myself to the world's derision, and wrecked everything I have to do here. Since permission has been given for 1000 men, and Lord Cranstoun will not be able to ship more than 500 to Stade this year, we are for the moment giving him no more than 6000 *riksdaler*, pending further orders from Y.M. and permission from the authorities here for additional levies. I presume (and I entreat) that my actions may commend themselves to Y.M., and that he may be graciously pleased to make arrangements for the money to be paid in Hamburg, so that Herr Coyet may not be reduced to ruin by reason of his loyal service.

The differences between this country and Spain have now reached such a pitch that they can hardly come to any other issue than open war; for the Spanish ambassador, Don Alonzo de Cardenas, has been recalled by his king. He called on me on the 17th to bid farewell, and we talked at length of the situation. He made no difficulty about answering all my questions. When I asked him why it had come to a rupture between England and Spain, he answered that his sovereign, and all Spaniards, entered this war with the greater content because they knew in their consciences that their cause was just, to which the whole world could bear witness; that they had the less expected any hostile designs from this country because they had done good offices to them more than to any other nation; that they had been the first to recognize them as a free republic; that they had manifested the greatest civility to their ships and subjects at a time when affairs were delicately balanced and could have been transformed by [the action of] even the weakest of foreign powers; that they might well say, in the words of Christ, *propter quondam beneficium lapidatis me*. Despite all this the English had fitted out a powerful fleet, attacked the island of St Domingo (otherwise called Hispaniola), taken Jamaica, and so under a pretence of friendship resorted to the most violent hostilities against a land which had been in Spain's peaceful possession for 180 years, and to which they had not the smallest claim; that it is vain and childish to suppose that one can be on terms of amity in Europe and wage war in America, or beyond the Line; and though that argument is widely used here he considers it only as the talk of the common people, and does not believe that those who sit in the government are prepared to make use of it; and even if they should be disposed to interpret agreements in such a sense he could only say that Spain neither can nor will concur in such an interpretation. For in the agreements between Spain and England it is expressly laid down that there shall be a general peace between the two crowns and the territories belonging to them; and also that if the peace should be broken they were obliged to grant time for merchants to withdraw their goods—three months on this side of the Line, nine months on the other; from which it is clear that the general peace is intended to apply to both sides of the Line (though Jamaica lies 8 degrees on this side of it!). That Spain's measures against the goods of the English had been no more than in the nature of reprisal: they had not been confiscated, but only detained until the English should give them some satisfaction and *restitutio damnorum illatorum*. If this should provoke a war, it can in such a case do no harm to Spain, since it is better to have an open enemy than a secret one who deprives them of their property without any sufficient cause. He recalled further that when that fleet was being fitted out he already had some suspicion as to where it was designed for, and had himself asked the protector if the fleet intended any hostile action against his sovereign; which question his highness took umbrage at, saying that he was not obliged to reveal his *arcana* to any foreign minister—to which he replied that he desired no more than what had been asked of him in the parliament's time, when Spain equipped a fleet in Dunkirk and they sent to him to ask for what that fleet was designed, and whether it was in any way directed against England. To this he had then answered that he did not know his sovereign's intention in that matter, but that he could assure them that it was in no way intended to be prejudicial to England, of which at their request he gave them a written assurance. He did not ask (he said) information on *arcana imperij*, but only whether his master had to expect from them the friendship which was implicit in their words. To this he could get no answer from his highness other than a reiteration that he was not bound to disclose his policies, and for the rest that he would do nothing but what was straightforward, justifiable and honourable. This was all the answer he could obtain. As a young man he had heard justice defined as *suum cuique tribuere*, and he could therefore find no justice in its *contrario*—namely, *suum cuique tollere*.

To this I replied that I had heard that the English agent had been murdered in their country, and whether that might not lead them to seek revenge?[1] To which he answered that they the [English] had no call to raise this issue, since they had been given the greatest imaginable satisfaction upon it. First, the agent in question was not murdered by a Spaniard but by an Englishman, and it was his own fault to the extent that he ought not to have left his house open for anyone to come and go before announcing his arrival to the secretary of state, in which event proper security for his person could have been provided. Next, what happened in regard to his murder was that six Englishmen entered his house and murdered him and his secretary, one of whom immediately made his escape and the other five took refuge in a church; and though the church is a *locus sanctus* and considered to be inviolable, the civil magistrate nevertheless thought the deed to be of such enormity as to deprive them of the right of asylum, and consequently removed them to such hard custody that one of them died there, and the others were condemned first to be racked and afterwards to lose their lives, the same sentence being pronounced, *propter contumaciam*, against him who had escaped. On the day fixed for their execution the archbishop had intervened and forbidden their execution upon pain of excommunication; and after a long debate it was decided that they should be put in the church again, since otherwise *jus ecclesiae* would have been violated. This was done, and a strong guard set upon the church-door: three nevertheless escaped and (he believed) are now in England; but one was taken and underwent his sentence. He wondered that they [the English] should make such a big issue of the affair, when all possible satisfaction had been given them; though when their minister in Holland was massacred,[2] and the perpetrators took refuge only in the house of the pretended king of Portugal—from which they escaped, and no great effort made to trace them—they spoke little of it, so that neither in the *causis belli* nor the *conditionibus pacis* [with the Dutch] was it so much as touched upon.

I enquired further whether there was any hope of a settlement between them. He answered that he had no orders to discuss it, but simply to remove out of this country. He had accordingly asked two or three times for an audience to take leave, which he would have liked to do in person, since he has been here for eighteen years; but since he could not obtain one he yesterday signified his departure in writing, and now waits only for a pass or safe-conduct, since it is his intention to depart without delay; and he hoped that he might not be detained, since it is contrary to *jus gentium* to hinder or delay the

1. A reference to the murder of Anthony Ascham in 1650.
2. Isaac Dorislaus, murdered in 1649.

journey of an ambassador. He said further that there was one thing that England perhaps would be disposed to plead in justification, alleging that it was Spain that first [broke the peace]: in the late king's time there was formed an association of noblemen and merchants who captured a little island by the name of Providence Island, which lies among the Caribbean islands and is situated near to the frontiers of [New] Spain, and they availed themselves of its position solely to commit piracy against the Spaniards. For this reason, about fifteen years ago, the Spaniards eliminated these buccaneers; and did so *vi pactorum* between the two countries, which forbid all piracy. And with that he left me.

I have discussed this business with some sensible Englishmen, and I am sure that they will not easily be able to justify their actions. They may no doubt claim that the papists act *infeste* against the protestants, but that alone is not sufficient reason for starting a war without adducing other grounds; and England will hardly escape the reproach that in beginning this war they are actuated more by greed than by religious zeal. For Spain there are two things of which they are so tender that they can make no concessions upon either: the one is the Inquisition; the other is the Indies; and anyone who attacks either of these touches them to the quick. They [the English] had assured the Spanish ambassador extraordinary, the marquis de Leda, that they would do nothing which was not *justum et aequum*; but at the very time that they were talking to him the fleet was sent off to fall upon their lands and conquests. The people here, and in the provinces generally, are very discontented at these proceedings: they say bluntly that the reason why their men had so disastrous an experience in Hispaniola recently was because they were employed in an unrighteous cause. Though they are all kept in such strict bounds that no agitation is possible to them, their affection—which was little enough before—is now cooled still further; especially among the merchants, who have not only suffered damage by the arrest of their goods, but are now to lose all their trade to all the Spanish ports, which is the best trade that England has, since it is based on the Dutchmen's quarrel with Spain. Men say also that the enterprise was very untimely begun: that if [the government] had amassed so great a hoard of treasure that they could think of no other way of using it, then would have been the time to think of new conquests, and to begin a war in which no danger was to be apprehended; but that the country is at present impoverished by great contributions and taxes, and the people oppressed by heavy burdens. No doubt the protector will do his utmost to carry through the work with reputation, and no doubt either but that he will give Spain occupation enough; but here in England the affair will not run its course without great difficulties. Regarding *spem compositionis,* everything turns on whether the English can maintain their hold on Jamaica, and in particular whether the reinforcements which were sent out four months ago have reached them: in that case peace is unlikely, for the protector will strain every nerve to retain it [Jamaica], and thence to get a foothold on the *terra firma* and *ex consequenti.* And Spain will rather fight to the last man than let anybody in to their treasure-chamber in the Indies. But if the Spaniards, with the united forces of those of their territories which lie close to Jamaica, were able to recover that island and consequently to extirpate the English in those parts, it might very well come to a peace; for to begin with such an expedition as Penn's would hardly be possible again: it is said that these Indies fleets have cost £20 million sterling, which is equal to 90 barrels of gold in *riksdaler.*[1] And besides, the Spaniards in those parts are now on the alert, so that no force from such a distance will be able to inflict any damage upon them. And for the sake of enjoying peace with England the Spaniards will accept any tolerable conditions if only their conquests in the Indies are safe and unmolested.

I send herewith a letter from the individual who was the writer of that which I forwarded by the last post.[2] It is the more worthy of notice because of the writer's character and ability: what he writes of the emperor's designs against Y.M. I shall do my best to unravel. I have moreover been told in confidence, by someone who is well informed on the subject, that England has now come to terms with Portugal, and that the Portuguese, to their considerable satisfaction, have obtained the terms they had been contending for;[3] further, that the protector's intention may be to make use of the Portuguese, of whom at least a quarter are resident in Spanish conquests in the Indies; but it is thought that they will hardly allow themselves to be used in that way. It is also said here that the Spaniards are disposed to use the king of Scotland against England: the more so since that might foment dissensions here; though others are of the opinion that this would only force [the government] to defend itself the more vigorously.[4]

---

1. On 12 October the commissioners for the Admiralty and Navy reported that wages due to the fleet amounted to *ca.* £120,000, and that they had not been paid for about twenty months. Cash in hand was less than £20,000, the remainder having gone to pay for Penn's and Blake's fleets. The total debt on the navy was *ca.* £657,835; there was a shortage of naval stores, and no chance of replenishing them unless further money was made available: Thurloe, iv. 79–80.

2. Missing in transcript.

3. Bonde's informant was entirely mistaken.

4. Nieupoort believed that the rupture with Spain would mean that England would at most commit herself to engaging Charles X to act against the emperor, as part of an anti-Habsburg alliance founded mainly on religion. But on 22 October (NS) Thurloe

Now that the peace with France has been concluded, it is said that a Colonel [Thomas] Cook (who is General Fleetwood's nephew and in great credit with the protector), being a French major-general, is to recruit 6000 foot for the French service, giving 18 *riksdaler* per man; but others who see a little deeper into the affair conjecture that since the people in this country are excessively unwilling to allow themselves to be employed against Spain, or in the Indies, the recruits are to be raised in France's name, and subsequently shipped off to fight against Spain: time will show which is true.

I shall soon be weary of waiting for these people, for I cannot induce them to get down to business; but since I have still had no answer from Y.M. I must bear it. I think that Sir Charles Fleetwood will be paying me a visit to-morrow, although it would appear to be contrary to their regulations; his main object being to convey his gratitude to Y.M. for the favour he has shown to his brother. When he comes I shall see whether I cannot, through him, do something to advance my business.

Coyet to Charles X

39

London, 19 October [in German]

[The protector and council meet frequently: it is supposed they have great and extraordinary affairs in hand; to which end they have recently held another day of prayer and fasting, privately, in Whitehall.

Blake was with the protector the day before yesterday, reporting on his cruise. Another strong fleet is being fitted out to sail for the West Indies next spring. Reports from New England that various frigates have arrived from Jamaica to take in supplies, and will shortly return with them.

The Dutch ambassador had this week an audience with the protector, and is said to have made a strong complaint that there has been no reparation for the losses inflicted on them by the English.

The Spanish ambassador likewise asked for an audience, to take leave. This was refused; so that he sent in his application in writing,

---

offered him private talks on the details of a joint Anglo-Dutch *démarche* to Sweden, and appointed the 29th for the discussion: *Brieven*, iii. 133. On that day Nieupoort reported that 'the lord protector roundly declared to me that in regard to Sweden he would accept no offers or invitation except in common with Holland': *ibid.*, 136.

and was granted the necessary safe-conduct. It was not framed to his satisfaction, so he now applies for another; and in the meantime makes courtesy valedictory calls.

Report of an encounter of an English frigate of Blake's fleet with a Spanish squadron, from which the frigate escaped with difficulty. Letters from Rohan [Rouen] of 13 October report that a declaration of the admiral in France orders all English ships and goods which are to be found anywhere in France, and have been taken into custody during the present controversy between them, to clear for sea without delay.

The marquis of Argyll recently arrived from Scotland, and a littler earlier also the earl of Lothian. On the other hand, Colonel Baron Cranstoun will in the course of the next week or so leave for Scotland to continue the recruiting which the protector has permitted, and will make every effort to ensure that a good number are transported to Germany this autumn.]

P.S. [in Swedish]
As to such other matters as may be passing here, and specifically how the Spanish ambassador complains of the actions of the English; how far progress has been made with Cranstoun's recruiting; and how I have pledged my credit to raise money for it; all this will no doubt have been conveyed to Y.M. more at large by his excellency the ambassador's report: to which I respectfully beg to refer to Y.M. I only implore most humbly that Y.M. will not leave me in the lurch, but that orders may be given for the accepting of my bills, either to Resident Möller, or to Herr Hoffstetter.

Bonde to Charles X

XVIII

London, 23 October 1655

Y.M. may be pleased to recall that on my departure for England he permitted me to try to persuade some young noblemen of quality to accompany me, and so to give to my mission the capacity to appear here with a lustre the more suitable to Y.M.'s great name and reputation. Among others I persuaded the person who carries this letter to undertake the journey with me, promising him that I would on his return humbly recommend him to Y.M., and assuring him that the time expended upon the journey would not be considered to have been wasted, but that Y.M. would take it into his gracious consideration. His name is Johan Sack, the son of Colonel Otto Sack. Since my stay here, somewhat against my earlier inclinations, is protracted by reason of the great changes that have occurred in Europe since my departure, and since he is very anxious to seek his fortune in the wars with Y.M., and has consequently requested me to allow him to leave, and to give him a good recommendation to Y.M., I have found his application so reasonable that I have not only been ready to release him, but also to permit him to carry with him this my humble recommendation to Y.M.[1]

XIX

London, 26 October 1655

Last Tuesday, the 23rd, I had a visit from the Lord Deputy of Ireland, Charles Fleetwood, and we had some interesting conversation. He began by expressing the great obligation which he and all his family felt towards Y.M. for the honour done to all of them by the numerous acts of grace and favour vouchsafed towards his brother, saying that though by the regulations which were now in force here he was not at liberty to visit or speak with public ministers, he was ready to break them rather than be supposed to be ungrateful, for he wished by deeds as well as words to manifest his constant purpose of showing his appreciation, in every possible way, of Y.M.'s gracious goodness; and he hoped that his highness had had such proofs of his fidelity that he would not take this amiss. I replied with a suitable compliment (mostly in praise of his brother), and added that Y.M. has always considered it his duty to love and esteem honour and merit wherever they were to be found.

I then took advantage of a remark of his to talk of my business here, and expounded the interest of both countries in maintaining a reciprocal friendship, in much the same terms as I had on a number of occasions used to the protector and Thurloe. To this he answered that the protector, and all who understood the situation, realizing very well that a close confidence and near alliance with Y.M. and the crown of Sweden was very necessary for England, were on that account very well disposed to it, and that the proposals I had made were much to England's advantage; but that he would tell me in confidence that the only reason for their long delay was that it seemed to them that the assistance which Y.M. was requesting in the Baltic was intended to be used against Holland, and that though they had indeed been at war with the Dutch, they had now concluded a peace which his highness, having given his *parole* and promise, felt himself bound as a man of honour to adhere to. And so continued with a long

---

1. *Cf.* Ekeblad, *Brev,* i. 426–7. Bonde had promised Ekeblad that he should be the first to be sent home, and his choice, first of Pär Bonde, and now of Johan Sack, was therefore a disappointment: *ibid.,* p. 416.

compliment about his desire to do everything in his power to forward my business here, and that I must let him know when any occasion arose in which I might be in need of his services, since he would always be ready to do what he could for me. On which he rose, and seemed in great haste to depart. I nevertheless made him an answer to all this, and said that I knew quite well that something of the kind had held up my business here, but that I had been so unfortunate as never hitherto to have had an opportunity to talk it over with his highness himself, or with his commissioners: if I had been able to do so I hoped that I should very soon have been able to remove their scruples on this point. He should bear it in mind, as a fundamental fact, that Y.M. had no grudge against Holland; that the crown of Sweden had invariably manifested nothing but good-will towards them; and that Y.M. had therefore no intention of offending them in any way. But that all the treaties between Sweden and Holland, Sweden and England, and England and Holland, include among other matters a basic provision for maintaining *libertatem navigationis et marium*; and that the assistance which Y.M. was now asking of them was to be employed only against anyone—whoever it might be—who created disorder in those seas; and if the Dutch had it in mind to do this they would be violating not only the treaties concluded between Y.M. and themselves, but also those concluded between England and Holland; and that therefore England, *vi pactorum* with Y.M., had an obligation, as we also had, to vindicate the freedom of the seas. But that the main motive [in my proposals] was this: that as he must certainly know very well, the catholics were trying to hurt the protestants—not only by force of arms, but to egg us on and incite us to quarrel with one another by all those devious practices of which they are masters; as they had shown in Germany in regard to the protestant princes and the crown of Sweden.[1] And that to prevent anything of that kind in the future the best and only means was that England and Sweden should so bind themselves together that none of the other protestant kingdoms or states would venture to meddle in such a manner as to give rise to disunion among us all, but that they might rather live in unity, and thus be able the more effectively to oppose the designs of the catholics. He seemed to take my answer well, and promised that he would press for my being able to get down to business with my commissioners. After I had recommended Lord Cranstoun's affair to him we parted for that time, with elaborate compliments on both sides.

The same day I sent my Secretary Barkman to Secretary Thurloe to remind him of my business, that I might for once be in a position

1. I.e. during the Thirty Years War, especially with regard to John George of Saxony.

to do something in it; pointing out that their differences with Spain must produce insecurity on the seas, and that it was consequently very necessary that some matters which had been deferred when the former [*sc.* Whitelocke's] treaty was concluded should now be settled; such as a form of sea-pass, passports, regulations about contraband, and so forth, so that there should be no disturbance of our trade; to which he answered that he could assure me that there had been much discussion of my proposals, both in the council and privately between the protector and himself, and that they had not merely discussed them, but had made such progress that the commissioners were to meet me in the very near future and settle all these questions in such a way as to give me satisfaction. How soon this will happen, and what their views may be, time will no doubt very soon reveal.

Meanwhile I have been working unofficially with a view to finding out what can be done for Y.M.'s advantage in regard to the Russia trade, and other branches of English commerce. In the time of the former kings, all foreign trade was restricted to particular companies, so that no one who did not belong to them, or at least had their leave, was allowed to trade to the places where they had a privilege; and among them was one called the Eastland Company, outside of which no one had leave to sail to the Baltic: their principal staples were in Danzig, Elbing and the places round about. But lately when the people took control in the time of the parliament, all these companies were abolished, as monopolies, and trade was opened to all. Now those same merchants of the former Eastland Company, taking advantage of the fact that I am here, and hoping that in consequence they may once more obtain some regulation of their trade on favourable terms, have met together and delivered a petition to the protector, together with the conditions which they desire his highness to ask of me. These papers I contrived to get the Company's secretary (who was for a long time resident in Danzig) to draw up, and I now send them to Y.M. in order that Y.M. may see what it is that they want. I humbly beg that Y.M. may be graciously pleased to let me know how far I may go in discussing it with them: my instructions mention that I may grant them a staple in Danzig and another in Riga; but state no specific conditions. I have drawn up, and attached to this letter, such explanations of my discussions with the secretary [of the company] as may be necessary, and my own opinions on every point, and now send them to Y.M.[1] I have used every means to encourage the members of the Archangel Company [i.e. the Muscovy Company] to ask for a staple in Narva; but they are somewhat slow to respond, on the ground that they would be exposed to paying dues at the Sound, and other hazards, while they have an unimpeded (if arduous) course to Arch-

1. Missing in transcript.

angel. Nevertheless, I shall use every endeavour; and if there should be new regulations about trade and Companies, and there is nothing to be done with the Archangel Company, I shall work to get the Eastland Company to fix their staple at Narva; in which case they may compete among themselves for the Russia trade. If this can be managed, I am hopeful that it will not prove unfruitful.

Coyet to Charles X

40

London, 26 October 1655 [in German]

[The treaty with France was signed on 24 October: its conclusion no doubt hastened by the extreme tension between England and Spain; vigorous preparations for war being made on both sides. Though so far there has been no confiscation of Spanish property, the protector has ordered the Spanish ambassador to leave within four days, and confiscation is to be expected then. Barrière, who has long been here as emissary of the prince of Condé, has been ordered to depart also. Captain Sydrack Black, who learning of Spanish detention of English ships attempted to escape it, is reported to have been fetched back by the governor of Vigo, who sent four frigates after him: he defended himself valiantly, killing 15 men and sinking one ship.

Penn and Venables still in prison, and have applied to the protector for a verdict to be pronounced upon their conduct. Blake is said also to have lost the protector's favour by reason of his failure to attack the Spanish fleet, and by his return to England without orders.[1]

When I recently visited the Venetian ambassador he expressed great joy that the Almighty had vouchsafed to Y.M. so great a victory over the Poles, at such small cost;[2] since once he had conquered Poland he would be a neighbour to the Turks, and so be in a position to turn his victorious arms to the advantage of Christendom, and he did not doubt that Y.M. would achieve immortal glory by doing so.

Refers to Christer Bonde's report on the Anglo-Swedish negotiations.]

P.S. [in Swedish]

Y.M. will have heard, through his excellency the ambassador's report, that I have raised some thousands of *riksdaler* on my own credit, and

---

1. There was no foundation for this rumour.
2. On 30 August Charles X entered Warsaw; on 7 October Kraków capitulated; Thorn was to surrender on 25 November.

on the other hand have drawn a bill for 3000 *riksdaler* upon Resident Möller, in the hope that he will duly accept it, especially since I had bills on him for 12,000 *riksdaler* for Cranstoun. I therefore humbly entreat Y.M. to order Möller to accept the bills I have drawn in Y.M.'s service, and to save my credit from being ruined. If I had not risked my credit, Cranstoun's recruiting could never have been successful this autumn, and this was a matter which could not be neglected without prejudice to Y.M. I therefore await Y.M.'s order as to where the means to continue the recruiting are to be found, since the resident now informs me that the money he has by him is to be allotted to other purposes, and the season does not admit [delay] if any troops are to be sent over before winter. I likewise humbly entreat Y.M. to be good enough to signify his pleasure as to whether I am to remain here longer, or not; so that I may make my arrangements accordingly, or otherwise the uncertainty will be my ruin. God knows my zeal to serve Y.M. faithfully: I desire only to know Y.M.'s intentions as to my person.

Bonde to Charles X

XX

London, 2 November 1655

Although I have perseveringly asked, in the appropriate quarters, that my commissioners should meet me so that I could get down to business with them, until yesterday all I got was large compliments, condolences and assurances that all would be well. But then my Lord Deputy Sir Charles Fleetwood sent his nephew, Colonel Cook, to inform me that after my last request to him he had managed to bring them to the point at which the commissioners are ready to talk to me at whatever time I shall appoint: I have asked them to come to me on Monday, if that is convenient to them. I am decidedly of opinion that the delay up to now has tended very much to Y.M.'s service; for his enormous successes in Poland will oblige this country to do for Y.M. what they might otherwise have had some hesitation in doing. The great uncertainty here as to Y.M.'s situation, which resulted from the fact that no certain tidings from the army had arrived for a long time, seems to have been a reason for their delay;[1] and another was their preoccupation with the treaty with France, which is now concluded. That treaty would seem to be pretty advantageous for England, since this last quarrel with Spain seems to have made no

---

1. Bonde was probably right: on 15 October NS Nieupoort reported that Thurloe had said to him that he heard that the Swedish navy was in a very bad state; that Wrangel was reported dead, having done nothing on land; and that the Swedes had suffered heavy defeats: *Brieven*, iii. 131.

significant alteration in the terms, which mostly remain as they were drafted seven months ago.[1] It is said that the Frenchman would not have signed so soon if he had not feared that if he did not this country might easily have been able to come to an agreement with Spain; but there are those who fear that before the treaty is ratified he may start some other objection, perceiving that there is now little hope of a settlement between Spain and this country. I had determined, in order to forward my business here, once more to solicit a private audience with the protector: I had it this morning, and will inform Y.M. of what passed in my next letter.

There is much discussion here as to what they are to do about the malignants (as they call those of the king's party). Some are of opinion that an attempt should be made absolutely to extirpate them, since no pardons, exhortations or good deeds can bind them to keep quiet, but they persist in attacking members of the government by their words, their writings and their actions; and that there is scarce one of them who, if his death-sentence were remitted to-day, would not thirst to murder the protector to-morrow, if he had the chance to do it. Moreover, vast sums of money are required for the great expeditions they have in hand, as also for the militia in this country, and it is thought reasonable that the money shall come from those who make it necessary to maintain such an army *propter pacem publicam*. And some persons in the government are timorous, and are afraid that they will never sit secure in their seats until these people are totally suppressed.

From the aspect of the world it looks certain that we are once again to have a war of religion. It is not improbable that the differences in the Swiss cantons may develop on that basis; and if they do, in my humble opinion it would be an opportunity, whatever happens, to have a regard to the protestant cantons in order to encourage them and unite them. There are those here who think that it would not be difficult to arrange a peace between France and Spain, if only the pope and the Spaniards were able to find a means to guarantee to Cardinal Mazarin his dignity and status; and since this is judged impossible, except France be engaged in war, they must find means to devise another war, less weakening to the catholic party. I had

1. The treaty was signed on 24 October, the negotiations having been saved at the last moment by the tactful persuasions of Nieupoort, who induced the English government to be content with the formulation '*Rex Galliarum*', instead of '*Rex Gallorum*', as they had desired: *Brieven*, iii. 138–9. Nieupoort considered that the treaty was a necessary preliminary to the 'Marine Treaty' which he was trying to negotiate, since until peace was formally established between France and England Dutch trade could never be secure from French privateers, or be able to establish 'normal' relations with England in regard (e.g.) to contraband and sea-passes: for the nuisance of French privateers, see E. C. Molsbergen, *Frankrijk en de republiek der Verenigde Nederlanden 1648–1662* (Rotterdam 1902), ch. vi.

been thinking that it was very necessary and sensible for this country to try secretly to get hold of somebody who might seek to warn the cardinal against giving any scope for a treaty between France and Spain; and I have said something to that effect to this person and that, as opportunity offered; but I have no means of knowing whether they paid any attention. But it seems worth while, since [Mazarin] is the only man who can block such a peace, to deter him from embarking upon it; for it would undoubtedly place the protestants in a very difficult situation. I have it on good authority that the emperor has consulted the pope as to whether to accept the Poles' offer of the Polish crown, and whether to undertake the defence of Poland against Y.M., and that the pope has advised him to it; among other reasons because it was impossible to go on for long winning these great victories, if only because Y.M.—like the late King Gustavus, of glorious memory—exposes his person too much, and an accident may easily happen to him: may the great God of His mercy bring their cruel desires and prophecies to naught, and preserve Y.M. to the honour of His name and the sole strength and stay of our dear fatherland, for many years to come.

Some here incline to the view that Spain now regrets having been so precipitate in the confiscation of English property, particularly since they now know that the English by reason of the reinforcements sent to Jamaica are stronger there in men and ships than they had supposed, and that it will not be easy to recover those places: they [the English] give out that, with reinforcements of 9000 men and 25 warships (besides 30 armed merchantmen) they are not only able to stand their ground there, but also to undertake some new enterprise. I send enclosed herewith two letters from the same person who wrote the letters I sent to Y.M. before: they give some food for thought.[1] At present there is much talk here of Brandenburg: it would seem that the old princess-dowager of Orange is meddling a good deal in the matter.[2] I have already used this, and shall continue to use it, to push this country into taking preventive measures, and I hope by the next post to give Y.M. a fuller report.

For the moment I can write no more than that I had to-day a very weighty conference with the protector, lasting for an hour and a half; in which by strong arguments I at last prevailed upon him to reconsider the resolution which he had previously taken, which was mainly directed to a mediation between Y.M. and Holland, either through me here, or by sending an emissary to Y.M. [I argued] that

1. Missing in transcript.
2. Amalia von Solms. A letter of intelligence from The Hague of 29 October NS reported that she was trying to arrange a triple alliance between the United Provinces, Denmark and Brandenburg: Thurloe, iv. 94.

there can be no mediation except with a view to concluding a peace; nor can any peace be negotiated where no war or other hostile act has occurred; and that therefore if the Dutch have any demands upon Y.M. they ought not to pursue them in the first place *praepostere* by taking overt action, to the embarrassment of other powers, but rather *amicabilibus*; and if these means proved inefficacious, that then, and not till then, was the time to think of other measures. And since he asked for my advice and opinion, I told him that what would most commend itself to Y.M. would be that he should give the Dutch seriously to understand that he could not suffer them to undertake any form of hostilities against Y.M., but that they should try to get what they wanted by agreement; and further, that we two should conclude a close alliance, so that if the one course of action proved of no avail, then the other would serve to keep the peace among the protestants. By this time I brought him to say that he would by his prayers, and by all amicable means, work to keep us in friendship, since the general interest of religion so eminently demanded it (this argument I was forced to employ, since it is that which is most effective here); and that if this did not help, he would be ready to consider any measures which might conduce to unity. We then parted, with great mutual satisfaction; and I think this was a good day. I hope that what I learned from him is what the commissioners intend to say, and that when I meet them again they may have received further instructions. As we had feared, though the post has arrived, I shall not have time to look at the letters before this goes off.

Coyet to Charles X

41

London, 2 November 1655 [in German]

[Since it is now a long time since I had the happiness to receive any letter from Y.M., or any answer to the questions which on various occasions (both before and after the ambassador's arrival) I have humbly directed to Y.M., and am in consequence uncertain whether my actions here have met with Y.M.'s gracious approval, or not, I do not know what more I have to do here; especially since his excellency the ambassador says that as far as he knows I am to be recalled as speedily as possible, alleging that my commission has been extinguished by his arrival. Would to God that I knew what Y.M.'s will in this may be, that I might with the greatest submission conform to it. The uncertainty in which I have been, since his excellency Herr Christer Bonde came here, has much hindered me from being as serviceable as I might perhaps otherwise have been, after being here for so long a time. Therefore, most gracious sovereign, it is my humble prayer to Y.M. that he will be pleased to make known his wishes as to my person, so that I may thereby be able, either to do some service here, or by proceeding to Y.M. may have the opportunity to present a verbal report on the course of affairs and the state of this country; the which cannot so well be done in writing, especially by reason of the war between Spain and this state which is now broken out, whereby it is to be feared that letters may well not go as safely as hitherto.

Baron Cranstoun still thinks that he may be able to bring 500 men to town from Scotland this autumn: he is going there himself to-morrow. The remainder he promises to forward with the first open water. It was certainly not his fault that the recruiting has taken so long, but the fault of the government here, which delayed issuing its written permission. I have, moreover, already made 3000 *riksdaler* over to him, which I raised at great risk to my credit; and also drawn a bill for the same amount on Resident Möller, not doubting that he will accept it, although so far he has made great difficulty about it, as I may have informed Y.M. already. And I humbly beg Y.M. to give orders that I may draw either on Resident Möller, or on Commissary-General Hoffstetter, for such amounts as I have advanced for Y.M.'s service, or have disbursed [for my subsistence], for it will otherwise be impossible for me to carry on here any longer.]

42

London, 2 November 1655 [in German]

[The former proclamation ordering royalists to retire to 20 miles from London between 5 November and 9 February is now reissued. The names of the Major-Generals, and their districts, listed: no royalist may for the present come here without their permission.

Bordeaux has sent his secretary home to obtain ratification of the treaty. The Spanish ambassador left last Monday: a proclamation issued justifying the war with Spain.

Penn is released from prison; it is said that Venables will be released also; though with the loss of his commission.

A new lord mayor of London installed last Monday, with all the usual solemn ceremonies, which have not been used since the troubles; the procession described in detail.[1]

The Venetian ambassador had a private audience with the pro-

---

1. Bonde's *Diarium* for 29 October reads: '*Vidi processum et pompam de* My Lord Maior; a silver white chariot drawn by six white horses *cui insidebat virgo sparsis crinibus quae virginitatem representare debeat*'.

tector the day before yesterday; the Dutch ambassador had one yesterday; Bonde had one to-day.]

Bonde to Charles X

XXI

London, 9 November 1655

In my previous letter, which was written in great haste, I gave Y.M. the gist of my last conversation with the protector; but since it was of considerable importance, by reason of the arguments employed on both sides, I have thought it necessary to recapitulate it for Y.M. in some detail.

After the preliminary greetings, compliments and congratulations to his highness on the recovery of his health, I reminded him that he had most recently offered to intervene in the matter of the Hollanders' naval preparations; and though at that time I could not understand as fully as I could have wished what his highness's intentions were, my ideas about it were afterwards clarified when Secretary Thurloe visited me a week later. I thought it necessary not only to remind his highness of this, but also more explicitly to ask for a reply to my former proposition. There had been a long delay about it, and I could well imagine that the reason for that was that there were those who wished to interpret the aid and alliance which his highness was being asked for, as being directed against the Dutch, and consequently tending to conflict with the recent peace with them. (I had indeed already formed the opinion that it was this view of the matter that had held up my commissioners; and subsequently my conversation with Lord Charles Fleetwood confirmed my surmise, as I may well have written to Y.M. a fortnight ago). I therefore requested that I be given an opportunity to remove this scruple; and I accordingly began by pointing out that Sweden (earlier than the Dutch) had made an agreement with England *de tutanda libertate navigationis et commerciorum contra turbatores quoscunque*; that the same provision had not been forgotten in the last treaty between Holland and England; and that it would be a serious reflection on their sincerity and prudence to say they [the English] had concluded treaties which were mutually contradictory. Y.M.'s policy was not to be considered as directed against any potentate or state in particular, but against those who made trouble on the seas, and the Dutch cannot do that without violating their treaty with England. The English are thus bound, *vi pactorum*, to help us to maintain the freedom of the seas, and cannot in consequence be held to be blameable should any rupture with

Holland follow, since it is the Dutch who have first broken the treaties. I then proceeded to demonstrate in detail how feeble was their excuse when they said that the purpose of their fleet was not to disturb trade but to safeguard it – as though it was for them to judge what potentate might attack his enemies, and by what means—a principle of which they had taken no notice in their war with Spain, when they blockaded all the trade to Flanders; and with more to the same purpose, which for the sake of brevity I omit. But although this argument is solidly based, I was well aware that it would have little effect on the considerable Dutch party in the council unless I touched them more *au vif* on the point where most of them (and especially the protector) are most sensitive. I therefore began by dwelling on the tremendous changes which have taken place in Europe in the short time that has elapsed since my coming here: Y.M. has overrun the whole of Poland; on the other side, his highness and this country have attacked Spain and the House of Austria in a vital spot, and though others spread the story that the expedition had turned out ill, for my part I judged that that place [Jamaica] was vastly important by reason of its situation, and that Spain with all its forces was incapable of evicting them from it (this happens to be true; but it is always wise to flatter, and especially when dealing with these people, as a means of conciliating them); and that consequently the catholics have been given great cause to rouse themselves and take thought for their safety. It was now more evident than the protestants quite relish, that the catholics have had more success by their intrigues, and by fomenting division among protestants, than by force of arms; and they were now beginning to play with Brandenburg the same game which had hitherto paid them so well,[1] and to incite others to stir up [the elector] with encouragement and [promises of] assistance; without which he would not venture to move. I know [I said] that Y.M. was much grieved that in these dangerous times some who profess the protestant religion care more for their supposed private interests than for *causam publicam*; and I could therefore see no other way of making them sit still than a junction between Y.M. and his highness, so that such as are not to be influenced by devotion to the honour of God must be constrained to it by our united forces. And if Y.M. should be attacked, or suffer too great injury, at the hands of the Dutch and the Brandenburgers, that I knew his generous spirit; and that whatever the case might be, he would not suffer it for long, but would leave incomplete the work which otherwise he might have designed to finish, and look to his situation on that side in the hope that by God's counsel he might be able to bring to reason those who in return for many benefits *injustissime*

---

1. Thurloe was receiving regular and apparently accurate information on the course of the negotiations between the Dutch and Brandenburg: Thurloe, iii. 447 *etc.*

attack him, even if it should entail *dispendium causae publicae*. If in doing so it should go ill with Y.M. (which Almighty God forfend), the English would then be forced to face the fact that when once the catholics and the House of Austria were freed from danger on that side, they would turn all their forces against them. If now the honour of God was a matter of concern to his highness (as I knew it was), I entreated him to take practical steps to promote the same, and not for any minor considerations to allow time to run on until affairs were no longer *in integro*; adding finally that he ought not, for England's sake, to suffer the designs which were at present preparing: there was talk that the Dutch were to occupy Pillau as a pledge;[1] and if once they got a foothold in the Baltic there was an end to any hope of England's drawing any of that trade into her hands, but that that state [the United Netherlands], which at heart was England's greatest enemy, would thereby (as I had said on a previous occasion) obtain a greater accession of strength than by a couple of conquests in the East Indies. That I was not minded to meddle in the great issues between them, nor did I press my wishes *à leur despens*; but all the same I was well assured that his highness himself knew that the last Spanish fleet was really Dutch, that in Amsterdam at this moment they were equipping ships which were to act against England under Spanish colours,[2] and that it was fear and not good-will that made them keep on friendly terms with England *etc*. And so concluded with an excuse for having been somewhat prolix.

To this he answered first by saying how much he had appreciated my discourse, and no excuse was necessary; and then began to expound the interest the Dutch had in the trade to Prussia, and that it was not strange that they should be concerned about it. He next spoke eloquently and at length of the situation as between catholics and protestants, saying that I had given a very good account of it. The theme of his speech was that the honour of God was the sole *but* of all his actions; he recapitulated the causes of his attack upon Spain, and the present condition of that enterprise; and he ended by saying that he would use every possible means with both sides [*sc.* Sweden and the Dutch] to preserve unity between them. I answered with a suitable compliment, and paid tribute to his good intentions; but explained that though I was well aware of the Hollanders' object, I was for that reason the more surprised that they should have proceeded *praepostere* to obtain it. That before Y.M. began his campaign this year the

---

1. The Dutch offered Brandenburg a loan at 6% on the security of the customs at Pillau: *Brieven*, i. 381; Ellen Fries, *Bidrag till kännedomen om Sveriges och Nederländernas diplomatiska förbindelser under Karl X Gustafs tid* (Uppsala 1883), p. 24.

2. Sagredo had the same impression: *CSP* (*Ven*) *1655–56*, p. 138, Sagredo to Doge, 12 November 1655.

attention of their resident [in Sweden] had been drawn to the fact that they would do well to negotiate with him in good time; and I could assure them that they could then have obtained terms such as they will hardly get in the future. To begin by demanding with threats and hostile gestures is never the right way to obtain things to which no other claim can be advanced than simply that one wants them: they ought first to try amicable approaches; and I could assure them that just as when the places in question were in the possession of a catholic king he could not, in his own interests, hinder their trade to them, so it was still more the case that they would be permitted by Y.M. to enjoy it. It was stupid to fear that Y.M. would try to draw all that trade into his own hands, as was demonstrated by my proposal to England on Y.M.'s behalf; and though no one can reasonably object to giving one's own ships some preference in regard to tolls, that cannot interfere with the trade, which is in bulky goods for which the freight is more important than the duty. I could consequently explain their actions only as arising from bitterness against us simply because we would not join them in the late war against England, and afterwards because we took some care for our own commerce.

He answered that all this gave him much pain; and although he considered a [Dutch] league with Brandenburg as a thing which might easily be of service to protestantism, he would nevertheless gladly see an end to the controversies between us and the United Provinces. Such an objective ought indisputably to be aimed at; but the means to attain it were more problematical, and he would be most happy, by mediation or other practicable means, to help to bring it about, either by action here or by sending someone over to Y.M. To this proposal of mediation I answered in the same terms as in my letter of [2] November; namely, that Y.M. acknowledges no ill-will, much less enmity, towards the Dutch, since up to the present we have lived in amity and done good offices to each other. Foreign potentates are not to be put to the trouble of interposing with mediation except when a peace is to be made; there can be no question of looking for a peace when no hostilities exist; and therefore in this matter I had no instructions from Y.M. If the Dutch find that they need something which God has given Y.M.'s righteous arms the power to dispose of, it is only reasonable that they make a friendly approach to him. Nor does it seem to be a prudent conduct to give offence, and then to imagine that they can extort *e manu victoris* something which with less *dispendio* they might obtain on friendly terms. He seemed somewhat taken aback at this, and looked at Thurloe; and I could perceive that this had been the answer that they had previously decided to give me; but he responded nevertheless by reiterating once again how necessary it was to the Dutch that their bread-basket (which is Danzig) should be open to them, and protested his desire to remain in unity with them and serve them by all practicable means; his overriding wish being to secure unity between the two of us, for the honour of God and the interest of protestantism, of which he spoke most earnestly, and in noble (*exquisite*) language implored me to believe in his sincerity and truth. And he asked me to tell him my thoughts as to how I considered that end might best be achieved.

After a short compliment I answered that Y.M. would take it best if his highness were to indicate to the Dutch, in all seriousness, that he was ill pleased with their absurd proceedings, which might cause extensive complications and disunion among protestants, and that if they persisted in them he would be obliged to take every measure to restore unity. Further, since an alliance for mutual defence such as I had proposed is the only means to compel the others to conform, he ought to embrace it. If my suggestion of commercial advantages for the English did not please him, as possibly giving the Dutch too much occasion for jealousy, and his highness might for various reasons think it inadvisable to offend them, we should be ready to find other means, and make an alliance for mutual defence in the Baltic and the Channel, with provision for as many ships, and as much money or other consideration, as should be agreed between us. He took this very well, and said he would reflect upon it; reiterating his inclination to oblige us [*sc.* Sweden and the Dutch] to be friends, and saying that 'there must by no means be any disunion between you: I shall ask both of you most pressingly to seek agreement; and if that fails, we must see about taking such measures as may be required'. With that we parted, well satisfied on both sides; and I have later heard that he was very happy about it.[1]

From all this Y.M. may gather that as I have always feared that the Dutch faction has been countermining my mission, so now it proves to be true; and for that reason I have always taken care not to be too precipitate, lest I should receive a rebuff, but have preferred to await [the news of] Y.M.'s successful campaign, and also other occurrences which may easily alter the posture of affairs. In this I have so far been fortunate that their quarrel with Spain, and the

---

1. In fact, the protector seems to have been in a state of painful indecision, to the exasperation of de Witt, who waited impatiently for some clear indication of what he might expect from England: de Witt to Nieupoort, 12 Nov. NS: *Brieven*, iii. 141. A week later Cromwell assured Nieupoort that he hoped for 'a still closer and more confident friendship' with the Dutch: Thurloe, iv. 178. On 29 November NS Nieupoort could report that the protector, in reply to an appeal from the States-General to signify his intentions with regard to the Baltic, had informed him 'That he had caused . . . to be proposed to the lord ambassador of Sweden so much, that he was of opinion, that all the protestant powers ought to cultivate among themselves unity and friendship'— an answer which left matters as uncertain as before: Thurloe, iv. 214.

attitude towards the catholics in general which that quarrel has constrained them to assume, force them to look to Y.M. more than to any other potentate, since they think that as a result of this war in Poland he may easily become involved in a war with them [the catholics]. I have talked of this with some leading personages, who are of the opinion that in such a case England might well make a descent on Flanders, assemble a strong army there, advance into Germany, so that we could, *unitis viribus*, attack the House of Austria and with the blessing of God have a good chance of overturning the power of the papacy: a vast prospect, which I do not altogether dismiss out of hand.[1] As I wrote some time ago, I find that these people are still not willing to accept my proposals for [commercial] advantages, from their fear of the Dutch. I have long been awaiting an answer to my letter concerning other means [of persuasion]; but not having received any, and the state of affairs becoming pressing, I have made bold to give them an opening for a mutual defensive alliance, basing myself upon Y.M.'s letter of 22 August from Koło, which suggested that such a proposal would not be unacceptable to Y.M. I beg Y.M. to pardon me for venturing to touch on that matter without express instructions: necessity, and international events, have forced me to it, and it seems to me that this proposal is less liable to objection, and more attractive to Y.M., than that which I put forward before.

I have written to Appelboom to find out how Louis de Geer proceeded in the matter of hiring ships for the war against Denmark,[2] and to see to it that I get some information about it. There is news from Holland of the exchange of ratifications of the late treaty between themselves and Brandenburg, and that the promised subsidies are to be paid to Brandenburg without delay; also that Pelz, the States-General's resident in Danzig, does his best to incite the estates of royal Prussia to accept the protection of the elector, encouraging them with the prospect of powerful aid from the States of Holland.[3] I have

1. *Cf.* Giustinian's report from Paris: 'everyone is agreed that the king of Sweden in the end will attack the states of his catholic majesty, as there is little for him to gain in Poland; and that Cromwell, by a mutual understanding, will invade the Indies and the provinces of the Low Countries which pertain to the catholic king ... The Dutch ... are afraid that with the opportunity England will approach too close to the United Provinces. The Dutch ambassador indeed spoke to me very earnestly about it, urging me to prepare the way and bring about peace between the crowns, as he foresees and dreads the expedition into Flanders that England will make if the first attempts are not stoutly resisted': Giustinian to Doge, 29 November NS 1655, *CSP (Ven) 1655–56*, p. 146.

2. In 1643. The enquiry obviously had reference to the possibility of Charles X's hiring of English ships.

3. Frederick William had tried as early as January 1655 to persuade Danzig to join the other towns of royal Prussia in defensive measures against a possible Swedish attack. The estate of nobles in royal Prussia reached agreement with the elector at Rynsk on

thought a good deal about how I should react to these clearly hostile proceedings of the Dutch. And although they might provide a reason for putting increased pressure on these people to take measures against their designs, I have been reluctant to say any more about it than I have indicated above; and I pretend not to know all the details, or to be in any apprehension, both because it may in that way be easier to arrive at a reconciliation between Y.M. and them [the Dutch], and also because it leaves Y.M.'s hands more completely free.

The protector is now starting to think of some regulation of trade in this country, and has formed a Council of Trade to take care of it. This post brings gratifying tidings of Y.M.'s incomparable successes in Poland; and the last, from the camp outside Kraków, written on 4 October, gives good hope that Kraków will fall.[1] I hope not only that this has happened, but also that Y.M. by this time is returning to Warsaw, and by the help of God has dealt with Prussia: Resident Kock[2] writes to me of the attitude of the estates to the elector, and if it is as he says I hope that the rhodomontades of the Dutch may prove vain. We have no great reason to thank these people for any friendly service, and may therefore attribute all these victories only to God, and to Y.M.'s prudence and valour. In order to counteract all the various stories about Y.M.'s situation which are circulating here, I had an English translation made of the account which came to me from Secretary Lilienthal[3] by the last post. I gave it immediately to Secretary Thurloe to deliver to the protector, principally to notify the death of his Princely Grace Landgrave Frederick [of Hesse]; but also so that I might comment on the news I had of the probability of the fall of Kraków, and of Y.M.'s good relations with Chmielnicki,[4] and other matters; which he received with great heartiness, made enquiry as to particular points, and protested his delight at the news; saying among other things that he hoped that Y.M. would be able to retrace his steps and reduce to order those enemies whom he had left behind him—significant words, in view of our earlier conversation.[5] He

2 November, but Danzig refused to participate: they distrusted the elector, and hoped for help from the Dutch: Cieślak, 'Gdansks ... betydelse', pp. 133–7. And *cf.* Bohdan Kentrschyńskyj, *Karl X Gustav inför krisen i öster 1654–55*, (Stockholm 1956), pp. 42–3, 113, for Charles X's anxiety at this possibility.

1. Kraków capitulated on 9/10 October.

2. Swedish resident in Danzig.

3. Johan Mayer af Lilienthal had been sent to Danzig in October 1654, and to Prussia and Poland, with instructions to attempt to assess the danger from Russia and the intentions of John Casimir and the Polish magnates: Kentrschyńskyj, *Karl X Gustaf*, pp. 41–2.

4. For this, see Kentrschyńskyj, *Karl X Gustaf*, pp. 12, 28, 68, 73, 80, 82; and *idem*, 'Ukrainska revolutionen', pp. 27–42, 56, 58.

5. Bonde seems to have taken this as implicitly approving Swedish designs on Danzig, or possibly Brandenburg.

offered condolences on the death of Y.M.'s brother-in-law [Frederick of Hesse], but observed that Y.M.'s great victories had well made good the loss. Whereupon, after commending my business to him, and asking for a meeting with my commissioners (which he promised me) I retired. There was really little in the audience beyond formalities, except that I reassured him about Y.M.'s situation, which I cannot but consider has been concealed from him by the Dutch faction. It must be two post-days since I wrote to Y.M. about the anxiety I was in regarding money for Lord Cranstoun's recruiting: we are now relieved of it, for Commissary Hoffstetter has promised to accept a bill for 4000 *rdr.* Cranstoun promises, if it is at all possible to come over before winter sets in, to send some men to Stade this autumn.

Coyet to Charles X

43

London, 9 November 1655 [in German]

[Another proclamation issued, denouncing at length the plots of royalists against the government, and announcing sterner measures against them. These cannot be carried out without an extraordinary military force. The protector therefore with the advice of his council has determined to establish a new standing army in every county; but in such wise that those who again engage against the government (but not those who live peaceably, or have been sufficiently dealt with already) shall be proportionably charged with the cost of this new force; though there shall be a general pardon for the adverse party, and all enmities be laid aside by both sides, but with the reiterated proviso that all give security for their continued good behaviour.

A new fleet of 40 warships is fitting out, to sail for the West Indies about Christmastide. Not yet known who is to command it: Penn and Venables (on the latter of whom almost all the blame for the mismanagement in Hispaniola is laid) are liberated; and although their commissions are taken away it is thought that Penn may sail on the projected expedition, under Blake's command.

The heavy expenditure involved in fitting out this fleet, and also in regard to the impending war against Spain in Europe, is to be met by doubling the monthly assessment throughout England from £60,000 to £120,000; so that there will be no lack of means to attack Spain in all quarters, though so far it does not appear that the Spaniards are doing the English much harm at sea (their hostility appearing only in ports and harbours), and they have not interrupted the post from here to Andorff [Antwerp?]; which suggests that Spain does not want war with England. Nevertheless, while the embargo on the English ships and goods continues, that will be considered on the English side to be a sufficient pretext for war, apart from other reasons.

The Spanish ambassador left a week ago from Dover, in an English frigate; a company of horse accompanied him to Dover. He entertained them handsomely at Canterbury, thus manifesting open-handedness at his departure, though in the 19 years of his residence here he has been extremely sparing and parsimonious. His priests he left to the Venetian ambassador, except for two Jesuits whom the ambassador refused to take. The laws against Jesuits being extremely severe, they had to be got out of the country without loss of time: the ambassador hired a ship to transport them and their baggage, which was however strictly visited by the customs-men.

Recently yet another new committee, or a '*Commerce Collegium*', was set up to improve trade and navigation: it comprises various members of the protector's council; the Commissioners of the Great Seal; the judges *supremis utriusque instantiae*; and members of the council of the City of London, to the number of 45. Richard Cromwell is to preside. It is to hold its first session in the Painted Chamber on 25 November. It seems that it will be concerned not only with trade and navigation, but also with customs accounts, in which frauds are suspected: yesterday Colonel [Edmund] Harvey, one of the Commissioners of Customs, was put in prison, accused of defrauding the state of large sums and applying them to his own use.][1]

Bonde to Charles X

XXII

London, [16] November 1655[2]

By my last letter Y.M. will, I presume, have had my lengthy account of my audience with his highness on the two preceding post-days. I

1. Abbott, iv. 17.
2. On 15/25 November Nieupoort had a long audience which clearly reflected Cromwell's indecision. In a lengthy and rambling speech he observed that Charles X was buried in the depths of Poland; no word had come from Rolt; could not he and Nieupoort negotiate jointly with Bonde? He agreed with Dutch objectives, protested his affection for Holland, remarked that the Swedes would deny any sinister intentions, compared Prussia to Naboth's Vineyard, doubted if he could find any suitable envoy to send to Charles, and promised to think it over: *Brieven*, iii. 145–6. De Witt's reply showed his impatience, and a suspicion that Cromwell would refuse to coöperate: moreover he had found that Bonde was well informed about Dutch approaches to Thurloe: *ibid.*, 148.

have had to some extent to accommodate myself to the feelings that obtain here, but I can assure Y.M. that I have not by doing so prejudiced his wishes and intentions in the slightest degree. Y.M.'s gracious letter of 30 September, from Casimir before Kraków, came safely to hand by the last post, with its news of Y.M.'s happy situation and his incomparable great success in his noble and laudable designs: may Almighty God, in Whom all power is vested, continue His blessings to Y.M., to the honour of His name, the immortal reputation of Y.M., and the great benefit and advantage of our fatherland. The same letter from Y.M. brings me also the information on various matters which Y.M. was pleased to give me: it is inexpressibly welcome, and I shall bear it in mind with all due reverence.[1] As to the taking of toll off Danzig, I have, as occasion offered, endeavoured to forestall any objections, on the grounds which Y.M. mentioned in his letters. And since the season is so far advanced, and in any case the customs-house in Danzig is closed, so that no duty is collected,[2] there is the less talk about it here.

What they are principally keeping an eye upon is how it may be possible to reconcile Y.M. and the elector of Brandenburg. If it should please God so far to bless Y.M. that he is able to realize his wish to reach agreement with the estates in Warsaw and in Prussia, now that he has finished with Kraków and (as I trust) reduced that part of Poland to subjection, then it is reasonable to suppose that these people will hold a more acceptable language than they have hitherto done, and move from general protestations to such more concrete points as Y.M. may, in that situation, think proper to put to them. Herr Appelboom's letters report the Hollanders' perplexity, and suggest that their anxiety about the toll in Danzig may easily result in their seeking the alliance with this country which they rejected before the war with England broke out. I hope, if Y.M. is pleased to make himself master of Prussia, that he takes such measures as he may think best and most serviceable for the promotion of commerce. I note from the same letter from Appelboom that they fear a discrimination in the matter of toll; which makes me much of the opinion that they have got to know of my overtures here; for I do not believe that they would be so disturbed at the prospect of Y.M.'s giving his own subjects a preference against the foreigners. If this is the fact, I am pretty sure that it comes from my commissioners, or from Thurloe, since I have kept it so secret that no one can have got it from me. I shall try

1. Carlbom, *Sverige och England*, p. 46. Charles X instructed Bonde to proceed *caute* in regard to any suggestion for a protestant alliance. He was to change his mind a month later.

2. This was Danzig's reply to the Swedish blockade: it deprived the Swedes of the tolls they had hoped to collect.

through every available channel to hinder their intrigues as far as possible; but I must admit that this country is in a somewhat confused state; and though the protector himself, and all his ministers, try to reassure me, with every conceivable protestation of their affection for Y.M. and the crown of Sweden, it is still true that so far little of any consequence has emerged, and that I am still not able to get together with the commissioners to negotiate anything. I should be very glad to know Y.M.'s views about mediation with the Muscovites. I have not spoken of it for a long time, and if they do not take to it, I shall let it drop as best I can. I shall also proceed *cautissime* in regard to the Evangelical Cause, and say nothing whatever to prejudice Y.M.'s policies in any way.

I had by this post a letter from my messenger to Y.M., Per Bonde, written from Switzerland on 19 October. He had been forced to make a long stop there, by reason of the roads' being unsafe, and complained bitterly that he cannot get hold of any convoy to continue his journey; which provokes him exceedingly.

Coyet to Charles X

44

London, 16 November 1655 [in German]

[The Major-Generals are beginning to apply actively the policy of proportionable contributions from the royalists, to the maintenance of the militia. The recently established Commerce *Collegium* has issued an ordinance ordering all receivers of revenue, and others who have had to handle public money at any time since 1642, to present their accounts. It is thought that *si respublica ex iis spongias fecerit* as much could be got from them as from the monthly contributions.

Differing opinions as to the objective of the fleet of 40 ships now fitting out: if for the West Indies, there would be difficulties, and the great expense scarcely justified. Some think they will be content to keep a foothold in Jamaica, and use this fleet against Spain nearer home.

Merchants report that two galleons of the silver-fleet are already in Cadiz, and the remainder expected immediately; and that the king of Spain has commandeered their cargo, to the prejudice of interested merchants: it would seem that he needs it. If indeed the fleet has arrived (which is doubted here) he has the English fleet to thank for it, which neglected its opportunity; for it is undoubted that if it had been longer delayed the English would not have allowed such a rich prize to escape them. Reported

also that the clergy in Spain have freely offered 4 million ducats
to the king.

No news of Spanish naval activities in these waters; though there
is a clamour that two Dunkirkers or Ostenders recently ventured
into an English port, in Norfolk, intending to capture some vessels,
but without success: they not only had to abandon their ships, but
had to pay for it with their necks. Reported also that some English
merchantmen from Brest have been snapped up, to the no little
indignation of merchants here that such acts of war should continue
after the conclusion of the treaty [with France].

The secretary whom the French ambassador sent to Paris to
obtain the ratification of the treaty returned yesterday, to the relief
of the ambassador, who had assured the government here that he
would be back within a fortnight. That it took him longer is
attributed to the renewed resistance of some governors in the French
frontier provinces, and to the suspicion that they were in league
with the prince of Condé. This caused the king of France, with the
cardinal, to hasten thither in person in order to deal with it, and
the ratification was consequently delayed until his return to Paris.

The Dutch ambassador recently had a conference with the commissioners: its purpose as yet unknown.

The protector has issued a proclamation that 29 November be
observed throughout England as a day of prayer and fasting.]

Bonde to Charles X

XXIII

London, 23 November 1655

Since the last post I have been very uneasy in my mind at the fact
that I am compelled to spend my time here virtually to no purpose,
and that after so many reminders I have still nothing to do. I have
therefore considered it necessary to draw up the enclosed remonstrance, and to deliver it to his highness in person, that I may see
what effect it may have. And in order to give it greater weight I asked
for an audience with his highness this week, so that I might speak
directly to him. I had it to-day at 10 o'clock this morning. In which
I took occasion (from the arrival of tidings from Brandenburg by
the last post) to begin by saying that although from the reasonable
expectations to be derived from Y.M.'s great successes in Poland, and
the taking of Kraków, I confidently expected that by this time Y.M.
would have come to a settlement with the elector of Brandenburg, I
had nevertheless thought it my duty to reveal to his highness that
there were those who alleged that the elector had good prospects of

coming to an understanding with his highness, and with this country, and to that end desired to send an ambassador hither.[1] That I was well assured of his highness's good affection towards Y.M., and therefore requested that he would make no statement which might be repugnant to Y.M., but rather address his mind to how Y.M. might be brought into a state of greater confidence with him, which I was assured would tend to the honour of God and the advantage of them both.

To this he answered that it was impossible for him to prevent people from talking and judging as might be most to their advantage: their intention was to lure others to embrace their party; but he could and would assure me that he would not only put no obstacle in the way of Y.M., and especially of his present undertakings against the catholics, nor would he by word or deed give countenance to any who might wish to thwart him; but he wished with all his heart that he knew how best to restrain all those who were minded to impede Y.M.'s progress against the conscience-forcing catholics. He then protested his sincerity at length; and said that as I had from the beginning talked to him honestly and truly, he would assure me that the character he was most jealous to preserve was the reputation of being an honest man, and if ever I detected any duplicity in him, I need never trust him more. Secretary Thurloe (who was the only other person present) reminded him that there was an envoy from Brandenburg in the country; but his highness said that he had never set eyes on him, nor received the smallest communication from him on matters of business; and he assured me that he would do nothing to conflict with Y.M.'s plans.

I replied that such a determination was no more than I had expected, and would expect, of his highness; and made a sort of apology. We then moved on to talk of Y.M.'s achievements in Poland. I informed him of the fall of Kraków; of the union between Chmielnicki and the Cossacks; and their good relations with Y.M.; of the agreement with Lithuania,[2] and so forth. He appeared astonished and delighted, enquired as to the length of Y.M.'s march, and said that if what I told him was true, a man travelling by himself could scarcely

---

1. Abbott writes of this audience: 'It seems to have begun with a suggestion reminiscent of the days of Gustavus Adolphus that England might invade Flanders, form a strong army there, and later, with increased power, enter Germany, and "with God's help make an end of the Pope's dominion" '. This is a reflection (in the wrong place) of the opinion—not of the protector but of 'some leading personages', reported in Bonde's despatch of 9 November: it was not a 'suggestion' made by either side at this audience: Abbott, iv. 28.

2. By the treaty of Kiedany, 18 August 1655, between Charles X on the one hand, and the Lithuanian hetman Janusz Radziwiłł and the Lithuanian estates on the other; whereby Lithuania was incorporated into a union with Sweden.

have traversed all those places more quickly than Y.M. had taken them.[1] He wished Y.M. all good fortune; asserted that all [his own] policies are directed against the designs of the pope and his adherents; and expressed his loyal support with many words. I then asked that my commissioners might enter into negotiations with me; in particular on matters of commerce and navigation, pending the time when he found it appropriate to treat of other matters. He said the commissioners were already appointed, and promised that they should certainly do so. I then took my leave, after recommending to his attention the business of some Swedish merchants in Barbados, and my Lord Cranstoun's affair in particular. I did not wish to enter more at large into the question of his interposition [with the Dutch], or into other questions; both because I had said enough to him on these matters already, and because I think it is sufficient, until such time as I am in a position to know how it may fall out between Y.M. and the elector of Brandenburg, to restrain him from giving any countenance to our enemies. I have good hopes that next week I may meet my commissioners; with whom I intend to treat both of recruiting in the future, and of those points which are postponed from the last treaty, and as to which I have instructions. I shall see to it that I am in a position to send Y.M. the draft of my first proposals by the next post.[2]

For the rest, these people are mainly preoccupied with the affair of the Indies. Many well-informed persons judge that however it may end, it is likely to tend more to England's injury than to its advantage. For they have already expended a great treasure upon it; and however well it may turn out it can be of little assistance to England in case of necessity, lying as it does at so great a distance, but will rather drain them of men and money, as is the case with Spain. And if things go badly for them there, they will have expended much money and lost many men, who might have been employed nearer home without risk and with greater advantage. The proclamation against Spain has now been translated into Latin, and I have sent Y.M. a copy.[3] I am reliably informed that Prince Robert [sc. Rupert] has been summoned to the emperor, and it is said that he is to take command of his forces:[4] he is considered in this country to be a gentleman of courage, but not of the calibre to have the supreme command of an army; and even those

1. Between 1 and 4 September Charles and his army marched 120 km. from Warsaw to Opoczno: Jan Wimmer, in *Polens krig med Sverige 1655–1660* (Carl X Gustaf-studier, 5) (Stockholm 1973), p. 344.

2. Bonde's *Diarium* of 28 November notes '*Composui articulos quosdam tractandos*'.

3. Possibly by Milton: see David Masson, *The Life of John Milton, narrated in connection with the ... History of his Time* (7 vols. 1859–64), v. 241.

4. There was no truth in the rumour: the emperor was not anxious to see him in Vienna.

who are of the king's party say that if his purpose had been to ruin the king's cause he could not have comported himself otherwise than he did.

His highness's envoy [William Prideaux] is returned from Russia; and I have reliable information that in his report he says much of the disorderly condition of that country and its government, and of their great fear of Y.M.; to whose person and splendid achievements he pays many honourable tributes.[1] If this may be of any assistance to my negotiation with them on the Russia trade, time alone will show; but in any event I shall say nothing on that head beyond what is contained in Y.M.'s orders from Casimir of 30 September. The terms which the Eastland Company have desired his highness to put to me I sent to Y.M. on 26 October, together with a short statement of my opinion of them; and I hope that they have reached Y.M. safely and that I may have an early reply to them.[2] Letters by this post have still not been delivered; whether the post has not arrived, or whether the letters are held up for scrutiny, I have no means of knowing.[3]

Coyet to Charles X

45

London, 23 November 1655 [in German]

[On 19 November the treaty with France signed by the protector, and ratifications exchanged. It is to be proclaimed on 28 November simultaneously in London and Paris, when it is to be hoped its contents will be made known. Soon afterwards the French ambassador (he informs me) will go to Paris to fetch his wife and family, and will speedily return.

A rumour that the king of Spain has raised the embargo on English ships and goods. The ground for this incorrect report is that two English ships carrying wine have arrived: they induced the

1. The tsar had given a reassuring reception to a mission sent to announce Charles X's accession, but privately spoke of him and the Swedes in terms of contempt: Kentrschyński, *Karl X Gustav*, pp. 106-7.

2. Missing in transcript; but printed in *CSP (Dom) 1655–56*, p. 97, and dated 4 January 1656.

3. The remonstrance appended to this despatch (wrongly inserted in transcript after Bonde's of 23 August) is in Latin. It appeals to the protector to hasten negotiations with the commissioners: Bonde has been awaiting their answer for more than three months; he fears that Charles X may take it ill, or put the blame on him; the period allotted for his mission has already elapsed, and it may well be that he may be sent immediate letters of recall.

Dutch at Malaga to allow them to sail in company with them, and it is expected that this may be practised in future by favour of the Dutch, in order to avert a possible shortage of Spanish wine as a consequence of the English edict prohibiting its import in foreign vessels. A Spanish ship from the Canaries, sailing from Dunkirk to Zeeland, and intending to proceed to Malaga under a convoy of several Dutch warships, was spotted by an English frigate lying in the Downs, and was brought up a few days ago, as was also a French ship laden with pipe-staves and destined for Malaga.

Great complaints by royalists over the decimation. The Major-Generals have peremptorily summonsed the leading delinquents and told them that proceedings will be taken against them without delay despite their opposition, and despite their appeal to the articles of war granted to them and the fact that they have made a composition for their property and been granted an amnesty. This rigour hits them the more hardly because the decimation falls not only on those actually involved in the late rising, but extends to the whole royalist party, which is now by presumption held to have been implicated. And the clergy and the episcopalian party greatly fear that on vexatious pretexts they may be treated with such severity that they may be not only extruded *a ministerio* but also be shut out *a paedagogiis* of those whose goods are sequestered, until they dare not venture to go about with the children of delinquents, or to earn a living in any capacity, *ne medicinae quidem.*

The Dutch ambassador last Tuesday gave a banquet and invited Bonde and Bordeaux: Bonde declined, in order to avoid the question of precedence between them. Coyet, however, accepted, and was flatteringly treated by the Dutch ambassador, who expressed his cordial wishes for good relations with Sweden. He gave pride of place to Bordeaux, with Coyet on Bordeaux's right, himself on Bordeaux's left, with the Danish resident next to him. He drank to the king of France, to Charles X, then to Bordeaux, then to the States-General, and finally to the king of Denmark, which so annoyed the Danish resident that he left in the middle of the meal.

P.S. Copy of letter from Barbados to the protector, and also of the French translation of the protector's manifesto setting forth the grounds of his war with Spain.][1]

---

1. Both are missing in the transcript.

Bonde to Charles X

XXIV

London, 30 November 1655

In my last letter to Y.M. I gave a full account of how I had an audience with the protector a week ago, principally concerning the elector of Brandenburg; when I requested, both verbally and in writing, to be allowed to meet my commissioners. Since then I have renewed my request both to Secretary Thurloe and to [Charles] Fleetwood, but have got nowhere.[1]

In the last few days the peace with France has been solemnly proclaimed, to the sound of trumpets; at which the French ambassador has manifested *publicum gaudium* with fireworks and a great banquet. Whether these festivities have somewhat delayed my business I cannot tell. But at least it is certain that since my last talk with the protector, when I upset his *consilium* of being a mediator between Y.M. and Holland, he has been so *en peine* that he hardly knows what he is going to do in the matter. And though I made as though I was prepared to allow my former proposals to be considered as a separate issue, and in the meantime to take up matters concerning commerce and so forth, it would seem that they are either irresolute or nonchalant; and they have had so much to do about the royalists, and how to keep them down, that they have not much time for anything else. Although the Dutch have many good friends here, they are treated no better, and the Dutch ambassador is so worried that he has no idea what steps to take about the Dutch ships that have been detained, having so far been given very little or no satisfaction. About three weeks ago he told the protector in very strong terms that his masters neither could nor would suffer it; but (as I am informed by one of my friends) the only result has been that some resolutions intended to be favourable to him which had been earlier decided on have since been held up, and not communicated to him; which has occasioned great bitterness between the Dutch and these people.[2] I can come to no other conclusion than that those who sit in the government have never dealt with affairs before, and particularly not with foreign affairs, and

---

1. As Whitelocke recorded: 'No commissioners being yet come to the Swedish ambassador, he grew into some high expressions of his sense of the neglect to his master by this delay; which I did endeavour to excuse, and acquainted the protector with it, who thereupon promised to have it mended, and to send suddenly to the ambassador': Whitelocke, *Memorials*, iv. 218. Whitelocke was appointed a commissioner on 5 December.

2. English privateers had taken 12 Dutch ships, and Nieupoort had put in a strong protest: *cf. Brieven*, iii. 159, 23/4 December NS, where he comments 'No one outside this country could have any idea what harpies there are here'.

that they blunder through ignorance; a situation which is not helped by the fact that they are much puffed up, rely on their advantageous situation and their great power at sea (of which they first became conscious in the Dutch war) and are consequently somewhat leisurely in their proceedings. And it is therefore certain that if the Dutch could find some way to obtain revenge, and to cut them down to size, they would not hesitate to take it—as no doubt Y.M. will have gathered from Appelboom's noteworthy reports.

For the rest, all persons of weight in this place are astounded by Y.M.'s great successes in Poland, and their effects will without doubt influence the policy they pursue here. I send Y.M. herewith a draft of the first of the points I intend putting to my commissioners: they will deal with recruiting and ships' cargoes. I have included the items which Y.M. was pleased to recollect, which I gather they will be prepared to entertain; and I have done so because if it were possible to obtain them it would in any event be as useful to Y.M. as if we were to engage with them on other, more controversial issues. And if Y.M. after settling with Brandenburg should come into possession of Prussia and Danzig, and *ex consequenti* come to terms with the Dutch, then both these formidable naval powers would be forced to make every effort to conciliate Y.M., since he would be able to tip the balance to one side and so ruin the other. I shall make every effort to carry this point, so that Y.M. may know in good time what can be done here next spring, and consequently can arrange for the necessary orders and the provision of means. I do my best to push them on, but I must nevertheless do it with courtesy, so that such good-will as I have acquired here is not lost. My greatest difficulty is that I have no money, and no means to obtain either private or public credit. If I had, I might win over some more persons, so that I could know what is going on, and also have at my disposal some people who would promote my business: I humbly beg Y.M. to turn this point over in his mind. The second point that I intend to present [to my commissioners] concerns contraband; which I hope will not occasion much difficulty, except that in the French treaty grain and provisions to places under siege are included; but I do not think there is much objection to granting that. Since I learn that in the French treaty it is provided that for the next four years 'free ship makes free goods',[1] I have inserted that also in the third point, which deals with sea-passes. For this purpose I have drafted three forms of pass: one for Swedish ships carrying Swedish goods, the second for Swedish goods in foreign ships, and the third for Swedish ships with foreign goods, and I will send the drafts of the latter two to Y.M. by the next post. I have decided to limit myself to these three points at this meeting, so that I may the

1. Bonde was misinformed, as he was to find in his negotiations later.

sooner have another conference with the commissioners. If I can carry this, it will be a great advantage and do much to promote our commerce, now that there is a war with Spain. I cannot tell what is to be hoped from these people, for they are so excessively dilatory; but I shall do my best as far as may be practicable and possible.

Bonnel's situation here is utterly wretched; and I shall soon be in the same predicament myself. Some small amount of money is promised me from Sweden, but so far I have not received any; and therefore, with great submission, I humbly beg that Y.M. may take steps, in Hamburg or some other place, to ensure that I am not left in need: among other inconveniences, it puts great obstacles in the way of Y.M.'s service.[1]

Coyet to Charles X

46

London, 30 November 1655 [in German]

[Peace with France proclaimed on the 28th; first before the council chamber in Whitehall (from which the protector and council observed the ceremony); then in Palace Garden, Westminster; then at Temple Bar, where the heralds were met by the lord mayor and council; then at the Exchange: the heralds bore the arms of the republic—a red cross with a harp. Copy of the proclamation enclosed. In the evening Bordeaux gave a banquet to the Swedish, Venetian and Dutch ambassadors, and other public ministers, with fireworks; and was the next day splendidly entertained in Whitehall by the protector.

The protector recently issued a proclamation ordering that no one who had engaged against the government should carry, use or keep arms; also that from 1 January 1656 no royalist may employ a preacher, professor, preceptor or similar person either in any public place, or privately except in his own house.

Despite the rigorous measures against the disaffected, another plot was recently set on foot, so that three persons (among them one Halsel [James Halsall], an agent of the king of Scotland who for safety's sake went under the name of More) were caught. They had secret letters of great and dangerous consequence concealed in the lining of their hats. They were betrayed by one of their accomplices and are put in prison. The method by which they

---

1. Bonde had already appealed to the Swedish council, through his brother, Gustav Bonde, for financial assistance: they sent him 3000 *rdr.* which it was hoped would be sufficient to cover a month's expenses: *RRP* xvi. 342, 391.

intended to pursue their design is kept secret, pending the seizure of the principal [in the affair].

Letters from St Kitts with news that Major Sedgwick and his squadron have presumably arrived at Jamaica, and that two ships with biscuit, brandy and other provisions have left the Caribbean islands for the same destination.]

Bonde to Charles X

XXV

London, 7 December 1655

I am assuming that Y.M. will have collected from my earlier letters that I have for some time been asking for my commissioners to investigate whether anything can be done regarding the matters on which Y.M. instructed me. I had a conference in my house last Wednesday, the 5th, with the commissioners appointed by his highness to meet me; namely Viscount Lisle (who had been appointed a commissioner on the previous occasion, but was absent through illness), Lord Whitelocke, and Strickland; and to that conference I brought with me Herr Coyet. I had explained to them why I desired to confer with them, thanking them shortly for their trouble in coming to my house, and proceeded to read to them the two attached articles, with a commentary on the advantages, and the marked strengthening of friendly ties, which would result from their acceptance. I apologized for the fact that they had been drawn as though they had already been agreed, explaining that I had not done so with the intention of prescribing anything to them, but with the idea of hastening our proceedings and setting out my views more clearly. They received them with a short compliment, and said that as they were still rela-tively unfamiliar with these matters they would ask time to discuss them among themselves, after which they would confer with me further; and with that we separated. I am very glad that Whitelocke has been appointed one of my commissioners, since he is particularly well informed on these questions, and I am at liberty to visit him, and he to visit me; which means that I am in a better position to give him the relevant information, and he has a better opportunity than was previously allowed to him to say what he thinks.[1] It seems to me, moreover, not improbable that they have now appointed other com-missioners than before in order that they may not seem obliged to give an answer to my first proposal.[2] As to the articles themselves, I

1. Since Whitelocke was not a member of the council, the rule against visits by foreign diplomats did not apply to him.
2. I.e. regarding the alliance, and Charles X's request for naval aid.

am sending the first of them, which deals with recruiting, to Y.M. by the next post; together with a short commentary explaining the reasons which led me to draft it in the form in which it now stands; and I hope that if I can get it accepted in this form it will, at less expense, partly realize what (among other important points) Y.M. has sought to obtain from this country. The second article, concerning contraband goods, is formulated strictly according to the tenour of my instructions, except that I have re-worded it more circumstantially in view of the fact that one cannot take too many precautions against this country's privateers, who are extremely mischievous. I have also discussed with Herr Coyet whether, when the time comes to raise the question of sea-passes, it might not be advisable to try to establish that 'free ship makes free goods'; since this was included, for the next four years, in the treaty with France; and, as I understand, the people here were disposed to accept a longer period.[1] But the French would not agree to that, because the dominions of the king of Spain are so situated that when there is any communication between them by sea it must pass the French coast—as for instance between Spain and Flanders, and Naples, Milan, Sicily and Spain—and consequently the French have always the possibility of harassing them at sea. They therefore hit upon four years, since they thought it likely that England's war with Spain would last at least so long,[2] so that for that period they did not need to fear that English ships would be active in the Spanish trade. The advantages which we judge Y.M. and his subjects might thereby obtain are principally (i) it provides against any possibility of stopping Swedish ships on any pretext whatever. Without such a provision they would hardly be safe, for [the English] would constantly be stopping and visiting them on the pretext of 'enemy goods', particularly during their war with Spain—as may be clearly seen from the example of the Dutch during the previous disputes between them and England, when over a hundred ships were stopped on the pretext of carrying French goods, and a great part of their cargo has still not been restored; (ii) it could be of great help to the trade and navigation to Spain this spring, especially in regard to cargoes consigned to and from those ports; (iii) we cannot see that it would work to the prejudice of Y.M. and the crown of Sweden in any way should Y.M. come to a settlement with Prussia and Danzig,

---

1. The truth was the exact opposite of what Bonde supposed: Article XV accorded free trade to English and French merchants trading to 'the Mediterranean, the Eastern Sea, or the Ocean' *except* that all sorts of war-materials were to be contraband for four years: Abbott, iii. 934.

2. The four years referred not to England's war with Spain, but to France's: Bonde's whole subsequent argument on the point was irrelevant, because it was throughout based on false premises.

which I feel pretty sure is already the case, or with God's help will be so before navigation starts again, for in that case Y.M. can have no enemy in the Baltic other than Denmark and Lübeck, and it is impossible because of the Sound to hinder navigation to Denmark, since all ships going in or out of the Baltic must pass the Sound, and can there lay up, or load whatever goods they choose, and no chance of preventing it as long as the Sound is in their [Denmark's] hands. There may indeed be a problem about Norway, but the inconvenience and risk is not to be compared with the convenience which [this provision] would afford to Y.M., especially in that for some years to come it will give a strong stimulus to Y.M.'s subjects to build ships and themselves transport such commodities as may be brought to their towns and ports. Should Y.M. be so unfortunate (though I hope that God may of His grace avert it) as to be unable to reach agreement with Danzig and Prussia, the situation would still be rather more than less to his advantage, in view of the fact that Y.M. is master of Poland, for whom it is important that trade continues through those channels; which will mean that England's commerce increases while that of the Dutch declines. I expect and hope that Y.M. may be graciously pleased to approve what I have done. Although I intend to bring forward other points about trade and compensation, I thought it inadvisable to say more on this occasion, both to avoid their delaying too long with their answer, and also so that they may not suppose that they have done enough if they give me satisfaction on some minor matters and reject the others. Besides, the matter of compensation is something they find it difficult to swallow, and I thought it better not to bring it forward until we are close to a settlement on other points.

I learned by the last post that God had called the incumbent in Örebro to Himself, and that there is consequently a vacancy there; and Dr Jonas Billovius, Court-Preacher to Y.M., whom Y.M. was good enough to allow me to take with me on my mission, has earnestly requested me to recommend him to Y.M., in hopes that Y.M. may be graciously pleased to prefer him to that situation; and since his praiseworthy behaviour well deserves that I should give him such assistance as I can, I make it my humble prayer to Y.M. that he may be pleased to give him his gracious approval. I am by this post writing in his favour to his grace the bishop, and to the congregation, and I expect that they will not reject his candidature, since he is of the same diocese and was born in Örebro, where his father for many years served as curate.

Two letters from Y.M. have this moment arrived by post, the one dated 25 October, from Proszowice, the other dated 11 November from Zacbenska, and I shall faithfully attend to their contents. Since the post is now due to depart I have no time at present to answer them, but must postpone it until the next post.

I have just learnt from a good friend that the Dutch ambassador, having received his letters at 11 o'clock, at 12 in great haste asked for an audience, and seemed to be much *en peine*.[1] I shall do my best to find out what he wanted to talk about. He was very agitated when he left the protector, and said that every means were being used to diminish the good-will and confidence between this country and himself. The Brandenburg envoy has still not had an audience, though the Dutch ambassador agitates for it as much as he does himself. I shall not neglect to elicit the object of his mission, and to countermine him as much as I can; but hope all the same that I can assure Y.M. that he has still effected nothing here.

[Annexed: Heads of proposals for negotiation. (In Latin)]

[1]. In terms of the treaty of friendship of 1654 each party may recruit soldiers and sailors at tap of drum, and ships *'tam bellicas quam onerarias'*, in all territories of the other subject to the following conditions:

(i) each party must notify the other which region it desires to recruit in, and the number of soldiers, sailors and ships;

(ii) the numbers collected for embarkation, or for exercise, not to exceed [...], in order to avert any suspicion that they may be a source of disturbance;

(iii) nor are they to be given arms until their ships have left port;

(iv) officers in charge may not take any person into their service who at the time is in the employ of either state, and troublesome persons may be restored to their sovereigns.

[2]. A form of certificate proposed to be granted by the authorities and council of each particular Swedish town, wherein the king declares that the ship was sent by him to the port specified, and contains so much copper, iron, copper wire, flax, so much corn, flour, barley, pitch, tallow, pickled fish, and so many cases of miscellaneous merchandise; in virtue of which certificate the owners may enjoy them without further inquisition.]

---

1. Nieupoort's letter of 17 December NS (*Brieven*, iii. 157) gives no indication of the reason for his agitation; but on that day he had delivered a strong protest against the seizure by English privateers of twelve ships from Zeeland: *ibid.*, 159.

Coyet to Charles X

47

London, 7 December 1655 [in German]

[Detailed description of the seating at the protector's banquet to Bordeaux: splendid vocal and instrumental music. Among those at table were Fiennes, Lambert, Claypole, Lawrence, Fleetwood.

Reported from Paris that when Mazarin called on the queen of France and the queen of England to explain the motives of the treaty of peace, it was very ill taken, in view of the fact that all their children and the principal Englishmen in their suite must now leave the kingdom; and they gave him to understand that they were not prepared to stay behind.

Yesterday the English commissioners resumed negotiations with Bonde, which had been interrupted by the conclusion of peace with France: they now seem anxious for a quick settlement.

Petition to the protector from some Jews, led by Rabbi Ben Israel of Amsterdam, to be permitted to live and trade freely in England. The protector has ordered some leading clergy to give their views on the proposal: decision postponed until to-morrow. Many think that they may be permitted to settle and trade, but on condition of paying a large sum annually, and of attending sermons at least once a week, in the hope that this may lead to their conversion, which is earnestly prayed for.

Yesterday was a day appointed by the protector as a day of fasting and repentance, and most preachers took texts suggesting that the recent failures were God's judgment on the nation. Another great fire yesterday: one preacher explained that the six or seven recent fires were to be seen as the beginning of God's judgment on the world, and rested his argument especially on the fact that next year's date—MDCLVI—came from the words *Conflagratio Mundi*, and that the first world would be drowned and destroyed in 1657: 'as if the destruction of the world was to be bound up with the Latin language!'.]

48

London, 7 December 1655

It is now a long while since I received a letter from Y.M., and I am therefore at a loss how to shape my actions; but in the meantime I have neglected nothing which it seemed to me might be of service to Y.M. here; and in particular I have discussed with his excellency Herr Christer Bonde how best to tackle relations with England. Among

other things, I could in my humble opinion come to no other conclusion than that the English would care little for any advantages in
Baltic ports that Y.M. might be disposed to grant them, above those
enjoyed by the Dutch; not least, because the assistance of some ships
was asked for in exchange. I explained this at length to Y.M. on
a previous occasion—indeed, before his excellency the ambassador
arrived in this country; and I accordingly notified his excellency that
I had done so, and entreated him not to raise the question of special
privileges until Y.M.'s answer to my humble letter should come to
hand; which was expected with every post. Nevertheless, since his
excellency had received no letter, he was constrained to put it forward;
as Y.M. no doubt learned long ago from the ambassador's report. But
how difficult it has been to bring the English to a resolution on this
matter is apparent from the very fact that so far they have made no
answer. The ambassador therefore at last found that it was best not
to press the point further, but considered it most serviceable to obtain
their assistance at sea, in case of need, by reciprocal permission to hire
ships and sailors, and also by an agreement permitting the recruitment
of soldiers in each other's dominions: all of which Y.M. will gather
from Christer Bonde's report, and the articles appended to it; and to
this I refer Y.M. I will add only this: that I certainly think that affairs
could soon be arranged along these lines, and Y.M.'s purposes be
effected with less loss of customs-revenues, with less embitterment
(and consequent opposition) on the side of the Dutch, and with greater
advantage to the navigation of all Y.M.'s faithful subjects.

Although up to the present I have received no special orders from
Y.M. in regard to myself, or as to how I am to act while his excellency
the ambassador is here, I have nevertheless thought that it might be
Y.M.'s wish that I should be joined in Y.M.'s commission to the
ambassador (but only in the quality of envoy); and this for the
following reasons: first, since I had a general credential to this state;
(2) since almost all *proponenda et hic negotianda* were entrusted to me
either in Y.M.'s instruction, or by his written orders subsequently; (3)
since I have neither been recalled, nor has his excellency had the least
instruction *in contrarium* regarding me from Y.M. I accordingly put
the point to his excellency, requesting that I might be admitted to the
conferences together with him; especially since it is not unusual, as I
showed by sundry instances both in Sweden and in this country, that
two ministers from the same sovereign—although differing in quality,
the one as ambassador and the other as envoy or resident—be joined
in the same commission, and be empowered to negotiate together. Of
which at last the consequence was that his excellency the ambassador—especially when he saw that I was not recalled, as he had at first
believed to be the case—permitted me to be present at the conferences.

If, in the uncertainty in which I was placed, I have happened [to misinterpret] Y.M.'s wishes, I desire with the greatest submission to have Y.M.'s clarification of them; at the same time most humbly assuring Y.M. that I have sought herein no more than to do Y.M. acceptable service to the best of my ability.

For the rest, as to how it is credibly reported that a protector shall [in future] be appointed by the casting of lots, Y.M. will be informed by his excellency the ambassador's written reports, he having undertaken to inform Y.M. in detail about it, so that it is unnecessary further to trouble Y.M. with it.

Since Baron Cranstoun left for Scotland we have had no news of him here; but I fear that by reason of the coming of winter he will not be able, as he had hoped, to forward any soldiers to Stade. But there is no doubt that next year, at all events, he will be sending the promised 2000 men for Y.M.'s service to the Elbe.

Bonde to Charles X

XXVI

London, 14 December 1655

Having by the last post received two letters from Y.M. (one from Proszowice of 25 October, the other from Zacbenka of 11 November), and Y.M. having in the former ordered me to dispose his highness to a closer alliance, in consideration of the catholics' meeting to arrange a league against the protestants;[1] and since in his last letter (which was a fortnight later than the former) Y.M. did not countermand that order; I determined, as far as might be possible, to carry it out. To that end I last Monday asked for an audience with his highness. It was appointed for Wednesday; but as his highness's daughter (who is married to Lord Claypole) was thought to be mortally ill, and was in pains of labour, it was postponed, with the explanation that his highness was so distressed at his daughter's condition that he could not undertake any business. However, she was that same evening delivered of a son, and I was told I could have an audience to-day. I have had it, and Herr Coyet accompanied me. Meanwhile, in order to prepare the ground for my business, I paid a visit to Lord White-locke, who at our last meeting was one of my commissioners, as I informed Y.M. by the last post. Among other topics I complained once again that at my first coming here, and often afterwards, I had desired to know, both from Secretary Thurloe and from his highness himself, what his highness's intentions were in regard to the cause of

1. Summary in Carlbom, *Sverige och England*, p. 47.

religion. I said that I hoped that Y.M.'s zeal and enthusiasm for the honour of God were sufficiently well known, nor could anyone doubt that his highness had given notable evidence of the same, but that Y.M. being at so great a distance could not be expected to shape his plans in regard to this great matter until he had to some extent been informed of his highness's attitude: for instance, in what way he was ready to ally himself with Y.M., and on what terms and reciprocal conditions *etc.* To this he replied that I had great reason to complain; and that if he had had to negotiate in Sweden in circumstances such as those in which I was placed here, he would never have been able to do anything. He himself much regretted that things were as they were; and afterwards observed that it was no bad thing that we could talk about it between ourselves, and that he would now discuss it not as a commissioner, or as one appointed by his highness, but in confidence between us. As his speech was somewhat lengthy I propose to give Y.M. only the gist of it. He spoke of the old, inveterate hatred of the catholics towards us, and how all their policies are mainly directed to the ruin of protestantism; and that for that reason the main and only goal of all our plans and actions must be the honour of God, as the most important consideration; and no trouble, nor any other worldly interest, ought to stand in the way of our pursuing it— especially now, when God seemed to have opened the way, through Y.M.'s great successes in Poland, and so afforded this country such strong reasons for not neglecting the opportunity, but rather for taking advantage of it: as Y.M. was in the highest degree justified in doing, in response to the insult offered by the catholics when they lured Queen Christina over to their hypocritical popish doctrines, and then dragged her round Europe as though to triumph in the ignominy inflicted upon the noble Gustavian family and the whole Swedish nation. The first thing to be done was to conclude *in hoc passu* an offensive and defensive alliance between Y.M. and his highness, and to define its purpose as being to destroy the papacy, and to strive towards making Y.M. emperor of Germany, and so perhaps to his following the path which the Swedes had taken aforetime. And the protector on his side might make himself master of those places which lie most convenient to him. Then all the other protestant kings and princes should be pressingly invited to join; and since Y.M. and the protector were already in full activity, no one could grudge that they took the lead. It was so necessary and Christian a work that no one who rightly professed Christ could reasonably hang back, and therefore no tergiversation or long delay was to be tolerated, but those who looked more to their own advantage than to the honour of God should be considered as *communes inimici.* The details as to how we should assist each other could be agreed on later in one way or another, according to how things turned out: the main thing was to decide on the principle itself.[1]

I should have been glad to bring him to be rather more precise about the details, but was not able to manage it; except that he said that the point I had drafted about recruiting would not then be necessary, since we should be helping each other on a much larger scale. I doubt if he has thought the thing through. Otherwise we talked a good deal about the differences between the lutheran and 'reformed' religion (which is what they call theirs), and the more so because those who are ill-disposed make a great clamour about them. I showed, among other things, that we agree in the basis of salvation, that is, *in puncto justificationis*, and that we had besides *communem hostem*, and more to the same purpose. We parted well content with each other, and he promised to do his best [about recruitment] as well as regarding the proposals I had formerly put forward.

Since I can judge both from Y.M.'s letters and Appelboom's that letters from these places must have a very uncertain passage, I send Y.M. herewith a duplicate of mine of 2 and 9 November, they being of some importance and in line with my last proposals. I have not failed to write by every post since I came here, and for a long time I have been using cypher, so that if my letters should have fallen into unfriendly hands there will not be much information to be gathered from them; but I hope very much that Y.M. may have received them, and that I may have Y.M.'s answer.

My audience with his highness was on this occasion of great importance, and no one else was present except my Lord Whitelocke and Thurloe. I shall send Y.M. the details by the next post: at the moment I have no time to write more than that his highness was strongly disposed towards such an alliance as has been proposed, and promised not only to do everything possible to forward it, but also (since I strongly pressed for a definite time) to communicate his views to me through commissioners within the next few days. I learn from reliable sources that the Brandenburg envoy's audience was mainly concerned with his wish to get his highness to intervene between Y.M. and his master.[2] I therefore to-day tried, without giving offence, to prevent this, in the hope that Y.M. himself, by the help of God, can come to a satisfactory arrangement. From Herr Appelboom I hear also that the Dutch are now holding a better language; which will I think be very conducive to a grand general system. I have this moment been

---

1. *Cf.* Whitelocke's entry for 23 January: Whitelocke, *Memorials*, iv. 220–1.

2. Schlezer reported this audience on 14 December. The protector, apart from expressing a general wish to be friends with the elector, seems to have confined himself to explaining why he preferred a French to a Spanish alliance: *Urk. und Act.*, vii. 729–30.

informed that Risingh has arrived at Plymouth from Nova Suecia, where all the Swedish settlers have been driven out by the Dutch.[1] I am much distressed to hear it, and I hope that when it comes to signing a treaty, Y.M. will bear it in mind against them. I have on a number of occasions written to Y.M. about money for my subsistence here, and I humbly beg that Y.M. will, if possible, arrange for some funds in Hamburg, since money can be had from Sweden only with very great delays and considerable loss. No letters from Hamburg have arrived by this post; but it is reported from Holland that Y.M. has captured Strasburg in Prussia, and had good hopes of taking Thorn. May Almighty God so bless Y.M.'s enterprises that before spring he may be secure from all enemies on that side; for I am sure that next year he may, in God's name, do great and glorious things.

Coyet to Charles X

49

London, 14 December 1655 [in German]

[To the treaty concluded between France and England, and now printed, was recently added an additional provision that the United Netherlands and all their dominions should be included, together with all allies of both parties who so request within three months of 23 November, O.S.[2]

The episcopalian clergy have everywhere strongly protested against the rigorous measures which are to be enforced against them as from 1 January 1656, and the various *doctores theologiae* have been answered that they need expect no softening of them unless before then they have given sufficient testimony of their affection to this state, and they must make the best of that. The forthcoming declaration as to the punishments to be given to transgressors has not yet appeared; but they have a foretaste of it in [the knowledge that] it will be applied *gradatim*: namely that those who presume to preach, or to administer the Sacrament, or to marry anyone, or to use the Book of Common Prayer, shall for the first offence be imprisoned for a month; for the second, for six months; and for the

1. The Swedes had established a colony on the Delaware in 1641; but after a promising start it had been neglected under Christina. In 1653 a reinforcement of colonists was sent out, and Risingh appointed governor; but at the time of its capitulation to the Dutch it still numbered only about 200 persons: C. Ward, *Svenskarne vid Delaware* (Stockholm 1938). Risingh was the author of a justly celebrated treatise on Swedish trade.

2. This was to conform to art. 15 of the treaty of peace between England and the United Provinces, which provided that each party be given an opportunity to be included in any alliance concluded by the other.

third be banished from the country. It is said also that house-to-house searches are to be instituted, so that anyone [suspected] of the use of the Book of Common Prayer (which is in part based on the popish Mass, and mixed with the Litany and *Antiphonis*, and therefore when the king and the archbishop tried to reintroduce it in Scotland, at the beginning of the troubles there, was by the Scots contemptuously referred to as the English Mass), is to be fined £2 sterling.

The question of giving the Jews liberty to trade has been debated for more than a week by the protector and his council, in the presence of leading merchants and theologians (who were summoned from Oxford), but a decision is postponed until next Friday.

Reported from Dartmouth that a Spanish ship from Ostend, with 200 Spanish soldiers aboard, was driven to that port by a storm: their objective at present unknown, but examination should soon reveal it.

The day before yesterday the Brandenburg envoy Schlezer, and to-day Bonde, had audience with the protector: Bonde's relation will give an account of what passed on that occasion.

Sends a translation of the protector's declaration explaining the decimation of royalists with a view to the support of the militia.

P.S. And also the articles of the Franco-English treaty.]

Bonde to Charles X

XXVII

London, 21 December 1655

As I had no time to give Y.M. a full account by the last post of the conference I had with his highness on that day, I beg to inform Y.M. that I was in the usual manner summoned to Whitehall at 10 o'clock, having with me Herr Coyet. After making his highness a little compliment and congratulating him on his daughter's happy delivery, I thanked him for the commissioners whom he had appointed for me, told him that I had transmitted various points to them on which I now awaited his highness's determination, and hoped that they would tend to the advantage of both nations and the glory of God; but that the main reason why I now wished to speak with him was to remind him of something which Coyet had asked for already before my arrival, and which I at various times had requested of his highness and of Thurloe. And that was, that his highness would be pleased to take into consideration the present posture of affairs, in which all the actions of the catholics seem to be principally directed to the prejudice and ruin of the protestants; and as by his piety and his zeal for the glory of God he had sufficiently manifested his serious intention to give them his protection, that he would let Y.M. know his views as to what steps he thought should be taken by Y.M. [and] himself, as the main buttresses of true Christianity, to forestall and defeat the catholics' plans. I referred him particularly to what I had said to him in my discourse of 2 November (of which I sent a second copy to Y.M. by the last post), when I spoke at length of their proceedings, not only as between themselves, but in regard to their manoeuvres to sow dissensions of one sort and another between protestants. I expounded it all again at still greater length, arguing that the glory of God must be the goal of all our actions, and that He had not endowed Y.M. and his highness with such power and wisdom in order that those who truly called upon His name should be suffered to undergo destruction, but rather that they should by their united forces protect them and enhance His glory. The great victories of Y.M. in Poland, and of his highness's forces in the West Indies, and his present great armaments, have so much the more awakened the jealousy of the catholics that we hear from all quarters of their great preparations; and therefore in such a situation time was of the essence. For these reasons I entreated his highness to take the matter into his consideration, and to give me his answer without delay; for he knew well that of all the rules of prudence the principal was to have a regard to times and seasons, and if this winter were allowed to pass without anything's being decided as to what to do upon the occasion we might upon the coming of spring be forced to confront great successes on their side, which with God's help might in time have been prevented.

To this he answered that nothing had been, nor should be, more dear to him than to devote all his care and resources to the advance of God's glory. That I well knew that he, no less than I, had warned of the danger of these times; that he had no greater wish than to avert the dissensions between the protestants which seemed about to arise; and that he sought by all possible means to constrain the one party and the other to unity. And he proceeded, with many eloquent (*exquisite*) words, to express his disposition to embrace *causam communem*; but it was essential for him first to know what Y.M. was minded to do, after which he would gladly agree to any practicable conditions that I might ask of him, to that end. I answered, that on behalf of Y.M. I must thank him for his great zeal and care for Y.M., and for his efforts to secure unity among protestants, and that I was now in a measure relieved of my anxiety, since I could see two means which it might be hoped would still the storm that had before seemed to threaten us. The first was, that I was confident that Y.M. himself, with God's help and without any subsequent complications, would see whether he could not come to an understanding with those who might have designed to trouble him. The second was that I hoped that since Y.M. was not conscious of having given offence to any, and for his part was not willing to believe that there were any that had hostile intentions towards him, therefore the great and imposing alliance which he intended to conclude with the lord protector would also be a means to keeping other protestants in unity; since none of them, in the present state of affairs, ought to prefer any consideration whatever to the duty he owed to God's service and His righteous cause. That Y.M. should make the first overture to the protector was very difficult for him at so great a distance, nor was it quite clear to him what might be his highness's intention in the present case; but I could say only this on Y.M.'s behalf, that Y.M. was resolved to enter *in hoc passu* into a reciprocal and strict alliance. But on what conditions, and in what manner the thing was to be done, were things that Y.M. wished in the first place to be informed of by his highness, so that this great and weighty affair might soon, with the help of God, be brought to a happy conclusion. It was a great advantage for his highness that he could negotiate in person, and so from hour to hour take *consilium ab re*; but for me it was difficult, Y.M. being so far away; and therefore it was the more necessary for me to have early notice of his highness's intentions, since it would be a matter of some months before I could have Y.M.'s answer and the relevant orders.

These arguments gave him rather more satisfaction; and he replied that what I had said was true, and that he both hoped and judged that before spring arrived, and the Brandenburger could receive any great assistance, Y.M. would make good use of his time, and with God's help make an end of that difficulty.[1] As to the other means which I had mentioned for ending those disputes [between protestants] he said nothing, either because he did not well understand me, or more probably because he deliberately omitted to do so since it trenched too nearly on the business;[2] but went on to say that he rejoiced greatly at the disclosure of Y.M.'s intentions that I had made to him, that he would gladly ensue that end as far as might be humanly possible;

1. On this same day Thurloe, after assuring Nieupoort that England would take no steps without informing the Dutch, and reiterating that the protector would listen to no proposals prejudicial to them, asked him what he would think if East Prussia were to become a fief of Sweden, as it had previously been of Poland: *Brieven*, iii. 163. This was a shrewd guess: by the treaty of Königsberg (10 January (OS) 1656) the elector became the vassal of the crown of Sweden for his duchy of East Prussia. Nieupoort replied that he would rather see things remain as they were. For the background to the treaty, see Wittrock, 'Fördraget i Königsberg', pp. 1–55.

2. Abbott translates '*emädan thet saken något nähr tracterade*' by 'since the subject touched *him* too closely', whereas what Bonde implied was that the protector felt that it anticipated the discussions to be held with the commissioners: Abbott, iv. 48.

would at the earliest moment take the matter into consideration, and would have *crebriores conventus* with me about it; and he would take care to lose no time (as I had done well to remind him), *nam post est occasio calva*. He began then to praise Y.M. to the skies, comparing Y.M.'s actions with those of King Gustavus, of famous memory, and saying that although like all other right-thinking persons in England he was then more moved with enthusiasm for his actions than for any other that had ever been performed, and that they had never desired anything more than to come to his aid, he must nevertheless admit that Y.M. had excelled him, and he was sure that God had appointed Y.M. to do great deeds. We fell now to talking of the tidings we had of Y.M.'s progress, and how that no news had come from Hamburg by this post, but that it was reported from Holland that Y.M. had already taken Strasburg, and that Thorn had entered into a parley with him. I thought it high time now to take my departure, and declared my private inclination to the great work, and to all other things serviceable to his highness; and he replied that he would wish my instructions to be as ample, or (as the English expression runs) 'as large as my heart': if so, we should certainly come to a satisfactory conclusion; and professed the very high personal regard he had for me. And so we separated, with very great satisfaction. My Lord Whitelocke was present at this conference, and there can be no doubt that the talk I had with him last week (of which I sent an account to Y.M. by the last post) proved of service on this occasion. Towards the end Lord Deputy Fleetwood also came in, having been appointed to be present.

Coyet to Charles X

50

London, 28 December 1655 [in German]

[No decision yet about the Jews. The protector proceeds very cautiously: the theologians strongly oppose it, from every pulpit. The proposals Rabbi Ben Israel put to the protector may be gathered from the extract enclosed.[1]

The decimation, and the ejection of episcopalian clergy and schoolmasters, are vigorously pursued; though it is hoped that the protector may be persuaded to use moderation towards many, in regard to their rank and their peaceful habits.

They press on with fitting out the fleet, to the extent that work

1. Missing in transcript.

continued over Christmas; and they have begun to press men for the navy. It is expected to be ready, unless there is an exceptionally severe winter, by the beginning of February.

P.S. Commissioner Risingh has arrived here, and hopes by this post to give Y.M. an account of New Sweden. He confirms that the Dutch have taken possession of it by force, [allegedly] because of the behaviour of the savages; but in fact the case was otherwise: we had different information, in the first place from Plymouth, that their [*sc.* the savages'] target was not Y.M.'s subjects, but the neighbouring Dutch, whom they have always looked upon as enemies. Commissioner Risingh has promised a more detailed account, to which I therefore refer. Y.M.'s proposals were to-day debated in the council: their determination upon them will be intimated later.]

Bonde to Charles X

XXVII

London, 28 December 1655

By my last letter I notified Y.M. of what passed at my last conference with his highness concerning the matters contained in Y.M.'s instructions to me in his letter from Proszowice of 25 October; and at the same time I sent duplicates of my letters to Y.M. of 2 and 9 November. Subsequently I have, through all possible channels, demanded an answer; but so far have not been able to obtain one, although both the protector and his council (or most of them) now seem to find my last overture to their taste, and every day give me promises of a conference of a more specific and practical nature. I have every reason to complain of the slowness of these people, and how they continually put me off from one time to another. I take Almighty God to witness with what diligence I have tried to advance my negotiation here (as my *Diarium* would confirm), and that I have neglected no occasion, however trivial, which might, directly or indirectly, have been useful for that purpose. But apart from my first conference I have not been able, except with great trouble, to bring them to the point of even giving me commissioners with whom I might negotiate. I then gave them some articles (of which I have already sent copies, and full explanations, to Y.M.); but since then it has been impossible for me to get speech with them. That things should advance so extremely slowly afflicts me more than I can express: among other things I begin to be afraid that Y.M., who treated the envoy from this country with the utmost graciousness and civility, may suppose that I have received reciprocal treatment here, and that the slow pace of business is in some way my fault. For some time back there have been many foreign ministers in this country, and not one of them has effected anything, though some of them have been forced to spend three, two, or at least one year here. But apart from this country's usual dilatoriness, and its small regard for the feelings of foreign ministers of high rank, the cause of the delay lies in the great alterations in the state of Europe—mostly on Y.M.'s side, but in great measure also in regard to this country. For some time now, the constitution of the government here, and the general state of affairs, have convinced me that they would be ready to accept Y.M.'s large offers of commercial advantages; and I have on a number of occasions written to Y.M. to that effect. Since Y.M.'s incomparable successes in Poland have so hindered correspondence that Y.M. has not been able to answer my letters, and I have consequently received no orders or instructions in the matter, I have thought it more prudent always to keep that business *in integro*, rather than by premature urging force them to give me a clear refusal, and so deprive me of all hope of rendering Y.M. any acceptable service. I entreat Y.M. most humbly to take a gracious view of the little I have done; and as the great uncertainty in which I have all this long time been compelled to remain (by reason of the paucity of information which has reached me as to Y.M.'s wishes) has often obliged me to write at great length—all judgments from appearances in this part of the world being to be considered as dubious—that Y.M. may be pleased to look with a favourable eye on my reports. With God's help I will carry myself here in such a manner as a due respect for Y.M., and the advancement of his service, may require; and I shall do my best, as far as may be in this difficult post, to carry out what Y.M. has ordered, and has entrusted to me. I await with great impatience the instructions which Y.M. tells me that he will send me.

The Portuguese resident was with me the day before yesterday, and informed me that relations between England and Portugal were not good, and that he was afraid that it might come to a rupture, although it had been supposed here that everything had been settled long ago;[1] and he asked me whether I would, as of myself, be willing to put in a word with his highness as to the expediency of securing Portugal's friendship, on the ground of the importance, both to Y.M. and to England, of that country's welfare, and of preserving it always in such a condition that it may not be obliged to side with Austria. The main point of difference between them lies in the fact that the former

1. The difficulty lay in John IV's refusal to ratify the treaty of 1654 unless the article conceding to English merchants and seamen free exercise of worship in their ships and houses was deleted.

Portuguese ambassador, whom the tragic fate of his brother had reduced to a state of deep affliction, hurriedly concluded a treaty with this country by the terms of which he seems to have conceded more with respect to Englishmen's religious liberty than his master in his condition of thraldom to the pope can ratify. There have this summer been various exchanges, but no decision reached other than that the king of Portugal has sent over ratification of the treaty as originally concluded, but with the proviso that the point at issue is confirmed only subject to endorsement by the pope. This is something which the people here will hardly consent to, since no nation in the world is more embittered against the papacy, and they are, besides, now at one with France. I have had great doubts as to how I ought to act in this affair. On the one hand I have no instructions from Y.M., and therefore cannot judge what interest Y.M. may have in it; on the other I perceive that it would certainly be a very acceptable service to the king of Portugal, and one which he would value highly whether I was able to effect anything or not. And as far as I can judge, his friendship is of importance to Y.M., both in regard to Swedish trade and also in general, if the catholics should now start anything against the protestants, as the reports that reach us indicate that they are all inclined to do. I have therefore discussed the question with Herr Coyet, and have thought that the most advisable line would be— since I know that I shall shortly receive news of her majesty the queen's happy delivery, and that a young prince has been born, to the great joy of Y.M. and his realms (a fact which has been reported from Holland, though I have as yet had no notification from Sweden)—to seek an audience with his highness to notify him of that event, and use the opportunity to see whether I may raise the point in such a manner as not to give offence.

The governor in Nova Suecia, Johan Risingh, has now come to town, and with him some thirty persons: they were brought to Plymouth in a Dutch ship, in terms of the accord which the Dutch by force of arms compelled them to make. From here they intend to proceed to Holland; and since I hear from Holland that a [Dutch] ambassador is to go off to Y.M. with all speed, it is necessary that Y.M. receive a detailed account of this gross act of war, and I therefore intend to lose no time in despatching Johan Risingh to Y.M. by the safest route.

XXIX

London, 4 January 1656 [from Bonde's *Register*]

Since my last letter I have twice this week spoken to his highness; first last Monday, when I notified her majesty the queen's delivery, and the happy birth of a prince.[1] I think it unnecessary to trouble Y.M. with my speech on this occasion. In his reply he expressed his exceeding pleasure, and said that he hoped that the birth of the young prince would be of great service, and increase the security of Y.M.'s person; for the Jesuits and monks had no more important design than the making of an attempt upon Y.M.'s person by violence, in the expectation of thereby annihilating all Y.M.'s immortal exploits, and had now recently set it afoot. But Y.M.'s royal throne being now by the birth of this prince secure against all human accidents, they would despair of ever effecting their evil purpose, and cease to proceed in it. He remarked also that the day on which the young prince was born was also the day on which Y.M. obtained possession of Thorn; which he took for a good omen.

I spoke also on this occasion of the Portuguese business; and reported how I had been informed by the Portuguese resident here that the peace which we had all along presumed to be agreed on between this country and them was now in some danger, since the king of Portugal, by reason of his dependence on the pope, had no power to do what his highness desired; and that in consideration of the general welfare it was of great importance that the king (whose hostility to Spain and the House of Austria provides a useful diversion, and who from the point of view of trade and other commodities can be of great service to the protestants) might not be brought to such extremities as to be forced to adhere to the catholics, to the great prejudice of us all.

He answered that he had every disposition to make peace with them; but the ratification that had been sent over alluded to the pope's confirmation of the point about religion, and I might judge for myself whether he could accept that. To which I answered that I could well imagine that such a thing was not desirable, but that if his highness were ready to permit some attempt to find an expedient, such an expedient might perhaps indeed be found.

He replied that he was very willing to try all means to reach an agreement, and that he could well judge (as I had said) how necessary it was to keep them from joining the House of Austria, especially as things were at present. I ended with a short apology, and therewith took my departure.

The next day, which was New Year's Day (which—like the whole Christmas season— is not observed here as a holiday) the Dutch ambassador Heer Nieupoort had two whole hours with the protector; after which the servant of Mr Fleming came to me to say that his highness wished to speak with me, and asked that I would accordingly come to him on the following morning at 10 o'clock, though it was later postponed to 4 o'clock in the afternoon. I did not know what he

1. The future Charles XI.

had in mind, but I judged that since on the previous day the Dutch-man had spoken to him for so long, and there seemed to be some urgency about our meeting, it must have reference to the offer of mediation which I had tried to avert on 2 November.[1] When Herr Coyet and I came to him, and his highness had sat down, he began a long conversation between us which lasted about a couple of hours. For the sake of brevity I give Y.M. only the essentials. He began with a little apology for my having been kept here for a pretty long time, but hoped that it might turn out to be all for the best for both of us. He then recapitulated my former remarks about the general state of protestantism, and said how happy he would be if by frank and confidential talks we might make plain the way in that matter; that he saw the necessity of preventing all quarrels and disunion among the protestants, and that we ought to take it into further consideration how best to tackle the business. From his lengthy discourse I took up these two points, and after excusing myself for not being ready with an answer to them (since I had not known what his highness was going to ask), said that I would nevertheless on the spur of the moment say this: first, that in the matter of the disputes between protestants, I perceived that his highness's main concern centred on Y.M.'s differ-ences with Holland and Brandenburg. As to the Dutch, I recalled the good offices which we performed for each other during the German war, and indeed at all times; I said that Y.M. had not opposed them in the slightest degree, and hitherto had committed no hostile act against them; it was true that they had this year had some talk of sending a fleet to the Baltic, and had contracted an alliance with Brandenburg somewhat unfavourable to Y.M., though they had not yet ratified it; and I therefore thought that the best means of settling these differences would be for them to send someone to Y.M., when I did not doubt that both for Y.M.'s interest and for their own it would be possible to reach a firm basis of friendship. As to Brandenburg, I explained at length what reasons the elector might have for opposing Y.M., and said that Y.M. would be ready to grant him the fief which

---

1. Bonde was mistaken. Cromwell told Nieupoort that he had had no objection to Charles X's attack on Roman catholic Poland, 'and though the king had thought fit to pursue his conquests as far as Constantinople, that he should have wished him from his heart good success', as also if he had directed his campaigns to lands where there were many oppressed protestants [*sc.* Silesia]; but added that 'he had already spoken seriously to Bonde and Coyet on the question of the king of Poland and Prussia; that he would take further action; and if the king of Sweden should desist, that would be well; but if he went on, something more than ambassadors would be required'. And that 'he would never receive anything separately and not in common with the United Netherlands in regard to any privileges, liberties or otherwise in the commerce and navigation of the east sea': *Brieven*, iii. 170–3.

he had formerly held of Poland on the same terms as before.[1] As to Pillau, the crown of Sweden had every right to it: it was first made a place of strength, at great expense, by the late King Gustavus of famous memory, and was handed over to Brandenburg on condition that [the elector] observed a 26 years' truce;[2] but since—as Y.M. has sufficiently made clear by his manifesto—this was not respected in the manner which Y.M. could have desired, he was not bound to restore to the elector a place which had been ceded to him *cum conditione ab illo non servata*. As to this particular dispute, I hoped that by this time Y.M. would have settled it one way or another, and that the common cause would consequently take no hurt from it. Moreover, I found it very difficult to act appropriately in these matters, since I have absolutely no information about how things stand in relation to Brandenburg, or to Holland either, except what I can obtain from the ordinary news-sheets, and from Herr Appelboom. What I especially wanted to know was his highness's views on the details of any alliance between us; and I said that [I hoped] that his highness would be pleased to reveal what he thought was to be done in relation to the great rally of the catholics against us: whether we should be considering a defensive alliance in case we should be attacked, or whether his ideas went further than that; with other precise points on which I should be glad to be informed.

He answered that I had rightly understood his mind; and as to Brandenburg he had no great anxiety, and no longer had an eye to that quarter except in so far as he was a protestant elector of some importance, who must therefore be encouraged to keep on good terms with other [protestants]. But Holland was a state very powerful at sea—and on land too—whose friendship could be of great assistance to the common cause, and its enmity capable of making things very difficult for us; and for that reason he was more concerned about them. He then expounded at some length how that republic was based entirely on merchants: they had so little land that it did not suffice for their subsistence, and for that reason they must look to trade as their only means of livelihood. And among other branches of their trade, that to catholic countries was of great importance; especially now, when owing to England's quarrel with Spain the greatest part of the Spanish trade had fallen into their hands. All this is something which they will hardly be ready to put at risk, least of all at a time when their country is in some confusion; so that although Holland—

1. Since the treaty of Königsberg between Charles X and the elector, which provided for this, was concluded only on 7/17 January, Bonde cannot have known it with any certainty. For the negotiations and the terms, see Ellen Fries, *Erik Oxenstierna*, pp. 244–49, and Wittrock, 'Fördraget i Königsberg'.

2. The truce of Stuhmsdorf, 1635.

which he considers the most reasonable of the provinces—might be well disposed, there are many of the prince's faction who are making trouble.[1] And if now, on top of all this, they should be deprived of the Baltic trade, or be put entirely at the mercy of another power by reason of the duties levied there, they might easily be brought to some desperate resolve, and ally themselves with the catholics. This [*sc.* relations with the Dutch] was of such importance that it must be decided first: the other conditions [for an alliance] might be considered later; and, as I had well said, we should think first of a defensive alliance, and subsequently proceed from there.

To all this I answered, after a short recapitulation of his long discourse, that his highness had certainly been right in saying that there was confusion in Dutch policy, as their dealings with Y.M. this year had sufficiently shown. If they had aligned themselves with Y.M. in time, and acted with that friendship which Y.M. had deserved of them, they would undoubtedly have obtained the best terms they could have wished for; and it can hardly be accounted prudent of them to offend him, for they might have reflected that it could very well happen that they must later come a-begging for them. But since what is done is more easy to be blamed than altered, there still seemed to me to be two ways of obtaining the unity which was desired, and hence of averting the danger which his highness feared from the present situation. The first was what I had already mentioned: that they should send an embassy to try by all means to obtain from Y.M. what they require, in which connexion I made the point that the interests of Y.M. and his realms demanded that the great quantity of merchandise which they produce be exported—a thing which can better be done by the Dutch, with their specially-designed ships, than by anybody else—so that they had no reason to despair; and though they had recently committed a monstrous deed in Nova Suecia, I believed that they would get what they wanted, provided they gave Y.M. adequate satisfaction. The second means of averting the danger he had alluded to, and for keeping them in union with us, was one which (in all humility towards both Y.M. and his highness) I thought might not be unserviceable to bear in mind in regard to the alliance for the common cause; namely that once Y.M. and his highness, as the most wise and powerful of protestant rulers, were agreed about the alliance, and appeared as its leaders, then all the other protestant kingdoms, states and princes would be drawn in to it, and that

---

1. Cromwell and Thurloe were both disturbed by the news that William Frederick of Nassau was being proposed as field-marshal of the United Provinces: *Brieven*, iii. 170. In the event, the proposal was not pursued: see Pieter Geyl, *Orange and Stuart* (1969), pp. 107, 110, 112.

consequently Holland might be brought to unite with us, *nam oderunt peccare boni etc.*

He skirted all this with great caution, and said that he would have been glad if in this connexion I had mentioned something about his coöperation; but as I had taken a quite different line he at last broke out and said that though he approved my last argument, and though it was indeed possible that it might produce the desired effect, there was no certainty that it would: the business was of such importance that there must be security against all eventualities. He would be happy to lend his assistance to it, but he lamented that Y.M.'s country and his were so distant from each other, and would rather that something were done nearer his own door-step; [and] once again spoke at length of his eagerness to establish a fast friendship. To which I replied that his zeal therein was highly laudable, and that since everything that comes from his highness was highly esteemed by Y.M., so his good-will in this matter would be esteemed also; but that I could not well understand how it might be possible to trouble other rulers and potentates in matters which were not preceded by any rupture or hostilities, and I hoped that this difficulty might be overcome by other means. Further, apart from the arguments which I had advanced already, I saw such reasons against any junction between the Dutch and the catholics that I could scarcely believe that they would bring themselves to it. In Spain they could never put any trust, since the Spaniards were an irreconcilable nation who would never forget their claims upon Holland; the French were their neighbours, and therefore the more dangerous to them if they should grow too powerful; and from all this I concluded that on that side with God's help everything would turn out well. At this he seemed somewhat taken aback,[1] spoke very slowly, and mostly to the effect that he wished it might be so; after which he promised me that I should have an answer to my propositions directly (which I had asked of him this time, as I did two days ago also), and so we parted.

It is certain that the Dutch make a great issue in this country of the duty which Y.M. has this year levied before Danzig, and this feeling is much reinforced by the increase (for the second time) in the rates imposed last year at Riga. This they denounce as intolerable; and as they have a strong party in the government here it is the easier for them to persuade his highness that the interests of England, no less than those of Holland, demand that trade be not burdened by heavy duties in the Baltic (where Y.M., with God's help, will soon be master): and it is not improbable that, as there is every reason to think, the protector's own interests (or what he supposes to be so) lie concealed

---

1. As well he might be, in view of Bonde's very different language as reported in his letter of 28 September, above.

behind this pretended cloak of religion; especially since he is now disinclined to accept any trade preference—as clearly appears from this conversation. What gives me small prospect of an early departure hence is that he said that the disputes among the protestants must first be resolved before anything can be done in the main question [*sc.* of the alliance]. I have still no answer to anything I have proposed or any draft I have put in, and God knows when I shall get one. I begin now to lose all patience with their long procrastination: I perceive that this country is in a state of confusion, and have great doubts whether any good result is attainable. The orders which Y.M. promised me have not yet arrived. I am very anxious to have them so that I may see whether it is possible to bring these matters to a conclusion.

Coyet to Charles X

51

London, 4 January 1656 [in German]

[News from Scotland is that the last chancellor of the kingdom, the earl of Loudon, has been ordered by the council of state to hand over the old Great Seal, so that a new Great Seal (and other reformations) can be expected. News also that General Monck has taken the earl of Glencairn (who was the king of Scots' *generalissimus* in the Highlands) into custody, for correspondence with the king and inciting new combustions, and lodged him in Edinburgh Castle.

Colonel [Thomas] Cooper, nominated to the council of state of Scotland, has been given the office General Venables had in Ireland; and Venables has been dismissed and broken for his mistakes in the West Indian expedition.

I am credibly informed that Monck is to be recalled from the army in Scotland and given supreme command of the fleet which is shortly to put to sea.

Scotland is reported to have had the worst weather for thirty years, and many shipwrecks in surrounding waters.

Bonde had audience with the protector last Monday and Wednesday; the Dutch ambassador on Tuesday: refers to Bonde's account for particulars.]

Bonde to Charles X

XXX

London, 11 January 1656

A week ago I was able to send Y.M. a long account of the two conferences I had with his highness in the course of that week. And as I was not well pleased that instead of any real negotiation, or of giving their views on the question of a general system, as I had wanted them to do, they only wasted time with offers of mediation and talk of the interests of the Dutch, I thought I would like to get speech with my Lord Deputy Fleetwood. This I contrived to do last Saturday, the 5th instant, when he came to me since he would not permit me to come to him. In a long and wide-ranging conversation I put him in mind of Y.M.'s serious desire for a relationship of friendship and confidence, and of the great importance of it for both countries, both in regard to the general protestant cause and to other, domestic, interests; and I pressed him, as strongly as good manners allowed, to embrace it. Among other matters he spoke of the Dutch, whose condition and intentions I represented to him in such terms that when he left me he was pretty satisfied. I need not detain Y.M. with the details, important though they are, since the effect of our conversation appeared two days later, on Tuesday the 7th [*recte*, 8th] instant, when his highness sent to me to ask me to come to him at 5 o'clock.[1] This I did, accompanied by Herr Coyet, and found with his highness Lord Lambert, Lord Deputy Fleetwood, and Thurloe. The conference lasted for an hour and a half; and since it is the most important I have hitherto had I think it necessary to report the gist of it to Y.M.

He began by giving information of the troubles in Switzerland, of which the protestant cantons have sent a detailed account to his highness's agent in Geneva, with the request that he would forward it to his highness and entreat him to give his support to the protestant interest in that country, since they feared that without it they might be attacked and swallowed up, not only by the catholic cantons but also by the forces of the pope, the Spaniards, and Bavaria. No doubt Y.M. has had the particulars of the origin of these disputes, and their consequences: how some catholics who live in Switzerland turned calvinist and took refuge in Zürich, and on that account alone had their property confiscated, some of their leaders arrested and executed, and some sent to the Inquisition in Italy, despite the fact that at the same time they were holding a meeting in Baden; all of which for the sake of brevity I omit. These tidings had further moved him to stand

---

1. Bonde's *Diarium* for 8 January 1656 runs: '*Desideravit colloquium mecum Dnus Prot. Quare hora 5 pomeridiana usque ad octavam maximi momenti discursum habui*'.

up for the general interest of protestantism, not least because these same [catholic] cantons had already a strong force on foot; and since from these proceedings, as well as from what had happened recently in Piedmont, it was plainly to be seen what the intentions of the catholics were, he had thought it necessary to notify me of them, and to take the opportunity to discuss with me, frankly and sincerely, what we were to do about the common cause. The main thing that made him hesitate was how our treaty was to be negotiated: whether it could be done here, or both here and by Y.M. The great distance between Y.M. and himself was a matter of much uneasiness to him, and he feared that at a moment when time was precious it might be wasted on sending missions to Y.M. and waiting for his reply; and he therefore desired to know my thoughts on the matter.

I answered with an appropriate compliment, thanking him for the information he had given me, which I would faithfully report to Y.M., to whom I was sure that his frank communication would be highly acceptable; and said that I rejoiced that his highness had shown such a serious determination to enter into an alliance with Y.M. *in hoc passu*, as being a thing to which Y.M. was strongly inclined. But since when I came to the meeting I had had no hint of the proposition he had made to me, I asked him to excuse me [for the present], so that I might have some days to consider it; after which I would take care to give him all possible satisfaction. (I could for the moment hit upon no other expedient than to gain time, as courteously as possible, for the arrival of at least one post, having been informed by the chancellor that I might expect Y.M.'s orders; and I did not wish him to know that my instructions and orders were deficient). I then went on to ask if in the meantime his highness might be pleased to give me some of his own ideas as to the details of the treaty [he proposed], so that I might turn them over in my mind. His answer was both lengthy and most remarkable. Among other things he said that he could indeed have negotiated with me in the usual way through commissioners, but that he believed that he could more clearly express his thoughts himself, particularly since he had great confidence in me, and had in many ways discerned my sincerity. His answer consisted of the following essential points. First, he said that he would tell me that he was, *realiter*, minded and determined to ally himself with Y.M. on the closest terms; a thing to which he was invited, not only for the honour of God (which was the first consideration) but also by the interests of our two countries, both of us being already involved, and it being therefore the more necessary that we should act together. As to the question against whom such an alliance should be directed, it must unquestionably be against the catholics in general, in the first place, but particularly against the House of Austria. As to its operation, in his view a defensive alliance was not sufficient, but it must be concluded on an offensive basis.[1] For the rest, all he could say was that he was ready to do all that Y.M. might be disposed to ask of him (and that he himself was in a position to undertake) in order to launch an effective and powerful attack upon our adversaries. There was only one point that gave him some concern, namely, that the power of the catholics is formidable, especially if they act in unison, and there was thus the greater danger that we might draw the whole swarm of them down upon the two of us, if we should reach an agreement without seeking to enlist other protestant kings, princes and states in it; and that without such a union the task might be too heavy for us. There was also the consideration that the other [protestants] might take offence at our proceeding without them, and might easily show their resentment; and it being common knowledge that the catholics make effective use of corruption and intrigue, there was a danger that they might draw those others over to their side. He then said that we must keep France in mind, being a country which, apart from its opposition to the House of Austria, contained many zealous protestants and good soldiers; all of which was worth remembering.

I heard his clear and open declaration with great satisfaction, and once again asked that I might have time to reflect upon it. But since Y.M. in his order from Proszowice of 25 October commanded me to induce him to a reciprocal alliance, and not merely to take soundings, I accepted his resolution with assurances that it would be most welcome to Y.M. But as to his last point I answered, speaking as of myself, and without prejudice either to Y.M. or to his highness, that it was certainly highly desirable, and undoubtedly attempts should be made, to draw in the other protestant states. But that I had my doubts whether it could be done in that way, for all rulers and states had so many other interests besides religion that zeal for religion would scarcely in itself be strong enough to induce them to adhere.[2] There were indeed some who had some regard for religion, but there were others who thought more of their interests and advantage; so that if the project were tackled by inviting all of them to participate, it was to be feared that we should lose the initiative even before we came to agreement on *praeliminaribus*; and the catholics would not neglect the opportunity to work upon them so that we never met together at all, and would thus attack and surprise us before we had

1. This is the first official suggestion from the English side of an offensive alliance: it foreshadows the terms Thurloe was shortly to communicate to Bonde.

2. In the audience which Cromwell gave to the Brandenburg envoy Schlezer on 7 January, the protector observed that 'it was nothing new to hear of religion's being used as a cloak for ambitious designs', *Urk. und Act.*, vii. 733.

organized ourselves. And even if agreement should be reached about spheres of action, success was doubtful, for the reasons I had just mentioned. It was reasonable to suppose that a much surer way of achieving it would be if Y.M. and his highness, as the two principal, most powerful, and wisest protestant rulers should first conclude an alliance and then invite others to join it, which some would do on principle, or because they were assured of powerful support. Inducements should be held out to the others; and if they refused their help they must be forced to adhere, for it would seem that all must be included, *ut aut nolint aut non possint offendere.* The German war offered a glaring example, it being impossible to draw the protestant estates into a *commune foedus evangelium* even though the catholics were at open war with them; and the only remedy was through the late chancellor's [Axel Oxenstierna] inducing the four circles of Upper Germany to unite in [the league of] Heilbronn to resist the enemy; and afterwards other circles and princes joined it,[1] and those that refused were considered to be enemies, which was the most effective means of bringing them to their senses. Apart from all this, it would be necessary, in a general alliance of this sort, that there should be somebody who had the *direktorium* and the management of it—an advantage which it was hardly likely that any one of the participants would agree to concede to any other. And there was the further point that in such a large gathering the requisite secrecy would be impossible to maintain, though it was of the utmost importance if the enemy were not to be given an occasion and a pretext to concentrate his forces. To this he replied, admitting that these were reasons of great weight, but nevertheless made some objections, though with the reservation that they were not to be understood as his considered opinion, but that he had to look well about him in this business. He gave it as his opinion that in the German business one important factor had been the pride of the electors, and went on to speak of the various protestant leaders, first of Denmark, then of the elector of Saxony, with some of the others; but suggested that now it would be possible to bring them to embrace the same common cause. Of Holland he said not a word; and I am glad that my arguments, both to himself and to Lord Deputy Fleetwood, seem to have cured him of being so concerned about the Dutch. I had been informed from a reliable source that his highness two days ago had said that he would unite with Y.M. *att desprit* [*sc. au dépit*] *de tout le monde*, and [that he trusted] that God would pardon them who, for the sake of the Dutch, had so long hindered him from doing so.

---

1. This was untrue: the Lower Saxon circle at first indicated willingness to join, but later refused; the Upper Saxon circle was never willing to do so.

He then pushed me hard for an answer, saying that he wished I was provided with orders and full powers, for in that case he saw nothing to prevent our coming to a settlement within a few days. I promised to let him know my reactions without delay. With that we parted; and what was very remarkable about my taking leave was that whereas his custom was to accompany me no further than to the door of the chamber where he gives private audience, he this time accompanied me through it as far as the door of his antechamber which lies beyond it, and my Lord Lambert and my Lord Fleetwood (who are the two leading men in England) went with me down to my carriage. This great and unusual civility must arise either from the fact that Y.M. has shown such graciousness to his highness's envoy [Rolt], or that now, having seriously made up his mind to unite with Y.M., he thinks to demonstrate his determination by outward courtesies to Y.M.'s minister. Whichever it is, it is certain that he has never done so for any other ambassador. He presses me strongly for an answer, and I must contrive how I may decently put him off, so that the Dutchmen do not shake his good intentions. In the meantime I await the orders which Y.M. has promised me.[1]

XXXI

London, 18 January 1656

By the last post I related to Y.M. what passed at my conference with his highness on the 8th, and among other things how he was urgent that we should make a serious start, since time was precious, and how on my side I asked for a delay of a few days, after which I would give him a further answer. I accordingly thought it necessary to ask for a

---

1. The tone of this audience as reported by Bonde contrasts markedly with that of the audience given to Schlezer on the same day. Cromwell is there reported as saying that 'he had no wish to point either to the king or to the elector, or to anybody else, nor to constitute himself a judge over the hidden counsels and thoughts of men; for he well knew that he himself must be judged by others as one that used religion and the name of God only as a pretext ... Of the reasons for the dispute that had arisen between the elector and the king he could say nothing definite, and it was not to be a matter of blame to him if he could not quite grasp it; for the places in question were far away, and had really nothing in common with this country: the interests, the *jura*, the *privilegia*, were pretty complex, and not so well known here': *Urk. und Act.*, vii. 733–4. The protector could not know that the treaty of Königsberg, which removed some of his difficulties, had been concluded some four days earlier. But he must have known of the petition of the Eastland Company, of 4 January, which asked for a better regulation of the Eastland trade, and expressed the view that Bonde's presence might facilitate a solution of their problems: *CSP (Dom) 1655–56*, p. 97. Thurloe told Nieupoort that when Bonde began to dilate on Charles X's zeal for protestantism, Cromwell (innocently?) interjected 'for instance, in royal Prussia?': *Brieven*, iii. 173.

conference with him last Saturday, the 12th instant, though I had
indeed had no further information as to Y.M.'s will in the matter. But
knowing as I do that Y.M. attaches the greatest importance to keeping
this government in a good humour with him, and to ensuring the
frustration of the plans of the Dutch to draw these people over from
Y.M.'s side by arts and insinuations and induce them to embrace
their interests in the Baltic, I have thought it necessary to touch
somewhat upon the only thing that seems able to tempt them, particularly since Y.M. in his orders from Proszowice of 25 October
appears to give it his approval.

I assured him therefore of the great satisfaction which I had derived
from his highness's last overture, and that I knew that it would be
most agreeable to Y.M. I would therefore do everything in my power
to promote it; and I could tell his highness that Y.M. was really
minded to enter into a mutual defensive alliance with him *in hoc passu*.
That Y.M. had not fully appreciated his highness's intention beyond
that; and that Y.M. must be allowed some time to revolve it, and to
take his decision upon it. His highness [I said] well knew that both
Herr Coyet and myself had all the time been anxious to know his
highness's views, so that Y.M. might be in a position to determine his
attitude. His highness had himself raised some queries, of the greatest
importance, as to the procedure to be followed; and I asked that if
there were any further details to be borne in mind, then his highness
would let me have some information about them in order to save time
and facilitate the negotiation. He answered at length, and showed
that his real intentions were the same as had obliged him to speak to
me so frankly on the previous occasion, but said that he could well
understand my request, and was in consequence well content with it.
He protested once again his great affection for Y.M., and said, to use
his own expression, that every step forward which Y.M. made in his
great campaigns gave him the utmost delight. As to the details which
I had asked to be informed of, it was his intention to confer with me
about them through his commissioners very shortly, and that we must
no longer deal *in generalibus*, since that was the way one proceeded
when the idea was rather to procrastinate than to deal seriously. [I
answered] with an appropriate compliment, thanking his highness for
being pleased to be at the trouble of so often conferring with me in
his own person; added that I was ready, and heartily desired, to meet
his commissioners; and with that I ended. And since I had previously
let it be known that I should like to see his fleet, which is now being
fitted out for sea, he offered me the use of his yacht, and said he would
send someone with me to supply me with information about it. On
which I thanked him briefly, and we parted.

On the following Tuesday I went to the fleet, and was treated with great distinction, as Y.M. may be pleased to gather from the attached relation.[1] I shall now make arrangements to meet the commissioners, if possible next week, and work out how to deal with them until I receive Y.M.'s further orders, for which I am extremely anxious. From Holland Appelboom informs me of their unusual [*owanlige:* qy. *owänlige*—i.e. unfriendly?] proceedings towards him; as also that they have paid the elector of Brandenburg the subsidy which they promised him. All of which has an ominous appearance. I shall accordingly lose no time in working hard to counteract their intrigues with this government.

Coyet to Charles X

52

London, 18 January 1656 [in German]

[The new fleet is to be divided into three squadrons. The first, of 40 great ships (mostly frigates) is to go to the Straits to attack the king of Spain (and by a recent report Naples has fortified its frontier and taken other measures of defence against an English attack). The fleet is to be commanded by Montagu and Blake, with *Naseby* as the ship in which they are to fly their flag; she carries 80 brass guns. Vice-Admiral Lawson is to sail in *Resolution*, of 80 guns; Rear-Admiral Born [Commissioner Nehemiah Bourne] in *Swiftsure*, of 60 guns (formerly Penn's ship on the West India expedition). The second squadron is destined for the West Indies: a few ships have already sailed, as reinforcements. The third squadron is to function as a home fleet, and will be employed on *ex tempore nascentes occasiones*.

The Dutch ambassador went to Chatham a fortnight ago to see the fleet, and took a sketch of it for his own use; but it was taken from him on the ground that it must first be seen by the protector.[2]

Last Tuesday Bonde, General [George] Fleetwood and Coyet were allowed to see the fleet, no doubt as a gesture of good-will: they were taken in the admiralty's best barges to Gravesend, then to Rochester, where they were met by Beth [Pett], the famous naval architect who built *Sovereign*, *Naseby*, *Resolution* and others, and there awaited the protector, who took them nearer to Chatham, showed them the principal ships, and handsomely entertained them aboard; on his departure he was saluted by all the ships. Pett escorted him back to Rochester, where he was met by the mayor and aldermen

---

1. Missing in transcript.
2. It was subsequently returned to him: *CSP (Dom) 1655–56*, p. 41.

in full state: he answered their compliments graciously, and continued by land to Gravesend. Next day he went by water to the Hope [Tilbury Hope], to view the ships there, and so back to London. As his excellency passed, he was saluted with fanfares and salvos of gunfire from Chatham castle, the blockhouse at Gravesend, the Hope, and Woolwich, in such style as no ambassador has been received since the king's death.

Last Saturday Bonde again had an audience in Whitehall, and no doubt will inform Y.M. what passed on that occasion.][1]

Bonde to Charles X

XXXII

London, 25 January 1656 [from Bonde's *Register*]

During this last week I have been asking about the commissioners which his highness himself promised me at his last conference; but they have not yet met me. I think the explanation lies in the fact that they have recently hit upon the proposal to send an embassy to Y.M. for the alleged purpose of negotiating about the general alliance. The reasons which moved them to this idea seem to be that they were afraid that I was not so fully instructed by Y.M. as is necessary for a matter so urgent, and of such consequence, and that on account of the remoteness of Y.M. from this place I might be compelled to waste much time by introducing various new points while waiting for an answer; and for this reason Mr Whitelocke, who was in the country, has been called to town. He was with me to dinner last Tuesday, and discoursed of various matters relating to the embassy to Y.M., though at first it did not occur to me that this was what he had in mind (for he has often jestingly told me that, being thoroughly discontented, he

1. Though the transcript has no further despatches from Coyet, he did not leave England until 14 June 1656. He continued to send a 'Relation' in instalments to Erik Oxenstierna, which was in fact a newsletter, and did not deal with policy, until the end of February, and was kept busy with arrangements for payments to Leven and Cranstoun, and with necessary correspondence with Commissary Hoffstetter in Hamburg. His departure was held up by exasperating delays in providing him with a frigate to convoy his ship; and while he was waiting he undertook a trip to Oxford and Bath, which was however cut short at Oxford by bad weather and a quarrel with his coachman about the fare: he was threatened with distraint for the amount due, but stood stiffly (and successfully) on his diplomatic privilege: for all this, see RA Stockholm, Coyetska samlingen, E. 3400 vol. 4 (unfoliated). At his audience of leave-taking on 3 May he was dubbed a Knight of the Garter. Giavarina noted that he was the first minister to receive a present on leaving since the beginning of the protectorate: *CSP (Ven) 1655–56*, pp. 215, 218.

would like to go to Y.M. and enter his service), until his attendant said the same to Marshal Duwall[1] and to my secretary, from which it was clear that he did so by order, and by way of sounding me. However, I did not let him see that I knew that he had been nominated for it, but talked in general terms of the question of the alliance.[2] He then admitted that such proposals were under consideration, but said that he had objected to them on the ground that the whole world, and especially the popish party, would have their eyes opened too wide, and might therefore be driven to coalesce against us; and for France especially it would be a serious matter, since they cannot deviate from our party without injury to themselves. Besides, Y.M. had me here as his representative, to whom the lord protector could disclose his private thoughts, and I could send an express to Y.M., await orders, and conclude the matter on the spot. Moreover, he had gathered that Y.M. was not best pleased at being disturbed by embassies in the middle of an onerous war.

I made not much answer to all this, since it came upon me somewhat unexpectedly, saying only that it might possibly be convenient for Y.M. to conduct the negotiations himself, and that I saw no more dangerous consequence of that than that it would be impossible to keep the business secret, since it would excite general suspicion; that it was indeed a little unusual to send an ambassador to a sovereign who had his own ministers at the place from which the embassy was to be sent; no doubt there was something to be said for it, and so forth; and so we parted. I cannot be sure whether that phrase 'the common cause' was intended to be a serviceable cloak for a policy of mediation between Y.M. and Holland. I think it not improbable, since at both the last and the preceding conference the lord protector touched on protestant unity as a *necessarium fundamentum* for all the rest, and I am certain that this is what Nieupoort has been trying for. Moreover, I detected in Whitelocke that they were anxiously awaiting the post in order to learn from it whether Y.M. and Brandenburg have reached agreement, or whether hostilities have broken out, and it was for these

1. One of Bonde's suite.
2. Whitelocke had been informed in confidence that it had been decided to send an extraordinary embassy to Charles X in the hope of preventing a quarrel between Sweden and the Dutch, and that he and Sir Christopher Packe had been selected. Though pressed by Cromwell, Whitelocke declined to accept appointment, remarking that Bonde probably considered himself sufficiently empowered to deal with the business. In discussion with Bonde on 23 January he suggested that the best procedure would be to conclude the Anglo-Swedish alliance first, and then invite other states to adhere to it (Bonde's own proposal). Bonde told him that 'he hoped within a very few days there would be an agreement between the king and the elector of Brandenburg' so that a special embassy would be unnecessary: Whitelocke, *Memorials*, iv. 219–21.

reasons that I reacted coolly to the idea [of an embassy]. I have subsequently thought further about it, and I cannot be certain whether it would be displeasing to Y.M. if I were to reach a settlement on the matters contained in my orders [i.e. the perfecting of White-locke's treaty], and that the other [i.e. Cromwell's proposals] should be considered as a new question and negotiated by Y.M. himself; especially if, by way of winning Y.M.'s good-will, they give me a satisfactory settlement.

By this post we have from Holland the good news that Y.M. on the 4th of this month concluded a handsome and advantageous agreement with the elector of Brandenburg, for which Almighty God be praised.[1] Discreet persons here judge that this treaty is of far more use to Y.M. and the Swedish crown than the winning of a great battle; for not only does it free Y.M. from an enemy of some consequence, but it reinforces his armies by [the elector's] coöperation. The Dutch will now be forced to eat humble pie; and since they have involved Y.M. not only in trouble and danger, but in vast expense, in order to maintain his fleet in the Baltic, and in other ways, and have otherwise manifested their *animum hostilem*, Y.M. may now with good reason force them *ad redimendam vexam*—to repay his expenditure, and additionally some millions in satisfaction. It will soon appear what this country's attitude is to be; and on the basis of all appearances here, and by correspondence from other places, I can come to no other conclusion than that they are most strongly in Y.M.'s favour, and are desirous of his success.

The commissioners are appointed to communicate with me to-morrow;[2] and I hope by the next post to be able to give Y.M. some report as to the effect produced by this latest news. My Lord

1. Bonde's *Diarium* records receipt of the news only on 1 February; but it was known at The Hague already on 28 January NS, and to Nieupoort soon afterwards. Thurloe's comment as relayed by Nieupoort was that he had always expected something of the sort, Brandenburg and Portugal being about equally trustworthy; and had added that Cromwell had always resented the Dutch-Brandenburg alliance, as having been made without consulting him. He deduced that Charles X would restore the king of Poland and annex Prussia and Lithuania; and disclosed (untruly) that Bonde had offered an off- and defensive alliance: *Brieven*, iii. 175–81. But Thurloe varied his comment to suit his audience: to Henry Cromwell he described it as a defeat for the Dutch; to Pell, as likely to advance the protestant cause: Thurloe, iv. 505; Vaughan, *Protectorate of Oliver Cromwell*, i. 315. As to the protector, he wrote to Charles X that 'we make no question, but the wresting of the kingdom of Poland by your arms from the papal subjection, as it were a horn from the head of the Beast ... will be of very great consequence for the peace and profit of the church': Masson, *Milton*, v. 250.

2. Whitelocke's recollection of the sequence of events is faulty: he dates the appointment of Fiennes, Strickland, Pickering and himself as commissioners to 28 January [OS]; and their meeting with Bonde to scrutinize Bonde's two draft articles of 5 December (*supra*, no. XXV, 7 December 1655), to 30 January OS.

Cranstoun's recruiting in Scotland is going well; and he hopes, as soon as there is no danger from ice, to send 1000 picked men to Stade: I have notified General Königsmarck of this, and I hope that the remainder will follow. Now that Y.M. is quit of this troublesome business with Brandenburg in such a highly satisfactory manner, I trust that Y.M. may find time to think of orders for me, and also some arrangement about my subsistence, both of which I await in all humility.

XXXIII

London, 1 February 1656 [from Bonde's *Register*]

The attached articles,[1] which were delivered to me (in English) by his highness's commissioners last Saturday [26 January], and on which

1. The draft, in Thurloe's hand, proposed that
    1. There should be an offensive and defensive alliance, directed against the House of Austria, 'whereof Poland is a chief branch'.
    3. The States-General 'and such other states as shall be thought fitt' to be invited into 'this confederacy', 'by such meanes as shal be thought convenient'.
    4. An army to be raised by the confederates 'for invading the said common enemy in such a manner, as shal be agreed upon'.
    5. No peace save by common consent.
    6. Freedom for England and Sweden to levy soldiers and hire warships and merchantmen in each other's territories.
    8. 'That in case either side be invaded by the sayd common ... enemy' the party so invaded be entitled to call for aid by land and sea from the other, at the expense of the requerant, regard being had to his circumstances.
    9. 'Noe declared rebell or fugitive from the one' to be tolerated in the dominions of the other.
    10. Ships carrying commissions for taking prizes 'from any prince, that hath noe territories, to be esteemed as pyrates'.
    11. No contraband goods to be supplied to enemies of either party: ships carrying them, with all their cargo, to be forfeit. A form of sea-pass to be provided, conformable to the twelfth article of the treaty of 1654. 'To the end, that the navigation and commerce may be encouraged, the tolls and customes shall not be raysed in the places now in the possession of each other; and in case of the conquest of any other places, noe greater toll, duty, or custome shall be imposed or set upon the people of either, than were due or payable in such places before the conquest thereof, and the same priviledges and advantages in all other respects continued. That if the tolls or customes be lessened to any other forreigner, or further priviledges granted to them, the people of either shall enjoy the like. That the States-General of the United Provinces, and such other of the confederates, as shall desire it within 3 months, shall be included in the treaty'.
    [and at the foot]
    Note of particulars to be added to the treaty with Sweden: 'all ships belonging to the one or other confederate, or the subjects of either [if provided with proper sea-passes] shall pass freely without any molestation...' [English ships in the Baltic; Swedish in the North Sea]: Thurloe, iv. 486–7.

there was little discussion (it being late in the day), astonished me no little; and the more I thought them over the harder and more unacceptable I felt them to be, so that I was unable to fathom what their intention was therein. I accordingly thought it advisable to seek a conversation with my Lord Deputy Fleetwood, both to manifest my resentment on Y.M.'s behalf, and most of all to find out what lay behind them; for I was determined not to discuss them with the commissioners without obtaining some explanation either from him, or from his highness.

At the request of General George Fleetwood, his brother came to me accordingly on Wednesday, when we had a long and wide-ranging conversation about them, of which I shall give Y.M. only the salient points. After making an appropriate compliment I said that I had received articles of such a nature that I was at a loss to understand what their intention might be in offering such things to Y.M., who is (thank God) a sovereign and a protestant, subject only to God, and responsible to no man. From their contents I judged that they were drawn up not by his highness, but by the Dutch, who no doubt supposed that even if the provisions included therein were of no direct use to them, such proposals might at least offend Y.M., and so instead of the good relations which already exist between our two countries, and which we are striving to draw still closer, they might the better play their own game and do a mischief to each in turn. During the long time that I had been here this consideration had always obliged me to suffer patiently the treatment I had met with in this place, and he could bear witness that throughout that period I had never said one word in irritation; but this was so gross that I was forced at last to resent it. I then turned to the tenour of the articles, and briefly reminded him that it was not customary to formulate them in English. I had given my views to them in Latin; and though I ventured to speak English, I was not so perfect in that language that I presumed to conduct negotiations in it; but I nevertheless did not believe that they had done so with any idea of assuming superiority. At this point he interrupted me, and protested that they had had no idea of giving offence; that it was a source of happiness to them that I could talk to them [in English]; that they had done it for their own convenience, since (moreover) they esteemed their language as good as any other; and entreated me not to take it ill. I answered that it could not be of any great consequence, but that I had wished to remind him of it because (among other reasons) in negotiations much importance might attach to a single word; and even if we should reach agreement in English it would be a tiresome business to translate it into Latin afterwards to the satisfaction of both parties, and we should then have the trouble twice over.

I then passed to *realia*, and spoke first of the inclusion of the Dutch in the treaty, which I found strange. I had been sent to England by Y.M., and had been accredited, not to the Dutch, but to his highness and the English nation. Y.M., moreover, had not supposed that England could have no other friends than the Dutch, or grant and receive any advantage in trade or otherwise without their being participants in it. He [Fleetwood] knew very well that the interest of both our countries (which I expounded to him at length) was rather to holding the Dutch *in officio* than to admit them to such exceedingly great benefits. Not that Y.M. had any intention of ruining them, but only of keeping them in such a condition that they might not have the presumption to aspire to dictate laws to other sovereigns and potentates, and to regulate all their actions. In relation to this point all the others were of the less importance, and I would mention only one or two of them. And first, that Y.M. should renounce the power he enjoys of giving his own subjects some preference and advantage over foreigners: a point which sufficiently demonstrated that it was drawn by Dutchmen and not by Englishmen; for England could not put it forward since they were in no position to object to what they did themselves: not only did they give their inhabitants a large preference in regard to customs-dues, as all sovereigns mostly do, but they expressly forbade anyone to import into England anything which is not the produce of the land in which he lives. But the Dutch (apart from the fact that we would not take their side against England) are jealous of us mainly because we have been trying, by the preferences to which I alluded, to emancipate ourselves from their thraldom. It was the more incomprehensible to me that England should wish to obtain this advantage for them, for if they had it they would ruin the Baltic trade of England as well as of Sweden, since their light ships and low freights would enable them to sail everybody else off the seas; and with Prussia, in particular, England had long and important trading connexions. It was true that Y.M. had offered England 'half-freedom' in Livonia and Prussia, but that was upon condition that they should undertake to preserve the freedom of the Baltic at their own charges, and help to defend it against all foreign fleets of war; from all of which he might judge what importance we attached to 'full freedom' in all the Swedish dominions, and how little we were disposed to abandon it to the Dutch at so cheap a rate. The second point I wished to mention was that Y.M. should renounce his liberty to dispose of the tolls and trade in Prussia: a suggestion not less strange than the former; and the Dutch would esteem it no small thing if—after using every effort to obstruct Y.M.'s actions, and if possible to incite all nations and sovereigns against him—they could obtain this point in Prussia by way of England without honouring Y.M. so far as to ask him for it. When I looked at what Y.M. is offered in exchange, I could see nothing but what Y.M. is offering to grant them in his own country: that is, permission to recruit and hire men and ships; and though it might be thought that this is at present of more use to Y.M. than to them, it is limited by a clause to the effect that the potentate in whose country the recruiting is done shall determine in which part of the country it is to be permitted; which means that Y.M. could refer them to Lappland, or they could pick Ireland, if either party were not disposed to accommodate the other.[1] This I demonstrated to be very inequitable, and the proposal therefore unacceptable to me; for Y.M., thank God, was not so short of men that he would be prepared to buy them at such a price. I argued further that it was a means to hinder the common cause, and would put too great a power and too many resources into the hands of the Dutch, who (as we know) hated that cause as a thing which would interfere with their trade to catholic places, and in any case called it *societatem leoninam*, inasmuch as both our countries understood each other too well, and were therefore able to keep them *in officio*.

I then frankly told him what my attitude was, and said without beating about the bush that if they insisted on the inclusion of the Dutch, or of anything about them, I had no wish to treat with them; but that the points which had been deferred in the former treaty might be settled, and that I hoped that since that treaty had been made without the Dutch it might be perfected without them also, after which I might take my departure; and so made it plain that I had taken offence. To this he answered that he felt that if I looked at the matter properly [it would appear] that they had not meant it in the sense in which I had taken it. It was certainly true that they had some ties with Holland, but they were of such a nature that the Dutch had more obligations to them than they to the Dutch. All the same, they were glad to do them good service if they could; they were their brothers in religion, and so forth. As to the points [I had raised] he said that he could not see why England and Sweden, since they intended to link themselves together by ties of closest friendship, might not enjoy the same conditions—they in our country and we in theirs— as the inhabitants of our respective lands did.[2] As to the Prussia trade,

1. Thurloe's draft includes no such limitation: Bonde is importing into the argument about alliance-terms a matter which was being discussed in relation to the undecided points in Whitelocke's treaty: *cf.* Bonde's draft terms on p. 214 *supra*.

2. If this argument had been accepted Charles X would have been debarred from extending the existing preference for Swedish shipping ('half- or full exemption') to match (e.g.) the Navigation Act. In the existing state of the Swedish mercantile marine this was only a hypothetical case, but it was the mercantile marine that Sweden was especially anxious to encourage. And it ignored the question what duties Charles might impose if he succeeded in capturing (e.g.) Danzig.

England had long been engaged in it, and Prussia could not do without English goods, so that he saw no reason why they might not expect to enjoy from Y.M., as their friend, the same conditions as they had previously enjoyed from the king of Poland. As to the recruiting and so forth, the points were rather a basis for discussion than articles, and on them they might well come to some agreement; with a good deal more which he developed at length. To which I replied that he was speaking for England, and if [agreement] was sought with England alone, it was reasonable enough for us to talk of it now, and debate the terms; but I told him once again that I had no business with the Dutch, and had not been sent to England by Y.M. to negotiate with them. In reply he said that he felt that out of consideration for England I might proceed with the negotiation in the order in which the articles were presented, and this was a clause about which we might well reach agreement later, it being the last clause to be considered; but when I reiterated that what I was asking of England, and what they were asking of me as Y.M.'s representative, bore absolutely no relation to the Dutch, and I must therefore know where I stood, he told me (but in strict confidence) that his highness had ordered him to come to me if I had not already desired to speak to him, and to tell me that what he was negotiating through the commissioners were only those matters which he considered as of minor importance, but that he had besides some business to transact so secret that he intended personally to conduct the negotiations with me. He therefore begged me only to allow the commissioners to come to me and proceed with the treaty: it would turn out all right. His highness and he had discussed the great interest of both countries in reaching a mutual understanding, and had gathered so much from me, that it was not to be neglected. And he told me that his highness— preferably while I was still here—would if possible come to a decision on all points; adding much to my advantage in regard to the esteem his highness had for my frankness and good conduct. And as I had earlier taken note of the fact that the French ambassador's secretary knew of everything I had said to his highness on public affairs, I said that I suspected that it had been passed on to the Dutchman, who had revealed it to the Frenchman in order to countermine the common cause; that what I said must remain secret, and that I was not prepared to treat with them if they were going to reveal everything to the Dutch, which [Nieupoort] boasts that they have promised to do. As to this he said once again that his highness desired to treat with me in the strictest secrecy, and asked me to let him know if there was anything which required it: in such a case he [Fleetwood] would come to me immediately, and I might repose absolute confidence in him. In this connexion he mentioned Strickland, who is one of the commissioners, saying that I was not to suspect him: all he asked of me was that I should proceed with the negotiations, and in regard to secret matters act as he had suggested. I promised to do so, and with that we parted.

From these last remarks I detected that in their hearts they are no longer so much inclined to the Dutch; but since they are in great need of money, and are busy equipping new fleets for the exceedingly long trip to the Indies, with no return from it, their power is greatly weakened, and they dare not openly offend the Dutch. But they hope by these proposals to make it appear that they are doing what they can for them; and to avert any suspicion on that side they always allow Strickland (who is their creature) to be present as secretary. But I am pretty sure that apart from this his highness has something else in mind, and of this I hope shortly to give Y.M. more definite information: it is a fact that by the 15th article of their treaty with Holland each side is bound to include the other in any [future] treaty.[1] I mean now to go on with my negotiation, and to see what I can make of it; and though I do not propose to speak against the Dutch in the presence of the commissioners, I shall nevertheless take such care as I can that they do not in consequence draw me into any obligation. I hope, all the same, with God's help to obtain an agreement, though it is a somewhat slow process; but on both sides there has been no firm policy hitherto, for everyone has had his eyes upon Y.M.'s exploits, and waited to see what the issue of them might be.

I had my Lord Whitelocke with me yesterday, but as he knows nothing of the most secret side of the business I spoke to him only in general terms:[2] he assured me that they would try to give me satisfaction. It seems to me that his highness follows the maxim that the best way is to deceive such of his ministers as are to act in the affair. I hope at least that he does so with Strickland: time will show. All is quiet with regard to the embassy I mentioned in my last letter: it will soon appear what resolution they have taken.

The Dutch have lost their bearings completely, as Y.M. can see

1. This was a misinterpretation of the article, as Bonde later realized: it did no more than bind each party to make provision for the inclusion of the other, should such inclusion be desired.

2. Whitelocke noted: 'The ambassador seemed much unsatisfied with divers parts of the articles, and said, that he had no commission to treat of any matters concerning the United Provinces to be included, and was much nettled at that business. In discourse touching a general union of the protestant interest, he said, it would be a difficult work; and for his master's falling upon the emperor, he said, that they in Sweden did not wish it to be so, because they doubted that then Sweden would be neglected. He declared his opinion to be, not to meddle with the great business of the protestant union ... but he said, that they might send to the king his master at their pleasure, and have a fitting answer': Whitelocke, *Memorials*, iv. 222.

from Herr Coyet's remarkable conversation with Nieupoort.[1] I learn by a good hand that tidings are come from Jamaica to the effect that although 8 ships have been at the mainland, plundered a town and taken 50 [prisoners?], they die off very fast: Fortescue, who was their principal commander, is dead, and things are in a bad way. It appears now that that enterprise was not as easy as it was considered to be: it is as though God put this project into their heads to humble their pride; and it seems very likely that if they had used a quarter of those resources in Flanders, where a good opportunity existed, they could have had great successes. However that may be, I still think it promotes Y.M.'s interests, even though it so exhausts them that they will hardly be able to advance the common cause as vigorously as they would otherwise have been inclined to do. I have to-day received Y.M.'s orders (with a letter to his highness)[2] and will faithfully discharge them, though I am in great need of money: I beg Y.M. to bear me in mind. I await most anxiously Y.M.'s [further] instructions, which are now very necessary, and fear that for lack of them I may not be able to serve Y.M. as duly as I could wish.

XXXIV

London, 8 February 1656 [from Bonde's *Register*]

Last Monday, the 4th instant, I had audience of his highness; and though for some time he had not been very well, which had prevented him from talking with me, this was nevertheless a notable conversation. I began by making a speech and delivering Y.M.'s letter to him; which he answered very well, and more eloquently than I have heard him speak before. It all turned upon his joy at the news of Y.M.'s successes, and with this I need not trouble Y.M. I then thanked him for the commissioners, and in this connexion said that I should have been much astonished at the articles they brought with them, if I had not found from my talk with my Lord Fleetwood that his highness would be pleased to communicate his thoughts to me regarding the most important and secret matters, which I for my part would be glad to be informed of whenever it should please him. I had nevertheless thought it necessary to tell him that Y.M. values so highly the confidence which exists between himself and his highness, that he will most willingly let it appear in anything that may be feasible; but that it had never been his intention to treat with the Dutchmen here in England. I therefore requested that he would not ask me to accept that clause; but said that if I might treat with his commissioners on

1. Coyet's report is not in the transcript, nor in the Coyet papers in RA, and Nieupoort does not mention it.
2. Not in Abbott, nor in SP 95/5B.

behalf of himself and England, I should be ready and happy to do so. To this he answered by reiterated protestations that it had never been his intention to suggest anything which he thought might be offensive to Y.M. or to myself: his only purpose had been to do the Dutch a service, if he could, or at least show them that he was doing what he could for them; not least because he believed that that might be a means to achieve and solidify unity among protestants; and also so that that state, whose existence was solely dependent upon trade, might not be led to pursue misguided policies: they had still many papists among their inhabitants. He then assured me with many words of the pleasure he experienced from Y.M.'s successes, and that there was not a man alive who rejoiced at them more than he did: if it might seem to me that he was fond of the Dutch, I ought to know that they were not very satisfied with him, having had no favourable answer to their requests;[1] but he had exerted himself to offer *bona officia* and to do good service to both sides, as far as he was able. I seized this opportunity, and said that he gave me cause to say what otherwise I had not intended, namely, that Y.M. knew all too well that the Dutch had attempted by all possible means to throw obstacles in his way: they had not only drawn the elector of Brandenburg into an alliance prejudicial to Y.M., and in addition assisted him with money, but they had done their best to detach his highness from Y.M. (who had accounted him for his closest friend), and to force him to embrace what they considered to be their interests; but since I had been assured of his faithful friendship I thought it unnecessary to show my resentment at this conduct. From all of which his highness might judge for himself whether Y.M. had cause to acquiesce in their demands here in England, which they had not done Y.M. the honour of putting to himself. They have now sent their ambassadors to Denmark to try whether they cannot arouse enmity to Y.M. in that quarter.[2] All of which was hardly calculated to induce Y.M. to show them any friendship. His [the protector's] design of working to bring about

1. Presumably in regard to captures of Dutch merchantmen by English ships.
2. The instructions of the Dutch embassy, of whom van Beuningen was the leading spirit, are of 6/16 November 1655 (though they did not reach Copenhagen till 4 February): printed in Becker, *Samlinger*, i. 91–3. They were to convey the anxiety of the Dutch at developments in the Baltic; to attempt to elicit how Denmark proposed to ensure freedom of trade there; to enquire, in the event of Charles X's levying tolls at Danzig in 1656, whether Denmark would join in an embassy to make remonstrances, or to mediate peace. The Dutch envisaged an alliance which should send a fleet, and possibly a land force, to Prussia, and wished to know whether, if a Dutch fleet were attacked, Denmark would come to its aid: Carlbom, *Magnus Dureels negotiation*, pp. 69–72. For de Witt's correspondence with van Beuningen, see *Brieven van Johan de Witt ... bewerkt door Robert Fruin* (Amsterdam 1919), i; *Brieven aan Johan de Witt ... bewerkt door Robert Fruin*, (Amsterdam 1919), II. i., and Thurloe, iv. 553, 564, 568, 585, 622–3, 628, 680; v. 149, 783. De Witt on 24 March NS firmly rejected van Beuningen's suggestion

unity among protestants, and so advance the common cause, was
certainly laudable; but I could tell him in confidence that I had
reliable information that the Dutch ambassador who was to be sent to
Denmark had had frequent discussions in Hamburg with the imperial
minister [Georg von] Plettenberg, who had depicted the strength of
the emperor's forces in very strong colours; from all of which he might
judge how far they were concerned about the common cause. [Y.M.'s]
intention was not to ruin them, for (apart from the matter of religion)
they are so situated that their forces balance those of Spain in the
Netherlands, and in any case they perform a useful service to many
nations as traders: it was designed only to keep them in such a position
that they should not imagine themselves to be appointed to be *censores*
over every king's actions. I made this last remark because the great
argument of the Dutch party here is that Queen Elizabeth raised
them up as a counter-balance against the power of Spain, and that
for that reason it is in the interest of England that they should be
supported.

He answered that he could not approve of their proceedings, and
said that the elector of Brandenburg must be laughing at them, having
upset their plans by the peace [of Königsberg], and asked whether
they had not sent an embassy to Y.M. (I cannot help thinking that
the Dutch party keep him in the dark as to what is happening); and
then continued *in terminis generalibus* to say how happy he should be if
he could do anything to promote unity; and for the rest said that in
regard to my first request he would be very ready to discuss matters
with me whenever I asked, and that nothing but ill-health would
prevent him from doing so. Whether it [*sc.* his reserve] arose from his
indisposition, or whether he is expecting more from me in the matter
of the common cause, I cannot be sure: it could be that they want to
try whether my teeth sit firmly in my head, or at least to make it
appear to the Dutch that they are doing what they can for them. At
this point I took my leave.

The following day the Danish resident[1] came to me, and I could
see that he was hoping to get something out of me. Among much
conversation about the Dutch, he asked what was the state of affairs

---

that the existing Dutch-Swedish alliance of 1645 be regarded as no longer binding.
Dureel's devastating description of the weakness and unpreparedness of Denmark may
well have influenced Charles X in 1657: Carlbom, *Magnus Dureels negotiation*, p. 94.

1. Simon Petkum. He had a trying and unfruitful time of it in London: on 25 April
NS 1656 he wrote to Rosenvinge 'I have sent continually for these last three weeks to
speak with the secretary of state, but he will never be at home'; and three days later,
'Sir Oliver Fleming is of late so much Swedified, that I hardly dare to speak to him':
Thurloe, iv. 698, 710.

in regard to the embassy from this country to Y.M., and remarked that no doubt its purpose was to mediate between Holland and Sweden. I saw well enough what he was after, and in general gave him appropriate answers, but on this last point I said that I hardly thought that the embassy would be well received if that was its purpose: it was customary to offer mediation *before* sending off an embassy, and it was odd to speak of embassies in a case where no hostilities existed. The crown of Sweden, like other powers, had considered it only politic, if they wanted salt from Portugal, wine from France and Spain, cloth from England, *etc.*, to seek the friendship of those who disposed of such wares as they might be in need of, and not to meddle in the private quarrels of those countries: it was nothing to them whether a duke of Braganza or the king of Spain should be king of Portugal, or whether the protector or the former king's family should rule in England: they let each country settle its affairs as best they can, taking care, however, to be on good terms with those who are in control.[1] And the Dutch should act in the same way. No ruler owed them anything, and still less is under their authority. If they wanted something over which Y.M. exercises control, it was no more than reasonable that they should ask him for it. And in any case I hardly supposed that Y.M. was disposed to accept England's mediation. When the English were engaged in a bitter war against the Dutch, Sweden had offered her mediation[2]—and that at a time when her position was such that she could perhaps have been able to decide the issue of the war in favour of whichever side she supported; but neither the English nor the Dutch accepted her mediation, and the same answer might reasonably be made [to the English] now. I know that he is going to retail all this to the Dutch, and I think that this may help to deflect any mediation, which I fancy will not commend itself to Y.M. I am told by a good friend that the protestant cantons in Switzerland are very anxious that Y.M. should do something for them, and that he should have some minister with them; and that they have written to Sir Oliver Fleming, who long resided there, to do what he can to press their case. I have therefore thought it not unserviceable to notify Y.M. accordingly. Yesterday evening the commissioners were with me, and they are coming again next Wednesday. We are working on the first point, concerning recruiting and the hiring of ships: the great difficulty is their demand for a proviso that those ships shall not be used against their allies [*sc.* the Dutch]. I shall do all I can to secure that they may be used against

---

1. He was to use this argument to Whitelocke later: Whitelocke, *Memorials*, iv. 225.
2. In May 1653.

all who propose to enter the Baltic with a fleet of war.[1] The English merchants in Danzig have loudly complained to his highness that their factors have been forced to participate in the watch, to pay the hundredth penny on all the merchandise they have on hand, and to pay the tenth penny on their own and their principals' property if they wish to leave; and his highness has written a stern letter to the town of Danzig about it, which I imagine may contribute something to Y.M.'s service.[2] The letter went off a week ago. I have this moment received Y.M.'s letter from Schlippenbeil. I shall give its contents my due attention, and send an answer to Y.M. by Johan Risingh, who leaves within the next two days, and also by the next post. By him I shall also send a letter which his highness has caused to be delivered to me through the commissioners. It is an answer to Y.M.'s letter to him, and to the notification of the happy birth of his royal highness.

XXXV

London, 15 February 1656 [from Bonde's *Register*]

Having had the great happiness to receive by the last post Y.M.'s orders of 6 January from Schlippenbeil, I thought it necessary to follow them as best I could;[3] and as my Lord Fleetwood has on various occasions faithfully discharged what I committed to him, and as moreover at my last conference with him he asked that if it should happen that there was something which I desired to be kept secret I would give him advance notice of it, I thought it necessary first to have a talk with him about it, so that he could prepare the way with the protector, and arrange that the protector might so manage it that what I intended to propose to him should be kept suitably secret; but since the protector was holding a day of prayer in secret at Whitehall (it is said, to pray to God for the fleet which is soon to set sail), [the

1. Bonde was ultimately defeated on this point.
2. For their complaints, Thurloe to Rolt, 10 January NS 1656: Thurloe, iv. 260–70; for the protector's letter, Abbott, iv. 91–2.
3. Charles's new instruction, dated Schlippenbeil 6 January, ordered Bonde to press the protector to conclude a *defensive* alliance *contra quemcunque*, with the special object of upholding the peace of Osnabrück: England to contribute an annual subsidy of 900,000 rdr., in return for which Charles would provide 30,000 foot and 6000 horse if the emperor violated that peace so flagrantly as to require the use of force. It communicated also a change of policy on commercial matters: Bonde was to make no further offers of special privileges at the expense of other countries, 'because we discern much jealousy in other countries, and because it provides an opportunity for cheating, and the diminution of our revenues'; nor was it necessary 'that you attempt with so much labour to induce them to forsake the trade to Archangel and sail to Nyen or Narva for Russian goods, since they may suspect that there is more in it than there really is': Carlbom, *Sverige och England*, pp. 64–6, and Thurloe, iv. 613–14.

audience] did not take place until after I had opened the matter [to Fleetwood], to whom I demonstrated the incomparable strength and security which would accrue to his highness and this government by such an alliance, and the advantage which they would gain in their war with one limb of the House of Austria by so powerful a diversion of the forces of that House;[1] and I argued finally that this was the best means of strengthening the foundations of our religion in general (which England throughout these times seems to have zealously striven for); and then proceeded to explain that Y.M. on his side asked no more of England than that they should assist him with a sum of 900,000 *rdr.* a year. I urged many arguments to prove that England should make no difficulty about such a sum. He replied that there might be some difficulty because of the Dutch, since England was bound by treaty not to enter into such an alliance without them. To this I answered that there might well be means of getting round that difficulty, and that they—and all other states—might be admitted to the alliance, once we had reached agreement.[2] He took this with satisfaction, and said that that was all they had wanted of Y.M.; but as to financial assistance he thought there was very great difficulty, and enlarged upon the present shortage of money. When I retorted that the English people, both in King Charles's time and subsequently, had shown a great readiness to grant what was asked of them in the name of religion, and that [on that plea] it would be easy to obtain large sums from them, he answered that such a thing could not be done without a parliament, which his highness was very reluctant to summon at this time; but he took it all *ad referendum*, assured me that secrecy would be observed, and so we parted.

In the afternoon, about 4 o'clock, I had an audience with the protector on the same business, Thurloe alone being present, when I put the case for the alliance and the points to be contained in it, and showed its consonance with the declaration which his highness gave

---

1. The orders from Schlippenbeil suggested that the agreement to defend the peace of Osnabrück was necessary in view of the possibility of an *attack* by the emperor; but though Ferdinand III gave moral support to Poland, and mediated the Polish-Russian truce of October 1656, he gave no practical assistance until the conclusion of the treaty of 21 November 1656, and one significant provision of that treaty was that it exempted the emperor from taking any action which constituted a breach of the peace of Westphalia: Bonnesen, *Karl X Gustaf*, p. 176.

2. In discussion with Whitelocke on 7 April Bonde argued that art. XV of the treaty of Westminster did not prevent the conclusion of an Anglo-Swedish alliance, but only bound England to give the Dutch an opportunity to join it: they read over the article together, and Whitelocke conceded that Bonde's argument was correct: Whitelocke, *Memorials*, iv. 240. For Charles X, a war with the emperor was no more than an unwelcome possibility: Bonde, both to Fleetwood and to Cromwell, was representing it as a possible option.

me at the beginning of January[1] (I sent it to Y.M. on 11 January, with a duplicate on the 14th); and I argued that it offered the most effective method of strengthening his position and his *régime*, by depriving its ill-wishers on the continent of all hope of doing him a mischief, and hence also of reconciling the spirits of malcontents here at home. I made much of the argument that the sum asked of England could in fact be recovered if their enemy's forces were weakened by so powerful a diversion, since the emperor would be rendered incapable of assisting the king of Spain in any way, and Spain would be compelled to join forces with the emperor against Y.M., as being the quarter from whence the greatest danger threatened; so that they [the English] would be able to save on their armaments an equal sum of money, or more. I mentioned finally the Swiss protestants, for whom his highness had manifested much compassion, as in the beginning of his discourse sent over on 11 January; when he had referred to the strife in that country [and said that] if Y.M. should resolve to attack the emperor, the catholics and both branches of the House of Austria would have so much on their hands that neither Bavaria nor any other of the neighbouring catholic states would be in a position to come to the aid of their co-religionists.[2]

His reply manifested much satisfaction at this overture, but dwelt mostly on the fact that in his view this was a matter which touched on Y.M.'s interests no less than upon his own, and it was therefore a question which party the greater reason to assist the other. He then protested his present great need of money, and the burdens to which the country had been subjected by the continuing taxes and impositions which had been levied for so many years, and so forth; but promised nevertheless to consider the matter with all the secrecy requisite in so important a question; and said that he was prepared to discuss it with a few members of his council. I replied that there was a wide difference in the interests of the two parties: that his highness was involved in a war with Spain, and whether Y.M. participated in it or not would be obliged to carry it on vigorously, while Y.M. was still at liberty to involve himself or not: it was now open to

1. This might pass for fair comment on the audience of 2 January, but it was a serious misrepresentation of that of 8 January: Cromwell's declaration on that day had been clearly for an offensive and defensive alliance; Charles was now offering a defensive alliance only.

2. On 9 February (the day after the arrival of the orders from Schlippenbeil) Bonde reiterated to Whitelocke that this was not the moment for a general union of protestants, but that 'if the king of Sweden and the protector made a conjunction first, they might fall upon the emperor and the house of Austria'. But the last clause was no doubt a sop to Bonde's interlocutor, and not a serious statement of possible policy: Whitelocke, *Memorials*, iv. 224.

him to consolidate his position in Poland and Prussia, and refrain from any further enterprises. Moreover, Y.M. would take risks in beginning a war with his neighbours, and incurred more danger by doing so than in the case of England, which had a strong wall of defence in the surrounding sea. And consequently that Y.M. could not determine upon such a course without substantial assistance. It was, besides, now so costly to make war, that whereas before it had been possible to have a soldier for 6 *rdr.*, the king of Spain was now having to pay 20 for every man recruited and transferred to Spain from the imperial dominions. To this he replied by arguing that Y.M. must inevitably fall out with the emperor, not only on account of the peace of Osnabrück, which had in many respects been violated, but also because the king of Poland had retired to Habsburg territory [i.e. Silesia]. He then made many excuses for having to some extent taken the Dutchmen's part, admitting that their proceedings could not be justified, and that it was only reasonable that they should make amicable approaches to Y.M. if there was anything that they desired of him, and protesting that the only thing that had forced him to take their part was that he was afraid that they might in sheer desperation take a resolution to unite themselves with our enemies. On the last point I answered him as courteously as I could, and in terms of Y.M.'s orders, and begged him to lose no time in giving me a good answer, so that Herr Coyet (who was present), having been recalled by Y.M., might be in a position to take some intelligence with him which would enable the business to be dealt with more expeditiously. And so we parted.[1]

I now have frequent meetings with the commissioners.[2] I am not

1. On this same 15 February Thurloe had a conversation with Nieupoort which illustrated the similarity of the difficulties which hampered the protector's dealings with the Dutch, and those which hampered an alliance with Sweden. Thurloe told him that they agreed in aim, but differed in method: the Dutch wanted a preliminary agreement with England on policy; Thurloe preferred independent action by their ambassadors to Charles X, and added that Charles would not tolerate being confronted by a joint Anglo-Dutch plan and being asked to adhere to it: *Brieven*, iii. 186–7.

2. On 7 February the commissioners debated whether the right of recruiting and hiring ships should be done only at places approved by local authorities: Bonde objected that in that case they might assign Finland or Ireland. An expedient proposed 'and not held unreasonable' that if one place were not approved by the local authorities, they should appoint another, as convenient and as near as possible: Whitelocke, *Memorials*, iv. 223; it was further agreed, on Bonde's insistence, that recruited troops might be employed defensively (e.g. in garrisons) against the friends of the other party. But Bonde insisted also that in the case of ships they might be employed offensively against disturbers of trade [*sc.* the Dutch]: this point left for consideration: *ibid.*, iv. 224. Neither of Bonde's demands was conceded in the treaty. On 13 February they met again; when it appeared that the council had inserted corn, hemp, pitch, tar,

entirely clear as to what I can expect from them, for we are still debating the articles among ourselves. I have been reliably informed that Nieupoort left his last audience with his highness (which he had some days ago) very dissatisfied: they had argued about the Swedish business, as to which he [the protector] had said that they should send to Y.M. themselves if they wanted anything of him; to which Nieupoort is said to have replied that he was ill-pleased with such an answer, and that he would write to his principals about it. On which the protector is said to have answered that he might do so, but that he could meddle no further in the matter.[1] The post from Hamburg did not arrive this week.

XXXVI

London, 16 February 1656

Since I have an opportunity to ensure that my letter comes safely to hand by the messenger Johan Risingh, who is leaving here immediately by ship for Hamburg, and intends to proceed as soon as possible to Y.M. (he has been delayed here some time drawing up a narrative of the unfortunate events that befel him in New Sweden), I have thought it necessary to avail myself of it to let Y.M. know that I received Y.M.'s letter, and his much longed-for orders, with all reverence and great joy, by the last post.

I gather that Y.M. has been pleased to read my letters down to the 25 November; and that he now orders that I shall hasten my negotiation in order that I may depart hence the sooner. I confess that I have been in this place longer than was expected; but I hope that the

---

money, into the list of contraband goods. 'The ambassador said, that if they would likewise add copper and iron, it would take in all the commodities of his master's dominions, and he might insist cloth to be added, which was as necessary for soldiers as corn and money'. Bonde took the line that the present situation (war with Spain) was irrelevant: what they had to look to was the situation in which Whitelocke had made the treaty. On passports, Bonde propounded 'free ship makes free goods, free goods make free ship'—'which was not held unreasonable': *ibid.*, 225–6. But controversy on both points continued.

   1. 'In discourse with the Dutch ambassador, he was passionate even to indiscretion, blaming the neglect of sending to the king of Sweden from the protector, and urging the necessity of yet doing it speedily. Being asked for what end, he answered, concerning trade': Whitelocke, *Memorials*, iv. 224. Nieupoort was especially disturbed by Cromwell's remark 'that we might be assured of his good faith and friendship for so long as we adhered to our true interests, and added, that he was ready to believe that we should not allow ourselves to be misled'. De Witt at once asked for an explanation of these reservations: Nieupoort replied that he could only suppose that the protector had meant 'as long as the Dutch do not turn to Orange': *Brieven*, iii. 184–5, 193.

detailed copy which I sent to Y.M. on 23 November, and all my subsequent letters, will have enabled him to appreciate that I have let no opportunity go unutilised which might forward my business. But as Y.M.'s orders, both from Alt Stettin on 28 July, and from Koło on 22 August, instruct me that Y.M. intended at all costs to maintain a firmer friendship with him [Cromwell] than with any other, and also that the contrivances of Brandenburg and Holland would prevent Y.M. from having security in his rear on that side, I thought it necessary to follow them strictly. And therefore, for reasons which I set out in my letters of 9 November and 28 December, I was induced the more patiently to suffer their delays; mainly so that I might not in the smallest degree give the Dutch party here any opportunity to provoke a refusal, and so entail my departure without receiving satisfaction: to the prejudice, and possibly the complete overthrow, of Y.M.'s necessary and politic designs. But I can assure Y.M. that all this was done without lowering myself in the slightest degree: on the contrary, I have here a higher reputation, and am more honoured by the lord protector, than in the case of any previous ambassador. I am greatly distressed that Y.M. writes that he is much astonished that I did not long ago, in accordance with his orders, sound the protector about the Protestant Cause, but that I have dragged my feet, and so lost Y.M. much precious time, now and in the future. I most humbly beg Y.M. graciously to take note of my most humble and truthful explanation. Although I cannot find, either in my instructions or in any other order from Y.M., that I was commanded to sound the lord protector on it, it is true that Herr Coyet long ago had Y.M.'s orders to do so, so that Y.M. might subsequently be in a better position to draw my instructions; but not only did he do his duty in that matter (as he reported to Y.M. before my arrival), but I too have pressed it as hard as I could venture to do, and spoken of it not only with Thurloe and Fleetwood (as reported in my letters of 31 August and 28 October), but also with his highness himself, particularly on 21 September (as mentioned in my letter of 28 September); but was never able to get any other answer than one couched *in generalibus terminis*, with a declaration that he must first know what Y.M.'s intentions were before he could give me his views in more detail. I beg that Y.M. may be pleased to note from my letter of 21 December that I courteously reproached him on this account. Moreover, I had not only Y.M.'s verbal command, but also his written orders of 30 September, from Kraków, to proceed with caution in this matter; which was why I did not venture, in so delicate an affair, to go beyond my express orders. But I imagine that from my letter of 21 December, and from his highness's declaration of 11 January, Y.M. will find that as soon as I received orders to pursue the question I not only pressed it, but received such a resolution upon it as—*in genere*—I could then hope for. Otherwise, I have done my best to discover what could be discovered of his highness's attitude towards Y.M.'s friendship, and always given Y.M. a faithful report of his own words; and though I have indeed still made little progress with the commissioners, it is nevertheless certain that I have had more discussion in private with his highness than all the ministers put together who have been here since the government was established upon its present footing. I therefore most humbly entreat Y.M.'s forgiveness if in all this I have in any way been in fault. I shall most punctually observe Y.M.'s orders to make no more offers to the English of preferences in the Baltic: I have in fact not made any mention of this for a considerable time, but have rather put forward other proposals to them which I hoped might give Y.M. what he wanted: of these I have written at length in my letters of 30 November and 7 December. Y.M. is further pleased to command that I shall not labour so much to induce them to abandon the trade to Archangel, so that they may not suspect that there is more in this suggestion than there really is. I did indeed at first rather emphasize this, in order to exaggerate the value of the Baltic trade; but when I found that they reacted coolly to the idea I let it drop, and instead privately incited the merchants of the Muscovy Company who reside here to ask for it, but in such a way as to suggest that they did not wish it to appear that I was aware of it. As to mediation between this country and the Russians, there has been no word of it for a long time, particularly since I learned from Y.M.'s letters of 30 September (from Kraków) and 8 November that Y.M. was not in favour of it. That Y.M. is graciously pleased to approve what I have done to prevent his highness's proffered mediation between Y.M. and Holland gives me great pleasure; and no doubt Y.M. will gather from my later letters to what great trials I have been exposed in this regard; but thank God no action has yet been taken, and still less will it be taken in the future.

I was with my Lord Whitelocke last Saturday, who confessed to me in strict confidence that the embassy for which he was destined was directed solely to a mediation, and that among others the Dutch ambassador himself had told him so; but he assured me that he would never allow himself to be employed on such a mission, and that it was disgraceful to make him such an offer, who had formerly been employed to negotiate between the crown of Sweden and this country: it was to make him the servant of the Dutch, who are the sole cause of his disfavour; and all that the Dutch party have brought up against him was because he was a person whom Y.M. and the crown of Sweden had both obliged and esteemed.[1]

1. *Cf.* Whitelocke, *Memorials*, iv. 219–20.

That Y.M. is graciously pleased to let me know what language I am to hold as to the Dutch is very timely information. In the uncertainty in which I have hitherto been in this regard I have thought it best to adhere to the same line; and though from time to time I have spoken somewhat strongly, it has always been with the reservation that Y.M. wishes them no ill, but simply that if they want anything of Y.M. they should ask it of him in a friendly fashion. In which, as (with God's help) in all other matters which may rise, nothing has been done otherwise than as is required for Y.M.'s due respect and reputation. I entreat Y.M., with great submission, to receive the *iudicia* and opinions which may have dropped from me regarding the protector and other matters graciously: I take God to witness that my intention has been, and shall always be, honest and faithful; and that I have taken pains to inform Y.M. in detail of what the state of affairs is, and how various people see it, so that Y.M., who is so far off, may thereby be the better informed. I thank Y.M. also, most humbly, for his promise to take measures for my subsistence. I shall spare no pains and effort to see to it that the expense is not applied in vain; and I hope that the means which have been afforded me have been so well and honourably laid out that they have redounded to the prestige of Y.M. and the whole nation. Of this, and of what has been passing here, Herr Coyet will no doubt report to Y.M., since I gather that he is now recalled. He has comported himself here well, and in a praiseworthy fashion; is highly esteemed by his highness and every-body else; and I have throughout received great assistance from him, both by his advice and otherwise; which is why in these last most important conferences I have always associated him with me, as being a respected minister of Y.M. at this place; so that he is the better able to give Y.M. a circumstantial account of what has been happening. Since by yesterday's post I had to inform Y.M. of how I had begun to execute Y.M.'s last orders, I think it unnecessary to repeat it all here; but I shall continue to advise Y.M. by every post of such progress as I may make. I desire only that God will grant me grace to carry out Y.M.'s most urgent orders with happy success.

XXXVII

London, 22 February 1656 [from Bonde's *Register*]

The last week having been occupied in preparing and celebrating the festivities which Y.M. has ordered,[1] both in respect of the happy birth of his royal highness, and of Y.M.'s incomparable campaigns; and

---

1. They seem to have been of a very splendid nature: Whitelocke was much impressed: Whitelocke, *Memorials*, iv. 226–7.

since in addition his highness has been preoccupied with the preparations for the departure of the fleet of Generals Blake and Montagu a week ago, there has been nothing worth reporting since my last letter, and I think it therefore unnecessary to trouble Y.M. with any lengthy despatch. General Fleetwood has been consoled not only by getting leave to recruit the 1000 men still outstanding for my Lord Cranstoun, but also by permission to raise an additional regiment of 2000 men on his own account, of which I hope to give Y.M. full details by the next post. I have learned from a good friend, in the strictest secrecy, that various extremely important secret articles were included in the treaty recently concluded between this country and France: I shall try to discover their tenour, and send them over by the next post.[1] Ambassador Nieupoort was with me, together with other guests, last Wednesday, and invited me to his house in return: to this I agreed, since he had first been a guest in my house. In general we are on a friendly footing, and in this I am encouraged by Y.M.'s orders to avoid showing any resentment against Holland. I hope to be able to say something of this by the next post.

XXXVIII

London, 29 February 1656 [from Bonde's *Register*]

The day after writing my last short letter I went to dine with the Dutch ambassador Nieupoort. Among other things he mentioned that he had had a letter from the States-General informing him that the king of France had indeed the intention of sending the duc de Rochefeaucaut [de la Rochefoucauld] to Switzerland to mediate in the war between the catholic and protestant cantons. He said that it was a matter of great importance, and that on the previous day he had imparted this information to his highness, who had assured him that he had ordered his resident in Geneva[2] to move to the place to which the Dutch minister who resides there had also had orders to go, and so do something to balance the power of the catholics. In this connection Nieupoort said that it would be a very good thing for the Protestant Cause if Y.M. were in some way to support [them], and send some minister to those parts—a thing which would be particularly desirable if all the present troubles should lead to a general war of religion, in which case it would be of the highest importance

1. Text in Abbott, iii. 930–8. They provided for the expulsion from France of Charles II, his brothers James and Henry, and seventeen leading royalists; and from England of Barrière and nine other adherents of Condé.

2. Samuel Morland, commissioner extraordinary at Geneva: *cf.* Abbott, iv. 141, 147.

that the protestant Swiss should remain under arms. Otherwise we talked only of indifferent matters, [though] as to the attitude of the Dutch in the present war in Poland he said that all they demanded was liberty to trade, for trade provided the means of subsistence for so many millions of persons in Holland, and he confidently expected that as a result of his embassy they would get it before many days had elapsed; adding, in the words of a proverb which is often on his lips, 'Friende konnen wel kyven, maer Friende mocten Friende blijven' [Friends may indeed fall out, but friends must still remain friends]. And since Y.M. in his last orders instructed me not to allow any resentment against them to appear, I agreed with him, and among other things said that they must ask Y.M. for what they wanted, and what it was in his power to arrange, in a friendly way, but that they might be sure that they would get nothing by constraint or force.

Although since [my last letter] I have tried to keep my negotiation going, I have not been able during this last week to have speech with the lord protector, by reason of the indisposition of his highness, and of Thurloe, nor was I able to meet the commissioners until this afternoon.[1] Nor could [General] Fleetwood obtain any authorization for the remaining 1000 men of Cranstoun's levy, still less for the further levy which he had solicited, although that had been promised us. I therefore thought it advisable to speak somewhat strongly, and asked General Fleetwood to tell his brother that I was by no means satisfied to be put off in such a manner, with more to the same purpose to demonstrate my ill-humour. On this my Lord Deputy, after making great excuses, and blaming everything upon the lord protector's indisposition, went to him at once; with the result that permission for the remaining 1000 men for Cranstoun's levy was issued yesterday and sent to Cranstoun, and for the rest the fairest promises made.[2] Since Herr Coyet has made over to him [Cranstoun] a part of the 12,000 *rdr.* which, by Y.M.'s orders, were to be paid to him according to the

1. Whitelocke records under 25 February: 'The Swedish ambassador came to visit me, and told me, that now the business of sending an ambassador from hence to Sweden was over, and there was at present no occasion for it; for this, their reasons, he alleged, were, a peace concluded betwixt the king of Sweden and the elector of Brandenburg, and the proceeding of the treaty here. Intimating, that he was sufficiently empowered to conclude what was at present requisite between his master and the protector; and that there was no likelihood but that there would also be a good understanding between the king of Sweden and the United Provinces': Whitelocke, *Memorials*, iv. 227. Abbott so far misunderstood this as to write: 'Bonde believed his chances of concluding an Anglo-Swedish treaty had been improved by the peace signed between Sweden and Brandenburg, which automatically eliminated [!] any close alliance between Sweden and the United Provinces': Abbott, iv. 109.

2. Cf. *CSP* (*Dom*) *1655–56*, p. 202.

agreement for recruiting the 2000 men, and since he [Cranstoun] has made such arrangements that he can raise them in a day or two, I hope that he will now exert himself and send over the 2000 in the immediate future. Y.M.'s letter, with its order to General Fleetwood to raise a further 4000 men, was received yesterday by him and by myself, and we shall both do our best to comply with it. If we can obtain permission, which I am pretty sure of, there is no doubt that there are men here who will be glad to enter Y.M.'s service. I hope to go on strongly with my treaty henceforward, now that the banquet which hindered me last week, and the press of business as Lord Keeper which hindered my Lord Fiennes, are both over.[1] The fleet is expected to sail shortly: what the plan is nobody knows for certain, but it is supposed that they will sail in company to the Portuguese coast, and that from there one detachment will make for Jamaica, some will sail to the Mediterranean, and the remainder stay on the coast of Spain looking out for the silver-fleet and otherwise doing what damage they can to Spain. There are some who fear that if Portugal changes its mind about confirming the treaty which their ambassador here was to conclude some time ago, they may attack the Portuguese, Brazilian or Indian fleets, and thereby delay the payment of the sum of money owed by Portugal to this country.[2] But this does not seem very likely, for the lord protector is in great need of Portugal's harbours in the present circumstances; and it is for that reason that he is sending the Latin Secretary Meadowe there shortly: a handsome and intelligent young man; one of the best I have seen here.

As I write this, General Fleetwood comes to me from his brother, and gives good hope of the recruiting which Y.M. by this post ordered him to undertake: he asks only that arrangements be made to ensure that the money is ready at Hamburg in time, since some time must elapse before any communication from that place can arrive here. Recruiting for the king of France is also afoot, which puts up the price of men, and he therefore asks that if possible the whole amount of muster-money be made available, for if half of it is to wait until the men are delivered he is going to be in difficulties. As to the price, he promises to see whether it is possible to manage with 12 *rdr.* per man, sea-transport included, and assured me that he will do his best in that regard, as I am sure he will.[3] I shall also write to the chancellor about

---

1. Sagredo reported on 25 February NS that there was a 'universal belief' that an offensive and defensive alliance would be concluded, and that the negotiations 'occasion no little jealousy in the Dutch minister': *CSP (Ven) 1655–56*, p. 180.

2. Admiral Montagu was in fact very eager to do this, but was ordered to confine himself to a demonstration off Lisbon: Corbett, *England in the Mediterranean*, i. 326.

3. On 12 March the council resolved to advise his highness to authorize Sir [General] George Fleetwood to raise a regiment of 2000 English (not Scottish) volunteers for the Swedish service: *CSP (Dom) 1655–56*, p. 221.

it, requesting his excellency's assistance towards a speedy despatch of the business; and I write similarly to Commissioner Hoffstetter by this post. The secret articles [in the Anglo-French treaty], or an extract from them, which I sent in my last letter to Y.M., I enclose also in this: they are kept extraordinarily secret.

I learn by reports that Y.M. and his army have moved from Łowicz to Lublin, there to seek out King Casimir, who has some forces in the area.[1] May the Almighty and all-powerful God be with Y.M. in his noble and incomparable actions.

XXXIX

London, 7 March 1656 [from Bonde's *Register*]

I have now once again got my commissioners to work steadily with me; and although there are various difficulties I nevertheless hope with God's help to disentangle them. It would be of great assistance to me, and would force them to give me better terms, if Y.M. were pleased to give me any information on the points put to the lord protector some time ago by the Baltic merchants, which I long since sent to Y.M., together with my opinion of them; but since Y.M. has not been pleased to do so I must exert myself as far as possible to do something about it.[2]

Yesterday evening I had a long and very notable conference with his highness,[3] the details of which I have no time to communicate to Y.M. Since Herr Coyet was present on the occasion he will be able to tell Y.M. about it when he arrives. When I asked for an answer to my last proposition, I found (or at least it appeared so) that he was resolved to reply to me with a refusal. His answer mainly consisted of protestations of his friendship for Y.M., long recapitulations of his attitude during the period [of my stay], and especially in regard to Dutch affairs. He said something of the legation which the Dutch (and he also) had wished to send to Y.M.; which—in view of the fact that it might not be agreeable to Y.M., and might seem to show a desire to put strong pressure on Y.M. to do what the Dutch

1. In February 1656 the Swedish forces in Poland attained their maximum strength (some 57,000 men); and on 8/18 February Charles X inflicted a severe defeat on Czarniecki at Gołąb.

2. Among the points debated was the English demand that they pay no more than Swedes in Swedish ports, though Swedes received no reciprocal treatment; and the question of diverting the Russia trade to Narva (on which Whitelocke was sceptical): decision on these points deferred: Whitelocke, *Memorials*, iv. 228–32.

3. The audience had been preceded by a meeting between Bonde and Cromwell in St James's Park: *Bondes Diarium*, p. 51; at which he probably communicated verbally the proposals for an alliance which were handed over to Thurloe on 17 March: Thurloe, iv. 623–4.

demanded—he had not allowed to depart; with more avowals of his great desire to be friends with Y.M. and to serve him. Such had been his conduct to the Dutch, though they had ill requited it,[1] and had allowed it to appear that they entertained suspicions that Y.M. and he had made some arrangement to their disadvantage—among other reasons because he had been unable to approve their unreasonable behaviour to Y.M., and had seriously warned them against approaching the question on those lines. He then came to the second point, as to which the substance of his answer was that their [sc. England's] relations with the House of Austria were such that he would not be justified in giving Y.M. any assistance in money; on which he enlarged at some length, alleging their necessities, which did not permit them to do what they would wish to do.[2]

I answered first by thanking him for his expressions of good-will, and acknowledged that his account of what had passed was true, and that Y.M. would always consider it as an expression of the friendship which existed between them; but for the rest I used so many and such strong arguments in rebuttal that after several exchanges had passed between us he burst out and made it clear that it was fear of Holland that mainly held him back; that he was afraid that if Y.M. entered into such an alliance with him the Dutch might easily turn to Spain and the Austrian party; and that as things stood at present he would be very reluctant to involve himself in trouble with them. To this I replied by confirming him in the nervousness he felt about the Dutch, since they detested this government, and I said that I could therefore see no means of security against them save by entering with Y.M. into an alliance to which they might afterwards be invited to adhere. They would then *sub nullo specie juris* have any reason to be alarmed; and when Y.M. embraced his interests, and the protector *vice versa*, it would be impossible for them to venture anything, since the two countries were so powerful that nothing could be more damaging to Holland than their enmity. I showed him this so plainly, that though I pretended to accept his negative answer and made as though to get up and go, he replied—animated by Thurloe and Pickering, who were also present—by asking me to remain, saying that he would be

1. On 4 March the commissioners for the projected Marine Treaty with the Dutch were ordered to speak to Nieupoort concerning information received about Dutch ships in Spanish service: *CSP (Dom) 1655–56*, p. 207; Thurloe, iv. 588–9; *Brieven*, iii. 203–7: *cf.* the account of Cromwell's strong remonstrance to Nieupoort, 3 March NS: *CSP (Ven) 1655–56*, p. 184.

2. On this day Giavarina reported that Cromwell had agreed to provide Charles X with ten powerful ships, Charles being to pay for them and retain them for as long as he wished: an extraordinarily belated (and inaccurate) reflection of Charles's proposal 1655: *CSP (Ven) 1655–56*, p. 190.

glad to hear my arguments and was ready to do anything that was possible; and after exchanging a few more words, it was decided that I should come to him again to-morrow or on Monday to discuss the matter further, he protesting all the while that he could assure Y.M. that he would never oppose him in his plans, but rather serve Y.M. by every practicable means. I then made him a little compliment on the granting of permission for Cranstoun's recruiting; and with that, although the conference had begun unpropitiously, we parted with much mutual satisfaction. I expect to be able to send over his resolution in full by the next post.

Herr Appelboom writes to me from Holland, and Swanenbärgh from Antwerp, that they are greatly alarmed there about a special understanding between Y.M., France and England.[1] May God Almighty give me grace to be able to do Y.M. acceptable service here: I shall apply myself to it with all fidelity, energy and zeal. We learn here by the post of Lieut.-Colonel Ascheberg's valiant action near Radom, and take it as an indubitable sign of God's blessing, *etc.*

XL

London, 14 March 1656 [from Bonde's *Register*]

During this last week I have pushed on my negotiations as best I could, have met the commissioners, and hope soon to have reached the stage at which the treaty may be put on paper.[2] I hope that it may provide for reciprocal recruiting of soldiers and seamen, and the hiring of cargo-ships and warships, and though it may include some restrictions, I do not expect that they will hamper Y.M.'s plans in any way. Otherwise I expect to get what I want, though progress is a little difficult.

1. *Cf.* Boreel to de Witt, 15, 23 March NS 1656: *Brieven*, i. 269, 279–80; *CSP* (*Dom*) *1655–56*, p. 209, Nicholas to Jos. Jane, 4/14 March. Mazarin informed d'Avaugour that he would be glad to see Sweden a member of the League of the Rhine which he was endeavouring to form: *Lettres du Cardinal Mazarin*, vii. 191 (25 February NS 1656). Rumours of such an alliance had been current for some time: *CSP* (*Ven*) *1655–56*, p. 122. The Dutch hoped rather for an alliance between the United Provinces, France and England, and put the idea to Thurloe on 7 April; who answered evasively. But Nieuwpoort urged that it was essential to split the very dangerous *rapprochement* between France and Spain by an alliance which would ensure the continuance of the Franco-Spanish war—though the States of Holland, replying to Thurloe's enquiries, made it clear that such a defensive alliance was to operate only against future aggression by Spain after that war was over: Thurloe, iv. 650, 712; v. 25; *Brieven*, iii. 216–19.

2. On 11 March Whitelocke noted that the articles on recruiting, passports and contraband 'were near agreed between us' (an optimistic assessment); the articles on trade, and on restitution and compensation for damage, were deferred: Whitelocke, *Memorials*, iv. 232. Soon afterwards (on 7 April NS) Nieuwpoort began his negotiations for a Marine Treaty: *Brieven*, iii. 213–15.

As to the principal question [i.e. the alliance], although in my last talk with his highness I had given him some ideas which might stir him to comply with Y.M.'s wishes, I thought it necessary to lay greater emphasis on them; and for that reason I yesterday had a long and very important conference with him. I thought the occasion demanded it, since at the previous one I had expounded [what I had to say] only piecemeal, and as opportunity offered. Herr Coyet heard it all, and I will therefore not trouble Y.M. with any account of it, since he can do that on his arrival, if Y.M. pleases.[1] I must inform Y.M. of only one thing, namely that he [the protector] was well satisfied with my arguments, and promised to communicate his answer to me within a few days. He scruples only one thing, and that is how to avoid offending the Dutch, while keeping them in officio. He is very afraid of them; and it would seem that they are now employing threats instead of all the good words which they used before. I hope to have given him such satisfaction on this point that he has grasped it. But our main source of difference is likely to be the amount of money.

Herr Coyet is still here. His stay has been prolonged by the need to provide himself with the money without which he cannot get away, and this has taken some time. As far as I am concerned I should be happy if he could postpone his departure until I was near an agreement with them on this last business [the alliance]; and if it should happen that they showed readiness to agree to what Y.M. wishes, I had intended to negotiate with them according to the tenour of Y.M.'s orders and induce them to conform to them as closely as possible, but not to conclude before Herr Coyet had carried [the draft terms] to Y.M., and I had received Y.M.'s reaction to them. If the differences between us proved to be too great, Herr Coyet could have informed Y.M., and I could take the measures which Y.M. has ordered [in such a case], conclude the treaty, and hasten home. But since Y.M.'s letter from Mosdovitz reached me yesterday, in which Y.M. commands that if I have not already managed to conclude a reciprocal alliance with the protector I am to urge him to send an embassy to Y.M. and make all haste to depart, Y.M.'s orders have somewhat altered my plans.[2] I have now brought the matter to a stage at which I can expect a favourable outcome in the immediate future; and since they are encouraged to proceed by (among other things) the intrigues of the Dutch, I am afraid that if this moment is lost, they may for various reasons become less amenable. It certainly looks as though

1. It was possibly for Coyet that Bonde wrote the long Latin *promemoria* which is printed in Carlbom, *Sverige och England*, pp. 69–70, *note*. It simply recapitulated the terms Charles had put forward in his orders from Schlippenbeil.

2. This was awkward for Bonde, who had been arguing that such an embassy was unnecessary.

my letter of 4 January may have animated Y.M. against them, since at that time he had not received my second letter of 11 January, which indicated that affairs had assumed a new aspect; and they have continued to do so, despite some difficulties. As to my remarks about Portugal, I can assure Y.M. that they have produced no ill effect in any quarter; but the Portuguese resident nevertheless sent home a report of them, which at the very least may confirm his master in his former friendship for Y.M., and be of service to our trade. I shall, according to how things develop, send Y.M. my views by the next post.

Things go on slowly here; but this is a state which stands on a very uncertain footing, and they therefore act with a good deal of timidity, and are fearful of anything either inside or outside the country which may turn to their disadvantage; but I hope nevertheless that Y.M. will find in the end that in these times the business here has to be gone about with patience, and without it might easily be wrecked. A week ago the lord protector showed me great civility in a spot to which men commonly resort for exercise [St James's Park]; which makes the greater *éclat* here since he usually goes elsewhere: as Y.M. will learn from the enclosed account.[1] General Fleetwood has got his permission to raise 2000 men, and it would be desirable to have the money ready, since he is to proceed with it shortly:[2] the other troops which Y.M. has asked for I hope to obtain, and not only that, but a general permission to raise as many as Y.M. may require. I heartily wish that I might be helped out with some money, otherwise I do not see how I can possibly get away. Bonnel's situation is now desperate, so that he dare not show himself out of doors for fear of being imprisoned; and I am in such a condition that it is impossible for me to help him. The agreeable news of Y.M.'s notable victory at Mosdovitz[3] is a source of great joy to us all here; and as I am sure of the lord protector's sincere disposition to be friends with Y.M. it will the more advance and promote our affairs.[4]

---

1. Cf. *Bondes Diarium*, p. 51.
2. *CSP (Dom) 1655–56*, p. 221: Whitelocke's version (31 March) is that he was given leave to levy 'two thousand more than the four thousand already granted ... in case the treaty here with the Swedish ambassador came to a good conclusion': Whitelocke, *Memorials*, iv. 232.
3. I.e. the battle of Gołąb, which Charles X had reported in his letter.
4. Two days later, on 16 March, Schlezer reported to Frederick William that in the course of an audience with the protector, at which Schlezer had suggested an alliance with Brandenburg, Cromwell had asked: with what object? with what advantage to England at a time when he was involved in a war with Spain? To which Schlezer could give only general replies. But he added 'Wie ihm aber sei, so wird man alhier je länger je mehr in der Opinion confirmiret, dass aus demjetzigen Wesen ein rechter generaler und pur lauter Religionskrieg werden werde': *Urk. und Act.*, vii. 740–1.

XLI

London, 21 March 1656

My two last letters will have informed Y.M. how far I had advanced with my negotiations a week ago, and also what passed in a couple of very remarkable audiences with his highness. This week I had Secretary Thurloe with me, and we talked at length on the same topics; and I am pretty clear from our discussion that they are well disposed to such an alliance. The most difficult point for them to concede is the subsidies which we are asking for. I demonstrated clearly to him that the money which they would thus give to help Y.M. would be saved ten times over by the powerful diversion of the forces of the House of Austria, which are now directed solely against them and France,[1] apart from the fact that the Dutch—who otherwise, to all appearance, are looking for revenge in England's present circumstances—would be kept in order. Besides which I argued that so powerful an alliance would give him security, as protector. Matters of great moment are at present under consideration here, and it is conjectured that they have to do with some alteration in the constitution, and that the protector is anxious to assume the crown; and so I thought it not inadvisable to encourage him to do so, since it would greatly strengthen this government, and consequently make it safer for Y.M. to link himself to it; but I did so mainly to oblige him by encouraging him to do what he was already desirous of doing; and so, perhaps, provide him with an argument for doing it. I therefore demonstrated to Thurloe the security which would accrue to England, and to his family, if he were of that mind, and that he could draw from our alliance such strength and advantages as no money could pay for. He replied with great civility; said that he must confess that England (as I had observed) could derive great benefit from the alliance; yet was at pains to show that Y.M.'s gains would not be less than theirs. He received my last overture with particular acknowledgement of the good-will to which it bore witness, excused himself politely, and dwelt mostly upon the stability of this government by reason of its large and well-disciplined forces on sea and land. As to this I made some few observations, and concluded by asking that whatever they thought of doing, they would hasten to do it: on this I laid great stress, and affirmed that it was my intention to leave at the end of April.[2]

1. *Cf.* Whitelocke, *Memorials*, iv. 225.
2. On 31 January Charles X had written to the Swedish council of state informing them that he had offers of alliance from France, Siebenbürgen and England, and asking their advice. On 27 March the council debated the question at some length. Some members were of opinion that an offensive alliance with England was to be

As to my other treaty, we have now got so far that I have been assured that it is in course of being copied. My Lord Whitelocke dined with me this week, to whom I handed some points in writing; the main ones concerned satisfaction and restitution to Y.M.'s subjects for damage inflicted during the late Dutch war. Y.M. will have learned by the last post that General Fleetwood has had permission to raise 2000 men, and is now waiting anxiously for the money, without which the work cannot be carried out. After receiving Y.M.'s last orders I have determined to expedite the conclusion of this treaty as much as I possibly can; and if I find that progress with the other is slow, to let it wait for some embassy that the protector may send to Y.M. If I do not receive some assistance from Y.M., or from the chancellor, I hardly know how I am to get away. My brother, in return for a private bond from me, has sent me money from [the estate of] the late Herr Conrad Falkenberg's children, but I doubt if I can get any more from that source. I beg Y.M. most humbly [to see to it] that the great hazard in which I am now placed here may not lead to my ruin.

XLII

London, 28 March 1656

Ever since my last conference with his highness I have asked, through the appropriate channels and in suitable terms, for my *congé*; and I have now certain information that it has been my business which this week has mainly engaged the attention of the protector and his council, so that I make no doubt but that I shall receive some written answer in the course of the next week. Although the state of affairs in Holland and Denmark, as reported by Herr Appelboom, together with many considerations here in this country (where they seem more inclined to Y.M.'s friendship than ever before), seem to demand that in this situation I should try to bring the matter [of the alliance] to

---

avoided, as they thought that Charles himself seemed to suggest in his letter, though he had added that 'a *defensivum pro mutua defensione rei Evangelicae*' had something to be said for it. Gustav Horn considered that Cromwell's object might be to 'conserve the title which all English kings have borne, i.e. to be called *"defensor fidei"*'. Johan Gyllenstierna held that any treaty should be with England rather than with the protector, since his children were unlikely to succeed him. Herman Fleming remarked that 'despite the fact that the protector gives out that it is to be considered *pro mutua defensione rei Evangelicae* ... it may well be a scheme to involve Sweden in England's wars'. Per Brahe alone seems to have been clearly for an off- and defensive alliance. The reply upon which they eventually agreed approved a defensive alliance with England, or with France, or Siebenbürgen, and listed Sweden's enemies (in order) as the emperor, the Muscovites, the Dutch, and Denmark: *RRP*, xvi. 422–5, 429.

some sort of issue, I nevertheless do not venture to await it here against Y.M.'s orders; especially in view of the fact that Y.M., who is every day engaged in great and fortunate undertakings, has not been pleased to reply to my letter of 11 January. I intend, all the same, to push it as far as I can, and to see whether I cannot obtain some written resolution upon it, after which he [the protector] can be encouraged to send an embassy, so that Y.M. may complete the work; contenting myself, for my part, with having laid the basis for it. I have good hope of a satisfactory settlement of the other matter [i.e. the completion of Whitelocke's treaty]; and General Fleetwood has already had leave to recruit 2000 men by tap of drum (as I reported to Y.M. on 14 March), which makes a great sensation here. Attempts are now made on all hands to content me with every sort of civility (of which some in these parts are jealous); and when to all this is added the fame of Y.M.'s incomparable progress and continued victories, I hope it may give certain persons food for thought, who might otherwise possibly intrigue against Y.M. I intend next week to speak to the protector to ask for my despatch, and to let him know of Y.M.'s incomparable achievements;[1] and so I hope to be able to write in more detail to Y.M. by the next post.

XLIII

London, 4 April 1656

Although when I wrote my last letter I had hoped to be able to send the full text of his highness's reply to Y.M., this was not possible on account of Secretary Thurloe's absence. I therefore had another audience with his highness on 1 April, in which I dwelt on the fact that time was now precious, and that Y.M. had ordered me to hasten my departure; and I tried by many arguments to remove everything that might seem to stand in the way of his giving me a favourable answer.[2] Afterwards I had a talk with my Lord Whitelocke, and

---

1. Cromwell was probably already informed of them through Rolt's letter to Thurloe of 4 March from Hamburg, which among other things reported that Charles X seemed likely to attack Russia when he had pacified Poland: Thurloe, iv. 575. In fact it was the Russians who began hostilities in June, by invading Ingria and Kexholm, thus virtually cutting off land-communications with Finland; and in July they over-ran most of Livonia: Bonnesen, *Karl X Gustaf*, pp. 168–72; Carlson, *Sveriges historia*, i. 323–9.

2. It must be to this audience that Whitelocke's undated entry for April refers: 'The Swedish ambassador had been at Whitehall, and was much discontented because he waited above an hour before the protector came to him, which brought the ambassador to such impatience, that he rose from his seat and was going home again without speaking to the protector'. Fleming, however, prevailed on him to stay, and he had his audience, in which Cromwell said 'that he was willing in case of a nearer alliance, or of an union concerning the protestant interest, to have our neighbours and allies in the

yesterday with my Lord Deputy Fleetwood, and courteously (though with some show of feeling) pressed for their definitive reply. They answered with all imaginable excuses and much civility; and the latter [Fleetwood] confessed in general that it was only lack of money that kept them back, and that though the diversion, and the other advantages which would fall to them by such an alliance, would undoubtedly be of great use to them, its sheer impossibility at present constituted an insurmountable obstacle. I asked that his highness might himself inform me of his decision as to how far he thought he might be able to go, [and said] that if I could have a talk with him I would see whether the difficulties which presented themselves could not somehow be obviated; and this was at once promised me. My main object is to extract from him, if possible, some assurance upon which one can rely, and to try to bring him to the point of making some money available.

I go round in circles with these irresolute people: sometimes I blaze away at them, at others I take them to my bosom. They cannot produce a single argument which I cannot show to be palpably erroneous, and in the last resort they are reduced to objections grounded on necessity. I cannot make up my mind whether I shall venture to stay here and see it out; for I am afraid that if it comes to their sending an embassy the *facies rerum* may easily have altered, either by some new involvement of Y.M., or by some change nearer home, in which case they would undoubtedly back away.

News reached me recently of the aid of 10,000 men which the emperor has made available to Spain in the Netherlands: it will be useful to me, since it enables me to show that Y.M. is free to make war on the emperor, or not to do so;[1] and it seems, indeed, that the emperor feels sufficiently sure of Y.M. to risk weakening his forces in so considerable a degree. All of which demolishes their main argument, which is that Y.M. must inevitably be involved in a war with him. They have great hopes here of the silver-fleet, and think that they have certain information that it has been ordered to sail for home about this time; and since their fleet has now had a good wind for the last week they hope that it may fall into their hands: if it does, it will certainly be a blow to the trade of all Europe, since business trans-

Low Countries included therein; and that he thought that it did become him to have a particular care of them, and to take them into any such treaty or alliance, and that he was not willing to do any such thing without them. These expressions of his highness did not a little startle the ambassador': Whitelocke, *Memorials*, iv. 234–5.
1. The figure of 10,000 was probably too high: see *Lettres du Cardinal Mazarin*, vii. 191.

actions and credit in all countries are largely dependent on it, either directly or *per consequentias*; but it would also put this country in a comfortable position to take serious action, and I am pretty sure that it would lead them to grant Y.M. a considerable subsidy, their good-will and disposition thereto being at the moment great. Both his highness and Fleetwood recently, as well as on previous occasions, showed this by their protestations; and his highness adduced, as one sign of it, the fact that he and all those who are of like mind with him ask God's blessing upon Y.M. in their prayers—indeed, it is certain that the clergy in a great part of their churches in England openly mention Y.M. in their prayers from the pulpit; which is very remark-able, as never having happened before in the case of any foreigner.

A duplicate of the letter which Y.M. wrote to me from Schlippenbeil on 6 January has reached me by this post from the chancellor. There have for some time been grievous tidings in circulation here of Y.M.'s situation; but as they originate from Danzig and Holland we take them to be fabrications, since letters from Breslau and other places say nothing of it.[1]

XLIV

George Monck to Bonde

Edinburgh, 10 April 1656 [in German]

[Has received his letter of 13 March; also a letter from the protector regarding the last thousand men to be recruited by Cranstoun. Will give Cranstoun every assistance in his power, and professes his devotion to Charles X. Cranstoun has been active in recruiting his first thousand, and has secured very good officers. The first 600 men have already been shipped off: the remaining 400 will follow soon. Cranstoun will then proceed to raise a further thousand. Tribute to Cranstoun's prudent conduct of the business; no com-plaints of the behaviour of his levies; no violence; and everything paid for in cash].

---

1. These rumours must reflect the desperate predicament of Charles X, who on 20/30 March found himself trapped, with 5500 men, in the triangle formed by the confluence of the San and the Vistula. On 27–28 March the force of Frederick of Baden, which had been summoned to the king's assistance, was heavily defeated—the first victory of the Poles in the open field in this war. But if it was indeed to these events that the rumours referred, the news must have travelled with unusual speed.

XLV

Bonde to Charles X

London, 11 April 1656

Of all the posts and all the news that ever were welcome to me, none could exceed this last.[1] For the last fortnight it has been generally reported here that Y.M. and his whole army were totally beaten and ruined, and that Y.M. himself was either dead, or not far from it. And not only that: the Dutch ambassador assured his highness of it as a fact; and last Wednesday he came to Coyet, who is now on the point of departing, expressly to tell him the news, and that in such impudent terms that it was disgraceful.[2] The reports brought by this post of Y.M.'s satisfactory position have now made public his untimely and unjustifiable animus, and cast the deepest dishonour upon him. God Almighty be eternally praised; may He reward our loyal prayers by preserving Y.M.'s noble person, and bring all his enemies to shame.

Next, I was by this post rejoiced to receive Y.M.'s letter and most welcome orders of 20 February from Siedlice.[3] I shall not only do my best to follow them to Y.M.'s satisfaction, but I am delighted to find that through God's blessing the line I have pursued here up to now is in entire conformity with Y.M.'s orders.

1. On 25 March/4 April Charles by brilliant tactics miraculously extricated himself from his predicament and headed north towards Warsaw: for these events see Wimmer, in *Polens krig med Sverige*, pp. 358–60.

2. Nils Brahe reported that Coyet, after denying the report, had added 'Nor have any such *portenta* been seen, as use to proclaim the deaths of great men'; to which Nieupoort replied 'We have seen *portenta* already, and it is *portenta* enough that the king should wish to be master of the Baltic, and should in so short a time overthrow so powerful a realm as Poland': Carlson, *Sveriges historia*, i. 288 *n*. 1.

3. Charles's orders from Siedlice made it clear that he desired an alliance in order to conserve his Polish conquests. It must therefore be directed against any who sought '*ratione belli polonici*' to attack him in the Baltic or elsewhere: thus a defensive alliance, if not *contra quoscunque* then at least against Holland and Denmark. Failing such an alliance, there was little point in an alliance to defend the Protestant Cause: an alliance based on religion was inexpedient while the position in Poland was still insecure. Bonde was therefore to contrive that the protector joined in a guarantee of the treaty of Osnabrück—which was '*in effectu*' a protestant alliance under another name. If the protector should be ready to accept this, Bonde could then proceed to negotiate for an annual subsidy, which Charles had the more reason to ask since in the event of a breach with Austria the greatest burden would fall on him. Though he concurred with Bonde's rejection of an alliance which would include other protestant powers, he conceded that once the alliance was made other powers would probably fall into line, and could be included by an accession-clause. If there seemed good prospects of the kind of alliance he wanted Bonde was to remain in England and continue working for it parallel with his negotiations for perfecting Whitelocke's treaty. But if the prospects for the alliance were poor, or too remote, he was to depart, referring everything to such embassy as the protector might later send to negotiate: the full text is printed in Carlbom, *Sverige och England*, pp. 75–7.

I have this week once again had meetings with my commissioners, and though the going was difficult I still hope that we shall soon reach agreement as to reciprocal recruiting and the perfecting of the former treaty.[1] As to the other matter [*sc.* the alliance], I work on it every day; and it is a remarkable thing, of which I hardly know any other instance, that I have conducted the entire negotiation with his highness personally, and without commissioners. Herr Coyet had intended to leave a few days ago, but as his highness excused himself from giving him his audience of departure until next Tuesday, he has had to remain. However, he is writing to Y.M. to-day about his encounter with the Dutch ambassador, and I therefore refer to his report: such impertinence and effrontery is unheard-of, and I hope it will do much to undermine his credit. The Portuguese resident was with me two days ago, and showed me a letter from his king expressing great satisfaction at the overture he made to me as to Portuguese dealings with this country, commanding him to discuss the whole affair with me in detail, and professing the friendship existing between Y.M. and himself, which it would always be his study to cultivate. He revealed to me further that there had appeared to be considerable likelihood of an agreement between Spain and Portugal; that Spain had offered all possible terms, but that Portugal, putting no faith in them, wanted strong guarantees which Spain was in no position to give; so that it had all been entirely abandoned. I shall take care to send to Y.M. an extract of that letter by the next post. It is moreover now certain that this country's envoy Mr Meadowe is empowered to conclude an alliance, and is said to be taking two forms of ratification with him, so that in case one proves unacceptable he may offer the other, which is likely to assist their mutual inclination. I have an

---

1. The negotiations had been made more difficult by the decision of the council that pitch, tar, hemp and flax were to be classed as contraband. But on 31 March the council changed its mind, and required only that they be deemed contraband during the war with Spain; and on 5 April Whitelocke was ordered to protract discussions with Bonde pending a reconsideration of the question: Whitelocke, *Memorials*, iv. 232, 237. This was in fact the compromise which was eventually agreed on. On 7 April, however, when Whitelocke called on Bonde, he found him in an intractable temper: 'he desired to know a certain answer, I or no, whether he [the protector] would do it [i.e. the alliance] or not'. Whitelocke, being ignorant of Charles X's terms, enquired what they were; and Bonde defended the guarantee of Osnabrück by observing that France was pledged to Sweden to maintain it, 'and England joining likewise therein, France would be engaged with them', whereas an alliance directed simply against Habsburg would probably reconcile all the catholic powers: Whitelocke, iv. 237-9. Meanwhile, on the contraband question, Whitelocke and Fiennes consulted with Thurloe, and they agreed that 'free ship makes free goods' was unacceptable—not because it would be a precedent which the Dutch would urge in the negotiations for their Marine Treaty, but because it would lead to an expansion of Sweden's mercantile marine: *ibid.*, 243.

audience to-day with his highness at 4 o'clock, but since I have no time to report on it to Y.M., that shall be done by the next post. But it is remarkable that the Dutch ambassador was appointed to have an audience at the same hour, but it has now been refused to him, and granted to me.

XLVI

London, 18 April 1656

As I had a long and wide-ranging audience with the lord protector on the last post-day, and therefore was not able to report on what passed in it, I think it incumbent upon me to inform Y.M. of the *essentialia* of that meeting. I began by assuring him that all was well with Y.M., despite the stories being spread about from Danzig and Holland, and informed him that I had had Y.M.'s letter, dated a day or two before that on which the disastrous action is said to have taken place;[1] and assured him in this connexion of Y.M.'s steady friendship. He replied that he was happy to hear it, in terms which sufficiently demonstrated that he spoke from the heart, saying how much he was upset by such malicious inventions. I then asked him to let me have a positive and constructive answer to the proposals I had put forward, pointing out how greatly they concerned his highness's interests, since it now appears, from the substantial support given to Spain by the emperor, that Spain is acting with Charles Stuart; which indicates that they intend to prosecute the war in earnest. I also laid much stress on what they had to expect from the Dutch, and so forth. To this he answered at length, declaring that it was his absolute wish and determination to enter into a mutual defensive alliance *contra quoscunque*:[2] it was only *in mediis* that we differed. As for instance (i) that he did not quite see how he could bind himself to maintain the peace of Osnabrück, and had no security that Y.M. would be prepared to do so; (ii) he endeavoured to argue that in this matter [of the alliance] there was an equality between Y.M.'s interest and his own; belittled the emperor's assistance to Spain;[3] and dwelt long on this

---

1. 'A day or two' was, to put it mildly, an understatement: 'a month' would have been nearer the truth.

2. This was an astonishing reversal of the line England had been taking since 26 January. Pufendorf (iii. 241) makes the protector introduce his declaration with 'In order that it should not appear that the whole alliance hung exclusively on the question of money...'; but this does not appear from Bonde's reports of 11 and 18 April, though it is clear that it is to this audience that Pufendorf refers.

3. Bonde wrote 'equality' (*esgalitet*), and 'belittled' (*förringhade*)—not, as Abbott has it, 'similarity' and 'stressed': Abbott, iv. 136.

point as being the one on which the whole business depends; (iii) he spoke much of what means could be used to attract France and other protestants to engage in it, traversing much of the ground which he had often gone over before, and promised me that commissioners would treat with me about it in the immediate future.

I replied by referring to our previous conversation, and in the first place showed him why the peace of Osnabrück was stated to' be the basis: (i) since *nomen religionis* would be too *éclatant*; (ii) the peace binds the emperor to grant freedom of religion to calvinists; (iii) and forbids him to assist Spain;[1] (iv) France can also be bound to maintain it, *vi pactorum*; (v) its violation is a *justa causa belli* in the eyes of both God and men; (vi) that the catholics had in fact sinned so much in that way, that we had *justam causam belli* whenever an opportunity presented itself to avail ourselves of it. As to equality of interest, I cited many of my talks both with him and with Thurloe and Fleetwood, but nevertheless pointed out once again (1) that the main burden of meeting the House of Austria would fall upon Y.M., as being nearest, and as being attacked by its strongest member; (2) whereas England had the sea for a bulwark, Y.M. lay adjacent to them on the continent; (3) Y.M. was already involved in war in Poland, and must consequently keep a considerable [field] army, and garrisons, in the country, which greatly weakened him, so that he could not venture upon any enterprise without assistance; (4) it was nevertheless one of the conditions that Y.M. should do so; (5) the diversion of his enemies' forces which his highness obtained was ten times more important than the value of the subsidy which was asked for, and in any case there was no obligation to pay it unless Y.M. took action against the House of Austria,[2] and [if he did not] they would still enjoy the *primum membrum* of the treaty, which was mutual defence *etc.*

As to the third point I recapitulated the arguments I had used on previous occasions, and showed how once we had reached agreement all the other states would be free to adhere to it, after separate negotiations with each one of them. On this I rose, being unwilling to detain him any longer, since he had been sitting from morning till night with some of the council, discussing matters of importance, and had not given himself time to eat or drink; but I accepted his offer of commissioners.[3] He said also that he was weary, but that before I left he could not omit acknowledging the very great obligation he felt towards Y.M. for his very gracious and honourable treatment of his

1. In fact, this was a provision of the treaty of Münster, not of Osnabrück, as Bonde must have known—though perhaps Cromwell did not.

2. This was more than Charles X's orders from Siedlice empowered him to say.

3. Cromwell had thus abandoned the idea of dealing with the alliance-question by direct personal negotiations with Bonde.

envoy Mr Rolt: this he said with many words and much emotion, and alluded once again to the great trouble he had been in at the reports which had been circulated of Y.M.'s having been defeated; and added that I had many times been welcome, but never so much as now, on account of the good news I brought him, and much more to the same effect. I took my leave with an appropriate compliment, and so we parted, well content with each other. I learn from a reliable source that Mr Rolt is now in high favour with him, and since he [Rolt] loudly proclaims Y.M.'s incomparable merits to one and all, he is now installed alone in his highness's chamber, and must relate to him for two or three hours every evening all the details of Y.M.'s behaviour, which he enquires about with the greatest curiosity, and which [Rolt] describes and praises; so that I can assure Y.M. that his highness loves and esteems Y.M. more than any other man in the world; and I do not doubt that he will do everything possible to serve and please Y.M.

But the news of the silver-fleet's safe arrival in Spain is said to make great difficulties for him.[1] He had great hopes in that quarter, and is so hard pressed for money that he is not in a position to do what he would like to do. There is a good deal of speculation as to what action England may take against Spain which may be of service to them if the fleet has come home, since their great naval armament has been extremely exhausting to them. One thing is certain, that their fleet will take every vessel they meet that sails under the Spanish flag; and this makes them less tractable in the negotiations we now have on foot in regard to contraband; for they now want it to include pitch and tar, and all kinds of tackle, masts, and sails, for the duration of the present war. So too in regard to sea-passes, whose provisions they claim be applied to other countries who may carry Spanish goods, and counterfeit such passes: a matter of the more importance since the Dutch are now engaged on a marine treaty with them, and wish to be accorded all that I may enjoy.[2] I have at last got the treaty

1. Blake and Montagu had been unable to leave Torbay until the end of March owing to the difficulty of manning so large a fleet: Corbett, *England in the Mediterranean*, i. 322. A letter of intelligence from Holland, 5 May NS, informed Thurloe of the fleet's arrival, and stated that it had been convoyed in part by de Ruyter: Thurloe, iv. 732. On 19 April there had been a serious clash in the Channel, when Captain William Whitehorn had stopped and searched four Dutch merchantmen escorted by de Ruyter: *CSP (Dom) 1655–56*, p. 284. On 19 May NS Nieupoort noted the strength of anti-Dutch feeling in the army, and in circles near the government: *Brieven*, iii. 289. Schlezer was very explicit about Dutch aid to Spain, and reported (most improbably) that with a view to a general alliance of protestants Cromwell was ready to support the Great Elector's claims to Jülich: *Urk. und Act.*, vii. 744–5.

2. At Bonde's meeting with the commissioners on 8 April he had objected to this (and also to the draft articles' being in English); but on contraband he was eventually to give way. Thurloe was reported to have blamed Whitelocke for making too many concessions to the Swedes: *Brieven*, iii. 224.

taliter qualiter on paper, but it is still so incomplete that I cannot yet send Y.M. a copy. Everything here goes excessively slowly; but this is the way they work—not least because everything must pass through Thurloe's hands;[1] but it gives me the idea that for some special reasons they want to keep me waiting—either because they wish first to complete their commercial treaty with the Dutch, or that they are still counting on the silver-fleet, in which case they would be in a position to come to a decision on my business, since they know very well that Y.M. will not accept their alliance without subsidies, although they, and his highness personally, are now very anxious for it. However that may be, I shall not fail to press them as much as I can; though I perceive that it will not be possible to leave this country at the time I had expected.

General Fleetwood is extremely anxious for money for his recruiting; and I much wish that I could have some also. Ever since my arrival I have had to wear mourning, which has meant that I could not honourably do less than order new liveries and an entire new outfit, all of which could not be done without great expense, for which I trust that Y.M. will reimburse me in my allowance, which otherwise will not cover it. I shall nevertheless economize as much as I can. And I hope that after all this trouble God will give me grace so as to execute Y.M.'s service that the great expenditure which this legation has involved may be repaid an hundredfold: to which end no pains and labour shall be wanting in me.

XLVII

London, 25 April 1656

In the course of the last week I have had two important conferences: the first, last Monday, with Thurloe and my Lord Fiennes (who is the principal person among my commissioners); the second with Thurloe alone in the Park.

In the first we discussed the matter of the strict alliance which has been so long under discussion. And in this we differed; because although his highness seems to be disposed to conclude it, he (i) desires a defensive [*sic*] alliance against the House of Austria, the king of Poland, and Charles Stuart; mainly on the grounds that the House of Austria is the principal prop of the catholic party, and the power that

---

1. *Cf.* Sagredo: 'all the acts of state are entrusted to a single secretary, who is so overwhelmed by the mass of business and the burden of so many different affairs, the perfect digestion of which demands an immense amount of time. For this reason their decisions move slowly ...': Sagredo to Doge, 5 Nov. NS 1655, *CSP (Ven) 1655–56*, p. 132.

the protestants have most reason to fear; (ii) thinks it unwise to make the alliance *contra quemcunque*, since that might give Holland and Denmark a suspicion that it was directed more against them than against the catholics, and this would make them incapable of interposing if any dispute arose between us and any [other] of the protestants, they being parties to it, and not neutral; (iii) [considers] that that party to the alliance which wishes the other to launch an attack against the House of Austria should negotiate the conditions upon which the other was obligated to do it; (iv) and that we should continue our negotiations until we reach agreement, but not conclude anything until we have invited the other protestants to adhere: if they are prepared to do so, well and good; if not, we could afterwards act by our two selves, and would have removed any cause of offence, or any ground for their associating themselves with those who might wish us ill.[1]

As all this is in direct contradiction of Y.M.'s principal intention in regard to this alliance, and as it suggests that their purpose is (1) to get Y.M. to name Charles Stuart as his enemy (as to which I have no orders and in any case think it unwise); (2) by such an alliance to give so much offence to the emperor that Y.M. will have no choice but to attack him, in which case they would not be obliged to give Y.M. any assistance; (3) to avoid paying the subsidy asked for, which is the main point. I therefore remonstrated with them on the danger and the unreasonableness of such proposals and procedures, and with this end in view I tried to obtain speech with Thurloe [alone], and yesterday managed it. I then told him plainly that I must, in accordance with Y.M.'s express orders, take my departure, and could stay here no longer; and if his highness should design any amendment of the terms of the alliance, it must be on the following lines: (i) the alliance must be defensive *contra quoscunque*, without specifying any, since that was the only means whereby all who might have any design against us, as well protestants as others, could be covered; and this to apply to the conservation of Y.M.'s conquests in Poland and Prussia, and to all that Y.M. holds in the name of Sweden, with the provinces and interests appurtenant, and likewise to the conservation of England and of his highness's own interests; (ii) the maintenance of the peace of Osnabrück must be the basis of the alliance against the catholics, since it unambiguously binds them to concede to the protestants their due rights and liberties; and if, moreover, it is broken, it gives us justification before God and men for any bloodshed that may ensue. That all the other protestants will be more readily disposed to maintain it than to do the same for any other alliance against one power

1. This represents a disavowal, on a decisive point (*'contra quoscunque'*), of the protector's declaration of 11 April.

in particular; since most of them have a great interest in its main-tenance. And that we now at once reach agreement as to how they may be of assistance on such an occasion. (iii) We must first agree between us before we invite anyone else to participate, lest the dis-closure of our purpose bring us enemies whom we are not ready to meet. And I declared that such were the orders I had from Y.M. If they were prepared so far to give way, and to conclude the alliance speedily, I was resolved to go on with the negotiations and bring them to a conclusion; but if his highness was of another mind, all I wanted was to complete the other negotiation in which we were engaged, and get away. If his highness should later desire to make such a treaty as that which we were now discussing, he could pursue the matter through ambassadors to Y.M.

He seemed somewhat staggered at this, protested earnestly that his highness's proposal was genuine, and that he had never seen him so disposed to friendship with anyone else; it was only that he wanted to go cautiously and not offend other powers, and thereby push them into an attitude of hostility. After this we went over every point in great detail, and I showed him by circumstantial arguments that this was the way it must go. And I could see very well that he was sorry to hear that I wished to be gone and to leave the ending of the business to his highness's ambassadors. For it seems to me that his highness is now very anxious for such an alliance with Y.M., if only he was not so desperately short of money. He promised me that I should certainly have his decision next week.

In the other treaty we have got so far that last Monday I handed them a draft, with the text as they had drawn it on one side of the sheet, and on the other the text as I would have it. He [Fiennes?] thanked me for putting it in order, and it would therefore seem that he approved [my wording]: (it is a scandal that now that Mr Meadowe has gone to Portugal they have no one who can write a decent line of Latin, but the blind Miltonius must translate anything they want done from English to Latin, and one can easily imagine how it goes).[1] If I get what I want with this treaty, as I now hope I shall, I shall be well content even though they should be unwilling to do anything in regard to the other. I think that the permission to raise troops and hire ships will be a great help to Y.M.'s plans, apart from the other facilities in regard to trade and navigation; and if they cannot make up their minds in regard to some other matters, it is probable that they will try to satisfy me in these, so that I do not leave in ill-humour, his highness being exceedingly well-disposed to friendship with Y.M.

---

1. It took Milton a fortnight to translate the draft articles: Whitelocke, *Memorials*, iv. 257. Ordinarily, the work would have been done by Meadowe. See the comment in Masson, *Milton*, v. 255–6.

I learn just now by the post that Y.M. may be presumed by this time to be in Warsaw, which leads me to hope that Y.M. may be pleased to let me have his decision on my request for money, and on General Fleetwood's recruiting. A thousand men of Lord Cranstoun's levies have already been sent from Scotland, of whom 600 have already safely arrived in Stade. If only General Fleetwood had the money, we should soon hear the drum beating in London for men for Y.M.'s service: they are coming forward in great numbers; which besides being of use to Y.M. would make a great sensation in the world and help to thwart the designs of Y.M.'s adversaries.

XLVIII

London, 2 May 1656 [from Bonde's *Register*]

The government of this country is at present much troubled as to how to proceed. It is not only a fact that the silver-fleet has reached home, but it is also certain that Admiral de Ruyter has arrived in Holland with 6 or 8 millions from it. The other two galleons which left Havana in company with those which have now arrived are thought to have been lost at sea, and small hope remains of their capture. I hear too from a reliable source that the king of Scotland, Charles Stuart, has reached an agreement with Spain, and has been given absolute command in Dunkirk and Ostend, with 50,000 gulden a month; and though the people here appear to make little account of it, they are nevertheless greatly cast down by it, especially since he will have at his disposal important ports so close to them that it is only a six hours' sail to England.[1] It is said also that the princess of Orange[2] has been in France to investigate whether it might be possible to form an alliance between Holland and France against England; but having no success in this, she has made up her mind to reside henceforward in Zeeland, as being a province well disposed to her son, and then to try whether she cannot bring that province over entirely to her side; from all of which discerning people judge that a disruption among the provinces might easily follow. I am also informed that the Muscovy merchants here have made strong complaint to his highness of the wrongs done to them by the Russians; and as his highness was ill-satisfied with the Russians' treatment of his envoy, who spent some time there, and as in the letter which the Great Prince [of Muscovy]

---

1. The treaty between Charles and Spain was signed on 12 April 1656 and ratified by Philip IV in June. It provided for placing 4000 foot and 2000 horse at Charles's disposal for an invasion of England: Firth, *Last Years*, i. 24.

2. I.e. Mary, the widow of William II and sister of Charles Stuart. But there is nothing in her letters from Paris (in *The Calendar of the Clarendon State Papers*, (4 vols. Oxford 1869–1932) iii) to suggest that her visit had any such political purpose.

wrote to him there was something which seemed to imply contempt, the protector is disposed to be revenged upon him—the more so, since the Muscovy merchants are offering, at their own charges, to harass the trade to Archangel so that it might very easily be stopped altogether. People here are saying that it would not be difficult, if Y.M. so desired, to persuade his highness to send to the Great Prince threatening him with war if he takes any action against Y.M.; and that if that had no effect that he [the protector] might attack him at sea in the manner suggested, and block all trade to Archangel, which would be no small blow to him. But since Y.M. has not so far been pleased to order anything of that nature I have not ventured to give it any encouragement, though I have thought it necessary to notify Y.M. of what their feelings are.

The protector is at present very downcast[1] about his position. He held a day of prayer in Whitehall the day before yesterday, and another today, the only effect of which is to give people the idea that his affairs are in a bad way; and though he tries by every means to demonstrate his keen desire for Y.M.'s friendship (as Y.M. will see from the attached report), I have not been able to make contact with any of them since my last conference with Thurloe, although I have pressed for it both through General Fleetwood and through his brother, who spoke to Thurloe in terms which were friendly, but also allowed some resentment to appear. Within a few days I expect to have a new livery for my suite ready, and then I intend to seek an audience with his highness and ask for my despatch.[2] I know that they, and his highness especially, set the highest value upon Y.M.'s friendship, but their situation is so bad that they scarcely dare to come to any real decision; which is why they are so excessively slow. Yesterday I received by the post a duplicate of Y.M.'s letter and orders from Siedlice of 20 February, and a triplet of Y.M.'s letter from Schlippenbeil of 6 January, to which I shall give all dutiful attention.

I am very troubled about General Fleetwood's recruiting. General-Commissary Hoffstetter writes to me from Hamburg that however willing he may be, he has not the means of furnishing money for it, unless I could raise a loan at six months' date. I will do what I can, though it is extraordinarily difficult to raise money here. I wish I could hit upon a way to promote a service which is so important to

1. The text has *förslagen* (cunning, wily), but the context suggests that this must be a slip for *nedslagen* (downcast): cf. Giavarina to Doge, 26 May NS 1656: 'They are indeed so fully occupied that they do not know which way to turn, and the protector has not a moment to call his own ... it is said, that when speaking recently in the council pointing out their difficulties, he could not restrain his tears as he spoke': *CSP (Ven) 1655–56*, pp. 221–2.

2. Bonde was now putting off his mourning for Maria Eleonora, widow of Gustavus Adolphus.

Y.M., not only for the men whom I hope may be raised here for Y.M., but also because it would make a great noise in the world if the drum were beaten here to recruit for Y.M.'s service.

We have had a proposal from the Prussian merchants to advance money against a drawback on the tolls at Pillau,[1] and if no other expedient can be found I am afraid I shall be forced to resort to it if they are prepared to agree to it; but since I fear that it might disturb some other of Y.M.'s arrangements, and I have not Y.M.'s leave to do it, it will be our last resort if all other means fail. I shall not hesitate to pledge my word and credit for that purpose, even though I am already very deeply committed, and shall inevitably be ruined if Y.M. is not pleased to help me. I send herewith an extract from the king of Portugal's letter to his resident here:[2] it deals with what I said to the protector on his behalf, and I hope that it may have done Y.M.'s service more good than harm. May Almighty God grant me His grace to be able to discharge my duty among this dilatory people; to which end neither zeal nor pains shall be wanting.

XLIX

London, 9 May 1656

Since I have found that the courtesy I have used towards these people this long time has done little or nothing to promote my early departure, and since the intolerable procrastination that they practise has made me suspect that they are simply trying to spin out time, or that this intricate and confused government has something else in view, I have manifested my extreme dissatisfaction, and accordingly asked for an audience with the lord protector. And having found that the Dutch are spreading such a quantity of malicious reports about Y.M.'s person, and his defeat, and that their persistence in doing so has made the protector hesitant and doubting, I put off our mourning-clothes and came to Whitehall with my suite in handsome livery, in a splendid coach, in the afternoon of the day before yesterday.

I spoke to him more forcibly than on any previous occasion, and made my dissatisfaction very plain. As the tidings of the despatch of the Dutch fleet to the Baltic have an ominous appearance, I took advantage of the opportunity; and after thanking him for the particularly gracious manner of his dismissal of Herr Coyet, which I accounted as evidence of his sincere friendship for Y.M., I said that I could have wished that as a sequel to it he had been prepared to hasten the conclusion of the business upon which I had been engaged

---

1. Charles X obtained a share in the tolls at Pillau in terms of his treaty of Königsberg with the elector of Brandenburg.
2. Missing in transcript.

here, and that he had paid a proper attention to that invaluable commodity, time. The objective of each of us had been the same, namely *communis causa protestantium*, and *ex consequenti* a state of trust and confidence among them; but we had differed somewhat as to the means to obtain it. His view seemed to be that we should try to bring them in [to the alliance] by luring them with good words, and so give them no cause for suspicion or pretext for breaking off. I had indeed approved this; but I considered that it did not go far enough. In view of the kind of people we had to deal with, we should have used *mascula consilia*, on the one hand gratifying them by our friendship, but on the other obliging them through fear of a defensive alliance to reconcile themselves to reality. However that might have been, the consequences of the policy that had been pursued were already apparent: the Dutch had now sent a fleet to the Sound;[1] and since there is no danger in the [Baltic] sea, much less on this side, it was perfectly clear that their action was intended, at least, to frighten Y.M. It was much to be wished that his highness and I had concluded the alliance between us two months ago, at which time I had made bold to assure him that they [the Dutch] would never have had the nerve to take it as they are now doing. And as it was known to God and all the world that Y.M. had given them no cause of offence, and had not only avoided all occasion for dispute but had genuinely done his best to promote a good understanding (as his highness well knew), I hoped that Y.M. might be excused, should he be forced against his will to abandon the struggle with *communem hostem* and address himself to his own defence. I trusted also that his highness would make no difficulty about testifying that I had faithfully and zealously urged [this policy] to him, since by all human reason it seemed to be the only one that could give effective security against all complications. And since things were now in a condition which bore an ominous appearance, and since he knew that it was better to extinguish a spark before it turned into a conflagration, I desired that he would soon make up his mind as to what he intended to do. I had some days ago told Secretary Thurloe my final opinion. I had not been minded to act like merchants who ask twice as much for their wares as they expect to get, but rather to state my views frankly: if his highness should be so disposed, I was prepared to settle with him; if not, and he desired to negotiate with Y.M. through an ambassador, I did not doubt that Y.M. would always be his friend. Since I had last Tuesday afternoon [6 May] had an answer [from the commissioners] to the points I had drafted, which

---

1. Obdam's instructions are printed in Thurloe, iv. 756–7; and *cf. ibid.* v. 29. On 21 April NS the States General had ordered that Appelboom be informed that the Dutch fleet was intended only to protect commerce: *ibid.*, iv. 689.

(except for the first of them, concerning recruiting) was clean contrary to my draft, or at the least differed widely from it,[1] I said that I had had to put up with this long delay for a whole year, and the least I could have expected was to bring this other treaty to a satisfactory end: most of it arose out of the former treaty [of 1654]; Herr Coyet had been sent over to complete that; he too had been here for a year; but I was conscious of such intolerable delays, and such wide differences between us, that I feared that there might be no more to be done in this negotiation than in the other. It would appear that God was not willing to grant us the grace to know what was good for us. The Protestant Cause was gravely endangered by such procedures. I showed him that it was not my fault, and finally desired that he would dismiss me: it might be that whoever he might send to Y.M. would be more fortunate than I in achieving some good. And with that I concluded.

In reply, he made many protestations that he had honestly meant well, and that it was a matter of great grief to him that his actions should appear to me in a different light; he had always been determined to strive for the establishment of a good understanding among protestants, was ready to solicit it of them, and would do everything that seemed to him to be useful, in order to forward it; he was not prepared to say which of our respective lines of action was the better, for he acknowledged that our views differed; but he knew that his own intentions were good, though it could be—as often happened—that a man was himself an obstacle in the road to the attainment of what he most desired. But on the main issue, in consideration of his own interests, he had thought that it would not be advisable at this time to give offence, but rather to do his best by all other means to avoid disunity, and he had made it clear to the Dutch ambassador as well as to me that he would not cease to use all good offices to that end. He was certain that the proceedings of the Dutch had had no encouragement from him. He would have been very ready to send ambassadors to Y.M., if he had believed that that would be acceptable to him, especially since he had learned that I had no powers to treat

---

1. The commissioners met Bonde on 6 May, and the question of pitch, tar, hemp *etc.* was again debated: Bonde pointing out that these commodities were not in the list of contraband goods given by the council to Bonnell in 1654—an objection which ignored the new situation which had arisen as a result of the war with Spain—and that in any case Sweden's trade with Spain was very small (an argument which the commissioners could fairly use against him): Whitelocke, *Memorials*, iv. 259. On 13 May Whitelocke and Fiennes proposed a declaration that pitch and tar be neither included nor excluded as contraband, until Charles X's pleasure should be known, and Bonde undertook to consider this proposal: *ibid.*, 262–3: this in fact provided the final settlement, as it would be laid down in the treaty.

of those differences.[1] He was prepared to admit that if the Dutch were to give offence to Y.M. through the pretensions which they were advancing, it would be unjust and unreasonable, but he could never believe it of them, for it did not make sense to send an embassy and a fleet of war, one after the other: however, if they did so, he would resent it as though it had been done to himself. It was his hope that he might be able to use his good offices in the matter, and that was why he had been anxious to keep himself in a position in which he could do this without partiality to the one side or the other. As to the other treaty, he had put it in the hands of commissioners, whose opinions perhaps were not reconcilable with mine; but if it came to him for decision he would gladly do what he could. He had been informed, moreover, that the cause of the delay lay more with me than with them; and he [turned to] Thurloe to ask whether he had not been told so. The rest of his speech consisted of great protestations of his wish for Y.M.'s friendship and his desire to serve him—which he was not unwilling to convey to Y.M. by sending an embassy to him; and he spoke a great deal to my advantage, by way of showing the great affection and esteem he had for me, and so forth. As to Herr Coyet, he said that he had much wished—both for his own sake, and especially for his master's—to do something to give proof of his faithful friendship; and though what he had done was of small account, he hoped that—as what one man puts into the hand of another is valued for the feeling that prompts the gift—so this would be taken in the same spirit.

I answered that I had not doubted his honesty, did not do so now, and would not do so in the future. It was not for me to pronounce judgment on his policies: the effects would demonstrate which line had been the better; nevertheless it was clear that *quis serio vult finem vult etiam media*. Regarding his mission to Y.M., I felt bound to tell him that my view was that it should be sent: assuming he was thinking of making any progress towards an alliance he could do it more conveniently now that he had been told what Y.M.'s present views were, and would be the better able to instruct his ambassador. I hoped and begged that he would at least let me know what he intended, so that Y.M. might have some knowledge of what he had to expect of him. I had made no mention of mediation; for Y.M. had shown them [the Dutch] all friendship, and they had no reason to be afraid of Y.M., or to make claims upon him; but just as Y.M., if he needs the

1. On 21 April NS Nieupoort had reported Thurloe as alleging that the protector would have sent an ambassador to the Baltic, if the Swedish-Brandenburg alliance had not upset everything; that the elector was still an Orange partisan; and finally that no suitable envoy could be found, Whitelocke being too committed to Sweden: *Brieven*, iii. 216–19.

wares of England, Portugal, France, and other countries, must stand on a friendly footing with them, so they [the Dutch] should do the same, and there was therefore nothing at issue between Y.M. and them. Still less had I any knowledge of what might be negotiating here to their advantage, for Y.M. had not thought it of service to give me any instructions in the matter, and I had the less desire to obtain powers to do so from Y.M. Regarding the other treaty, and the commissioners, I felt obliged to disclaim the responsibility for delay which was laid upon me, and to say what otherwise I might have hesitated to say. It was a month or five weeks since I saw any of the commissioners; and I was then handed a draft of the treaty, on paper, to which I had immediately sent a written reply embodying my views as to how the terms ought to be framed, which Y.M. could hardly suppose would occasion any difficulty. But neither then nor later had I been able to arrange a meeting with them to discuss it.[1] And I was obliged to add that what annoyed me most was that I must sit like a prisoner in my house, and could neither get anybody to come to me, nor might I go to any of them;[2] and so time goes by without anything's being done, though a day was now as precious to me as a month. I begged pardon for having to say all this. He was aware that I had always taken pains to use all due civility and to refrain from any observations which might be critical of himself or his ministers. And then once again I asked that he would expedite my despatch.

To this he replied with the same protestations as before, and apologized for his remarks, saying that he did not think any fault lay with me, except possibly in the fact that I had not sent a request to the commissioners, who had orders to call upon me when I asked for a meeting. I was not disposed to wrangle with him on this point, but took my departure with an appearance of much *froideur*, with the idea of trying whether such a cloudy countenance might not expedite my departure better than the other [tactic]; but I felt compelled to disabuse him of the idea which Secretary Thurloe had put into his head, that the blame rested with me; whereas the main reason was that he [Thurloe] monopolizes business in his own hands.[3] There are a number of things which make my negotiations here very burdensome, and among them the fact that Secretary Thurloe is an absolute factotum, and even the most trivial thing cannot be done except through him; which makes him excessively slow in everything that he has to despatch, besides which he is very ignorant and clumsy in

1. This was scarcely true: he had met them on 6 May.
2. This was true in general; but there had been numerous exceptions.
3. Abbott's version makes it appear that it was Cromwell, not Thurloe, who monopolized all business: Abbott, iv. 159.

dealing with foreign ministers—as evidenced by the case of the Venetian resident, who has now been soliciting an audience for six or seven weeks in order to present his credentials on his replacing the ambassador, and has still not had it, and gets only irrelevant answers. I cannot assert it as a fact, but it seems to me very probable that my business has got involved in some intrigues against the protector's family by persons who, not being anxious to see it strong and stable, thwart it *quibuscunque artibus*. I am certain that his highness himself, and the Lord Deputy of Ireland, Fleetwood, desire nothing better than to align themselves with Y.M.; and there must therefore be some other powerful obstacles in the way. Among other devices of which they avail themselves not the least effective has been the dissemination of rumours of Y.M.'s death and the army's certain defeat; and these rumours are asserted with such insistence that men will by no means allow themselves to be disabused; which is why I myself and my suite have laid aside our mourning-clothes. By this post we have certain tidings that Y.M. has arrived at Thorn in good health, and that his army is in good shape after having had the better of various encounters with the enemy; for which God Almighty be eternally praised.

Yesterday the commissioners were with me again, and as last Tuesday I received their written answer to what I had lately sent them, we are now labouring to reach agreement on the various points. I send Y.M. herewith the first article, concerning recruiting, on which we shall at last shortly come to an agreement: it is true that it is limited by certain reservations, but I hope they will not affect the main point, particularly while there is firm friendship between us; and since they could be as useful to Y.M. as to them. But as I wrote to Y.M. in April, great difficulties have appeared regarding contraband goods, and regarding sea-passes, as a result of their war with Spain, and I have much trouble to resolve them, since they will by no means allow any nation to carry to Spain any commodities which are necessary for fitting out a ship; and they protest that they would rather allow all the goods which are listed as contraband to be carried thither, than permit hemp, rope, sails, pitch and tar, and masts.[1] I am afraid that the only expedient I can hit upon is to make a separate and secret article whereby those commodities are to be neither contraband nor free, but that they try to obtain Y.M.'s consent to reckoning such goods as contraband solely for the duration of the Spanish war.[2] They

---

1. In the course of the negotiations for the Dutch Marine Treaty Thurloe gave Nieupoort an assurance that the Swedes would not obtain this concession: *Brieven*, iii. 224.

2. This was the solution eventually agreed on. On 8 May Fiennes had propounded another expedient: that English merchants should buy up all those commodities around which controversy on contraband centred: to this Bonde raised many practical

likewise argue much about what form the sea-passes are to have, and contend that the right of visitation should remain unaffected, because of the great opportunities for smuggling which would otherwise be left open.[1] I find this the more troublesome because it had been thought that it would present no difficulties: God guide me aright in

---

objections: Whitelocke, *Memorials*, iv. 259. The question was left open in the convention attached to the treaty. Charles X accepted the convention, and it was probably in consequence that there was drawn up (early in 1657) 'Consideracions and Propositions to be represented to His Highness the Ld Protector for the manageing the Trade of Sweden and the King of Denmark' (PRO, SP 95/5B, fos. 154–6). It proposed the formation of a joint-stock company for three years, in which members of the council should have 'a considerable share'. It was to have the sole right to buy Swedish iron, copper and tar: the king of Sweden was to forbid such purchase to anyone else. During the three-years' duration of the contract he was to be prohibited from permitting the erection of any new mills or furnaces for the manufacture of iron or copper, except with the consent of the company. The company was to have the right to import these commodities, and to re-export them, free of duty; it was also to have the sole right to vend them at any place in the Swedish dominions. Prices were to be pegged at the lowest current rate; quality was to be guaranteed by the Swedes. Company ships importing salt into Sweden were to pay no more in duty than the Swedish Salt Company, and if possible leave was to be obtained to import salt into Sweden's Baltic provinces. As to Denmark, the king was to be forbidden to raise the Sound Tolls, or to detain company ships on the pretext of visitation: if possible, full exemption from the Sound Tolls (as in the case of Sweden) was to be obtained. These preposterous proposals would have reduced Sweden for three years to virtual economic servitude, and would have violated Denmark's sovereignty. Not surprisingly, no more was heard of them; but it was probably to them that Thurloe was referring when he wrote 'There was a particular treaty on foot with Sweden for pre-emption of all their copper, to prevent the Dutch of that commodity': *Somers Tracts*, vi. 332. The idea arose from a petition on 15 January 1656 by Jacob Momma, a Swedish merchant resident in London, who manufactured brass and brass wire (Whitelocke, *Memorials*, iv. 249–50), which asked for the raising of the duty on Swedish copper to balance the quadrupling of the export duty which Charles X had ordered in order to protect the Swedish brass industry against foreign competition. Cromwell referred it to the Council of Trade, where Whitelocke, pointing out that England had almost a monopoly of calamine, suggested buying up all Sweden's copper output, and so giving England a monopoly of brass. The Committee strongly supported him; but on 13 May reported that it would be difficult at present to include any moderation of the Swedish duty in the terms of Bonde's treaty: *CSP (Dom) 1655–56*, p. 318. For Momma, see Per Sondén, 'Bröderna Momma-Reenstierna. Ett bidrag till den svenska handelns och industriernas historia på 1600-talet', *Historisk tidskrift* (1911). The 'Propositions in Order to a Treaty with Sweden' (PRO, SP 95/5B fos. 152–3), which date evidently from about the time when Cromwell began to ask for Bremen, were slightly more realistic: all they demanded was equality of dues and duties in Sweden as between English and Swedish subjects, and the abolition of the Swedish Tar Company's monopoly; but this was to ask more than any Swedish king would have been prepared to grant.

1. The Council had suggested, in order to avert complaints against the Admiralty Courts in future, that Boards of Commissioners, equally composed of representatives of England and Sweden, should assess claims for compensation, and should also scrutinize passports; and this Bonde seemed prepared to consider: this arrangement was eventually agreed upon: Whitelocke, *Memorials*, iv. 247–9.

it. I cannot very well reject all their arguments, for then they might very well retract on the point of recruiting.

Since I did not manage to have the extract from the king of Portugal's letter to his minister here translated into Swedish in time, I send it to Y.M. now. It is a long time since I had any answer to my letters either from Y.M. or from the chancellor. I am anxiously awaiting them, as also for what is needed for General Fleetwood's recruiting, and some consolation for myself, so that I can get away.

L

London, 16 May 1656 [from Bonde's *Register*]

After I had last week spoken somewhat strongly to the lord protector, and shown myself very dissatisfied with their delays and irresolution (of all of which I gave Y.M. a full and circumstantial account by the last post), affairs seem once again to have taken a somewhat more favourable turn. Though it is clear to me that the conclusion of the great question of a closer alliance must depend upon his highness's sending his own mission to Y.M., I hope nevertheless to obtain reasonable terms in the other treaty. The main difficulty I have to encounter lies in the specification of contraband goods, of which I have already written to Y.M. This week I have been meeting my commissioners, and have now given them a new draft of the whole treaty. Next Tuesday we are to meet again. And yesterday I had a conference of some importance with my Lord Fleetwood, in which I told him, briefly and courteously, the reasons which had prompted me to complain to his highness of the dilatoriness with which they use me. And as at that time letters from Holland had given a full account of how the Dutch fleet had already sailed for the Sound, I had thought it my duty to tell the protector how dangerous it would be for the Protestant Cause that such a thing should happen; but since it was now learned that the fleet had not yet sailed I wished that he would persuade his highness to try to prevent it by sending a serious warning to the Dutch.[1] Secondly, since I perceived that there was little prospect of my effecting anything in regard to the defensive alliance (though I was quite prepared to conclude it, if the protector wished it) that he would persuade his highness to communicate his views and intentions to me in writing, so that Y.M. might know what he had to expect, and so that I could show Y.M. that neither zeal nor pains had been wanting on my part loyally to carry out Y.M.'s orders. Though these were the reasons that I gave him, my main object was to obtain from him [the protector] a written assurance that Y.M. may be certain of

1. Thurloe's intelligence from The Hague, of 26 May NS, was to the effect that the fleet, of 48 ships, was definitely to sail: Thurloe, v. 29.

his constant friendship, so that after I leave neither the Dutch nor anybody else may be able to constrain him to take any steps repugnant to Y.M.'s wishes. Lastly, I asked him to help me to bring the other treaty to a conclusion, since I was very anxious to take my departure. I explained some points in it, and told him that in the last draft which I had that day handed to my Lord Fiennes, I had gone as far as I could, and hoped that the matter might rest there.

To this he replied with the greatest politeness, making many excuses for their dilatoriness, and assuring me that it did not arise from any lack of good-will towards me, and still less towards Y.M., but from many other obstacles. He promised to exert himself to carry out everything I had asked of him, and made many apologies for the fact that the protector was unable to conclude the alliance with me, protesting that from the high esteem his highness had for me he would rather have concluded it with me than with any other; but that it was only in *modus operandi* that we differed, which led him to think that it might more easily be settled [directly] with Y.M.; that his highness would not fail to use such good offices as he could to avert any ill-will between Y.M. and Holland; and that he believed his highness would prime me with information about the legation which he was to send to Y.M. Lastly, he spoke of the other treaty, and promised to use every effort in that regard. After which we parted, with many compliments on both sides.

Up to the time of the last post, and until I met the commissioners last Tuesday, I was more worried than ever before in the whole of my life; one reason for this being that I did not know what to do for money if I should have to depart immediately because I had fallen out with them, and so take my leave on bad terms with them; but I now feel somewhat more cheerful, after my last conference with the commissioners and my conversation with Fleetwood, which have given me once more good hope of finishing this troublesome business in such a way as to serve Y.M.—and (I sincerely hope) to Y.M.'s satisfaction. I am encouraged also by the good news of Y.M.'s and her majesty the queen's happy arrival in Prussia: God Almighty be praised and thanked for it. I should have been very glad to send Y.M. the draft of the secret article regarding the goods which his highness insists must not be sent to Spain during their present war with that country, but since they have not yet seen my proposal I am unable to say whether they are prepared to be satisfied with it. The only commodities I specified in it were sailcloth, hemp and rigging; with the suggestion that his highness was at liberty, either by pre-emption or by other means, to arrange with Y.M. that these goods be not sent there, though they are not to be designated as contraband. I hope that this solution may not be prejudicial to Y.M. or his subjects, but that they [the English] may be reasonably satisfied on this point, which they consider essential to the conduct of their war with Spain; and that for the rest I may obtain pretty satisfactory terms, and leave this country with good-will: which is something that in the present situation seems to me to be very necessary. I shall use every effort to finish this business as soon as possible and make my way to Y.M. in Prussia, so that I may give Y.M. an account of everything that has passed here.

LI

London, 23 May 1656

A letter from Y.M. reached me by this post; but as it bore no date (no doubt because it was written in haste) I am not able to judge how old it is, nor the place from which it was written. It is none the less with the greatest pleasure that I learn that Y.M. has arrived back in Prussia in good order and good health, though many who are ill-disposed have been for some time vexing us with tidings to the contrary; but God be praised, who has turned their malice to their own shame and disgrace.[1] I am very worried to learn from the same letter from Y.M. that some of my reports to him have been intercepted by the Poles, so that Y.M. has been unable to obtain information as to the state of affairs in this country, and I for my part have been the less able to receive news from Y.M. But I am glad that all my letters were written in cypher, so that they can hardly have been of any use to them. But since the chancellor no doubt reached Y.M. long ago, I hope that Y.M. has been able to obtain some information about my affairs; for on the most important matters I have sent him duplicates of my letters to Y.M., in view of the fact that Y.M. was so far away that it was likely to be a considerable time before I could obtain any intelligence from Y.M. himself about my business. I hope that the accounts of my most important meetings here since 28 March may in fact have come to hand, and that I may receive Y.M.'s orders concerning them. I greatly long to have them, among other reasons on account of General Fleetwood's recruiting, which has still not started, for lack of funds, though both I, and Hoffstetter in Hamburg, have made every effort to raise money; but hitherto with no success. By the next post I shall take care to send to Y.M. duplicates of the letters which, to judge from the dates, may have gone astray.

---

1. Charles X, turning his back for the moment on the partisans in central Poland, was concentrating on establishing a firm control of royal Prussia. On 8/18 February the Swedes had captured Marienburg; but this was their only substantial success, and Danzig proved defiant: Wimmer, in *Polens krig med Sverige*, p. 361.

As to the course of affairs here, I informed Y.M. in my letter of 25 April of my conversation with Thurloe, and that I proposed as an *ultimum remedium* that his highness should send a legation to Y.M. Since then I have mostly concentrated on getting agreement on the other treaty, in which the most delicate points are the articles on contraband, and on satisfaction for the losses sustained by Y.M.'s subjects. I have this week been hard at work with the commissioners, and am still trying to push them on.[1] Apart from Herr Coyet, who leaves next week for certain, I have had the greatest assistance from Herr Appelboom in Holland, both in the way of information and advice. He has sent me the draft of the Dutchmen's Marine Treaty, which is secretly in agitation here; and the fact that it has been mooted adds no little to the difficulty of my negotiation, for they are afraid that the Dutch may demand—and have more reason to demand—what they concede to me. I have been forced at times to indicate my annoyance, as Y.M. will have seen from my letter of 19 May, and again (though somewhat toned down) to Deputy Fleetwood, as I reported by the last post. Their affairs here are in a state of complete confusion, and I am reliably informed that relations between them and Holland have a very ill appearance: they are now absolutely convinced that Admiral de Ruyter has brought the king of Spain's silver to Holland, and then sent it on to Flanders; and, what is more, Ambassador Nieupoort protests strongly to the protector because the English wished to visit their ships. In other respects the Dutch have given Spain all the assistance which can injure England at this time,[2] so that they have done more damage than Spain has: indeed, it is said in so many words that the Dutchmen's naval armament is directed more against England than to the Baltic. They therefore now insist upon complete freedom of navigation, and if the English stand upon the pretension to visit their ships, they will defend themselves by force: in which they are much influenced by the fact that England is no longer as strong as she was in relation to Holland.[3] The English on

1. When Bonde met the commissioners on 20 May, they informed him that the council stood firm on the inclusion of pitch, hemp and tar as contraband for the duration of the Spanish war, and used Bonde's own argument against him: that there was little Swedish trade with Spain. To which Bonde replied that he certainly could not wait (as Fiennes had suggested) for an answer from Charles X on this point. They appointed to meet next Tuesday; but Whitelocke has no mention of such a meeting: Whitelocke, *Memorials*, iv. 264–9.

2. De Witt wrote to Nieupoort on 9 May NS: 'the Vice-Admiral de Ruyter is arrived in Zealand, being come from Cadiz with 7 men of war and 30 merchant ships richly laden, for which God be praised: here is extraordinary joy shown at their arrival': Thurloe, iv. 729.

3. Presumably on the ground of the wide dispersal of English naval forces at this time.

their side now realize that they can gain no advantage against Spain if Holland obtains such freedom; so that it appears very probable that things may come to a crisis between them. I am informed, from a pretty reliable source, that the protector has given orders to General Blake to come home with his fleet, which cannot be possible unless they have some particular design in contemplation.[1] I shall use every possible means to get at the truth of all this. It is at all events certain that the protector and his council are extraordinarily preoccupied, and that the day before yesterday they once again held a day of prayer at Whitehall, mainly to ask God's guidance in this Dutch business.

This development makes me ponder what attitude to take towards it. If relations [with the Dutch] continue to deteriorate, the protector will find that what I have so often warned him of has proved true, and that the means [I suggested] to ward it off were sound. And undoubtedly, unless he is totally blind, he will seek to embrace the alliance which I have been offering to him. This reflection is in some measure confirmed by a talk which Secretary Thurloe had with Herr Coyet last Saturday, in which he ingenuously confessed that the cruel tidings which have been spread abroad of Y.M.'s defeat and death have been in no small degree an obstacle to our business. Though it may seem odd that he was willing to admit it, it is not unreasonable to conclude that he wished to make it apparent now, when the earlier news has proved false, and the welcome good news of Y.M. and his victories has been received, that opinions have altered. If the Dutch now decide that they must court Y.M., and settle the differences which seem to exist between Y.M. and them, it might seem a fair question whether we should commit ourselves further with England than they seem to be prepared to commit themselves with Y.M. (that is, by interposition, and offices of that kind) unless there are particular advantages to be gained; since it is very likely that England has now greater reason to seek Y.M.'s friendship than Y.M. has to seek theirs.

But all this is highly speculative, and so I have thought it best to stick to Y.M.'s orders; and having already aired the possibility of their sending a mission from his highness to Y.M., to leave it at that, taking note of whether they show more desire for the alliance than before, while at the same time steadily asking for my *congé* (which is the only way of forcing them to take any decision), and meanwhile to work away at concluding the other treaty, of which I shall send the particulars to Y.M. by Herr Coyet. Since it was not possible for my

---

1. The rumour was untrue. Cromwell did not send orders to Montagu to return until 29 August, and even then Blake and twenty frigates were to remain on station off the Portuguese coast: Corbett, *England in the Mediterranean*, i. 333. The recall had nothing to do with internal affairs, but was decided upon on the grounds that nothing material was now to be effected.

instructions to cover every detail, I have had to yield on some points which they do not specifically mention, as Y.M. will see in the article regarding recruiting which I sent over to Y.M. on 9 May; but I shall take care that nothing is done which contravenes Y.M.'s orders, wishes or interests. The fact that Y.M. is so far off has been a great affliction, since—unlike the ambassadors of France and Holland in their negotiations here—I have not been able to obtain information from Y.M. every week as to the progress of events, but have been forced to trust in God and act to the best of my understanding; and for that reason I trust that Y.M. may be pleased to put the best construction on it all, and I humbly beg him to do so.

Although such is the state of affairs, the audience with his highness from which I am this moment returned went in such a way that I cannot but think that I must depart without having achieved anything. The protector argued that he must remain neutral, and must in no way offend either Y.M. or Holland; and therefore their *spiritus*,[1] which they must follow as their best counsellor, could not allow them to conclude with Y.M. on the basis that had been proposed. As to the other treaty, here too he found that nothing was to be done, since I would not agree to their demand that hemp, tackle, sailcloth, masts, pitch and tar, should be contraband. In answer, I showed them the unreasonableness of this, but being unwilling to allow it to appear that I thought it of especial importance, I accepted it in part, (*eendeeles*), and thereupon took my leave. By the next post I shall send Y.M. a full report of this encounter; for the moment I can only say that I fear that nothing may be able to be done in regard to the proposed alliance because of their fear of the Dutch. But in any case, even if they were allied to Y.M., I doubt whether much reliance could be placed on them, at any rate on this confused government. The Dutch call the English *stertmen*,[2] since they always preserve to themselves some loophole, which means that those who imagine they can rely upon them can never be sure: it has always been their way, with the French protestants and others also. If I find that they are fully determined to allow me to depart leaving unfinished business behind me, and if we can agree on the other points, I see that the ultimate *remedium* is to leave the whole article on contraband out, as being the course least prejudicial to Y.M., and at the same time giving no cause for ill feeling between Y.M. and his highness—though the fact that I have never been able to get from them any categorical

1. I.e. conscience; though Abbott (iv. 150) translates it 'state of mind'.
2. Neither *stert*, nor any compound of it, is listed in *Woordenboek der Nederlandsche Taal*, xv (1940). I am indebted to Professor André Brink for the information that this is a slightly vulgar word, meaning 'tail', or in this context 'backside': *cf.* Swedish *stjärt*.

resolution, but am put off from day to day, might well have given Y.M. good reason for it. But rather than suffer the smallest indignity I shall immediately express my displeasure and depart, according to Y.M.'s orders, that being the only method available for dealing with this troublesome business.

LII

London, 30 May 1656 [from Bonde's *Register*]

Towards the end of my last letter I mentioned something of the unfavourable course of my encounter with the protector at my last conference with him, and promised to give a detailed account of it by this post. I have therefore humbly to inform Y.M. that being most anxious to get away from this place, and seeing that the commissioners proceed with extreme slowness in the concluding of this treaty, and make great difficulties in everything that is to be decided, I thought it necessary to speak with the lord protector and demand my despatch. I did so last Friday afternoon. I began by reporting the certain tidings I had of Y.M.'s favourable situation, and mentioned that I had received letters from Y.M. himself. I then expressed my desire that his highness would despatch me, since I was extremely anxious to depart; and as I gathered that in the great affair of a closer alliance there seemed little chance of anything's being done, I asked his highness to be good enough to let me know what he proposed to do, and whether he intended to pursue the matter by a legation to Y.M., so that Y.M. might be the better able to shape his plans when he knew what he had to expect from his highness. In the second place I asked also that he would help to get the other treaty finished: I had recently put in another draft, which I hoped his highness would find reasonable, and which I believed required no alteration; and said that I was sure that he would not expect me to treat him as the Portuguese did (whose treaty his master refused to ratify), adding that though I had hoped to be of service in the common cause, since that was now out of the question I thought no more of it, but desired only to have a favourable answer on the two points I had propounded.

In his reply, he said much about his pleasure that the rumours had been proved false, hoped the news about Y.M.'s victories was confirmed, and dilated on the joy the tidings gave him; but for the rest he showed that in regard to the closer alliance we proceeded upon principles that were so divergent that he did not see how we could negotiate with each other upon it. Although I had thought that my proposal would have been the best way to attain the end upon which we were at one, they could not find it in their *spiritus* (which they were bound to follow, as their best counsellor) to embrace it. As to the other treaty, he had been informed by the commissioners that there was such a wide difference between us, particularly in matters which it seemed to them could do little hurt to Y.M. but were of vital importance to them during this Spanish war, that in this matter also he saw little likelihood of achieving anything. This led him to the conclusion that this was not the appropriate moment to effect anything; and he lamented the fact that we must part in this fashion at last.

At this I was not a little taken aback, though I did not show it, but answered that I had gathered from his highness's commissioners, some time ago, that there was not much prospect of our agreeing on a closer alliance, and it was for that reason that I had suggested, as an expedient, the sending of a mission to Y.M., and that I hoped that my request to know what his highness intended to do about it might not be thought unreasonable. As to the other treaty, I must admit that I had wished to conclude it, and it had never occurred to me that the point about contraband, which now appeared to be the *lapis offensionis*, would cause any difficulty, for during their war with Holland they had not then contended that the same commodities that are now in question were contraband, although the Dutch had maintained that they were; which was why the council of state at that time had drawn up a schedule of contraband goods and given it to Mr Bonnel, which I had presented to them [the commissioners]; moreover my Lord Whitelocke on his return to England had written to Mr Lagerfelt that his form of passport and specification of contraband goods has been approved and endorsed. Apart from all this, I begged his highness to consider what the consequences for us would be if we should consent to all the products of our country, and the source of all our wealth, being deemed contraband: a thing we have never yet conceded to any country, and have not the slightest intention of conceding now. He should also reflect that his demands in this matter would not be satisfied by my quitting the country in ill-humour: the business would be left in a state of uncertainty which might easily lead to disorders, if they were to class goods as prohibited and we were to refuse to accept this. But if the situation here was that there was no more to be done about it, then I was his humble servant. I paused a little at this point, in case he should wish to reply; but all he said was that he hoped that before I left I would visit him a few times at Hampton Court and join him in killing a stag or two. I replied that I should like to talk to him before my departure, but if such were to be the upshot of the matter I should not linger here very long; and with that we parted.

Although I did not allow it to appear that I was disturbed by these difficulties, I cannot adequately describe the embarrassment of my situation; and what makes it most disastrous is that I can get no letter or answer from Y.M. to what I send him by every post, and have here such an uphill game to play; so that although some time ago Thurloe talked of this treaty as an easy business, things have so altered since then that I hardly see how we can reach agreement with them. I might have considered that this was only a feint of the protector to scare something out of me; but when I came to examine their attitude it appeared to me that since Spain is carrying on the war against England with vigour and determination, while England's attacks on the Indies and the Spanish silver-fleet have turned out badly, they see no other way to inflict damage on their enemy than by hindering trade, and stopping the supply of those commodities which Spain cannot do without, and that therefore they cannot by any means acquiesce in the articles on passports and contraband goods which I am instructed to obtain. Add to this a great misfortune, in that the Dutch are simultaneously in negotiation with them for a commercial treaty; and as the greatest part of the trade to Spain is in Dutch hands, they [the English] aim to disrupt it as far as they can, and so the same issues which have arisen between me and them are a matter of discussion between them and the Dutch. And so they think that if they were to concede anything to me, the Dutch would demand the same treatment, and if on the other hand I were to make a concession to them, then the Dutch must do the same. But if I thought of leaving before the business was completed, and thus departed with a show of displeasure, or if I should allow things to come to the extremity of demanding my recall and asking the protector to allow me to go, I am confronted with weighty arguments: the most important of them is the intrigues of Denmark and Holland against Y.M., of which I am warned by Herr Appelboom, and which make it clear that no faith is to be put in them, and that there is nothing they more desire than that some ill-will, or at least a coldness, should arise between Y.M. and the lord protector. For the main consideration which has hitherto restrained them from taking overt action against Y.M. is the belief that an especially close relation exists between Y.M. and the lord protector; if this were to cease to exist, Y.M.'s negotiations with them [the Dutch] in Marienburg would be made more difficult,[1] and they

---

1. A reference to the protracted negotiations between Erik Oxenstierna, (the Swedish chancellor) and the Dutch ambassadors, which led eventually to the treaty of Elbing on 1 September. A Dutch embassy to Charles X arrived in Marienburg on 9 May; but tentative negotiations did not begin until the end of June, and the first formal conference was held on 14 July, once Charles X (by the treaty of Marienburg on 15 June) had obtained a firm promise of military aid from Frederick William of Brandenburg. They were given additional urgency by the arrival of a powerful Dutch fleet in Danzig Roads on 17 July. For the negotiations see Fries, *Erik Oxenstierna* pp. 291–300.

on their side would become bolder and more insupportable. Although I cannot doubt that the lord protector is in his heart strongly inclined to friendship with Y.M., it is nevertheless the case that the Dutch use many artifices to draw him away, offering all sorts of conditions, and flattering him that they will join him in attacking Spain if only he will—if not injure, then at least abandon—Y.M.[1] To this may be added that this *régime* is riddled with intrigues, and with such jealousies that I have some reason to doubt whether there may not be those who deliberately confuse sensible policies so that matters may go ill. For these reasons I have thought it inadvisable to make a public demonstration of my dissatisfaction, but still to find means to mend matters, or at least to hold on until I can get some orders from Y.M.; and so I have sought speech with my Lord Fiennes, who is the leading figure among my commissioners, and a very reasonable man. This I managed last Monday [26 May], explaining to him with some resentment that it was not Y.M.'s fault, nor mine, that our business did not go smoothly, and courteously putting the blame on them. I then suggested some expedients which might serve to bring it to a good conclusion. On Wednesday afternoon he gave me some papers or drafts, to which I returned an answer on Thursday morning. I now send Y.M. the treaty as it stands at present, with my own annotations to each of the articles, with a request that Y.M. may be pleased to consider it; and though I do not well know whether I can stay for Y.M.'s answer, I beg that Y.M. will be pleased to let me have it. I hope shortly to receive from Y.M. some answer to my former letter on the same subject, which presumably will give me some guidance. The greatest difficulties I have met with have been on the questions of contraband goods, passports, and satisfaction. As to the last, I think we shall reach agreement; in regard to the other two I have consistently stuck to my position, until we reached a stage at which I began to be afraid that by doing so I should forfeit all good-will; for among other arguments they said that they knew that Y.M.'s subjects at present had little or no trade with Spain, so that the terms they proposed could be of no prejudice to them, while the protector, on the other hand, would be gratified in a point on which his whole war with Spain depended; and if Y.M. would not meet them on this they could have little hope that he would help them on any more important occasion. What chiefly moved me to relax my previous rigid attitude was the special consideration that by doing so it might easily be a

---

1. On 19 May NS de Witt had written to Nieupoort informing him that at a special meeting of the States of Holland it had been made quite clear that they would not engage in any offensive alliance directed against Spain, nor in any way violate the peace with that country: *Brieven*, iii. 227.

source of disunion between this country and Holland, which I think is something very necessary at this moment. The Dutch insist strongly on the article regarding contraband goods, on free passes, and that free ships make free goods and may not be subject to visitation, and the English fight against these things *tanquam pro aris et focis*; and if Y.M. were to make some concessions on these points it would undoubtedly cast a *pomum Eridis* between them, for England would then have all the greater reason to stand firm upon them. If Holland nevertheless refuse to give way, that would give great offence on this side; and if they did give way, that would equally cause a coldness in Holland, as being a thing that their principal interests do not permit; with the result that these people here would be driven to bind themselves more closely to Y.M., and to keep the Dutch (who are now insupportable) on a tight rein. I am given great hopes of obtaining a favourable decision in our great affair, if only I will give way a little in this; or at least of getting a written declaration by his highness of what he proposes to do in it; which may in any event be necessary to Y.M., to give him security on this side.

Y.M. may have collected their views on passports from the article *De Conservatoribus Commerciorum.*[1] They cannot now refuse the granting of passports, since that was expressly agreed in the treaty of Uppsala;[2] but they have concocted a form of passport which it is impossible to comply with: I hope to send Y.M. a copy by the next post. I am quite sure that I could contest a great number of points [of the treaty]; but I am afraid that it may not be possible to reduce them to the form which has been permitted to me. If Y.M. were prepared—solely for the duration of the present Spanish war—to relax some of his most rigorous conditions, that would not only be well taken here, but would also greatly assist in the design mentioned above [*sc.* of sowing dissension between England and the Dutch]. I shall bend all my efforts to doing what may be for the best, in which nothing would be of greater help than if I were so fortunate as to know Y.M.'s pleasure. Both General Fleetwood and I have been greatly longing for the arrival of this post; but it has not yet turned up, so that we do not know if it is bringing letters to us from Y.M. Herr Coyet sets off tomorrow morning by way of Holland to Y.M., and he will give Y.M. an account of everything that has happened here. I send with this a duplicate of a letter of 1 February: I have not been able this time to fair-copy any others, having been constantly busy all week.[3]

---

1. The article on passports was to become article IV of the eventual treaty.
2. Art. XII.
3. Schlezer reported on 6 June that Bonde was very discontented at his lack of success (which Schlezer attributed to the 'Dexterität' of Nieupoort, 'der jetzt à toute force regieret'), and was probably not very well disposed to Brandenburg either.

LIII

London, 6 June 1656

Since my last long letter I have been engaged all week with my Lord Fiennes on various drafts of the article on passports, though we still have not settled it. His highness is so extremely busy with his council, and so worried, that neither he nor they give themselves time to eat, but are meeting every day with the Major-Generals of the provinces (who are as it were governors) to discuss how they shall deal with the situation. Some are for insisting that a parliament be summoned; and as this is a matter of great consequence and very debatable wisdom, they have the more trouble in coming to a decision about it, though the situation is now such that without a parliament the war against Spain cannot be prosecuted with the energy that is required, for lack of money. These obstacles have much delayed my negotiation this week, though I press on through good and evil; God knows how it has happened that no letters have reached me from Y.M. I cannot suppose that Y.M. thinks that I have already taken my departure, for I have written an account of our progress by every post. What makes me most anxious to receive Y.M.'s orders is that it is essential for me to know how far the friendship of this country is necessary to Y.M., now that nothing is to be done with them in the great affair [*sc.* the alliance], and that the other treaty goes so slowly and with such difficulty. For a long time I have had no information about the defensive alliance, apart from Y.M.'s original order [from Siedlice?], and this makes it the more difficult to decide what to do in the matter. If this state is not put upon a stable footing by a parliament, or by some other means, not much reliance can be placed upon it; and it is almost impossible that they should do anything *a bon essein* [*à bon escient*] and without any loopholes (*eschappader*). They are moreover so anxious that they scarcely know what to do; for they stand in so uncertain a condition, and all their attacks on Spain go so badly for them, while the king of Scotland and Spain neglect no opportunity to make the best of their advantage. On top of all this, there is in the country little—or rather no—affection for this government. These considerations move me on the one hand to take myself off without concluding any further agreement, contenting myself with the fact that my apparently confidential footing with his highness has throughout my stay restrained many adverse proposals; but on the other

---

Further, that Cromwell was seeking information (under art. 15 of the treaty with the Dutch) on the terms of the alliance between the Dutch and Brandenburg: *Urk. und. Art.* vii. 748–9.

hand Y.M.'s negotiation with Holland[1] (which establishes at best a lukewarm friendship) has implications which—as between Y.M. and England—might undoubtedly be prejudicial to Y.M. Between these two dubieties my opinon vacillates, so that I intend in the course of the next week to try what can be done and then come to a firm decision, for I am desperate to get away, and my means are very straitened.

I have just returned from a meeting with the commissioners, and there seems to be a good prospect that it will all turn out well. By the next post I shall send Y.M. a draft of the treaty: I hope it may arrive safely. My only comfort is the news of Y.M.'s favourable and fortunate situation,[2] which I get by every post from various places—except from those where Y.M. is: whether this is because of the uncertainty of the posts or the roads, I cannot tell.

LIV

London, 13 June 1656 [from Bonde's *Register*]

I have with the greatest delight this week received two letters from Y.M.: one, of 9 May, from Marienburg, containing Y.M.'s order to let his highness know the reasons which have forced Y.M. to attack the city of Danzig, and to warn the English not to drive any trade there for the time being; the other, of 16 May, from Schneebloch, in which Y.M. is pleased to communicate his instructions as to the closer alliance, now that he had learned by my letter of 25 April of the obstacles which seemed to be holding things up on this side.[3] I cannot adequately express how welcome to me these orders have been; among other reasons, because Y.M. has been graciously pleased to approve

1. I.e. the negotiations which were to result in the treaty of Elbing.
2. In reality, Charles's position was anything but favourable. He had indeed, by the treaty of Marienburg (15/25 June), constrained the Great Elector to renew—for the last time—his agreement (in return for large territorial concessions) to give military assistance, but only until the end of the year; but after the battle of Warsaw the elector was not to be persuaded to participate in any further campaigns deep into Poland. Charles was in fact now desperate to come to some agreement with the Dutch.
3. Charles's orders (which arrived on 11 June, according to Bonde's *Diarium*) approved Bonde's actions on the completion of the treaty of 1654. In regard to the alliance Charles was prepared, since it seemed mostly to stick on money, to lower his demand from the 5 *tunnor* of gold (which was the amount of the former French subsidy) by one-third: i.e. to 333,333.4 *rdr. per annum*, or even to 300,000 if agreement could be reached on the other terms, payable annually in two instalments. But regarding the protector's demand that the alliance be directed against the House of Austria Bonde was to represent that 'at present it is not appropriate in that form, but we think it best that it be *in terminis generalibus contra quemcunque*': Carlbom, *Sverige och England*, pp. 103–4.

what I have done; and I could wish for no greater consolation for the difficulties and setbacks I have experienced here. It puts fresh heart into me after a period in which I was greatly troubled at not receiving any letter from Y.M. for a long time.

The difficulties which have for some time held me up will, I hope, have been conveyed to Y.M. by my last letters, and especially by that which was sent off just a fortnight ago enclosing a draft of the treaty which was under negotiation. Since then I have met my commissioners again, and handed them the treaty re-drafted for the second time, in which some words are inserted in the interests of clarity; and in particular I have taken care that what is provided in article 5 may be without prejudice to treaties formerly concluded with other countries:[1] this was in order that nothing should be done which might be prejudicial to Y.M., for though I have no instructions as to this article, it is one which cannot be avoided; and also because in Sweden's treaty with Holland[2] it is laid down that each country shall be free to bring their prizes from the other's harbours. They have been considering it this week, and I hope soon to have their answer. Meanwhile I thought it necessary to speak with my Lord Deputy Fleetwood, which I did on Tuesday morning. And since I had perceived that the long delays to which I had been subjected were not fortuitous, or the result of indifference, but à dessein—the jealousies occasioned by my presence being very useful to them in the present posture of affairs—I told him something of my last encounter with his highness, and said that although there was not much left for me to do in regard to this last treaty, since I felt pretty indifferent about it now that I had not been able to get my definition of contraband goods accepted, nor the principle that 'free ship makes free goods', I did not wish to take my departure without more ado, and leave the country (as I very well might have done) in an ill-humour, since in view of the present state of affairs and the condition of the Protestant Cause that might be a great embarrassment; but that I was exploring other possibilities, of which my Lord Fiennes was now fully apprised. But though my presence in this country could not be said to be useless either to Y.M.'s service or to theirs, if only for the disquiet it caused to those who wished both of us no good, nevertheless I asked him to push for my despatch, since my private circumstances could no longer brook delay. If his highness were to send a legation to Y.M., it would probably be

---

1. Article V, as finally agreed, provided that ships of one ally, if taken as prize by an enemy or rebel, should not be admitted to the ports of the other; but if so admitted, they and their cargoes were not to be sold, the passengers and crew were to be liberated, and the ship to quit the port immediately.

2. The treaty of 1645.

able to make a good agreement, which would make an equal, if not a greater, *éclat* in the world.

He answered me with the greatest courtesy, made many explanations of their attitude on the contraband controversy during the present war with Spain, and hoped that now that I had made some concession on that point there would be no difficulty with the others. He added that he had not abandoned all hope of being able to treat with me about the closer alliance, with many protestations of how much his highness wished to negotiate it with me; and then touched shortly upon some particular points, mostly relating to the considerations which restrained them, on account of Denmark and Holland, from entering into an alliance *contra quemcunque*; but since he was in something of a hurry I replied briefly, and we agreed that he and my Lord Fiennes should come to me and talk further of the matter; and so, with many protestations, took his departure in good humour. At this point arrived Y.M.'s most agreeable order, which coming on top of this conversation encouraged me to try once again what chance there was of doing anything in the business. I therefore had to-day an audience with his highness, in which I first presented to him Y.M.'s orders to me regarding Danzig, and then spoke to him of the treaty which I was engaged in negotiating, and finally indicated my readiness to discuss the great business with him if he seriously desired to embrace it, however great the difficulties attendant upon the long delay might appear. He answered me with strong assurances of his joy at Y.M.'s successes; and since I had promised him on Y.M.'s behalf that the English in Elbing should have favourable terms and friendly treatment, he took that as a great sign of amity, and promised to arrange that the English should give no assistance, or carry any supplies, to the Danzigers, and for the present they should stop their trade with them. He mentioned that they wanted to force the English there to serve them against Y.M.; that he had let the Danzigers know of his displeasure at this;[1] and that the English there were determined to do nothing in opposition to Y.M. (I am moreover reliably informed that the English have no love for Danzig, on account of its harsh treatment of them). For the rest he affirmed his exceeding inclination to the closer alliance, admitted that he found Dutch policy to be concerned only with their own presumed advantage, and very little with the common welfare, and that he was now quite as much disposed to such an alliance as before, if not more so. He would get his

1. Printed in Abbott, iv. 928–9. Danzig had appealed to the protector for aid in (?) March: Thurloe, iv. 663–4; and a month earlier to the Dutch: *ibid.*, 499. A copy of the protector's protest was read to the Swedish council on 29 May: *RRP*, xvi. 466. The orders from Schneebloch were written just when Charles X—for the first time—was giving serious attention to preparing a regular siege of Danzig.

commissioners to meet me, and would think I was an angel from Heaven if I could indicate to them ways and means to attain that longed-for goal. I answered briefly that I had long ago told him what would happen, and if he would be pleased to examine the proceedings of the Dutch—on the one hand towards himself, and on the other towards us, by their sending a fleet to the Sound—he would be able clearly to perceive that nothing was further from their thoughts than to embrace the Protestant Cause. If he were ready to ally with Y.M. *contra quemcunque* I would gladly concede what I could in other matters.

He took this with great cordiality, and then enquired what I knew about how Holland stands with Denmark, [saying] that the Dutch were now growing pressing[1] in their correspondence with Denmark; and since I have good information through Herr Dureel[2] I told him frankly that (as far as I or Y.M.'s minister on the spot could divine) there had been some signs of it while the false rumour of Y.M.'s defeat and death was in circulation, but that latterly relations had become somewhat cooler, and that Denmark seemed to have qualms about offending Y.M., particularly as long as things went well with him; but that he might take it as an indication of their plans, and that it became all the more necessary for him and Y.M. to be allies: the Dutch would spare no pains to thwart us, and only such an alliance could check their designs.[3]

Among other things, he offered excuses for the former audience; and we parted accordingly with great protestations of friendship. So we have become good friends again in spite of our previous quarrels.[4] If I see that they are at all in earnest I intend to treat with them, in accordance with Y.M.'s last orders; if not, I shall finish the other treaty, and leave the rest to his embassy, but at the same time contrive that the news of the intimate correspondence between Y.M. and him shall make the greatest possible impact; which can do much good. Herr Coyet left last Monday. It is a great pity that the best season for General Fleetwood's recruiting is coming to an end: I long to hear the drum beating in London for Y.M.'s service.[5]

1. The text of the transcript has '*prokade på*': qy: a mistake for '*pockade på*'?
2. Magnus Dureel, the Swedish minister in Copenhagen.
3. Bonde's assessment of the position in Copenhagen was already out of date. The first detachment of Obdam's fleet arrived at Helsingör on 15 June, and Frederick III lost no time in giving permission for it to sail on into the Baltic. Its coming caused near-panic in Stockholm, where it was feared that it might attack Öland or Gotland. On 6/16 August Denmark agreed to coöperate with the Dutch in naval operations off Danzig, and did actually send a squadron to join Obdam. Already on 4 July NS de Witt could inform Nieupoort that 'our ambassadors report that we have nothing but good to expect from Frederick III': *Brieven*, iii. 248–9.
4. *Cf.* Whitelocke, *Memorials*, iv. 270, for Bonde's optimism after this meeting.
5. On 17 June the council of state ordered that Cranstoun's Scottish estates be desequestered, at Charles X's request: *CSP (Dom) 1656–7*, p. 14. But when on 29 April

LV

London, 20 June 1656

As agreed at my last audience with his highness a week ago (which I reported to Y.M. by my last letter), my Lord Deputy Fleetwood and my Lord Fiennes called on me last Tuesday. And as their purpose was to discuss with me how we might come to a closer alliance, they asked me to let them have my thoughts about it. I therefore summarized for them the substance of what had been said on various previous occasions, enumerated the reasons which seemed to both of us to be arguments for a closer relationship, as well those which related to the particular interests of our two countries, as those which concerned the common cause; and by way of demonstrating the most effective means of maintaining a mutual good understanding among all protestants, in the first instance, and afterwards with France, I explained the interests, the situation, and the inclination to such an arrangement, of all the states and nations to be considered. But in view of the fact that I had hitherto found little real concern for it on their side, and had moreover small hope that they would take it any more seriously than before, they being persuaded that Y.M.'s Polish war must in the end involve him in hostilities with the emperor (in which case they would be prepared to give Y.M. only a little, or no, assistance), I thought it necsssary to affect an entire indifference, in order to see whether by such an attitude they might not be stung into embracing the common cause more effectively—particularly since it is certain that such an alliance with Y.M. is as necessary to them as it is to Y.M., if not more so.

I accordingly observed that the posture of affairs had greatly altered since I spoke of the matter last winter and spring:

(1) Y.M. was now in no danger from the emperor and Spain: they had their ambassadors with Y.M., and were offering to keep on good terms with him;

(2) the emperor himself was in very bad health; and since neither his son, nor any other of the House of Habsburg, has as yet been elected king of the Romans, and a considerable section of the German princes would oppose such an election, his thoughts and energies were so preoccupied with that problem that he would be glad to take care to remain on friendly terms with Y.M.;

1657 a bill was introduced to grant a pardon to Cranstoun, as having done good service to Sweden, Thurloe intervened with the remark 'I doubt that Cranstoun hath not done such good service as is moved. It is true, he raised some men in Scotland for the king of Sweden, but I hear they are since gone to Middleton', and the bill was laid aside: *The Diary of Thomas Burton*, ed. J. T. Rutt (4 vols. 1828), ii. 76.

(3) nor did protestantism seem to be in any danger, Spain proclaiming that she was forced to fight England for the sake of the Indies, rather than on grounds of religion;

(4) the situation of the protestants in France was stable; and though the emperor had to some extent persecuted them in his hereditary lands, he had now ceased to do so, lest the plight of the protestants should force Y.M. to take action against him—which, as Y.M.'s affairs now stand, might inconvenience him [*sc.* the emperor] considerably.

(5) Y.M. had now little danger to fear from Holland and Denmark: the hand of God, which is over Y.M. and leads all his actions, restrained them. And if ever it should be necessary, Y.M. could soon satisfy the Dutch ambassadors, and afterwards they could be very good friends. Or, in the event of their embarking upon any enterprise against Y.M., he could easily make peace with the king of Poland, and then, with God's help, be a match for anybody who might try to do him an injury.[1]

But on the protector's side the face of affairs had so altered that Y.M. might with good reason hesitate to take his part. He was involved more and more deeply in his war with Spain, who lost no opportunity [*à*] *bon escient* to make trouble for him, and among other things was making use of the king of Scotland for that purpose. And the emperor, by his excuse [*sic*] to the king of France, had declared himself England's enemy. Apart from this, there were many other considerations which might hold Y.M. back. Nevertheless, if his highness were really minded to do something, I was ready to conclude with them; but only if they would accept the following terms:

(i) that we ally *contra quoscunque*, in which case the best issue could be expected, as I had demonstrated to them at large;

(ii) that we pledge ourselves to maintain the peace of Osnabrück (and I explained the reasons which bound us to do so);

(iii) that we agree immediately *de modo auxilij ferendi*, as to which I was prepared to reduce my former demand for money by fifty thousand pounds sterling a year. On these terms I required a decision, since they had had time enough to deliberate, and I desired that they would make up their minds without delay.[2]

1. The first four paragraphs of Bonde's argument were no more than the plain truth, now bluntly thrown at the English negotiators for the first time. Not so paragraph 5, which was partly based on Bonde's ignorance of the real situation, and partly bluff. Though the treaty of Elbing, soon to be concluded, might paper over the cracks with Holland, Charles X never ceased to expect trouble from Denmark. As to Poland, he more than once attempted a negotiated settlement with John Casimir, but before 1659 his attempts never had any hope of success.

2. Pufendorf (iii. 247) mistakenly makes Bonde say that Charles would be willing to conclude the alliance without any subsidies.

They answered me at length, and sought to show that Y.M. could not look forward to any constant friendship from the emperor. They said that they knew nothing of the emperor's declaration against them, and even if it existed he could not do them much harm, and so forth; but the main point of their answer was that it was inadvisable to antagonize Holland and Denmark at this moment, least of all by conditions that touched on trade and other interests; but that if Y.M. would enter into a defensive alliance with them against the House of Austria, the king of Poland, and Charles Stuart the king of Scotland, that would answer the same end, since Holland and Denmark would not attack Y.M. except in alliance with Poland, and if they wished to inflict damage on England they would not do so without allying with Spain, in which case we should be better able to give each other effective aid, since they embraced the interests of those against whom we should be allied.

To this I answered that no defensive alliance of that sort was possible, for they were already involved with Spain, and with the emperor also; and as soon as Y.M. bound himself to act with them against the House of Austria that would be tantamount to declaring war against the emperor, and to do it on terms which left him ignorant of how far he could rely on the protector's help: they might judge for themselves whether such a course was advisable, especially when (as I had before explained) he had no need to take it. I said further that it was a matter of no little astonishment to me that they should be so nervous of offending Holland, though it was in any case impossible to avoid a war with them: they knew that Holland supplied their enemies with all they required, and that all the ships in Dunkirk and Ostend, which inflicted so much damage on them, were fitted out by the Dutch, and all their crews came from the same quarter. Either they must put up with all this, or come to a breach with them; and although they might wish to plead that it was all the work of privateers, and that the Dutch had done as much when fighting their own enemies, I could prove to them clearly that ships belonging to the States-General had transported the Spanish silver to Flanders. The reason why their ambassador insists so strongly on the principle that 'free ship makes free goods' was so that they could assist Spain at their will and pleasure. At this they were taken aback, and could make no answer; and the point was not pursued. But their policy still seems to be to get Y.M. involved with the emperor, and afterwards to give such assistance as they may think proper; and with this I am by no means satisfied.

They then spoke of the other treaty; and though I had before thought that they would now be prepared to compromise, I found most of it tied up with so many limitations and clauses that I could not accept it. I therefore took it extremely coldly, and said that for me the treaty was of no great consequence: if they were not prepared to sign a treaty on a basis which would bring safety and security to both sides, I would not ask them to sign one at all, but would take my leave and let it appear how unreasonable it was that they should have detained me for upwards of a year (an experience to which there is scarcely an example of any extraordinary ambassador's being subjected), and had then let me go with my business unfinished. They promised to discuss the matter again; and with that we parted. I have subsequently heard that they have met again about it, and are said to have decided, among other things, that an embassy must be sent to Y.M. without a moment's delay.[1] I am very pleased about this. Not only will the impression produced by such a mission be an effective deterrent to Y.M.'s ill-wishers, and Y.M. will thereby have the great advantage of a respite, but it will hasten my despatch, since I shall take care to settle what I can, and postpone what cannot be settled advantageously, for them [the mission] to deal with on their arrival.

The Portuguese resident has this moment been with me and reported that all is now settled between England and Portugal, which is of great service to all our affairs.[2] I hope now to leave shortly, when I shall at once make my way to Y.M. to present an account of all my actions, and of any other matter that it may be necessary for him to know.

LVI

London, 27 June 1656

By my last letter I gave Y.M. a detailed account of what passed between me and the commissioners last week concerning the closer alliance. As to that, nothing more has subsequently transpired, though I am informed by a sure hand that his highness is fully determined to send an embassy to Y.M. as soon as I have departed, and that there has been some consideration of which members of the council should be sent. I intend now to have another audience with his highness this week in order to press the question, and to find out what he thinks about the action of the Dutch in sending their fleet to the Sound. Although I have done everything to make them take some action

1. On 19 June the council of state minuted: 'To remind His Highness to speed an ambassador to Sweden': *CSP (Dom) 1655–56*, p. 387; and already on 21 June NS Thurloe had assured Nieupoort somewhat airily that 'although the embassy might arrive somewhat late, he could assure me ... that it would be proceeding forthwith': *Brieven*, iii. 251.

2. Ratifications were exchanged in Lisbon on 31 May, the approach of Blake's fleet having persuaded John IV to yield at all points.

about the alliance, I still see no sign of their doing so, partly because of their fear of the Dutch, but mainly because of the uncertain condition of affairs in this country. For some time past they have been the subject of much discussion; and though strict secrecy is observed it is thought that they have been debating on what footing this government shall stand: some want a king, lords and commons on the pattern of England's old constitution; some of the anabaptists seem to be disposed to have a king, but without lords or upper house (as it is called here); but there is much doubt whether any decision has yet been taken. If there is nothing more to be done in the affair [of the alliance] (as seems to be the case), I hope all the same to have laid the foundation for something which may be to Y.M.'s service; and it is reasonable to suppose that the impression produced by their mission to Y.M. will presently have as much effect as would have been produced by an alliance, and that in the meantime it will give Y.M. time to see how things develop in one quarter and another.[1]

I have been with the commissioners several times this week about the other treaty, and have now at long last reached agreement with them; so that I expect the final text will be available next week, after which I shall lose no time in taking my departure. I shall forward it to Y.M. by the next post; and I hope it may, with God's help, commend itself to Y.M. Although I have been obliged to agree to the fifth[2] article, which provides that the enemies of one party may not seek refuge with prizes in the harbours[3] of the other; and also the second article, which provides that one party shall not assist the enemies of the other by leasing ships and so on in such a way as to be prejudicial to his interests, I nevertheless hope that these two articles will not conflict with Y.M.'s interest and intentions; and that even if this should in some measure be the case they will be held to have been satisfied by the permission of free and open recruiting of soldiers and sailors; freighting of ships; precise definition as to passports, and consequent security of commerce; a reasonably adequate satisfaction for losses in the Dutch war;[4] permission to trade to Barbados and

---

1. It may have been some rumour of Bonde's improved relations with the protector that provided the basis for the startling letter from Dureel which was read in the Swedish council of state on 24 July. That letter (of 17 July) reported that Cromwell had 40 warships ready in the Downs to proceed to the Sound, and had given orders that all Dutch ships were to be visited in the Channel. The rumour had no foundation, and the council seems to have passed over the letter in silence: *RRP*, xvi. 560. For similar rumours, *CSP* (*Ven*) *1655–56*, p. 190; Thurloe, iv. 584.

2. Transcript mistakenly has '*främpte*', for '*femte*'.

3. Transcript has '*kammar*', for '*hamnar*'.

4. Article VII of the treaty would indeed establish regulations for the settling of claims; but controversy was not thereby ended.

America;[1] the right to fish for herring and other fish without hindrance or payment of duty; permission to dry nets on the coastline and to obtain food and all other necessaries; and so forth.[2] As to what I promised them in regard to trade to Poland and Prussia, and I hope it may not be to Y.M.'s disadvantage.[3]

Herr Coyet is safely arrived in Holland, having been honourably conveyed there by three frigates. At Herr Hoffstetter's request we have ordered a quantity of powder here, and I intend to speak with the lord protector next week about its free export. I presume that Herr Coyet and Hoffstetter will find some means to get some money for General Fleetwood's recruiting: he is very anxious for it; and as I am well aware of his great zeal and his desire to do Y.M. acceptable service, I cannot doubt his exertions in that matter, nor that he himself will have informed Y.M. of them. What I can do to help him in it shall be communicated to Y.M. by the next post. By this post I have had no letter from Y.M.

LVII

London, 4 July 1656

Since my last letter I have been mainly occupied with the preamble and final paragraph of the treaty which we have agreed upon: I hope we shall soon have completed it. I indicated that I should then like to talk a little with his highness about the alliance, and at least to sound him as to his opinion of these proceedings by Denmark and Holland. I accordingly had an interview with him yesterday evening, in which I showed him how dangerous was the present state of affairs,

---

1. Article IX of the treaty would, on the contrary, reiterate the English claim to a monopoly of trade to America; though it added the somewhat illusory qualification that individual Swedes, if provided with Charles X's recommendation, *might* be allowed to trade thither 'as far as the state of his [the protector's] affairs and of the republic will for that time permit'.

2. This was an important concession to the Swedes, and one which had been denied to the Dutch at the peace of Westminster. It had been foreshadowed by Cromwell's additional instruction to Whitelocke of 7 April 1654; but at that time with the proviso that they should pay a recognition of the tenth herring, or at worst of the twentieth herring: Whitelocke, *Journal*, ii. 196. The proviso was now dropped.

3. By article VIII it was provided that the English should enjoy all the 'prerogatives' which they had formerly had in Prussia, Poland, or elsewhere in the Swedish dominions, 'in preference to other nations'. If Sweden were to grant greater privileges to any other nation than the English, or to people who were not [at present] Swedish subjects, England should also enjoy such improved privileges. This met Charles X's insistence on his right to grant specially favourable terms to his own subjects, and implicitly to those who might afterwards become so. And any edict published since 1650 which might have been burdensome to English traders to Poland or Prussia was to be cancelled in the Swedish dominions [e.g. in a Swedish-controlled Danzig?]

and how all that disunity among the protestants which Y.M., not less than he, had previously feared, might now very well be the consequence of Holland's entry into the Baltic with Denmark's permission; and that it would have been advantageous if his highness had been pleased to accept Y.M.'s favourable offer long ago, in which case I would almost venture to assure him that the Dutch would never have gone so far. But since that had not happened, I would only say, by way of bringing him to a realization of the state of affairs, that he should consider the situation and the inconveniences which might undoubtedly follow if Y.M. should become involved in any dispute with Denmark and Holland: the Protestant Cause would be abandoned; the emperor would obtain a breathing-space in which to resolve his problems; the other catholic powers would be free to coalesce, to our destruction; and while the protestants savaged each other England would be left alone to deal with the House of Austria, and—what was more than all—those who were the enemies of us both would be in the happy situation (should any misfortune befall Y.M.) of destroying us one after the other. I added that I wondered that his highness had such consideration for Holland: he knew that they hated this government more than anything else in the world, and as long as he left them alone he must suffer greater injuries from them than from Spain itself. I therefore suggested that he reflect whether it was not still easy to form an alliance, and *obstare principiis*, rather than to allow the fire to grow so fierce that it could not be put out. I alluded to England's devotion to the Protestant Cause, and *ex consequenti* to Y.M.; and since he had now made up his mind to summon a parliament, nothing was more calculated to cement the feelings of his subjects with his own, than that they should see that he was really concerned for the honour of God and the welfare of the country. All of which, and more, I developed at some length.

To this he made a lengthy reply, to the effect that his actions had been consistent and sincerely meant; and that though both Holland and Denmark had done their utmost to alienate him from Y.M. he had not only turned a deaf ear to them, but had manifested to each his strong disapproval of their schemes, as being unrighteous and unreasonable; that they had never had any encouragement from him to embark upon them; and he still found it hard to believe that they would be so foolish as to undertake anything of that nature. He must admit that it had been his intention to conclude an alliance with Y.M., and he was not sure that he would not have been glad if it had been done long ago; but things had turned out for them so that it had not been possible to do it: they had a fleet off Spain of between 43 and 50 ships, another of 36 at Jamaica, and some 40 or 50 here at home on their coasts; and this pressed them so hard that they dared not take the risk of other ventures. They would have offered mediation, if it had been acceptable;[1] and he knew very well that their hearts had for the most part been with Y.M. With that he ended, confessing that the state they were in, and the way affairs had gone, had been what hindered him; that their fleet costs them so much that they are practically living from hand to mouth; and that he was sure that we wished them as much good fortune in their enterprises as they wished us in ours; and so forth.

I answered by acknowledging his sincerity of purpose, and could not but admit that their expenses were very great, so that I was surprised that they were able to meet them; but I put it to him whether, as he could hardly carry on his war with Spain successfully, it might not be better to go on a little more slowly on that side, put affairs at home upon a secure bottom, and then with so much the greater energy, *coniunctis viribus*, fall upon the House of Austria: it would be quite easy, either supposing the impression made by our alliance still came in time to halt their [*sc.* Denmark's and Holland's] plans or, if before that they had already gone too far, then nothing would be easier than for England to station a fleet on this side of the Sound and block the Dutch fleet's return home, or to attack it when it was weakened by autumn gales and a long period at sea—for it would scarcely be able to find harbour in the Baltic in winter. And if the Dutch lost this fleet it would not be so easy for them to fit out another. In this connexion I did my best to show that he had as much danger to apprehend on this side as on the other—or even more; however, I said that if he found that he could not conclude the alliance with me [I trusted] that he would send to Y.M. without delay.

He answered by saying that *nunc lupum auribus tenent*, and that any relaxation of the grip on him would give him a chance to do them evil; but at all events he hoped for the best, and promised that he would send off the embassy, and perhaps the more speedily in regard to the present posture of affairs. He spoke also of the parliament; that they had resolved to summon it, and hoped that as honest men they would carry through the business with Spain: everybody in the country loved the Protestant Cause as patriots should (apart from the king's party, and they would not be permitted to attend); and so gave many protestations of his affection, as he usually does. And after I had thanked him for cancelling the sequestration of Lord Cranstoun's estates, in consequence of Y.M.'s intercession and my request,[2] and

---

1. Abbott (iv. 200) translates 'they ... would have offered mediation if it had been advantageous to them'; but the Swedish is not *förmånlig* but *behaghlig*.

2. *CSP (Dom) 1655–56*, p. 375, and *ibid.*, *1656–57*, p. 14 (10 July 1656) which notes that the order was 'confirmed in person'.

had begged permission to export a quantity of powder for Y.M.'s use, we parted, with compliments on both sides. His remarks cleared up two points on which I had been doubtful all the time I have been here: one was, that the king of Denmark has been making secret moves, through the Dutch, but that he has been given no answer of any kind; the other, that when last winter they thought that the Spanish silver-fleet would not be able to escape them, they had been disposed to ally with Y.M.,[1] but that they had postponed doing so until they saw how things would turn out, and if affairs had gone well for them instead of thoroughly badly, they would undoubtedly have concluded the alliance. Since I see that there is now nothing to be done in that matter, I shall hasten away as quickly as the slowness of those who have the business in hand may allow, and still contrive to leave the best impressions behind me. If parliament can agree about the constitution of the government I have good hopes of them, since the affection to Y.M. is very great in this country, and everything depends on it—if only they knew their own interests. My Lord [sc. General George] Fleetwood, who remains here, can do much in that matter by reason of his opportunities to talk with his brother, and I shall therefore leave him full information before my departure.

The draft of the treaty which we have agreed upon will be carried to Y.M. by Herr Coyet: I shall send it to Hamburg, where he now is, in order to make sure that it reaches Y.M. I have had no letters or information from Y.M., which troubles me unspeakably.

LVIII

London, 11 July 1656

By the last post I sent Y.M. a detailed account of what passed at my last audience on the 3rd instant. I afterwards thought it necessary once again to emphasize the importance of this affair, and I had therefore a long conference with Secretary Thurloe at my house, last Monday, in which I repeated what I had said to his highness, but rather more freely and at length, and showed him how dangerous would be the consequences for them, and particularly for this government, if Holland and Denmark were to coöperate in attacking Y.M.[2] I also depicted in strong colours the great advantages of Y.M.'s offers from the point of view of his highness's own interests, and the use it

---

1. Abbott (iv. 200) paraphrases this: 'The other was that in the preceding winter the English in order that the Spanish silver-fleet should not slip away from them, had been inclined to ally themselves with the king of Sweden'—which makes nonsense.

2. Denmark's treaty with the Dutch bound Frederick III to send a squadron to collaborate with the Dutch fleet off Danzig; and this was in fact done.

might be to him when parliament meets, especially if his highness were minded to settle the government in himself and his family—to which I see that both he and the greatest part of the country are inclined. He answered me very frankly, protested that his highness's main object in the course he had taken had been to avert all ill-feeling among protestants; and though I had always maintained the contrary, he ingenuously avowed that he had never thought that the Dutch would be capable of doing what they had done, nor could he say what they might have done if we had joined forces as I had desired; but this he would say to me in confidence, that he had learned by a sure hand that though the Dutch have a suspicion that something of the sort may have been settled between us, they had nevertheless resolved upon this enterprise. As to Denmark, he said that his highness had had no proposal from them worth communicating to me, except that last winter there had come a letter from the king of Denmark *in generalissimis terminis*, with the remark that the aspect of affairs all over the world was everywhere extraordinary, and that in consequence he would be very glad to know what the protector's attitude might be expected to be:[1] to which they had found it most advisable to return no reply. For the rest, he laid great stress on the difficulties which they confront at this time, and that they were not easily to be persuaded to fall out with Denmark and Holland; thereby indicating that it was their reverses last year and this, and the uncertain state of affairs at home, that were the sole reasons which had restrained them from allying with Y.M. He promised that he would, as I had requested, work faithfully for Y.M.'s service during the time of the forthcoming parliament; and said also that his highness was minded to send an embassy to Y.M., though he was a little troubled to hit upon a suitably capable person. And so we parted, with great assurances of friendship on both sides.

The following day I had my Lord Whitelocke with me; and since he is a person highly regarded in parliament, I did my best to prepare him to give his support to anything which may tend to Y.M.'s service: which he promised faithfully to do.[2] I also learned from him that he was in favour of his highness's assuming the crown, though parliament must reserve to itself the rights which pertain to the estates in well-ordered kingdoms; and as far as I can gather from one person and another it seems likely that in the course of this parliament his highness

1. Printed in Abbott, iv. 104.

2. Abbott (iv. 200) states that at a date 'a week later' than the audience of 3 July Bonde 'suggested Whitelocke for the post' of ambassador to Sweden. I cannot identify the basis for this statement: see the reference to Whitelocke in the letter of 11 July, *supra*.

will become king; and if he does there can be no doubt that he will collaborate with Y.M. in the closest possible fashion. For the rest, I have reached agreement on the preamble, the conclusion, and everything else about the second treaty, and shall now make every effort to get away with the shortest possible delay, and to force his highness to give me a promise that he will send an embassy to Y.M. immediately afterwards. As to the state of affairs in this country in other respects, I refer Y.M. to the attached account.[1] I have had no orders from Y.M. by this post, nor for a considerable time past.

LIX

London, 18 July 1656

I have now got so far that I am able to report that the treaty between Y.M. and this country was yesterday signed and sealed, and copies of it exchanged, and that it has now, thank God, been brought to a favourable conclusion.[2] Assuming that all my letters have not been intercepted, I hope that Y.M. will by the last of them have been apprised of its contents. I had in fact intended to send a copy of it to Y.M. by Herr Coyet; but since the places through which the post goes grow every day more hostile to Y.M. and to the crown of Sweden, and since moreover I myself hope to be able to take my leave of the lord protector, and then betake myself with all speed to Y.M., I have thought it wiser to retain it until my arrival. We have been greatly depressed by the news which comes with this post of Warsaw's being taken by the Poles, and the great danger from the barbarous population to which those good gentlemen who are in the city are exposed.[3] All our hope now lies in some happy stroke with which Almighty God may be pleased to bless Y.M., and so in spite of all make everything well again. We learn from Sweden that the Russians from Ladoga have fallen upon Nyen, and not much good is to be expected from our neighbours on that side;[4] and though well-

1. Missing in transcript.
2. Text in Abbott, iv. 904–11. Art. I gave each party the right to recruit; art. IV accepted the 'preheminence' of each in its own waters, and regulated passports; art. VIII dealt with English trading privileges in Prussia and Poland (see p. oo note oo, *supra*); art. IX gave individual Swedes the right to seek special license to trade to America, if circumstances permitted; art. X gave Swedes the right to fish herring on the British coast, provided the number of ships did not exceed 1000. An attached convention provided (subject to Charles X's agreement) that no Swedish naval stores be exported to Spain for the duration of the Spanish war in Swedish ships, but suggested a conference to determine prices of these commodities, should England wish to buy up Sweden's total production of them: (see p. 290 n. 2, *supra*). Cromwell ratified the treaty on 5 November; Charles on 30 December.
3. The Swedish garrison in Warsaw surrendered on 21 June/1 July.
4. Nyen fell to the Russians on 5 June.

informed people judge that the Dutch will scarcely venture upon overt hostilities to Y.M., they are credited with every reason to do so; which others magnify, and use to incite them. It is also very bad news about the great defeat of the French at Valenciennes, and there are many who fear that it may lead to a change in French policy, and that a peace between France and Spain may easily be the consequence, especially since opinion in France inclines that way. What line the people here will adopt in the present state of affairs will scarcely be clear before the meeting of parliament. I cannot help deducing from their general behaviour that the lord protector must have as his secret maxim a wish to see England in some danger, and the protestant interest likewise, so that this state of affairs may the better advance his private interests with the parliament; this is however no more than a guess, though it remains very probable. In my private audience of leave-taking I intend once again to lay stress on the dangers of the situation, and to see how far he can be brought to confront them. Meanwhile I have been informed that in my recredentials mention is to be made of the mission which his highness designs to despatch to Y.M., and this I shall do my best to encourage. I am unwilling to weary Y.M. with tiresome business, and with my own situation here, but God knows that I am hard pressed for money, apart from Bonnel's wretched situation, and several other difficulties: God Almighty help me to get out of this place honourably and come to Y.M.; when I look forward to Y.M.'s listening graciously to my troubles and saving me from inevitable ruin. What adds unspeakably to all my other anxieties is that I have had no letter from Y.M. for some months: I pray to God with all my heart there may be no grievous reason for it.

LX

London, 1 August 1656

I was forced, on account of my solemn leave-taking, to miss writing to Y.M. by the last post; for which I entreat Y.M.'s forgiveness.

I think it needless to trouble Y.M. with particulars of what occurred on that day, and on the following day at Hampton Court, in the way of outward pomp and unusual demonstrations of friendship: I refer Y.M. to the attached narrative of Commissary Barkman.[1] But as on the previous day the post had brought me letters from the chancellor

---

1. Missing in transcript; but Bonde's *Diarium* for 25 July has: '*Habui solennem audientiam valedictoriam* ... played at bowls for two hours; *bibit mihi sed secrete adeo Dns Prot. in memoriam Regiae Maiestatis, quod adeo contra morem ipsorum est, sed nunc maximam amicitiam annuebat*': *Diarium*, p. 52.

which made it apparent to me that at the time they were written
Y.M. did not consider my departure from here to be as urgent as I
had believed;[1] and since there was no time to cancel the leave-taking
audience, for which great preparations had already been made; I feel
I must acquaint Y.M. with the reasons which induced me to press on
with my leave-taking. The main one was, that I had had no orders
from Y.M. since the spring, apart from that from Schneebloch on 16
May, either in response to my enquiries, or in modification of the
orders which were then sent to me. Those orders laid it down that I
should lay the basis (as well as I could) for ensuring a relation of
confidence between Y.M. and his highness; should do what I could
in the matter entrusted to me [i.e. the completion of the treaty of
1654]; and allow all the rest to be dealt with by an embassy from his
highness to Y.M., which I was to endeavour to persuade him to. This
has been the line which I have followed ever since; and though I have
not had the success I could have wished in the matter of a closer
alliance, I have by God's grace surmounted the obstacles I have had
to encounter in negotiating the other treaty (of which I sent Y.M. an
account on 30 May, with a draft of the proposed treaty); and I hope
that I have, with God's help, concluded it upon terms which may be
acceptable to Y.M., and to the great service and security of his faithful
subjects: of which I subsequently (and in particular on 27 June) gave
Y.M. detailed information. And as I considered that I had so far
provided Y.M. with the assurance that Y.M. might not only rely on
this country's doing nothing to his prejudice, but rather that the
feeling here was that when circumstances would permit it they would
gladly enter into a closer alliance with Y.M., I thought it might be
better to encourage them to pursue the initiative towards the conclusion of such an alliance through their embassy, rather than that
I should remain here unfruitfully. I had moreover to give serious
consideration to the great expense which Y.M. incurs by my mission,
which must undoubtedly be a burden at a time when money is
generally so scarce. I could therefore reach no other conclusion than
that Y.M. might well suppose that I was already on the way home,
in view of the fact that I have repeatedly written that I intended to
finish my treaty and then hasten away, and in view also of the fact
that I had had no other letter from Y.M. for a long time. And since
no other way was open to me, I thought that I must talk further with
his highness at Hampton Court last Saturday, especially since the
chancellor's letters gave me some light on the state of affairs. I have
always thought that in conditions as they are at present, and in view
of my own present uncertainty, a mission from his highness is of vital

---

1. For the letter from Erik Oxenstierna, see Carlbom, *Sverige och England*, p. 112.

importance; for it may facilitate Y.M.'s negotiation with Holland,[1] and the impression it makes may put an obstacle in the way of the adverse party's violent animosity against Y.M., and also make Denmark think twice about involving itself in their plans, it being well known that for Denmark fear of England is a great deterrent. This is why I have welcomed the fact that I have been treated here with unusually conspicuous friendship and confidence, since it is something to cause apprehension in those who do not wish us well. It occurred to me also that if his highness's embassy should happen to coincide with that of the Dutch, they might (if they were [men] upon whose fidelity Y.M. could rely) be of great service in the negotiations with Holland. And since Denmark is close at hand, and can be relied upon to make no trouble without England's or Holland's assistance, it might well be that they could be induced to send an embassy also; in which case all ill-feeling among the protestants would be averted, and a coalition between them would follow; which is his highness's dearest wish and the main objective of his plans.[2] But in this connexion it has also occurred to me that although by such means Holland and Denmark might for the moment be kept quiet, they nevertheless will always be jealous of Y.M., and of any increase in the power of our dear fatherland; which means that it is essential to continue to maintain close friendship between Y.M. and this country in order to preserve a reasonable balance against them. And to promote that friendship I have thought that it would be useful if their [the English] interest in the trade to lands in Y.M.'s possession, and their profits from it, were such that their own advantage, as well as other considerations, would oblige them to cultivate it. If now their ambassador were on the spot during the present negotiations with the Dutch, they might then (without its appearing invidious) receive those advantages which Y.M. might be prepared to grant them in preference to all other nations; and which, if they were not on the spot, Y.M. might perhaps be unable to avoid denying them, in order to conciliate the Dutch.

1. Obdam's fleet had arrived off Danzig on 17 July, and was soon to be joined by a Danish squadron; and Charles X was by this time desperately anxious to come to some arrangement with the Dutch. His anxiety (and his change of objectives) was reflected in his letter to Erik Oxenstierna of 12 July: 'We must have the Baltic safe: we consider the crisis which could follow the failure of this negotiation of more importance than anything that Poland and Prussia can do against us'; and on 24 August: 'God knows what the condition of our affairs is here at present. I do not believe that our country has for many years been in such a dangerous situation: humanly speaking the only means of salvation is a quick settlement with the Dutch': Carlson, *Sveriges historia*, i. 314, 316.

2. On 16 April the Dutch ambassadors at Copenhagen had reported that Denmark would probably agree to send embassies to Poland and Sweden, provided Cromwell did so. Also that Frederick III had written to Cromwell concerning proposals for an alliance with Denmark, and was awaiting his answer: Thurloe, iv. 680.

I therefore expounded to him [the protector] the present dangerous position of protestantism:[1] how Y.M., who (together with his highness) is its principal support, has without reason been subjected on the one side to an attack by the Russians, fomented by his enemies, and how relations with Denmark and Holland had an ill appearance; so that the intrigues of the catholics, and their tactic of *divide et impera*, may well prove effective if we get to the stage of quarrelling among ourselves, and so become a more easy prey for them; and on the other side the heavy defeats of France both in Italy and Flanders[2] greatly raise the hopes of those who work for peace between France and Spain—a thing which the common people in France, and the clergy, are so anxious for that they rejoice at France's defeats. I therefore begged his highness to take it [the common cause] to heart with all speed and seriousness; and since I had now taken my leave mainly because my departure might the sooner impel him to send an embassy to Y.M.—which I had earlier wished him to do, as seeming to be a useful means to forward the cause, provided there was no delay—that he would lose no time about it. I laid stress in this connection on the validity of such arguments as were likely to be effectual with him; urged once again all the ways and means which might occur to him to bring about unity, since there was nothing Y.M. more desired than to maintain a cordial relationship with all protestants; and from this proceeded to large protestations and thanks for the affection he had shown me for Y.M.'s sake, and said that since he had so much loved and esteemed me as a private person, and shown me such confidence as none before me had enjoyed (as to which, for his honour, I cannot be silent), I offered him, in appropriate terms, my faithful service.

To this he answered with great protestations, and began at once to censure the Dutch, or rather that party among them which, he said, cared neither for religion, honour, fatherland, or honesty, but contrary to all *principia, divina* no less than *humana*, foster much evil, to the ruin of the protestants and of themselves. He insisted that his affection and his heart had always been on Y.M.'s side; so that when to his great chagrin he saw how the Dutch rejoiced at the cruel tidings of Y.M.'s death, he considered making demonstrations of joy in London when it was found that these rumours were false, and fabrications. He emphasized that it was no lack of inclination that had deterred him from concluding the closer alliance, but that he had feared that it might reinforce the enemies' evil designs; and that a contributory

1. Contrast his argument to the contrary, in his recent interview with Fiennes and Fleetwood: *supra, p.* 309.

2. The defeat of the French forces attempting to relieve the siege of Valenciennes, 16 July (NS) 1656; the raising of the siege of Pavia by the Marquis of Caracena soon afterwards.

cause had been their financial straits and the troubles at home; but
he nevertheless gave an assurance that the Protestant Cause, and its
security, was the basis upon which he had proceeded, and upon which
he would always stand as long as he had any say in the matter; and
therefore he would willingly himself apply, and suffer others to apply,
all reasonable remedies to cure those disorders, even though it might
be considered and accounted to be contrary to his own interests. He
therefore promised, if I thought good, to send an earnest (*mouuant*)
letter of remonstrance to the United Netherlands, in the hope of
bringing them back to the right way; and he hoped that it might
bear fruit, since not all men in the Netherlands were of the same
inflammatory tendency: there were still many who clung to their old
principles and were not seduced by Spanish propaganda. As to France,
he must confess that if that country were to ally with Spain he
perceived that the consequence, humanly speaking, would be the
inevitable ruin of the protestants; but he would tell me, in strict
confidence and absolute secrecy, that he saw no reason why France
and England should not stand together as one man: the French might
be catholics, but they were not so bigoted as the House of Austria,
and in any case there were many protestants among them. That was
why he was at present treating with them; and he hoped shortly to
bring the negotiation to a successful issue; which he thought would
effectually prevent any conjunction between France and Spain. He
said also that he expected to be able to give me a notable piece of
news before I left, which would sufficiently indicate his intentions in
regard to the common cause. And ended with extraordinary demonstrations of regard for me in my private capacity. And so, after I
had returned appropriate compliments for his offer and his confidence,
had urged him to send that letter to the Netherlands as soon as
possible, had touched once more on the embassy, and had made
arrangements for correspondence with him, we parted; with the
utmost content on each side.

By the last post I had from Herr Appelboom a remonstrance which
the Spanish ambassador in The Hague had handed in to the States-
General. I at once had it translated into English and communicated
it to him [the protector]; and though Thurloe also had a copy, it was
nevertheless of use, in that it gave him an idea, and encouraged his
suspicion, of the faction that now rules in Holland, as being bought
by Spanish money and entirely under Spanish influence.[1] In order to
obtain further information on these matters I spoke with Secretary
Thurloe last Wednesday, on which occasion he assured me that his
highness's embassy would be sent off as soon as possible, and certainly

1. For Spanish activity in the Netherlands, and especially in Amsterdam, see
Molsbergen, *Frankrijken ... Nederlanden*, pp. 157, 160.

before its journey can be plagued by winter weather; also that the embassy is mentioned in his highness's letter to Y.M. [i.e. in Bonde's recredentials]; and further, that his highness was minded to impart to me the matter of it, and the project for mutual defence of each other's country, which he has committed to his ambassador; with a request that I would prepare the way for their smooth transaction on Y.M.'s side.[1] He promised also that his highness would write an urgent letter to the Netherlands at the earliest possible moment, taking occasion from the remonstrance of the Spanish ambassador mentioned above; and said that his highness would be very anxious that Y.M. should also write to them pointing out, on the same lines, the unreasonableness of Spanish policy, particularly since Y.M., although he is at peace with Spain is [in that remonstrance] severely animadverted upon. He promised that all this, and whatever might be necessary for my departure, should be ready next week. Since matters on this side are now as far settled as is possible at present, I intend if God wills to set out in the week after next, around the 14 or 15 August, and to betake myself to Y.M., where (by correspondence with this place) I can do Y.M. more service than by longer remaining here, at great expense to Y.M.

P.S. Y.M.'s letters of 4 and 6 July from Novodvor [Nowy Dwór] arrived after I had written the above.[2] I had to-day an important conversation with his highness about them; and though he pleaded his *impuissance*, I got him nevertheless to promise to write strong letters to Holland and Denmark immediately, and also to give some thought to what more he is prepared to do. I found him very much concerned about France; and no doubt he will immediately give them substantial assistance. My departure, which cannot now be put off since matters have come so far,[3] puts great pressure on him to make up his mind: of this I shall inform Y.M. by the next post.

---

1. No trace of any such project seems to have remained; if, indeed, it ever existed.
    2. Bonde was ordered to obtain some sort of help from England—by a diversion, a loan of troops, or a subsidy—now that Charles was attacked by the Russians and that the emperor was appearing more clearly his enemy; and especially to ask what England would do if Denmark and Holland should combine to attack in the Baltic. Mediation was to be ruled out; but (a notable indication of his weakening position) if it were actually offered 'it might go ahead': text in Carlbom, *Sverige och England*, pp. 117–18.
    3. The orders for the presents to Bonde had already been placed: *CSP (Dom) 1656–7*, pp. 50, 79, 95, 115; but the jewel (estimated at £1850; actual price £863.18.0) could not be ready in time: hence Bonde's departure had to be delayed. He was also to have £1200 of cloth.

LXI

London, 8 August 1656

I mentioned at the end of my last letter that in consequence of Y.M.'s letters from Nowy Dwór of 4 and 6 July I had a talk with his highness. His answer was mostly concerned with excusing himself from giving any real assistance, on the ground of lack of money. But he said that he expected that some moderate and honest persons in Holland, not to mention the remonstrances which he intended sending to them and to Denmark, would avert any ill effects, and for the rest promised to think about it again, and let me know his views before I departed.[1] With a view to having some opportunity to do more about this I called last Monday about dinner-time on my Lord Lambert to take my farewell of him. This gave me a good opening to dilate to him (and also to my Lord Lawrence, who is president of the council) on their interest in this matter; to which my Lord Lambert, who is a very sensible man, replied by frankly confessing that a strict alliance, offensive and defensive, between Y.M. and this country might be arranged: he protested that he wished for it, and hoped that his highness's embassy to Y.M. would be able to do much in that matter, and that the opportunity might be taken to establish a solid league of protestant princes. When I remarked that the state of affairs was such that wishing and talking would get nowhere but that what was needed was action, this made a great impression on him, and they both promised to lend a hand towards bringing it about. When speaking of their embassy to Y.M. I try to avoid the word 'mediation', so that it may be thought of principally as designed to establish a closer alliance between Y.M. and the lord protector, which is indeed what they really intend. As to making any diversion against the Russians, I have thought it wisest to sound only Thurloe, who seemed not unwilling that something might be undertaken from here on a purely private footing; but since the year is so far advanced that it is imposs-

---

1. On 4 August Bordeaux told Nieupoort that he had seen Cromwell on the previous day and offered good offices about the Marine Treaty; that Cromwell had professed optimism, but had added that the sending of the Dutch fleet to the Baltic was another business; that he looked on it as 'very considerable'; and that other proceedings were 'a great reflection upon the crown of Sweden'. Nieupoort was surprised at this last, since the protector had said nothing of it two days earlier; and he said that he would speak to Cromwell about it. Bordeaux advised him to 'let it alone' since with Cromwell he would be speaking through an interpreter: better to raise it with Thurloe privately. Nieupoort did so, and Thurloe said that he had not heard a word about the Baltic from Cromwell during Bordeaux's audience, though he had been present all the time; 'but he did observe and find, that there was a very strict confederacy between Sweden and France': Nieupoort to [?] de Witt, Thurloe, v. 247. In this he was mistaken.

ible that anything can be done this summer, and since there is still some doubt whether the reports of the Muscovite's attack upon Ingria are true (and of the unreliability of such rumours I have now, thank God, had confirmation from all quarters),[1] and lastly to avoid the possibility that the protector may merely use the opportunity and afterwards do nothing on occasions of more importance to the cause, I have thought it best to enter into no negotiations upon it, but rather privately to sound the attitude of particular merchants to such an enterprise. They seem to be very keen on it, and there is no appearance that the protector will interpose any obstacles if Y.M. should wish next year to freight[2] some ships here and recruit soldiers in terms of the treaty I have made with them, in order to use them in action of this sort, or if Y.M. should wish to give encouragement to these merchants. But as the whole question of the interests of the merchants, and indeed the whole question of the constitution, depends upon the decision of this parliament, no decision in principle is likely to be taken before it meets. As far as I could gather from my Lord Lambert, there is now no general disinclination to his highness's becoming king. All the principal nobility in the country desire it; and if it comes about it is not to be doubted that as his authority and security increase he will follow his principal inclination and desire, and link himself closely to Y.M. Having this week taken leave of the public ministers and other good friends here, I likewise called upon the Dutch ambassador, who made great protestations of their wish for amicable relations and a close alliance with Y.M., England, France and Denmark. From the chancellor's letter I find that Y.M. would not disapprove if I were to stay here a little longer; which I heartily wish I had known before I took my leave. However, I shall postpone my departure for another week beyond what I intended, and meanwhile see how far I can push our business here; leaving the management of the details to General Fleetwood and Commissary Barkman, who I am confident will be capable of building on the foundations already laid, to the advantage of Y.M. What Y.M. commanded me to do here with regard to the Act of Seclusion[3] I reported at large to the chancellor a week ago; it is a very salutary measure, and his highness seems not averse to it—indeed, rather to incline to it so far, that on my advice he is thinking of sending a young Count Hohenlohe over to Holland in secret on the pretext of private business,[4] for the purpose of discreetly stirring up

    1. The reports were true.
    2. 'Freight' (*frachta*) not 'hire', in the transcript.
    3. Presumably to induce the other provinces to follow Holland's example, and adopt it, though this does not appear in Carlbom's paraphrase of the text.
    4. This was the Count Hohenlohe mentioned in Coyet's no. 26, *supra*. Nothing seems to have come of this idea: Hohenlohe left England (with £100 journey-money from Cromwell) on 19 October 1656 to go to Germany: BL Add. MS 38100 fo. 29.

trouble behind the scenes. In which I hope that he may do a great deal, for he is a sharp young man for his age. I have this week obtained permission to export 500 *centner*, or tons, of powder, whose purchase Herr Coyet negotiated on Y.M.'s behalf, and I shall bring it with me to Hamburg. By the next post I hope to be able to let Y.M. see some effect of what I have been doing here. And with that I bring this letter to a close.

LXII

London, 13 August 1656 [from Bonde's *Register*]

Although I have used every possible means with his highness himself, and with other leading personages, to obtain some sort of implementation of his highness's promise as to the remonstrance he intended to send to Holland and Denmark, and also of his promise to reveal his intentions to me, I have been forced to stand idly by while everything was protracted, and time running out, until they had no hope of being able to keep me here for some time longer. It was for this reason, and in order to be able to secure (at the very least) the despatch by this post of a remonstrance to Holland, that I yesterday morning had a notable audience with his highness at which (by my request) some of the leading members of the council were present. My first step was to present General Fleetwood, who at the time of my arrival had not presented to his highness the credentials which Y.M. had given him, but intends now on my departure to do so, both because he will thereby be better able, in conjunction with Commissary Barkman, to serve Y.M., and also because this seems to be what Y.M. intended, as intimated in Y.M.'s letter of last winter.

I had on previous occasions tried, by arguments based on the Protestant Cause, on Y.M.'s alliance with him, and so forth, to move his highness to face the present situation; but I was now resolved to show him the danger into which he and England were running as a result of Dutch actions. And as we stand upon very frank terms with each other, I appealed to the desire I had to serve him as a thing which bound me to reveal to him the perils which I saw approaching him if he did not take serious precautions against them in good time; and added that it must be considered as a fundamental fact that the plans of the Dutch are to attempt to get into their hands a monopoly of the trade of the whole world, and that in order to achieve that end they have discovered a special technique for wresting it from the hands of their friends—namely, to couple their negotiations with powerful fleets of war.[1] I then showed him at length the irreparable damage to

1. A technique which Cromwell had successfully deployed in the case of Portugal.

England which has arisen from the fact that the Dutch have by Danzig been granted *jus indigenatus*,[1] and which would become still more serious if Dünamünde and Putzig were to fall into their hands, since it would mean not only that all English trade to those places would be at once shut out by the Dutch, but the consumption of English woollen cloth—which is England's sole, or at least principal, source of wealth—would be hindered to those who have been used to take the greater part of it. I then pointed out to him how, upon the same basis, they have consistently demanded of him that free ships shall make free goods, and that their ships be not visited—a matter upon which his highness had very recently caused a serious and well-argued remonstrance to be drawn up, in order to demonstrate the unreasonableness of that demand. They took that for a sign that he was afraid, and as late as 5 August had resolved that Ambassador Nieupoort should insist on these points, since they were of importance to their trade—which with them is an unanswerable argument. And I put it to him that if they cared so little for him now, at a time when they had still not safeguarded themselves on our side, and when a union of forces might still easily occur between Y.M. and him—if they were so bold as to do this now, what reasonable ground had he to expect that once their fleet had achieved the effect in the Baltic which they hoped for, it would not come—with forty others now being fitted out—and force him to grant the concessions which they now demand? I developed all this at length, and incidentally mentioned next Wednesday as the day on which I intended to take my departure. He was deeply moved; and answered that God, to Whom all things are possible, and Who shows thereby that He alone reigneth, concealeth from men that which is to come to pass. He said that it had never occurred to him that they [the Dutch] would for their own advantage ignore all the obligations of a Christian and an honest man; and he hoped, therefore, that God would punish their unrighteous proceedings, and bless his own upright intentions. And he was of opinion that whatever they might think of England, she would always be able to defend herself and beat off any move calculated to hurt her. [And added] that the outcome of Y.M.'s designs had not altogether answered the expectations that had been entertained of them, and that this had been a great obstacle in the way of resolutions which they might otherwise have taken; and more to the same purpose. Although I might very well have answered that I had often told him all this before, I was not anxious to argue with him, but replied that though I hoped that England would be able to put up a good defence,

---

1. By the terms of the Dutch-Danzig treaty of 30 June/10 July. But in fact Danzig disavowed her negotiators, declined to grant parity of treatment for Dutch merchants, and refused to ratify the treaty: Cieślak, *Gdansks ... betydelse*, pp. 138–9.

these were *extrema remedia*, and that it would be better to cure the wound by plasters, for if they neglected it they might find that they had no other resort but to amputate the whole limb. I invited him to recall what I had said in that room (pointing to it), that if our enemies once managed to contrive that our two countries became no more than indifferent friends, then they would have won the game; and to prevent that, we must have a regard to time, as the most precious resource that remained to us. I hoped that he himself would be my witness that I had given him fair and frequent warnings, and had before told him what I foresaw might possibly come to pass; so that I had done my duty and satisfied my conscience, should any misfortune follow in the future. At this he answered that his remonstrance to Holland would certainly be ready to be sent off by this post, and that he would communicate it to me:[1] as to any other steps he might take, I should certainly be informed of them next Monday or Tuesday. At this point we parted, with the strongest protestations on both sides; and I have since learnt, by a sure hand (and General Fleetwood had the same information), that what I said to him had so great an effect upon him that he cancelled his decision to hold a day of prayer at Hampton Court to-day, and has remained here and brought his family back.

My impending departure is among the things that force him to make up his mind; and I hope for that reason that it may prove very serviceable to Y.M. General Fleetwood and Commissary Barkman are fully informed of everything; and if Y.M. should be pleased hereafter to send his commands to them, I hope that they will be properly attended to, and with less cost to Y.M.

Ambassador Nieupoort was with me the day before yesterday to take leave of me, with the strongest assurances of the States-General's desire for Y.M.'s friendship. He gave me the full text of their recent decision that their ambassadors to Y.M. should ask for nothing new, but only insist on the confirmation of the former treaty,[2] with great protestations of good-will. By this post we received the splendid news that Almighty God has blessed Y.M. with a quite magnificent victory;[3] for which His Divine Majesty be for ever praised and honoured by us all: it will undoubtedly strengthen Y.M. in all quarters, and confound

1. It was not ready till 21 August: a letter informing Charles X of its contents is dated the same day: Abbott, iv. 233–4.
2. This was scarcely correct: the treaty of 1645 had had an implicit point against Denmark.
3. The three-days' battle of Warsaw, 18–20 July OS: see Stanislaw Herbst, in *Polens krig med Sverige 1655–1660*, (Carl Gustaf-studier, 5) (Stockholm 1973), pp. 255–94. The strategic effects were *nil*, but politically it administered a temporary cold douche to Denmark.

the designs of his enemies; and I am certain that it will give his highness better courage (who hitherto has been much troubled), and will force him to address himself to what the present posture of affairs seems to require. Although I had assumed that his highness's remonstrance to the States-General would have been sent off to-day, I now learn that it has been decided to send it off by express next Monday or Tuesday; and I hope that the news of Y.M.'s great victory, together with the more moderate line to which the States-General now seems to incline, may bring an end to all troubles on that side.

LXII

London, 22 August 1656

As I mentioned to Y.M. in my last letter, the reasons I previously reported to Y.M., and the impossibility of my remaining here any longer after taking leave and making all preparations for departure, have determined me to set out this week. I leave behind me not only feelings exceedingly well disposed to Y.M., but also General Fleetwood and Commissary Barkman, fully informed on all points, and able after my departure to perform Y.M.'s service. And so I have no choice but to adhere to my resolution, and intend, if God will, to start to-morrow. As to the honours and courtesies shown to me by his highness, I cannot now give a full account of them: I can say only this, that as they exceed everything not only in the time of the parliament, but also under some former kings, they make a very strong impression, and give to all surrounding nations a lively realization of the confidence which has been cemented between Y.M. and this country. I have this week been visited by my Lord Lambert, my Lord Deputy Fleetwood, and Secretary Thurloe, who all came to take their leave of me: they have never done the like to anyone else. On which occasion they all manifested an extreme desire for close links with Y.M., and a hope that his highness's embassy to Y.M. may with God's help be able to achieve it. And I am assured, not only verbally but in writing (in my recredentials from his highness to Y.M.) that he [the ambassador] is to follow me directly. I have besides arranged for a safe correspondence with those leading persons already mentioned, so that after my departure I can keep them informed of everything they need to know for the service of Y.M. The results of Y.M.'s glorious victory at Warsaw have greatly brisked up Y.M.'s interest here: it had been considered to be in a very precarious condition, in consequence of the hostile moves of Poland, Muscovy, Denmark and Holland; and I can assure Y.M. that his highness, and all those who wish Y.M. well, have rejoiced at it as though it was their own victory. I mentioned in my last letter how I spoke with his highness last week: since then it has in fact happened that the Dutch ambassador has insisted on 'free ship makes free goods'—to which I am assured by my Lord Deputy Fleetwood, my Lord Lambert, and Thurloe, that England will never agree.

I have this moment taken my final leave of his highness: I have not time now to retail all the particulars to Y.M., except that it went with such exorbitant protestations of affection that I can give no full account of it.[1] The essence of it was that he promised to send a person in the immediate future to treat further with Y.M. on everything that may conduce to the advantage of the Protestant Cause, and also to prevent attacks upon us by our neighbours. In which connection he manifested great displeasure with Holland, and was increasingly disposed to admit the correctness of my predictions. This morning he assured me that he would send off his letter to Holland by express, and promised me a copy of it. And so I hope that all that Y.M.'s service required has been faithfully done, and that this letter, together with these last happy tidings, may have a good effect in Holland. General Fleetwood and Commissary Barkman I have to-day once more recommended to his highness; and I am sure that they will be able to do what is necessary here as well as I. The outward pomp of my despatch will be no small cause of chagrin to the Dutch. His highness has given me a considerable present, as well as some horses, and in exchange I have given him the black carriage-horses which Y.M. entrusted to me: they are somewhat old; but they look well enough, and I hope that Y.M. may not disapprove.[2] I shall do all I can to bring a good horse with me for Y.M.'s service, and hope very soon to be able to have the pleasure of seeing Y.M., crowned by Fortune and by Victory, and to be able in Y.M.'s presence to make my humble profession of how much I am

Your Majesty's
faithful and most humble
servant
Christer Bonde.[3]

1. Full accounts of these last audiences, and the ceremonial which accompanied them, up to the time of Bonde's final departure, are in Barkman's letters of 1, 8, 15, 22 and 29 August, in BL Add. MS 38100, fos. 1–10v.

2. A somewhat cheeseparing requital for his own lavish treatment; but he was clearly in financial straits.

3. After a somewhat troublesome voyage he caught up with Coyet in Hamburg, where the financial difficulties of each of them were relieved: they landed together at Pillau, 16 October 1656: Carlbom, *Sverige och England*, p. 131.

INDEX